Studies in Urban History

The urban past has never been so closely identified with the problems and tendencies of modern life as it is today, nor so full of interest and promise for historical research. The town, for so long the unconsidered container of industry and trade and the anonymous masses, is now assuming a new importance in its own right. Historians are addressing it *directly*, partly to understand urban changes better for their own sake but chiefly in order to relate them more coherently to economic, political, and cultural developments on an altogether wider plane. 'Biographical' studies of individual towns are thus laying the basis for more comparative analysis of the differences between them and the urban systems they comprise; investigations of urban life in microscopic detail are being matched by far-reaching research into the fundamental social processes leading toward the urbanisation of the whole world. Historians are on common ground here with other disciplines, for towns have always embodied their own history with peculiar tenacity, and this is now causing scholars across a wide front to look at the urban past with growing curiosity. Among them are geographers, economists, sociologists, demographers, archaeologists, civic designers—each of them having distinctive approaches and techniques, all of them sharing the problem of interdisciplinary communication.

The present mood of urban history is therefore experimental and exploratory. The field is wide open and world-wide, as much concerned with concrete detail where it matters as with imaginative hypotheses wherever they lead, as readily approached by the geographer as by the sociologist or the historian. **Studies in Urban History** is a series designed in this mood. The volumes have a standard format but in all other respects remain completely unstereotyped so as to give free rein to the most promising ideas, from whatever quarter or however remote their reference to time or place. Their forerunner was the work published in 1968 and edited by the General Editor of the new series, *The Study of Urban History*. This book was immediately acknowledged as 'having put British urban history on the map', and the volumes in the new series are all selected with the object both of filling important gaps in our knowledge and of demonstrating particular techniques of research or approach.

The Council House, Birmingham, the new municipal focus for the Chamberlain administration as it appeared about 1880 before the addition of the Art Gallery at the rear. It was designed in a rich Renaissance style by Yeoville Thomason, a local architect, and begun in 1874. From an unidentified print in the Birmingham Reference Library.

About the Book

The chief political challenge of the new urban civilisation of the nineteenth century took the shape of municipal reform. Virtually the whole effort of making the expanding industrial towns fit to live in had to be channelled through the municipalities. Their task was twofold: to finance ever-growing commitments without losing democratic support and to find volunteers equal to public office.

This book is the first to probe systematically the social composition and leadership of town councils in this country as they underwent their initial ordeal. It examines particularly Birmingham and Leeds between 1835 and 1914 as a means of elucidating how far town councils really conformed to widely-held notions of what such bodies should ideally be. This investigation leads on to a searching discussion of its present day aspects in the light of the Redcliffe-Maud inquiries into local government, and concludes by comparing English experience with that of the United States and Germany. It is a long-awaited work of major importance, not only for political and urban historians but for all those engaged in either the study or the practice of local government today.

About the Author

E. P. Hennock was born in 1926. Having served in the army from 1944-7, he became a scholar of Peterhouse, Cambridge, took the History Tripos and obtained his B.A. in 1950. Three years as a research student under Sir Herbert Butterfield were followed by ten years teaching at the newly founded University of Keele, first jointly in the Departments of Political Institutions and of History, later entirely in the Department of History. He obtained his Ph.D. from Cambridge in 1956. Since 1963 he has been teaching at the University of Sussex. He was for some time chairman of graduate studies in History and is a Reader in History in the School of English and American Studies. He was a Visiting Fellow of All Souls College, Oxford, in 1966-7 and British Academy Visiting Fellow at the University of Tuebingen in 1972.

The jacket shows Chamberlain Square, Birmingham, as it appeared about the time at which Birmingham became a city in 1889. The Town Hall, designed by J. A. Hansom and E. Welch after a Roman temple, was started in 1834 but not completed before 1849. The Council House, at a right-angle to it, is the most grandiose example of a style much used for commercial buildings in the city: it was begun in 1874 and augmented ten years later by the addition of the Museum and Art Gallery. The Chamberlain Memorial Fountain occupies the centre.

To
My Wife and Children

Fit and Proper Persons

Ideal and Reality in Nineteenth-Century Urban Government

E. P. Hennock

Reader in Modern History
University of Sussex

McGILL–QUEEN'S UNIVERSITY PRESS
MONTREAL
1973

© E. P. Hennock 1973

First published 1973
by Edward Arnold (Publishers) Ltd.,
25 Hill Street, London W1X 8LL

ISBN: 0 7735 0154 1

Library of Congress Catalog Card No. 72–96448

Legal Deposit 1st Quarter 1973

Printed in Great Britain

Foreword

Sixty years ago four-fifths of Britain's population could be classified officially as urban. It might be said of this country at least that the process of urbanisation had already come to an end, since the proportion of the population living in towns and urban districts was to remain more or less constant down to the present time. It appears to us now, looking back, as something of a paradox that the study of the urban past, though never totally neglected in this country, should have been held in abeyance for so long after that phase of urbanisation had closed. And if we widen the horizon to include, not merely growing numbers, but changing attitudes, movements, structures, images, the fact of the matter seems to be that an urban culture has arisen without an historical tradition that might explain it. Yet it was Britain which led the world, however unconsciously or even prodigally it may seem to have done so in human terms, in establishing a type of urban culture in the nineteenth century which has been transplanted or transformed over a much wider field in the twentieth. How surprising it therefore seems that it is only within the last generation, perhaps within little more than a decade, that urban history as such should have come to be recognised in this country as a proper and distinctive field of study and research.

So recent are these developments that their very limits and the techniques for discovering what they were about are still in a state of flux. So multifarious are the possibilities now opening up that most of the practitioners at work in this field are not yet rid of their initial sense of confusion. Nothing could, in fact, be less surprising. What they see before them is a field in which they must pay attention, not only to particular towns in all their peculiar detail—to urban societies fixed more or less in time and space—but a field in which they are being called upon to investigate historical processes and trends that completely transcend the life-cycle and range of experience of any

v

single community when viewed in isolation. The global demographic sweep of urbanisation is already overturning our notions of what cities are or might soon come to be. Sociological concepts of urbanism are forcing us to look deeper for the generic differences between urban and agrarian life that common experience has led us so often to take for granted. The political realities of facing urban problems that have fewer national characteristics than fundamental human ones are suggesting inter-cultural comparisons of a type which historians grounded in empirical traditions have generally viewed with alarm. The interconnections between the growth of cities and the rise of industrialised societies have thrown into the study of their economic relations searching questions about the extent to which urbanisation itself may be regarded as an initiator or a product of economic growth or decline.

The town, which was to historians for so long the unconsidered container of industry and trade and the anonymous masses, is therefore now assuming a new importance in its own right. Historians are addressing it *directly*, partly to understand urban changes better for their own sake but chiefly in order to relate them more coherently to economic, political, and cultural developments on an altogether wider plane. Purely 'biographical' studies of individual towns which leave no lasting impression when set in a void offer a basis for making their differences indelible when studied comparatively; investigations of urban life in microscopic detail are being matched by far-reaching research into the fundamental social processes leading towards the urbanisation of the whole world. Historians are on common ground here with other disciplines, for towns have always embodied their own history with peculiar tenacity, and this is now causing scholars across a wide front to look at the urban past with growing curiosity. Among them are geographers, economists, sociologists, demographers, archaeologists, civic designers—each of them having distinctive approaches and techniques, all of them sharing the problem of interdisciplinary communication. The present mood of urban history is therefore experimental and exploratory. The field is wide open and world-wide, as much concerned with concrete detail where it matters as with imaginative hypotheses wherever they lead, as readily approached by the geographer as by the sociologist or the historian. *Studies in Urban History* is a series designed in this mood. The volumes will have a standard format but in all other respects remain completely unstereotyped so as to give free rein to the most promising ideas, from whatever quarter or however remote their reference to time or place.

Foreword

The main challenge of urban history is not only one of exploration but of communication between disciplines that are not so much disparate as disconnected. For this reason every volume in this series is being selected with the object not only of filling some important gap in our knowledge but of demonstrating particular techniques of research or approach.

The forerunner of these volumes was what now appears to have been a seminal conference, held in 1966 by the Urban History Group operating in this country, in an attempt to promote the exchange of ideas between scholars occupied with problems of urban analysis within different disciplines. From it came the volume I edited in 1968 under the title *The Study of Urban History*, which might be said, as one reviewer remarked, to have 'put British urban history on the map'. That book was an unconscious anticipation of the series now taking shape. In his Foreword to it Asa Briggs looked forward to the time 'when the field will have been cultivated still more and when the fascinating projects described in these pages have reached completion'. It is fitting that the first studies in the series should come from members of the group that came together in 1966 and who have since taken up one of the challenges thrown out at the time by François Bédarida. 'Historians', he said, 'should try to respond to as many of the questions thrown up by sociologists, demographers, geographers, town planners as they can. As brilliantly expressed by Lucien Febvre, "the present offers us a lot of questions to be put to our beloved documents".' The first volume in the series* explored a contemporary problem— the fate of the modern city centre—in terms of the constraints imposed on one major city by the legacy of its own past. This second volume is occupied with another perennial problem—the exercise of municipal democracy in an increasingly complex urban society—and it does so, to begin with, in terms of the aspirations and experience of two contrasting industrial towns of the nineteenth century. The heart of Dr. Hennock's study is the council chamber, for it is there that the forces that gave a place most of what mattered to the community as a whole came together, even though they seldom stood fully revealed. Part of the enormous achievement of this book is to have uncovered the structures of political power which underpinned the municipal programmes that were carried through, in such mutually illuminating ways, in Birmingham and Leeds, and to have analysed so closely their

* Anthony Sutcliffe, *The Autumn of Central Paris: the Defeat of Town Planning 1850–1970* (1970).

social characteristics both on their own terms and by comparison with many other places. No work that I know in this field has penetrated so far into the political workings of the urban machine as it set out on the terrible task of civilising the first nation of city-dwellers. Yet what is in many respects more valuable still is to have broken through the thicket of statistics which must inevitably guard the entrance to any real understanding of the machinery of modern society, and to discover the human material behind it. Here, in a specially sensitive way, we can watch the political figures themselves, not merely the marks they made but the quickening of their energies, the fastening of their beliefs, the personal beginnings of the whole municipal ethos. We get in this way a much more convincing perspective of the evolution of that form of collectivism which was being embodied in English local government at that time, embroiled fully as it was in the ineluctable demands of the day.

Dr. Hennock is in all this a knowing guide, taking us by some new and more rewarding paths over territory that has been surveyed in rather broader outline before, but in the last part of his book he offers us an entirely new viewpoint. Here he provides the link between the ideals and the actualities of nineteenth-century urban government and the historically-derived expectations we still have of the role of the town councillor in the changing structure of local government at the present time. The fundamental re-ordering of municipal life now going on in the wake of the Royal Commission on Local Government in England (the Redcliffe-Maud inquiry), which reported in 1969, marks the end of a complete cycle in these affairs. The towns that stood so small and unreformed in the shires of England before the Royal Commission on Municipal Corporations, which reported in 1835, have come to dominate our national life, and the old boundaries between them and their counties are being removed. This is therefore a most timely book, enabling us both to enter more imaginatively into the earlier era of municipal reform and to see what is now happening in more comprehensive terms. Not only so, for in providing an historical commentary on our own affairs Dr. Hennock has also looked further afield. His framework of comparison includes the traditions and practices of urban government in Germany and the United States, and he offers us thereby some valuable insights into the historical origins of contemporary cultural differences. We need more studies that can embrace so much.

University of Leicester H. J. DYOS
August, 1972

viii

Preface

This book begins with a grateful acknowledgement to the four universities with which I have been associated since I first embarked on the work which is here presented. My previously unpublished thesis for the Cambridge Ph.D., submitted in 1956 under the title 'The Role of Religious Dissent in the Reform of Municipal Government in Birmingham 1865–1876', provides the material for book I, part II. It was done under the supervision of Sir Herbert Butterfield, and I owe much to his wisdom as a teacher and to his great kindness. The subsequent research was begun in my last year at the University of Keele and continued intermittently during my time at the University of Sussex. Although I cannot recommend the experience as ideal for the pursuit of historical research and the writing of books, I count myself fortunate to have been involved in the early years of these two university foundations. Finally I wish to thank the Warden and Fellows of All Souls College, Oxford, for electing me to a Visiting Fellowship for 1966–7, which gave me a much-needed opportunity to reflect on what I was doing and to work uninterrupted by teaching and administration.

I am greatly indebted to the Director and Trustees of the Leverhulme Foundation for the grant which has financed much of the work, and to Mr. John Sykes M.A. and Mr. T. L. Burton for their valuable help in the research at Birmingham and Leeds respectively.

My choice of Leeds as the second town to be studied was strongly influenced by the existence of Mrs. Brenda M. Baxter's (née Powell) M.A. thesis, 'A Study of the Changes in the Social Origins, Political Affiliations and Length of Service of Members of the Leeds City Council 1888–1953', Department of Social Studies, Leeds, 1958, and particularly by her generous offer to allow me to use the biographical card index on which the statistical conclusions of her thesis were based. It was only after I had committed myself too far to make a change of plan feasible that it turned out that this card index had been left in the care of her former supervisor, who was by then teaching at another university. Further investigations established beyond a reasonable doubt that the card index had been thrown away when the person in question vacated his room at the University of Leeds. This mishap has added very considerably to the work and may well have affected the completeness of the information which it was possible to assemble.

For permission to use manuscript records my thanks are due to the Chamberlain Trustees, the Passfield Trustees, the Corporations of Birmingham and Leeds, the Leeds Conservative Association, Mr. Michael Meadowcroft (the Leeds Liberal Party agent), to the Ministers of the Church of the Messiah, Birmingham, the Church of the Redeemer, Birmingham, and Mill Hill Chapel, Leeds, and to Sir Donald Finnemore, who many years ago gave me access to the records of the People's Chapel, Birmingham. I wish also to express my thanks to those who have helped me to use the collections of historical material in their charge, especially to Miss D. M. Norris and Miss Dorothy McCuller at the Birmingham Reference Library, Mr. D. R. Denman at the Leeds Civic Hall, Mrs. Horne at the Leeds Central Library and Mr. C. G. Allen at the Library of Economic and Political Science. I have explained on p. 365 what this book owes to the cooperation of Mrs. Barbara M. D. Smith of the Faculty of Commerce, Birmingham University. Others from whose advice I have profited include particularly Professor Asa Briggs, Mr. D. N. Chester, Professor E. M. Sigsworth, Professor D. E. C. Eversley, Mr. F. R. Beckwith, Professor Frank Bealey, Professor J. F. C. Harrison, and Mr. Maurice Hutt. Professor H. J. Dyos has been an indefatigable editor and the source of good advice and encouragement. An interim report on the research for this book was given to a conference which he organised at Leicester University in 1966, and was published in *The Study of Urban History*, ed. H. J. Dyos (Edward Arnold, 1967). Some of the figures contained in that paper have subsequently been re-worked and are superseded by those contained in the present book. Finally I wish to thank Miss Brenda Magurran who undertook much of the typing, and Mr. T. Garfield and Mr. D. Orme who drew the maps.

Contents

Contents

Tables

Plates

Unless otherwise indicated, plates 1–17 come from illustrations contained in the Birmingham Collection in the Birmingham Reference Library and plates 18–34 from the Local History Department in Leeds City Library. Permission to use this material is gratefully acknowledged, as it is for each of the following: the Librarian, Birmingham University Library for plates 8, 14 and 15; Messrs. Lewis & Randall, Birmingham, for plate 16; the Leeds Civic Trust for plates 20 and 21; the Thoresby Society for plate 22; the Lord Mayor of Leeds for plates 18, 24, 27, 28, 29 and 30.

Figures

Maps

Abbreviations

A.G.	*Aris's Birmingham Gazette*
ald.	alderman
B.C.P.	*Birmingham Council Proceedings*
B.G.	*The Birmingham Gazette*
B.J.	*The Birmingham Journal*
B.M.N.	*The Birmingham Morning News*
Chlain.MSS.	Chamberlain Manuscripts, University Library, Birmingham
clr.	councillor
D.P.	*The Birmingham Daily Post*
L.I.	*The Leeds Intelligencer*
L.I.C.	Leeds Improvement Commission
L.M.	*The Leeds Mercury*
P.P.	*British Parliamentary Papers*
W.P.	*The Birmingham Weekly Post*
Webb Loc.	*Webb Local Government Collection*, British Library of
Gov. Col.	Political and Economic Science, London School of Economics
Y.E.N.	*The Yorkshire Evening News*
Y.E.P.	*The Yorkshire Evening Post*
Y.P.	*The Yorkshire Post*

Note : Abbreviated titles have been given to works appearing more than once in a given chapter. The place of publication of all books cited is London, unless otherwise indicated.

Introduction

'This meeting considers . . . a fit and proper person to represent the . . . Ward on the Town Council'

These words have been used in support of candidates for election to the town council ever since election became the rule in 1835. They stand at the beginning of this book not least on account of their ambiguity. They beg more questions than they answer, and both kinds are encompassed by this study. To what ideas of fitness did men appeal when recruiting town councillors? To what degree did the actual composition of any council reflect these ideas? We are concerned with the relation between ideal and reality, as it affected the recruitment of citizens to serve on town councils. The book deals specifically with the experience of two big towns, Birmingham and Leeds, in the years between the Municipal Corporations Act of 1835 and the outbreak of the First World War.

To confront what men had hoped for with what they actually achieved is both chastening and instructive in whatever sphere of life we meet it. In the case of the government of towns in the nineteenth century there are additional reasons for regarding it as a matter of significance.

In 1801 only 17 per cent of the population of England and Wales lived in towns of more than 20,000 inhabitants. By 1911 that figure had risen to 61 per cent. Not only did the population become increasingly urbanised, the size of towns became larger. In 1801 only London exceeded 100,000 inhabitants; in 1911 forty-four towns did. They accounted between them for 38 per cent of the population. Again in 1801 London contained just on 865,000 inhabitants and the largest provincial town 90,000. In 1911 the respective figures were four and a half million and 746,000.[1]

---

[1] A. F. Weber, *The Growth of Cities in the Nineteenth Century* (New York, 1899), tables XVIII–XX; *Census of England and Wales*, 1911, I, tables VII, IX.

These are familiar facts. They indicate that in the nineteenth century the bigger towns were the growing points of the new society. It was there that men confronted the complex tasks which made it possible for large numbers to live together.

There was no successful precedent to which to turn. Europeans had never yet lived in large towns without poisoning themselves with their own waste products. Life had survived only through immigration from the healthier countryside.[2] The growth of the urban population depended therefore on constant improvement in sanitary administration, if a relapse into disaster was to be avoided. Nor was this all. Beyond the issues of survival lay a whole range of other problems, many of them connected with the creation of a civilised urban way of life which would not be limited to the few but was adapted to large numbers.

It was ironical that England should have been the first country in which these issues had to be faced. For there was much in their social experience that unfitted Englishmen for the task. For centuries the most successful of them had graduated into the rural gentry and aristocracy. The ease with which the English nobility had opened its ranks to talent had saved the nation from much social strife. It had also greatly enriched the culture of the upper ranks of English rural society with new talent and wealth. In 1800 English civilisation was rural; towns were the playground not the homes of the English upper class. To become a country gentleman was the aspiration of every successful town dweller. Not only the accomplishments but also the aspirations of English culture were rural.[3]

Such a situation brought great advantages as long as towns were a minor element in the society. But it proved a poor foundation on which to build an urban way of life when the balance tilted away from the countryside. The English equivalent of the rich and cultured patricians, who dominated Hamburg and Frankfurt, Florence, or Amsterdam were merchants of two generations' standing, casting a speculative eye on a landed estate, and hoping for a place on the county bench. Some Unitarians or Quakers were a little more resistant to the pull of the gentry and in some instances provided towns with a slightly longer experience of an established patrician house. But the difference that this made, though significant by English standards, is paltry by comparison

[2] R. Mols, *Introduction à la Démographie historique des Villes d'Europe du XIVe au XVIIIe siècle* (Louvain, 1954–6), II, 329–38; III, appendix, Table 10.
[3] In this connection see the very interesting comments in Ruth Glass, 'Urban Sociology in Great Britain: A Trend Report', *Current Sociology*, IV, 4 (1955), 14–15.

with the long-standing patriciate in many areas of continental Europe.[4]

These are circumstances which the student of English urban history has to accept as given. They affect his subject everywhere and at all times. Not one of the three generations which we shall examine escaped the lure of the country-house ideal. The last of them found itself in addition exposed to the pull of the metropolis, and from the point of view of their native town that only made the situation worse.

The social implications of urbanisation form one of the great themes of modern British history. This book is intended to make a contribution to that theme, not to encompass it. The means by which the threat of death and disease was mitigated and a new urban way of life created include a multifarious range of institutions, many of them those voluntary associations that are among the most fascinating features of England in the nineteenth century. By concentrating on the action and composition of public authorities we are therefore bound to abstract one set of institutions from a network of great complexity. The two detailed case-studies, particularly that for Birmingham, attempt to remedy this one-sidedness and to explore the inter-connection of public authorities and voluntary associations of different kinds. It has not been possible to do this for the period 1835 to 1914 as a whole. Since it is, however, by what they choose to omit that historians most often mislead, it should be stressed that this is due solely to the limitations of time. It is therefore important to guard against the anachronism of seeing the past through twentieth-century collectivist spectacles.[5]

The reader will find much in these pages that resembles contemporary discussion and anxiety about the inadequate recruitment of talent into elected local councils. Some of those anxieties have had a long history. Nor has the calibre of elected representatives in the past been always as high as has been suggested by some, who see the present position as an ominous decline from past glories. The remarkable continuity in the formal structure of urban local government since 1835 seems to invite such comparisons between the past and the present. Although municipal corporations have acquired numerous duties and shed some others, their structure is one that an early Victorian would recognise. Mayor,

---

[4] See for instance Helmut Boehme, *Frankfurt und Hamburg* (Frankfurt, 1968); Percy E. Schramm, *Neun Generationen. 300 Jahre deutscher 'Kulturgeschichte' im Lichte des Schicksals einer Hamburger Buergerfamilie* (Goettingen, 1963–5).

[5] In the long run, however, public authorities enlarged their role in one field after another at the expense of other associations. The growing demand for compulsory regulation and the pressing need for revenues larger than those to be raised by voluntary subscriptions were two powerful forces driving in one and the same direction.

aldermen, and councillors are chosen now as then at the same intervals and in the same manner. The principle of unpaid service by citizens without special training, which was a central feature of the system then, is still scarcely modified today, in spite of the payment for loss of earnings that was introduced in 1948. These resemblances are, however, merely a part of the picture. There is good ground for arguing that the recruitment to service on the town council was between 1835 and 1914 more far-reaching in its effects for good or ill than is the case today.

We need to bear in mind two features of local government in that period which have been greatly modified since. The first is the vastly greater reliance on local initiative, which characterised parliamentary legislation for much of the nineteenth century, as indeed it had done throughout the eighteenth. Up to the 1830s it was assumed that almost any action that required legal sanction, i.e. anything that tampered with established rights, would originate from the particular circumstances of a locality and be applicable to it alone. The method of legalising such actions was the local Bill (or in even more limited circumstances the private Bill) introduced into Parliament by the local M.P. on the petition of the substantial inhabitants of the locality. Local and private Bill legislation formed the great majority of the legislative work of Parliament.[6] The great legislative work of the 1830s with its recourse to general acts shows that the earlier assumptions were under pressure, but in practice local acts remained the standard procedure in most matters. We shall find the Leeds street commissioners between 1840 and 1842 obliged to draft their own act by the refusal of the government to contemplate general legislation for the sanitary needs of towns and the inappropriateness and ultimate failure of the efforts of private M.P.s in this field.[7] In fact the years 1836–48 were a great period for local acts.

The practice was now no longer without its critics. 'It is surely a hardship', wrote an assistant commissioner of the Royal Commission on Municipal Corporations,

> 'that the inhabitants of each town should be compelled to purchase at their own charge one code of laws at least; to buy separately in each particular instance regulations, that are not of private but of public concernment, and that are, or ought to be, applicable to

[6] Frederick Clifford, *A History of Private Bill Legislation* (1885), I, appendix A.
[7] See below, p. 190.

4

every town in the kingdom, as the matured result of general legislation. If a return were made of the total sum that has been paid for Police Acts, its magnitude would rouse the most listless and would astonish everyone.'[8]

The expense was indeed a great burden, and as it became apparent that the requirements of towns were really very similar, the practice grew up of taking over in their entirety clauses from the local acts of other towns. The practice became formalised in the Clauses Acts of 1847. Thereafter certain clauses taken from the local acts of pioneering towns could be incorporated into local Bills by a greatly simplified procedure, which did much to reduce the cost.[9]

Before the late 1840s the initiative of the larger and wealthier towns had been almost the sole driving force behind attempts to control the rapidly changing urban environment. After that date Parliament increasingly resorted to general Acts, whose powers could be adopted at the discretion of local authorities. But it was still the locality that decided whether to do so or not. The powers were available, the procedure had been simplified and cheapened, but there was seldom any compulsion. Localities were still expected to know what they needed and for what they were prepared to pay. Nor did the older practice of specially drafted local acts fall into disuse. On the contrary, towns continued to be faced with problems to which the sparse general legislation provided in their opinion no suitable remedy. They continued to draft their own Bills either supplementary to general acts or in preference to them, particularly if the latter carried with it any form of supervision by the central government.[10] Most of the work of identifying and defining new statutory needs still fell therefore to local authorities, especially in the bigger towns which were in the forefront of the new social experiences.

Although much of the general legislation remained optional, compulsion became more common towards the end of the century, particularly in the fields of public health and education. This meant that over some of the most important spheres local authorities lost the power of initiative that they had enjoyed for so long. Even in the twentieth century it has not been entirely lost, but the contrast with the past is

[8] *Municipal Corporations in England and Wales. Royal Commission Reports on certain Boroughs* (by T. J. Hogg), p. 135; 1837–8 (686) xxxv.
[9] Clifford, *Private Bill Legislation*, II (1887), 526–9.
[10] This was the case with the Public Health Act of 1848. Many of the larger towns including both Birmingham and Leeds refused to adopt it but obtained their own local improvement act instead. The average number of local acts in the fifteen years after 1850 was 230 per year, compared with 155 per year in the fifteen years before 1850. Clifford, I, appendix A.

very great. For all but the last few years of the period to be studied, initiative lay overwhelmingly with local authorities, whether this took the form of independent legislation or the adoption of optional powers. Especially was this true of large towns such as those with which this study is concerned.

The second feature that characterised local government in the past was its independence from supervision by central authorities. This also gave to the negligence or efficiency of local bodies an importance which has since been greatly modified. From the beginning of the eighteenth century to the 1830s this independence was absolute. The period under review saw the development of various means whereby the central government could impose minimum standards on the localities. But the development was patchy. It occurred first in the sphere of poor law administration and there took a form which raised much opposition and thereby probably hindered the adoption of similar detailed control in other fields of administration. More indirect means had to be found. After 1856 Exchequer grants were used to enforce minimum standards on the borough and county police forces, and the same device played an important role in the history of education. But outside these spheres the use of grants to enforce minimum standards was negligible before 1914 in the areas for which municipal corporations were responsible, although the total amount given in grants increased considerably towards the end of the period.[11]

In matters affecting the death-rate the right of the central government department to investigate and publish its findings proved important even in the absence of any powers of enforcement. After 1866 the central government did obtain powers to compel sanitary authorities guilty of gross neglect. Although the ultimate sanctions were seldom used, their existence added effectively to the supervision of the weaker authorities. However, the bigger towns were little affected by the Act of 1866.[12] Treasury control over the borrowing powers of local authorities occasionally prevented a locality from doing something they would in other circumstances have done. Otherwise there were only the courts of law. Although a cumbersome way of applying pressure, legal action could be most effective, to judge from the history of Birmingham and Leeds.[13] Yet when every allowance has been made, the fact remains that the

---

[11] Maureen Schulz, 'The Development of the Grant System', in C. H. Wilson, ed., *Essays in Local Government* (1948).
[12] R. J. Lambert, 'Central and Local Relations in Mid-Victorian England: The Local Government Act Office 1853–71', *Victorian Studies*, VI (1962–3).
[13] See below, p. 107 ff. and pp. 212–3.

determination of standards depended on the efficiency and conscientiousness of local authorities to a far greater extent than has been the case in recent decades. Missing was the systematic supervision by the departments of central government and the purposeful use of the financial power.[14] Only the Boards of Guardians felt the heavy hand of government, and their exclusion from this study serves to sharpen the contrast between the present and the past.

This book could well have been accompanied by a systematic study of the place of salaried officials in the history of municipal government. By 1908 the American writer, A. L. Lowell, thought that their position was so central to the whole process that the excellence of municipal government was roughly proportional to the amount of influence that the salaried officials were allowed to exercise. The motive force behind English town councils was, according to him, to be found mainly in the officials.[15] Like other foreign observers of English local government, Lowell was liable to magnify the importance of those features which he wanted to persuade his own countrymen to adopt. By comparison with the American officials, who were primarily political partisans and made way for their opponents when their party lost control of the city hall, their English counterparts must have seemed powerful figures and beneficent experts. Not all Lowell's assertions on this point should be accepted as proven. But his American perspective helped him to focus attention on the bureaucratic process and there can be no doubt that for the twentieth century this was a fruitful emphasis. How far the same applies also to the nineteenth century is less clear. In the absence of any systematic study of the subject what follows is no more than an impression. But it provides good reason for focusing on the elected members in the first place.

It is one of the differences between M.P.s and members of local authorities that the latter have always exercised administrative powers, while the former, unless ministers of the Crown, have not. A town council is both a representative assembly and an executive body, and in the committee system it has a means of performing its executive duties. In this respect it is more like the government than like Parliament. Like the government it employs servants subordinate to it to carry out its policy. According to the formula that became orthodox in the twentieth century, the committee was responsible for policy and the official for

[14] See D. N. Chester, *Central and Local Government: Financial and Administrative Relations* (1951).

[15] A. L. Lowell, *The Government of England* (New York, 1908), II, 178–80.

administration. In recent times it has been a common complaint that the officials encroach on policy-making. For a long time it was the other way about and the committee members 'encroached' on administration, although they did not think of it in that light.

In the early 1850s the Darlington Board of Health expected the members of its inspection committee to visit an allotted area of the town regularly.[16] In the 1860s and 1870s the members of the visiting sub-committee in Leeds and of the borough inspection committee in Birmingham were expected to do the same, supplementing and supervising thereby the work of the salaried inspectors of nuisances. Indeed one Birmingham councillor died from an illness contracted in the performance of his duty. In Manchester as late as 1913 members of the audit sub-committee were regularly checking entries and initialling passbooks and ledgers. The chairman of the housing sub-committee personally inspected condemned houses and conducted interviews with their owners.[17] The active role played by the elected members for a long time in administration was particularly marked in the crucial area of finance.[18] Until 1855 the Leeds borough treasurer had been little more than a cashier, receiving and paying out money as he was told, while the whole burden of drawing up estimates fell to the chairman of the finance committee. In Birmingham in the late 1860s it was the chairman of the finance committee who devised a new system of accounts as well as a cheaper method of raising loans. Much of the financial success of the purchase of the gasworks and the water-works in the mid-seventies, not to mention the Birmingham Improvement Scheme, was due to Joseph Chamberlain's skill as a negotiator.[19] For another generation powerful chairmen of the finance committee, drawn from the circles of big businessmen, continued to control the municipal finances in great detail.[20]

Nowadays the influence of salaried officials is due mainly to two factors, which reinforce each other. One is the personal quality and effectiveness of the individual. The other is the existence of an organised profession with minimum standards of competence and remuneration, active in the dissemination of professional knowledge. This second factor hardly comes into the picture during the period under review. It

[16] Public Health Act, *Report to the General Board of Health on Darlington 1850*, Introduction by H. John Smith (Durham County Local History Society, 1967), p. 10.

[17] Ernest Simon, *A City Council from Within* (1926), pp. 60, 31.

[18] On this subject see my 'Finance and Politics in Urban Local Government in England, 1835–1900', *Historical Jl.*, VI, 2 (1963), 212–25.

[19] See below, p. 117 ff.

[20] Evidence of the Birmingham town clerk in 1900, quoted in Conrad Gill and Asa Briggs, *History of Birmingham* (1952), II, 126–7.

was as individuals that officials influenced policy and set standards of administration. The extent to which they did so varied therefore very much from person to person and from place to place. The choice of the official and his dismissal lay in the hands of the council, as did the determination of salaries, which differed widely even in places comparable with each other. Although there were exceptions, councils must often have got the officials they deserved, and they were not beyond dismissing men who were too good for them, as happened in Birmingham in 1857.[21]

Such are the reasons for a historical study of the recruitment of members of town councils. Who served on the councils of these two large towns at different periods in the nineteenth century? From what sections of the community were they drawn, and in what proportions? Did the composition of the council remain fairly stable over three generations or fluctuate considerably? Did the composition of the councils in these two towns resemble each other or not? If not, what explanation is there for the contrasting experience? How did the experience compare with what people at the time would have wanted a town council to be? These are some of the questions to which this book provides the answers. In the two case studies of the Municipal Gospel in Birmingham and the New Era in Leeds we can follow both the formulation of standards and the attempts to implement them.[22]

These two reform movements form the focus of the book. They are treated in detail in order to show both the sources of the movements and their consequences. What is more, the rest of the book is intended largely as a commentary on them. The long-term studies in Books I and II place them in a historical perspective in terms of the difference that they made to the composition of the councils. Book III is primarily concerned with the ideas themselves. Although the two reform movements occurred in different towns and at different times, they share the same point of view. We shall see that the creation of this point of view was largely the achievement of the group of men around Joseph Chamberlain in the Birmingham of the early 1870s. Their concept of what a council should be has proved long-lived, dominating thought on the subject almost to the present. But like all ideas it arose out of a particular set of circumstances. We shall examine it in relation to earlier views and then trace its tenacious survival into the twentieth century. The final chapter

---

[21] See below, p. 33.
[22] Readers are advised to consult the 'Note on Methods' on p. 361 before going on to Books I and II.

of the book shows the strains that have resulted from this survival under circumstances that are in many respects far removed from those under which it had been formulated.

RECRUITMENT: THE PROCESS AND THE PROBLEM

Under the 1835 Municipal Corporations Act there were two conditions with which a candidate for election to the borough council had to comply. He had to be on the burgess roll and to satisfy a further property qualification.[23] The burgess roll, the list of all qualified voters, was limited to occupiers of rateable property in the borough residing within seven miles of it, who had paid rates for the previous two and a half years. In addition to these qualifications, which they shared with all municipal voters, candidates had to own real or personal property worth £1,000 or else occupy property of a rateable value of £30. In smaller boroughs, not large enough to be divided into wards, the relevant figures were £500 and £15 respectively. This property qualification was not always strictly enforced, nor was a man required to resign if his property fell below the amount specified. At least as important in limiting the sections of society from which councillors could be drawn was the fact that their service was unpaid and council meetings held during normal working-hours when employers were unlikely to permit an employee to be absent. In consequence even Chartist candidates tended to be small masters, shopkeepers or publicans.[24]

These barriers kept out others than wage or salary earners. They tended also to exclude most of those in process of building up their business, the young men on the make. The council was for those who could spare the time, who had arrived where they were content to be. There were exceptions, however, particularly in the early decades, and the graphs in appendix II do not all display the expected time-lag between the establishment of a new industry in the town and its appearance among the occupations of the councillors.

The widening of the municipal franchise automatically enlarged the numbers qualified as councillors. Two additional changes affected the candidates only. In 1869 the area of residence was extended from seven to fifteen miles beyond the borough, and in 1882 the property qualification was abolished for all but those living in that outer ring beyond seven miles. This small anomaly, which however mainly affected

---

[23] The authority for the next five paragraphs is B. Keith-Lucas, *The English Local Government Franchise. A Short History* (1952).
[24] See below, pp. 197–8.

wealthy people, was not remedied until 1918. After 1882 there were therefore no legal obstacles to the candidature of manual workers, whatever the practical difficulties may have been. Even before that date they had not proved an insuperable barrier. In 1872 the action of the Yorkshire Miners' Association, who lodged £1,000 temporarily in the bank in the name of a candidate for the Barnsley Borough Council, showed what could be done for a trade union nominee.

The municipal franchise was altered in three principal ways during the period 1835–1914: by the enfranchisement of compounding ratepayers, by the reduction in the ratepaying period required before admission to the burgess roll, and by the enfranchisement of women.

In the years after 1835 rating authorities did not normally trouble to rate the smaller houses. If they did, they resorted to compounding, which became very widespread after the mid-century. This was an administrative device for the convenience of the rating authority, who would have found it difficult and expensive to collect paltry amounts from the often shifting occupiers of small houses. They therefore levied the rate on houses below a certain rental on the owner, and left him to recoup himself from his tenants when he drew the rent. In such cases, in which the landlord had acted as an unpaid rate-collector, they levied less than the full rate. Although the tenants paid the rate in fact, they did not pay it in law. Since their name was not entered in the rate-book, they did not qualify for the burgess roll. The rental below which compounding occurred varied widely from town to town. It was £13 in some parts of Birmingham, £7 or £8 in others, £20 in Brighton, and £6 in those boroughs that adopted the Small Tenements Rating Act of 1850. Where that Act was adopted the compounding occupiers qualified for the franchise and this greatly increased the municipal electorate. In other boroughs the compounders often had no right to the vote. In Birmingham an attempt to put them on the burgess roll in 1864 was declared illegal. In such boroughs the electorate was markedly increased in 1869 when the Municipal Franchise Act put their rights beyond dispute. The same act also reduced the period during which rates had to be paid from two and a half years to one, and enfranchised women provided they met the other qualifications. The courts decided that this did not include married women since they at that time still had no property rights independent of those of their husbands. Their right to sit on borough councils was not established until 1907, their right to the municipal vote not until 1918.

The size of the municipal electorate relative to population varied therefore considerably from one borough to another before 1869 and much less so thereafter. 1869 saw an increase everywhere, but where voting qualifications had been low it was much less startling than where the qualification had been high and the electorate small. Birmingham and Leeds offer a marked contrast in this respect. In Leeds the municipal electorate was quite exceptionally large almost from the start. After standing at about 5 per cent of the population in the first two years and being enormously increased in 1837 due to an error in the registration procedure, it stood at about 10 per cent when this had been put right and remained at about that level for many years. It was 9 per cent in 1851 and 13 per cent in 1861. In 1871 it had risen to 19 per cent and remained at that level for the rest of the period under review. Leeds is therefore an exception to the general rule that despite the democratic appearance of the 1835 Act compared with that of 1832, the municipal electorate was usually smaller than the parliamentary electorate. In Leeds both in 1838 and in 1850 it was between two and three times the size of the parliamentary electorate. Birmingham on the other hand had a particularly restricted municipal electorate before the legislation of 1869 drastically changed the position. Both in 1851 and 1861 it comprised a mere 3 per cent of the population. By 1872 it stood at 18 per cent, having risen from 9·5 thousand to 62 thousand in a decade, most of this increase taking place in 1869. Thereafter the municipal electorate was much the same in both boroughs, standing for the rest of the period at between 18 and 20 per cent of the population. The experience of both cities seems to have been extreme by comparison with the two medium-sized towns investigated in Brian Keith-Lucas's book on the English local government franchise, as the following figures show.

TABLE 1. *Municipal electorate as a percentage of population*

	Birmingham %	Maidstone %	Ipswich %	Leeds %
1841	3	6	8	10
1851	3	6	8	9
1861	3	9	10	13
1871	18	13	15	19
1911	19	18	20	20

The qualification for the municipal franchise is important, and not only because it largely coincided with the legal qualification of councillors. For there was after all one final condition for becoming a town councillor, the process of election. Large boroughs, such as Birmingham and Leeds, were divided into wards each of which was represented by three or six councillors. Elections were held annually at the beginning of November, one-third of the councillors retiring each year. Since the wards were the municipal constituencies, it was in them that municipal politics was organised. Ward meetings were called to nominate candidates, ward committees set up to fight elections, first on an *ad hoc* basis and from the 1860s onwards as part of the regular party organisations. There were normally several meetings before a contested election and these were reported in the local press. Although politics could differ widely in character from one ward to another, it was not usually considered essential for candidates to be either residents or employers in the wards they wished to represent. For this purpose the borough was the prime unit of politics both before the establishment of permanent party associations and after.[25]

So much for the councillors. Aldermen were elected by the town council for a period of six years. They were assigned to a ward for which they acted as a returning officer. Aldermen could be chosen from any person qualified to sit on the council, and for the first reformed council it was not uncommon to select distinguished citizens who had not fought an election. The same happened occasionally at other times, but it was most unusual. In most boroughs it became the convention to choose the aldermen from the more senior councillors, who were thereby saved the trouble of further popular elections. In practice therefore the normal path into the council was through popular election.

It was this that distinguished the recruitment to borough councils from the processes that had existed in the unreformed corporations. It also distinguished it from the practice that pertained in the counties until 1888. There social position was decisive. The nomination of the Lord Lieutenant, which was normally accepted by the Lord Chancellor, was made according to standards that appeared proper to those already on the county bench.[26]

In practice, elections frequently proved an obstacle to the recruitment of the leading citizens of the borough. But this in itself requires explanation. Nothing deterred such citizens from wishing to stand for

[25] Such a generalisation does not quite do justice to the strong sense of local identity found in Leeds south of the river, and there may well be other towns of which the same is true.
[26] That matters became more complicated after the creation of elected county councils is indicated by the case of Cheshire. J. M. Lee, *Social Leaders and Public Persons. A Study of County Government in Cheshire since 1888* (1963), studies county politics from a very similar point of view to my own.

2

parliamentary elections, which were usually far more expensive and unpleasant than municipal ones. These factors were no obstacle where the prize was large enough. It is just here that we find the great difference between the Palace of Westminster and the council chamber. All studies of the parliamentary representation make it clear that, except for a certain deflection caused by the uneven distribution of seats, the nineteenth-century House of Commons mirrored the country's social and economic elite. This is exactly what cannot be taken for granted in the case of town councils. We need to investigate the composition of these councils in relation to the social structure of the town, and should not be surprised to find great diversity in this respect from time to time and from place to place.

BOOK I
BIRMINGHAM

Part I
The Composition of the Council 1838–1914

I

The Council in the Victorian Age

For all the similarities between the two towns, we must begin by stressing a difference. In 1835 Leeds already had a municipal corporation; Birmingham did not. As an unincorporated town it lay outside the scope of the Municipal Corporations Act. Its government, by Court Leet and Street Commission, remained unchanged until 1838. Then, on the petition of the inhabitants, the Crown granted a municipal corporation on the model of the 1835 Act. The first election for a council did not take place until December 1838. The three years' delay had, however, done little to change the nature of Birmingham politics. With some reservations, which will become apparent later, the municipal election was a late manifestation of the alignments that had been formed between 1830 and 1832 around the issue of Parliamentary Reform. Birmingham's first Town Council was a creation of the politics of Reform as truly as those elected in 1835 for Leeds and other established boroughs.

Since the beginning of the decade the town had been dominated by a body formed in 1830 to agitate for Parliamentary Reform, the Birmingham Political Union. After the victory of 1832 it lost its momentum for the time being and ceased its official existence in 1834. But even before it was formally re-founded in 1837 it emerged spasmodically to initiate public meetings.[1] The economic crisis of 1836–7 once again provided the conditions for a more permanent existence, and in May 1837 the Union was formally reconstituted with a large paid-up membership and an elected council. The Birmingham Radicals had been assured by their political adviser in London that the government itself would rectify the anomaly of large unincorporated towns. It was therefore only

[1] The fullest treatment of the Birmingham Political Union is in the V(ictoria) C(ounty) H(istory), *The County of Warwick*, VII, *The City of Birmingham*, ed. W. B. Stephens (1964), pp. 296–303. The fullest treatment of the movement for municipal incorporation is in Conrad Gill and Asa Briggs, *History of Birmingham* (1952), I, chapter XI.

after their hopes had been disappointed by the legislative programme for the parliamentary session of 1837 that they roused themselves to action. A town's meeting was called in March 1837 and a committee appointed to take all necessary steps to obtain a municipal charter for the town. An interview with the Home Secretary followed and led to nothing. The way to success would have to be by means of a petition to the Crown. They began to organise the collection of signatures.

In their desire for municipal incorporation the Radical leaders did not speak for all sections of the town. The movement to obtain what is now considered the normal machinery of local government was then a highly controversial political manoeuvre. Nor was this peculiar to Birmingham. In Manchester and Bolton petitions for a municipal corporation also provoked counter-petitions from the opponents of the move. In Birmingham this counter-petition was organised by the local Conservative leaders. The existence of a Conservative organisation, the Loyal and Constitutional Association, made it easy for them to take the initiative, but the opposition was by no means limited to Conservatives. Many Whigs, who had co-operated with the Political Union over the question of Parliamentary representation, were lukewarm or openly hostile to the establishment of a corporation.[2] The rival petitions indicate that a majority of the ratepayers desired incorporation, but what the opposition lacked in numbers it made up in wealth. The rateable value of the property occupied by the rival petitioners is estimated very differently according to different methods of sampling, but that of the opposition was either slightly more or else considerably more than that of the incorporation party.[3]

This strong opposition among the propertied is explained by the fact that the municipal corporation was scarcely thought of as an administrative device. The enthusiasm for it was enthusiasm for representative institutions. Thomas Attwood of the Political Union regarded a corporation primarily as a device for petitioning Parliament on the questions of the day, an extension of the Union but with a recognised legal status and a continuous existence. When Richard Cobden subsequently advocated the incorporation of Manchester, he also stressed this aspect of the case.[4] In its early years the Town Council in fact made a point of passing

---

[2] See speeches by James Taylor and David Malins at the meetings held on 3 and 12 January 1838, *A.G.* 8.1.1838, 15.1.1838.

[3] Gill and Briggs, *Birmingham*, I, 225–6.

[4] A Radical Reformer [Richard Cobden], *Incorporate Your Borough! A Letter to the Inhabitants of Manchester* (Manchester, 1838), reprinted in W. E. A. Axon, *Cobden as a Citizen* (1907).

resolutions on most of the major issues of national politics and forwarding them to Whitehall or Westminster. The town councils of other boroughs did the same. The control over the urban environment, in so far as this was being attempted, was in the hands of the Street Commission for the parish of Birmingham and of similar bodies in the outlying parishes.[5] The establishment of a municipal corporation was not intended to supersede them. The only administrative function to be assumed by the new Corporation was the creation and control of a police force. The opposition argued with much force that this could be done better and more cheaply by a stipendiary magistrate. It is clear that the Corporation was not strictly necessary for administrative reasons, but desired or rejected on account of its representative character. What was at stake was the principle of representative government.

> 'At present the authorities were self-elected, self-delegated, and irresponsible; and hence they had no authority, and commanded no respect, or not such respect as they ought, as rulers of the people to enjoy.'[6]

Although the existence of the Birmingham Street Commission was not directly threatened by the granting of a municipal charter, the logic of such rhetoric pointed towards a clash between the two bodies. To William Redfern, the most active advocate of incorporation, the ultimate effect would be 'the consolidation of all the local Acts, the concentration of all powers in one body and their administration by one set of officers'. At the dinner to celebrate the granting of the charter he called on his fellow Radicals never to rest satisfied 'until every oligarchical system throughout the town was utterly abolished and all its rights, powers and authorities were transferred to the Town Council'. This was an open challenge to the Whig-dominated Street Commission as well as to the Church-dominated governing body of the Grammar School.[7] Indeed within a fortnight of the grant of the charter the law-firm of Redfern, Bray and Barlow gave notice of their intention to bring a local Bill before Parliament in 1839 to vest the powers of the three street commissions of Birmingham, of Deritend and Bordesley and of

---

[5] There was a street commission for Deritend and Bordesley and another for Duddeston-cum-Nechells. There were also surveyors of highways for Deritend, for Bordesley and for Edgbaston.
[6] George Edmonds, speech at the town's meeting 30 October 1837. *B.J.* 4.11.1837, in J. T. Bunce, *History of the Corporation of Birmingham* (Birmingham, 1878), I, 117.
[7] *B.J.* 21.10.1837, in Bunce, *Corporation of Birmingham*, I, 108; *B.J.* 23.2.1839, p. 4, partly quoted in Gill and Briggs, *Birmingham*, I, 273.

Duddeston-cum-Nechells in the Corporation.[8] Nothing was to come of this gesture.

Some Radical members of the Birmingham Street Commission had recently withdrawn from active participation, but in any case Radicals did not form the bulk of the membership. Although the Commission included Tories, the body was effectively run by a small but influential group of Whigs, known in the town for their public spirit as well as for their economic and social status.[9] Whiggery was not a militant cause in Birmingham politics and possessed no organisation of its own. In national politics the local Whigs had been content to go along with the Political Union in the politics of Reform. They had supported the two Liberal Radical candidates, Thomas Attwood and Joshua Scholefield, the twin leaders of the B.P.U., who now represented the town in Parliament.[10] But at the municipal election there would be forty-eight elected places to be filled as well as the sixteen aldermanic seats that were in the gift of the Council. As the Radical leaders prepared for the election, the question began to be asked, whether prominent merchants, who owed their position in the town to their social and economic role but were not identified with the Radical leadership, could be regarded as acceptable candidates.

The charter had been received on 1 November, the preparation of the burgess roll was fixed for 11 December and the election for 26 December. On 5 November twenty-five of the most active members of the committee that had conducted the campaign for the charter constituted themselves a central committee to fight the election. Eleven days later they issued a list of approved Liberal candidates for the wards in the parish of Birmingham. Those for the outlying parishes appeared a few days later. On the principle that those most active in obtaining the charter would make the best councillors, the central committee had nominated seventeen of its own members. It would presumably have nominated more, if five others had not preferred to canvass for the various salaried offices which were about to be created.[11]

This high-handed action did not go unchallenged. In St. Peter's ward

[8] *A.G.* 12.11.1838, p. 3.
[9] See the evidence of *The Birmingham Journal, B.J.* 21.11.1837, p. 4.
[10] At the time of the general election of 1837 it was estimated by the Liberal leaders that there were 300 Whig voters, 1,000 Whig-Radical voters and 2,000 Radical voters. On the other side there were 1,000 Tory voters. Speech by P. H. Muntz, *B.J.* 10.11.1838, p. 2.
[11] *B.J.* 10.11.1838, 17.11.1838, 24.11.1838. Dr. Birt Davis subsequently withdrew his candidature for St. Paul's ward and was nominated for the coroner's office, thus making six. Five of them obtained a salaried office and the sixth became town clerk when his successful rival resigned in May 1840.

a protest meeting of burgesses was held a mere two days after the publication of the list. The sponsor of the meeting was a Liberal, and the chair was occupied by a resident of standing in the ward who, like most of the speakers, was also in sympathy with the Liberal cause. They protested about two things—the nomination of candidates by 'a self-elected body' without even the pretence of consulting the burgesses of the ward, and the choice of political activists to the exclusion of widely respected citizens of standing. They accepted only two out of the six names put forward and rejected the others in favour of men who were active street commissioners and Whigs. The sponsor of the move explained that

> 'he had but one object in view, and that was to prevent the Tory party from outvoting them. That they could not do unless fit and proper persons were offered to the burgesses. . . . He for one should not stand nice as to a shade in the politics or religion of any man who might be otherwise well qualified.'[12]

One of the rejected nominees, a small bookseller and printer and a strenuous Reformer of twenty years' standing, pointed out that he was a poor man and added that a person ought not to be elected solely on the grounds of his standing in society. But the meeting was clearly against him. In a spirited leading article the editor of the *Birmingham Journal*, who was one of the most prominent members of the central committee, repudiated the notion of ransacking the list of street commissioners for suitable candidates. But in the face of the eminent names that had been put forward he concluded lamely that it was in any case an insult to ask such men 'to submit to the every-day and humble labours of a common-council man'.[13] However, the lesson had been learned, and within the next week ward meetings were held in which the original list was frequently amended. In St. Peter's the result was a compromise: the Radical bookseller was retained, one of the four street commissioners was accepted, and the remaining places filled by two men of standing in the ward, one of whom stood in the first rank of Birmingham businessmen.[14] But three of the Whig street commissioners had been excluded, and the most prominent among them allowed himself to be nominated

---

[12] *B.J.* 24.11.1838, p. 7.
[13] *B.J.* 1.12.1838, p. 4.
[14] Charles Geach, then aged thirty. He had already helped to found two local banks, was at the time manager of the Birmingham and Midland Bank and only at the beginning of a great career as an entrepreneur. Eliezer Edwards, *Personal Recollections of Birmingham and Birmingham Men* (Birmingham, 1877), p. 128.

by the opposition. Similar compromises occurred elsewhere. Five candidates were accepted by both sides, but in at least six wards respected Whigs or even Reformers were standing in opposition to the official Liberal list. It did them no good, for at the polls the official Liberal list was voted in without exception.[15]

This complete triumph is a testimony to the hold which the Political Union had acquired over the town, as well as to the concessions that had been made. It was the last occasion on which Birmingham politics were to be untroubled by the impending split within the Union between middle-class and working-class Reformers, although parliamentary and municipal elections continued to be won, as before, by Liberals.[16] That the opposition should not have obtained a single seat on the Council was also due to the clever way in which the ward boundaries had been drawn. The Radicals were strongest among the small occupiers in the outer parts of the town; the Conservatives were chiefly found among the larger occupiers in the centre. A central ward, such as was customary in many boroughs including Leeds, might have returned one or even three opposition candidates. But in Birmingham several wards were drawn in strange funnel-shapes from the centre outwards, thus cutting up the town centre and swamping its voters with those from the remoter parts ⟨*see* map 1.⟩ The contentious St. Peter's ward is an extreme case. The only ward in the parish of Birmingham to have six councillors instead fo three, it linked the wealthy area between New Street, Anne Street, Colmore Row and High Street by a narrow corridor with the poorer parts around the railway depots and the canal wharfs.[17] The sympathetic Joseph Parkes, well briefed in the politics of the town, had presumably used his position in the Privy Council Office to good effect.[18]

Birmingham was not the only borough in which such gerrymandering had taken place. In Bristol it had worked in favour of the Tories. The barrister appointed by the Crown to decide on the ward boundaries, being pressed for time, largely accepted the recommendation of the churchwardens that wards should coincide with parish boundaries. The result was the creation of some wards with markedly fewer electors, and six more Conservative councillors than in equity was justified. In a

---

[15] *B.J.* 8.11.1838, p. 4. For the final list of candidates see Bunce, I, 153–6, which gives no hint of the conflict over the nominations. For this the source is *B.J.*, which reported the ward meetings.

[16] For the split see T. R. Tholfsen, 'The Chartist Crisis in Birmingham', *International Review of Social History*, III (1958), pp. 461–80.

[17] See A Burgess, *Ten Objections to the Birmingham Corporation* (Birmingham, n.d. [1839]).

[18] For Joseph Parkes see Jessie K. Buckley, *Joseph Parkes of Birmingham* (1926).

very evenly divided Council this deprived the Liberals of the majority which they would otherwise have had.[19]

When the original elections in Birmingham were supplemented by the choice of sixteen aldermen, all but two were chosen from among the councillors. At the subsequent bye-elections the vacancies so caused were filled by more Liberals. The two exceptions deserve a comment. One was chosen to heal the breach among the Reformers of Duddeston-cum-Nechells between those who believed in nominating party militants and those who wanted men of standing and substance. The other must also have been chosen in a spirit of concession. A Whig, a street commissioner, a county J.P., and a gentleman of independent means, John Towers Lawrence for all his Unitarianism seems to have had more in common with those who had been defeated than with the victors. His tenure of office was short.

In its occupational composition the new Council mirrored therefore largely that of the Liberal party in the town, led as it was by a few bankers and substantial merchants, and consisting of the bulk of those small manufacturers and tradesmen for which Birmingham was renowned. The small gradations by which these were separated from those above and those below—so favourable to the creation of a democratic sentiment, and so difficult for anyone attempting to sort them into categories is a commonplace among all who have commented on the social structure of Birmingham and the political consequences that flowed from it.[20]

There were no members of the learned professions on the Council, but one Captain R.N., who was also secretary to the London & Birmingham Railway Company. There was one banker and eight fairly large merchants, as well as the gentleman of private means already mentioned, who was himself from a merchant family. Of this group three were certainly Whigs and another had been acceptable to both sides at the election and so presumably not closely associated with the Radicals. Birmingham merchants had small businesses compared with the mercantile houses that dominated the economic and social life of Liverpool or Leeds. But in terms of the Birmingham economy they

---

[19] G. W. A. Bush, 'The Old and the New. The Corporation of Bristol 1820–1851', unpublished Ph.D. thesis (Bristol, 1965), pp. 340–42.

[20] Richard Cobden to Joseph Parkes, 9 August 1857, in John Morley, *The Life of Richard Cobden*, 9th ed. (1903), pp. 663–4; Asa Briggs, 'Thomas Attwood and the Economic Background of the Birmingham Political Union', *Cambridge Hist. Jl.*, IX (1948); T. R. Tholfsen, 'The Artisan and the Culture of Early Victorian Birmingham', *Univ. Birmingham Hist. Jl.*, IV, 2 (1954), 146–66; Alan Fox, 'Industrial Relations in Nineteenth-Century Birmingham', *Oxford Economic Papers*, n.s., VII (1955); Asa Briggs, *Victorian Cities* (1963), pp. 187–92.

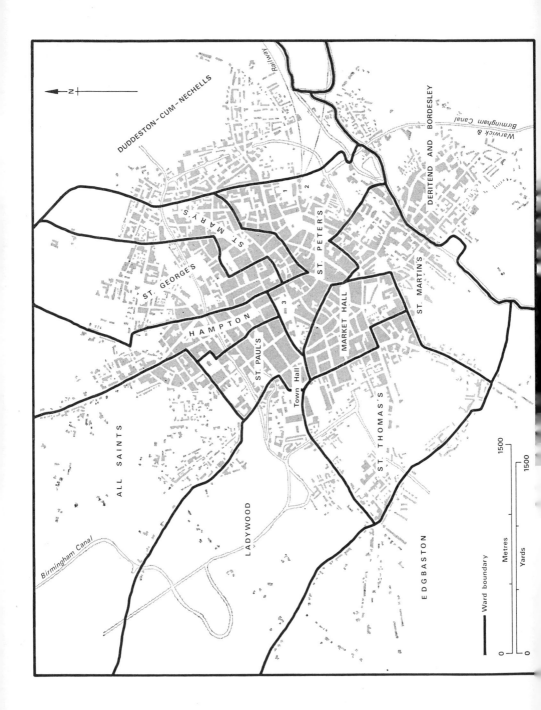

were the leading figures and, together with the most respected attorneys and physicians, largely constituted the social elite of the town.

At the other end of the scale there were thirty-five owners of small businesses, comprising about 55 per cent of the whole Council, of whom twenty-three (36 per cent) were manufacturers of one kind or another. The latter were concentrated in particular in the outlying wards, Ladywood, All Saints', Deritend and Bordesley, Duddeston-cum-Nechells, and in the two wards, St. George's and Hampton, whose peculiar funnel shape joined the jewellers' quarter to the outlying areas of north Birmingham.[21]

In view of the mutual distrust between the leaders of the movement for incorporation and many prominent members of the Birmingham Street Commission we should not expect to find a large overlap between the two bodies. It must also be borne in mind that the Street Commission operated only in the central parish. If we therefore exclude the twelve councillors for the out-parish wards, we are left with a town council of fifty-two members, of whom eleven were also street commissioners. Taking the membership of the Street Commission in 1839, 1842, and 1851, first, the overlap can be put in tabular form.

TABLE 2. *Members of the Birmingham Town Council who were Birmingham street commissioners*

Date	No.	Per cent of Council less out-parish wards
1839	11	21·2
1842	10	19·2
1852	12	23·0
1856	8	15·4
1862	4	7·7

This result was not due to a boycott of the new Council by the others, for there were a further seventeen commissioners among the thirty-two

[21] The statement in Gill and Briggs, I, 233 that the manufacturers on the first Town Council 'represented outlying wards where most of the industry was established' is true only if Hampton and St. George's wards, with their funnel-shape, are regarded as outlying. In fact the jewellers' quarter lay close to the centre of the town to the north and east of St. Philip's church ⟨see map 1⟩.

MAP 1 (opposite). *Borough of Birmingham 1838.*
Source: Local History Collection, Birmingham Reference Library.
1 and 2 railway depots, 3 St. Philips Church. The canal wharfs are South-West of the depots.

candidates defeated in the relevant wards. The remarkably high total, therefore, of twenty-eight out of thirty-four commissioners, tried successfully or unsuccessfully to serve on the new body. The reason for the relatively small overlap between the two bodies was political: a high proportion of the public men of economic and social standing in the town were excluded by the control which the Radicals exercised over the politics of the borough.

The Birmingham Street Commission is of interest both because it carried out administrative duties important for the welfare of the town, and because it was composed of many of the economic and social elite. The same grounds justify a look at the Guardians of the Standard of the Wrought Plate who were responsible for the Birmingham Assay Office. The prosperity of one of Birmingham's principal trades depended on the absolute reliability of the local assay mark, and the Assay Guardians were therefore chosen for their known public status. They were drawn from the local business community who considered the position a mark of honour and from the peers and gentry of the district.[22] Once again we find a relatively small overlap with the Town Council, although the overlap with the Street Commission was considerable.

TABLE 3. *Assay Guardians on the Birmingham Town Council and the Birmingham Street Commission 1839–52*

		Subsequently appointed as Assay Guardians	Total
Total No. of Assay Guardians 1839	38		
No. on 1839 Street Commission	11	7	18
No. on 1839 Town Council	2	3*	5
Total No. of Assay Guardians 1842	41		
No. on 1842 Street Commission	10	4	15
No. on 1842 Town Council	1	4*	5
Total No. of Assay Guardians 1851	39		
No. on 1851 Street Commission	7	4	11
No. on 1852 Town Council	1	3*	4

* Including P. H. Muntz, who became a Guardian only in 1875.

By 1842, the next sample year, thirty-five of the original sixty-four members had left the Council. A turnover of just under 55 per cent in

[22] Arthur Ryland, 'The Birmingham Assay Office', in *The Resources, Products and Industrial History of Birmingham and the Midland Hardware District*, ed. Samuel Timmins (Birmingham, 1866); The Birmingham Assay Office, List of Guardians 1773–1942, Typescript in Birmingham Reference Library.

three years is rather high. Just how high would be indicated by a comparison with Leeds. Unfortunately a straight comparison is ruled out since six years elapsed there between the election of the first reformed council and the 1842 sample. But if one assumed the same rate of change in Birmingham over the next three years as over the first, this gives a notional figure for Birmingham of 80 per cent compared with 64 per cent for Leeds.[23] These high figures cannot be explained by any major electoral come-back on the part of the Conservatives. But during these years the strain on the Birmingham Town Council must have been enormous. In the first place the legality of its municipal charter was challenged in the courts. Secondly a hostile government, uneasy at the connection between the local Chartist movement and many members and officers of the Council, deprived the Corporation of its control over the local police force. With the maintenance of order vested in a commissioner responsible to the Home Secretary, the Council had little to do beside making political gestures and trying to speed up the legal proceedings upon which its very existence depended. The year 1842 saw the turn of the tide. The legal status of the Corporation was confirmed and its police functions restored.[24] The next decade saw it consolidate its position in the town. Turnover in membership for the years 1842–1852 was 75 per cent compared with 86 per cent in Leeds.

In spite of the turnover in personnel, the social composition of the Council had changed little between 1839 and 1842, and not so greatly even by 1852.

TABLE 4. *Birmingham Town Council 1839–62 : selected occupations*

	1839	1842	1852	1856	1862
Large businessmen	9	8	10	8	5
Gentlemen	1	1	—	—	—
Naval officer	1	—	—	—	—
Lawyers	—	—	3	4	4
Total	11(17·2%)	9(14·0%)	13(20·3%)	12(18·7%)	9(14·0%)
Small businessmen	35(54·7%)	30(46·9%)	24(37·5%)	28(43·5%)	21(32·8%)

[23] Since the information for this study has been collected systematically only for the sample years, it is not possible to make the more straightforward comparison of 1836–9 in Leeds with 1839–42 in Birmingham, nor of 1836–42 in Leeds with 1839–45 in Birmingham. However, the notional figure for Birmingham probably errs on the low side, since turn-over would probably have been higher among the councillors who had already served more than three years than among those who had not. For the methods used in studying the membership of the Council and all definitions of terms used throughout the book, see 'A Note on Methods' on p. 361.

[24] See Gill and Briggs, I, chapter XII.

The number of large businessmen hardly varies, and if we include the gentlemen and the naval Captain in order to round off the representation of the economic and social elite, the consistency is equally striking. Three of the 1852 elite were stalwarts from 1839; the remaining seven had all been recruited during the previous decade.

What was new by 1852 was the presence of attorneys, i.e. solicitors.[25] It is strange that this had not happened before. The sort of position held by attorneys made them commonly members of town councils, and the Birmingham Council was never again to be without them. The profession was represented on the Leeds Town Council during this period, and the same was true for instance of Nottingham, Bristol and Exeter.[26] Of the three attorneys Thomas Hodgson ranked among the leading professional men in the town, and remained on the Council until he became Deputy Clerk of the Peace in 1864. Henry Hawkes had begun his career in Joseph Parkes's office, one of the outstanding figures in Birmingham Liberal politics. Hawkes himself had been prominent in organising the party in Duddeston-cum-Nechells and was elected a councillor for that ward as soon as he had made himself professionally independent in 1846. He was to be a prominent figure in Birmingham municipal politics well into the seventies, and was finally appointed to be Coroner as a reward for his services. The absence of political lawyers such as Hawkes from the Council in its early years is probably due to the single-mindedness with which the dominant party had used its power of patronage to reward its supporters.[27] The third attorney in 1852 was of no importance and did not remain long. Strictly speaking only Hodgson belonged to the economic and social elite of the town.

As yet nothing startling had changed in the relation between the Town Council and the upper ranks of Birmingham society. The overlap was still rather small not only when compared with Leeds, or indeed with

---

[25] They were not the first members of the learned professions on the Council. In 1842 there had been a surgeon, i.e. a member of the lower ranks of the medical profession.

[26] For Leeds see table 12, p. 194. In Nottingham there were at least three lawyers on the first reformed Council (5·4 per cent) and five in 1843-4 (8·9 per cent). In Bristol the profession provided 9·2 per cent of all the Council members between 1835 and 1851. There were 10 lawyers (15·6 per cent) on the Council in 1845. Exeter with a social structure very different from that of Birmingham furnishes an extreme case. From 1836-47 17·4 per cent of all Council members were lawyers. They made up 25 per cent of the Council in 1848-9. G. W. A. Bush, *The Old and the New*, pp. 575-6; Robert Newton, *Victorian Exeter 1837–1914* (Leicester, 1968), appendix I.

[27] See above, p. 20 fn. 11. The firm of Redfern, Bray and Barlow, which did most of the electoral business for the Liberals and had handled all the work in connection with the campaign for incorporation, provided the first two town clerks. George Edmonds, the Radical stalwart, became clerk of the peace. Arthur Ryland, who had done some of the registration work in 1838, became clerk to the borough magistrates and only later became a town councillor.

Liverpool, Bristol, or Nottingham, all of them places with a long established municipal corporation, but also with Manchester, where the
Corporation dated from the same time and had passed through the same
vicissitudes.[28]

Much greater changes seem to be occurring in the Birmingham Council at the lower end of the social scale. Of course there is much less information about those who figure in the statistics as small or small/medium
businessmen, so that the margin of error in allocating them into categories is probably greater. But even so it looks as if the medium-sized
businesses are providing an increasingly larger proportion of the Council, while the immense preponderance of really small businesses is
lessening. In 1852 the balance between the two categories is for the first
time equal. From 1862 it was to shift increasingly against the small men.
This is what we would expect. After about 1860 the Birmingham
economy entered a new phase in which economic growth showed itself
by an increase in the average size of firms and not mainly, as in the past,
by an increase in the total numbers of enterprises. The development from
1839–52 is more surprising because it does not so obviously coincide with
what is known about the economic history of the town.[29]

1852 is not merely a sample year in the decennial series, it is in any
case the beginning of a new phase in the municipal history of Birmingham. For the Birmingham Improvement Act of 1851 had finally
established the municipal corporation as the principal local authority.
It had endowed it with all the powers of control over the environment
and provision of civic amenities which had previously belonged to the
Street Commission, and it had added greatly to them. This was the consequence of investigations into the sanitary condition of the town, which,
here as elsewhere, led to a new 'sanatary conscience'. They convinced the
inhabitants of the need for a local board of health with far greater powers
than had been possessed by the Street Commission. These powers were
required for the whole borough and not for the central parish only. In
addition it was obvious by 1851 that Parliament would grant such

[28] For Liverpool see occasional hints in B. D. White, *A History of the Corporation of
Liverpool 1835–1914* (Liverpool, 1951), especially pp. 17, 88–9. For Nottingham my own
investigations confirm R. A. Church, *Economic and Social Change in a Midland Town.
Victorian Nottingham 1815–1900* (1966), pp. 181–2. Shena D. Simon, *A Century of City
Government: Manchester 1838–1938* (1938), and 'Manchester 1838–1900' in *Webb Loc.
Gov. Col.*, volume 158 provide information on the early Manchester Town Council, but
it is only impressionistic.

[29] V.C.H., *The City of Birmingham*, pp. 81–208; G. C. Allen, *The Industrial Development of Birmingham and the Black Country* (1929), pp. 113 ff.

far-reaching powers of taxation only to an elected body. The street commissioners, for whom the years since 1838 had been a period of great activity, recognised that their day was past. They cordially co-operated in the drafting of the Act which put an end to their existence.[30]

This co-operation owed much to the work of a few men who had belonged to both bodies.[31] When the control of market and town hall, of road improvement, lighting, paving and drainage passed to the Corporation, more members of the Commission became town councillors. In 1852 there were twelve former street commissioners on the Council ⟨*cf.* table 2, p.25⟩; at least three more had joined by 1855.

There was therefore good ground for assuming that the relation between the upper ranks of Birmingham society and the Town Council would in the future be closer than it had been in the past. In 1839 such prominent merchants as William and Clement Scholefield, leading figures in the Political Union, had been brought into the Council by their embattled commitment to the creation of representative government in the town. The ease with which after the resignation of these pioneers their places were filled by partners in some of the most prominent firms in the town was a sign that the Town Council had become an acceptable forum for public work.[32] So was the willingness of the former street commissioners to be recruited around 1852. In such a situation social emulation often builds up a momentum of its own. It is easy to imagine the process whereby municipal service as councillor would come to rank with that of an Assay Guardian, a governor of hospitals, schools or similar bodies, a church or chapel warden as a normal claim on the town's leading citizens, and election to the bench of alderman as scarcely inferior to the distinction conferred by appointment to the bench of magistrates.

In fact the opposite happened. The tentative beginnings were nipped in the bud by the course which municipal politics took in the

[30] Conrad Gill, 'Birmingham under the Street Commissioners, 1769–1851', *Univ. B'ham. Hist. Jl.*, I, 2 (1948), pp. 255–87; Gill and Briggs, I, chapter XV.

[31] Particularly Aldermen Henry Smith and William James. Smith, a Whig, was mayor in 1845 and 1851 and a street commissioner until 1850. He was a brassfounder, an Assay Guardian and a member of the closely knit network of Unitarian families. His father had also been an important figure on the Street Commission. In 1838 his nomination for St. Peter's ward had been rejected by the Liberal Central Committee. He was nominated in the election for aldermen in December 1838 but defeated. James, a Tory, had been a strong opponent of incorporation in 1838. clr. 1849–50, ald. 1850–November 1851. By 1850 he had realised that the Street Commission could not hold out against the Council. An accountant, Assay Guardian and chairman of the Birmingham Waterworks Co., he just fails to be caught in the sample for January 1852.

[32] E.g. Abraham Dixon of Rabone Bros., merchants; Ralph Heaton senior of the Birmingham Mint; Charles Reeves, sword cutler.

1850s and early 1860s. The effect of this on the recruitment to the Town Council can be seen in the figures for 1856 and 1862 given in table 4 ⟨p. 27⟩. The number of large businessmen went down, a development not at all compensated for by the increase in the number of lawyers, of whom only two out of four were partners in leading firms. At the lower end of the scale 1856 sees a temporary reversal of previous trends, and among the twenty-eight small men were more licensed victuallers than ever before. In fact the drink trade as a whole increased its representation to nine, i.e. 14 per cent of the Council ⟨figure 1, p. 36⟩. How had this come about?

Between 1852 and 1856 the Council passed through a political crisis, which was the direct consequence of the new duties it had assumed.[33] The cost of the programme of drainage and road construction on which it had embarked had, here as elsewhere at the time, been gravely under-estimated. By 1853 there was a serious deficit in the Improvement Account. In 1854 the purchase of the Birmingham Waterworks Company, for which provision had been made in the 1851 Improvement Act, was prevented by a determined group of 'Economists', i.e. econo-misers, on the Council who were acting as spokesmen for a Ratepayers' Protection Society. This body reappeared in November 1855 as the Independent Association of Ratepayers, when the same men tried to stop the Corporation from going to Parliament for powers to raise additional loans needed for its programme of drainage, paving and street improvement. Defeated in the council chamber, they rallied sup-port in the town. In December the ratepayers voted in a town's poll and refused to sanction the new Improvement Bill. It had to be with-drawn. The proposed Bill would have increased the rates to 3s. 9d. : £, a figure that was still less than the sum of the various rates levied in the parish of Birmingham before 1851. But this did not prevent the Economists from launching their campaign and seizing effective power. Representative government, it was widely felt, ought to be cheaper than the irresponsible Street Commission. It could not be per-mitted to add to the rates.

The decision of the ratepayers immediately precipitated a financial crisis. The Birmingham Banking Company refused to increase the Corporation's overdraft, and faced with a veto to their policy, both the finance committee and the public works committee resigned *en bloc*.

---

[33] The next two paragraphs largely follow Gill and Briggs, I, chapter XVIII. Professor Gill, however, confused two issues, the opposition to the purchase of the waterworks in 1854 and to an Improvement Bill in 1855. The original sources are *A.G.*, *B.J.* and *B.C.P.*

The Economists now took responsibility, and their leader, Joseph Allday, became chairman of both committees.

Allday was to be the dominant figure on the Council for the next four years. He had been an active popular Radical since 1832. In 1828 he had launched an anonymous scandalmongering newssheet which at one stage led to his imprisonment for libel. On the collapse of the paper he set himself up as a small manufacturer and retail ironmonger, but his preoccupation with public life swallowed up the time needed to keep his business afloat in the difficult conditions of the early 1840s. Thereafter his wife opened an eating-house, which became well known for its tripe suppers and prospered. This was the perfect vehicle for his ambitions. It became a centre for the airing of political views and local grievances. In 1848 Allday became churchwarden of St. Martin's, the nominee of the Radical opposition to church rates and clerical control. By virtue of that office he was a guardian and overseer of the poor. In 1849 he became a town councillor and in 1853 achieved local fame by a successful campaign to expose abuses in the Court of Requests and in the borough gaol. An attempt by the borough magistrates to hush up the case was defeated, a royal commission investigated the details whose publication caused a national scandal and led to the dismissal of the governor and the prison surgeon. The Report censured all but one of the magistrates responsible for visiting the prison for having failed to exercise any real supervision. Allday's action was popular Radicalism at its best, a fearless exposure of abuses sanctioned and condoned by those of rank and power. He was the hero of the hour, his aggressiveness, his meddlesomeness and sheer persistence had triumphed. The episode became the subject of a well-known novel *It's Never too Late to Mend*, which Charles Reade wrote in 1856 and which was also turned into a play.[34]

This was the basis of Allday's reputation in the years immediately after 1853. It helps to account for his great power on the Council and the ease with which he could outface, insult and defeat his opponents, who included borough magistrates and leading figures in the public life of Birmingham, veterans of the struggle for the municipal charter.

The other leaders of the Economy party were a cabinet maker, a draper with a shop in the High Street, and an attorney-cum-vestry clerk.[35] The reliable core of the party consisted of another 18 members:

[34] *P.P.* 1854[1809] xxxi. The case is described in S. and B. Webb, *English Prisons under Local Government* (1922), pp. 169–75. For Allday see *B.M.N.* 6 May 1878 and a revealing character sketch in Eliezer Edwards, *Personal Recollections*, p. 70.
[35] John Gameson, clr. and ald. 1850–70. George Turner, clr. and ald. 1851–72; J. W. Cutler, clr. and ald. 1853–71.

10 manufacturers—7 small and 3 medium-sized;
5 small tradesmen/shopkeepers, including one wine and spirit
     merchant;
2 licensed victuallers;
1 coal dealer.

It was clearly a party of the small men. Those whom they replaced from
power by and large belonged to a different section of the community.
Their most prominent spokesman owned what was probably the largest
corn-milling plant in Birmingham and was a former street commissioner.[36] The chairman of the previous finance committee was a
merchant in the America trade[37], that of the public works committee
was Hawkes, the attorney. The twelve most reliable adherents of the
group consisted of

9 manufacturers—1 large, 4 medium-sized,[38] 3 small-medium,
     1 small;
1 leading attorney (Hodgson);
1 wine and spirit merchant;
1 licensed victualler,

This conflict had important consequences. In the first place the
victory of the Allday party, determined as they were to keep the rates
down to 2s. 6d. : £ meant a general reduction of the estimates. Work on
the drainage scheme was stopped, the paving activities of Piggott Smith,
the borough engineer and former servant of the Street Commission who
had a national reputation for his roads, were severely curtailed. In 1857
he was dismissed altogether and replaced by his assistant at half the
salary. Not all the policy of the new regime was equally cheap. In 1857
the Corporation had to pay £7,500 compensation to the governors of
the grammar school for breaking an agreement into which the Corporation had entered in 1851, to continue the construction of Albert Street.
In the end the street was completed after all, but not until 1864.

It is difficult to tell which was more disastrous for the town, the short-
sighted penny-pinching policies adopted, or the bitterness of the conflict in the Council chamber. Already in 1854 the faction-fighting had
driven the town clerk to resign his post. The debates of 1855 were
memorable for the invective of the attacking Economists, and the tone

[36] William Lucy, mayor 1849, 1850, borough J.P.
[37] G. V. Blunt, Incorporation Cttee 1838, councillor and alderman since 1839.
[38] Including P. H. Muntz, incorporation committee 1838, mayor 1839, 1840, borough
J.P., M.P. for Birmingham 1868–85.

of debate did not improve when they were in control. Some of the defeated party fought back; many withdrew from the Council. Three of the large or medium-sized manufacturers, including P. H. Muntz, retired in 1856. Neither Lucy nor Blunt lasted until 1862. In the Allday era municipal service lost what limited prestige it had begun to acquire among the respectable section of Birmingham society.

In its extreme form the policy of 1855 was bound to be a passing phase, for processes had been started in the early 1850s that could not just be stopped. In 1852 an outlet had been constructed for the town's sewers into the river Tame. By 1854 the first complaints were received about the fouling of the stream, and in 1858 C. B. Adderley of Hams Hall, a large landowner in the Tame Valley, obtained a legal injunction, restraining the Corporation from connecting further sewers to the outlet. In consequence the Council was forced to spend money on filtration works and to direct its attention once more to the drainage of the borough. 1859 was the last year in which the Economists had it all their own way. Two years later the Corporation went to Parliament for an Improvement Act giving it power to raise additional loans. The reversal of the policy of 1855 was achieved only after a struggle and owed much to the financial ability and rasping agressiveness of Robert Wright, an accountant elected in 1858. Unfortunately ill-health forced him to retire from the Council in 1862. He died four years later, too soon to see the long-term consequences of his work.[39]

The best way to bring out the significance of the next phase in the history of the corporation is to compare the composition of the Council in 1862 with that of twenty years later.

TABLE 5. *Birmingham Town Council 1862–1902: selected occupations*

	1862	1882	1892	1896	1902
	No. %	No. %	No. %	No. %	No. %
Large businessmen	5 7·8	15 23·4	17 23·6	16 22·2	12 16·7
Small businessmen	21 32·8	11 17·2	11 15·3	11 15·3	12 16·7
Drink trade	5 7·8	1 1·6	1 1·4	— —	1 1·4
Medical men	— —	4 6·3	7 9·7	5 6·9	4 5·6

[39] Gill and Briggs, I, 416–27. On p. 427 the reference to J. S. Wright ought to be to Robert Wright. For details of the difficulties over drainage, see J. T. Bunce, *History of the Corporation of Birmingham*, II (Birmingham, 1885), chapter IV.

The sharp reversal of the situation created by the events of the 1850s is very clearly shown in the first two columns of table 5. When the figures for 1882 are compared with those for 1839–52 〈table 4, p. 27〉 they show that this was not just a reversal of the special situation created in the 1850s. The proportion of large businessmen was now considerably higher than it had ever been before, while the proportion of small businessmen had continued its previous sharp decline.

It is not merely by comparing large and small businessmen, however, that we shall understand what was happening in these twenty years. Hence the inclusion of the figures for the presence of the drink trade and of the medical profession. As a percentage of the total membership of the Council these groups had never been large, but their importance was symbolic. Their presence related to two controversial issues in local government during the mid- and late-Victorian period, the control of the drink trade and the improvement of public health. The almost total disappearance of councillors directly connected with the drink trade, when they had constituted 7·8 per cent in 1862 and 14 per cent in 1856, points to changes in the nature of municipal politics. It is in marked contrast to what was happening in other towns at the same time.

From the 1860s onwards militant temperance organisations with political, not merely educational objectives intervened in the municipal politics of many towns. This in turn led the drink interest, which had always played an important role in politics, to organise itself and to counter-attack. As the providers of the most commonly accessible social facilities, publicans had always played an important role in the formation of political opinion and had been well placed to act as representatives. Even when they remained in the background, they were all but indispensable as the providers of committee rooms and of the traditional liquid lubricants of the electoral process. The Licensing Act of 1872, by emphasising the role of the police in the detection of licensing offences, made influence over the watch committee of the Town Council a coveted prize for both temperance militants and publicans, second only to the Licensing Bench.

In Leeds the proportion of the Council drawn from the drink trade rose from 7·8 per cent in 1872 to 16·9 per cent in 1902. 〈*See* figure 1.〉 In Wolverhampton it was 10 per cent in 1889 and again in 1904. In Exeter, where the trade had been strong in local politics for many years, it reached a peak with 22·9 per cent in 1871 and was still 13·3 per cent in 1899. In Newcastle-under-Lyme the drink trade provided as many

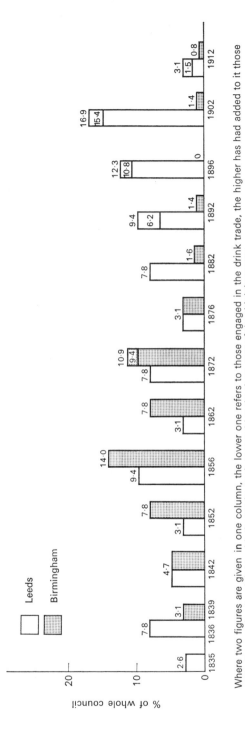

Where two figures are given in one column, the lower one refers to those engaged in the drink trade, the higher has had added to it those with close professional links with the trade, such as would make them part of the drink interest:

Leeds 1892 one accountant, one architect
1896, 1902 one auctioneer and valuer
1912 one architect
Birmingham 1872 one lawyer

FIG. 1. *Representation of the drink interest on the Town Council 1835–1912: Birmingham and Leeds*

as 20·8 per cent of the successful candidates at municipal elections between 1872 and 1899.[40]

Of course councillors other than publicans, brewers and spirit merchants could be, and were, in favour of leniency in regulating the sale of alcoholic drink. Similarly, others than medical men were advocates of a vigorous policy in the field of public health. Indeed the number of Council members drawn from the medical profession was very small even at the best of times. That is understandable, for doctors were busy men. It must have been far more difficult for them than it was for lawyers to keep several hours at a time regularly free from professional calls for attendance at Council or committee meetings. In view of this the figures for the Birmingham Council in this period are remarkable, although not unique. In Wolverhampton, where there were four medical men on the Council in 1888–90, i.e. 8·7 per cent, the picture was comparable. A very different pattern, however, is found in Leeds ⟨*see* figure 6, p. 206⟩. The contrast between the two towns is one of timing. At its highest the proportion of medical men on the Leeds Town Council was not much below the Birmingham figures. But in the period 1882–96, when the Birmingham figures were so high, the percentage in Leeds never rose above 3·1, i.e. two members. The pattern in Leeds is fairly similar to that found in Exeter. In both places an established corporation had attracted merchants and professional men before 1835 and continued to do so in the years that followed. The number of medical men was highest in the first few years after Reform, and thereafter fell to insignificant proportions until the very end of the period.[41] In Birmingham such men were valued as experts by the electors and by their colleagues, and nearly always served on committees dealing with aspects of public health or lunacy.

Table 5 indicates the contrast between the Council in 1862 and 1882. It also shows that what had happened by 1882 was no flash in the pan, but the beginning of a phase that continued at the very least until 1896. By 1902 the position had in some respects become more ambiguous. The proportion of small businessmen continued much as it had been, nor did the drink interest re-establish its former position. The number

---

[40] G. W. Jones, *Borough Politics. A Study of the Wolverhampton Town Council, 1888–1964* (1969), p. 368; Frank Bealey, 'Municipal Politics in Newcastle-under-Lyme 1872–1914', *North Staffordshire Journal of Field Studies*, V (1965), 66. Bealey's figures of successful candidates over a series of years are not directly comparable with the other figures drawn from the whole council in sample years, but they make the same general point.

[41] G. W. Jones, p. 109; R. Newton, Appendix I.

of medical men did not significantly decline, but the proportion of large businessmen fell sharply. As we shall see, the high proportion of these large businessmen had been considered the special hallmark of Birmingham municipal affairs in the previous thirty years, and the drop caused anxious comment at the time.

2

Greater Birmingham

The Council in 1912 does not lend itself to straight comparison with what had gone before. The creation of Greater Birmingham in 1911, a city of 68 square miles, had drastically altered the situation. In 1938 the borough had covered 13 square miles, and 17¾ square miles since the boundary extension in 1891. On that occasion the size of the Council had been increased from 64 to 72. But the extension in 1911 was on a different scale altogether, and the Council now consisted of 120 members.[1] The inclusion of areas with a social structure different from that of the central area and with their own established patterns of local politics and representation, naturally produced a city council that was not merely the old one writ large. We shall have to distinguish between the representation of the old area and that of the new, if we wish to know to what extent contrasts between the Council in 1902 and in 1912 were the result of boundary extension, and to what extent they were due to factors operating within pre-1911 Birmingham.[2]

In respect of the indices mainly noticed so far there was little strikingly new within the area of the old wards. The percentage of large businessmen remained much the same at 16·9 as in 1902, although it was only 15 for the Council as a whole. This came as a disappointment to some of the advocates of the Greater Birmingham scheme. Like Lord Simon of Wythenshaw later, they had hoped that the inclusion of the

[1] C. A. Vince, *History of the Corporation of Birmingham*, IV (Birmingham, 1919), chapter 2. This is a continuation of the work by J. T. Bunce.

[2] In 1902 the Council represented eighteen wards. By a reorganisation of ward boundaries the area of the pre-1911 city was in 1912 represented by sixteen wards. The newly incorporated area was divided into fourteen wards. The custom whereby aldermen, although elected by the Council, were each assigned to a ward, meant that some aldermen elected before 1911 found themselves, as a result of the reorganisation, without a ward. They were therefore assigned to other wards, and three of them to wards in the newly incorporated area. Since they were really members of the old Council, elected originally to represent pre-1911 wards, they have been counted with the representatives of the old area. This results in sixty-six members for the old area and fifty-four for the new, making a total of 120. Percentages given in the text and tables are based on these figures.

new residential areas would bring more people of this kind into the Council, and so re-establish the position that had existed in the eighties and nineties.[3] At the other end of the social scale we find a startling contrast between 1902 and 1912, if we take the Council as a whole. The percentage of small businessmen rose from 16·7 to 20·8, a return to a position such as had not existed since 1876. But this change was entirely the consequence of boundary extension. In the old wards the proportion had remained the same; in the new wards it was as high as 25·5 per cent.

Among the professional men the change that had taken place was even more remarkable. Of the four medical men on the Council in 1902 only one, a dentist, continued into the new era.[4] The new wards contributed one doctor (retired) who had been for many years a prominent member of the Erdington Urban District Council.[5] But two in a council of 120 was a mere 1·7 per cent, a marked contrast to the 5·6 per cent in 1902 or the 9·7 per cent in 1892.

If we look at the professions as a whole, the picture is very different. Apart from lawyers and doctors, the councillors from the established professions had been numerically insignificant before the creation of Greater Birmingham.[6] There had been one accountant in 1862 and 1902, one architect in 1892, one consultant engineer in 1896 and one graduate teacher in 1892 and 1896. But in 1912 the enlarged Council had a sudden access of these miscellaneous professions. Now there were five accountants, three teachers and one consultant engineer. The number of lawyers had also risen sharply, and between them they more than compensated for the practical disappearance of the doctors. In 1902 the professions had provided thirteen members or 18 per cent of the Council, in 1912 twenty-eight members or 23·3 per cent of the greatly enlarged body. If we take the pre-1911 area, the percentage was 22·7. The difference is small, for although the lawyers were more heavily

[3] For Simon's expectation from a Manchester boundary extension, see p. 323 below.

[4] Alderman W. H. Bowater, the only dentist caught by the sampling method throughout the whole of the period. He was a Conservative and a leading figure on the City Council then and for many years to come. The first Lord Mayor of Greater Birmingham, he became Lord Mayor for the fourth time in 1914, and was knighted for his services in 1916. He remained an alderman until his death in 1932.

[5] Dr. Alfred Paget Evans M.R.C.S., ald. Erdington North.

[6] For a definition of the professions as used in this study, see 'A Note on Methods', p. 362.

MAP 2 (opposite). *Greater Birmingham 1911.* Based on Conrad Gill and Asa Briggs, *History of Birmingham* (1952), II, pp. 156, 169.
1 Aston, 2 Lozells, 3 Duddeston-cum-Nechells, 4 St. Mary's, 5 St. Paul's, 6 St. Bartholomew's, 7 Market Hall, 8 Ladywood, 9 St. Martin's and Deritend, 10 Balsall Heath.

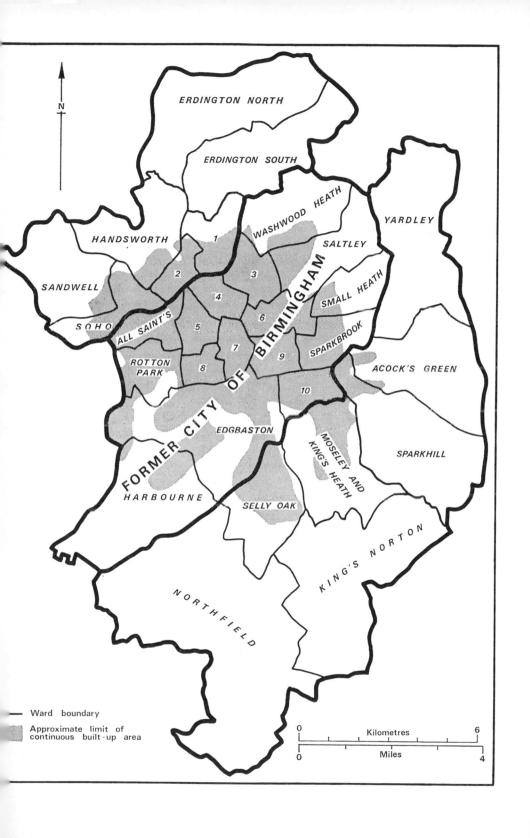

N

ERDINGTON NORTH

ERDINGTON SOUTH

WASHWOOD HEATH

YARDLEY

HANDSWORTH

SALTLEY

1

SANDWELL

2

3

SMALL HEATH

SOHO

4

6

ALL SAINT'S

5

SPARKBROOK

ACOCK'S GREEN

ROTTON PARK

7

9

8

10

FORMER CITY OF BIRMINGHAM

EDGBASTON

MOSELEY AND KING'S HEATH

SPARKHILL

HARBOURNE

SELLY OAK

KING'S NORTON

NORTHFIELD

— Ward boundary

Approximate limit of continuous built-up area

0   Kilometres   6

0   Miles   4

concentrated in the central area, the accountants and more particularly the teachers tended to sit for the new wards.

Figure 2 ⟨*see* pp. 44-5⟩ provides the evidence for a comparison with the past. Although the percentage in 1912 was the highest ever reached, the really significant increase had occurred in 1892. The years 1856–76 had seen the percentage steady between 6·3 and 7·8. 1882 saw a transition to a higher level, which was then held from 1892–1912 at between 18 and 22·7 per cent.

One possible explanation for this new plateau could be economic, i.e. a marked increase in the proportion of professional men in Birmingham. There was such an increase, as one would expect in view of the function of the city as the regional centre for the west Midlands. Table 27, appendix 1, is drawn from the series of Birmingham directories, and shows the number of independent professional men practising in the city. This source comes nearer than do census returns to indicating the size of the group from which the professional members of the Town Council were drawn. The classification used in the occupational tables of the census is not discriminating enough to make any figures calculated from them comparable with the professions on the Council as defined in this study. The use of directories has another important advantage. By counting those who practised in the city, even if they resided just over the city boundary, it overcomes one of the most obvious difficulties that the use of census statistics presents to the urban historian. Line (iii) indicates the changes in the percentage of professional men in the adult male population of the town, and (v) shows the degree to which this factor contributed to the changes in the composition of the Council. Had its composition merely kept pace with the changes in the community, the ratio in (v) would have remained unchanged. Instead it rises considerably between 1871/2 and 1892. To have retained the same ratio as in 1861/2 and 1871/2 would have reduced the professional element on the Council as follows:

> 1882 by 1
> 1892 by 7
> 1902 by 5
> 1912 by 6 (for the pre-1911 area).

It is therefore clear that the marked contrast between the earlier and the later period is overwhelmingly due to changes in the municipal politics rather than in the occupational structure of the city. But the same is not necessarily true for the increase in the professional element on the Council that occurred between 1892 and 1912. This could have resulted from the changes in the occupational structure of the area covered by the pre-1911 city, providing as it did professional services for the growing population outside its boundaries.

We have already noticed the increase in the miscellaneous professions on the Council of 1912 compared with previous years. But this alone would not have compensated for the sharp fall in the proportion of doctors that had occurred since 1892. That the total for the professions remained so high was due to the continued recruitment of lawyers. There had never been so many of them before, even in percentage terms. Since 1852, when they had first appeared in the sample, their share of the Council changed hardly at all until 1892. Thereafter each sample year recorded a steady increase, rising from 6·9 per cent to 14·2 per cent in 1912 for the Council as a whole and 15·4 per cent for the old wards taken alone.

The one exception in the series 1852–92 is the year 1876, when the percentage fell to 3·1 only to recover again by 1882. ⟨*See* figure 2.⟩ At first sight there seems no reason to pay much attention to a single erratic figure in mid-decade. But in this instance there are grounds for thinking it significant, and for suggesting that the turning-point from a fluctuating level to a steady rise occurred not in 1892 but already in 1876. The explanation for the low figure in 1876 is that the mid-seventies saw a change of generation among the lawyers on the Council. Figure 3 plots the careers of the men involved and shows what happened ⟨*see* p. 47⟩. Hawkes, Hodgson and Ryland had all sat out the troubled years of the 1850s and given long service on the Council. Together with Cutler, a leading member of the Allday party, they made up the 6·3 per cent in 1862 as they had done in 1856. But by 1876 they had all retired. At the same time Maher, who had taken Cutler's place as a prominent Economist, had his municipal career prematurely cut short by electoral defeat.[7] 1876 is therefore a year of transition.

Almost at once there began the recruitment of a new generation. One in 1875, two more by 1882, three more by 1892, two more by 1896, six more by 1902. Of these many remained on the Council for a considerable time, giving service comparable in length with that of the stalwarts of the 1850s and 1860s. Therefore as the recruitment continued, so the total rose. Figure 3 shows the steadiness of the recruitment, and the length of service, anything from twelve to twenty-seven years, that had become normal. It also shows something else that the new recruits from 1875 onwards had in common. Most of them were leading members of their profession in the city, in contrast to the earlier generation who had

---

[7] See below, p. 152.

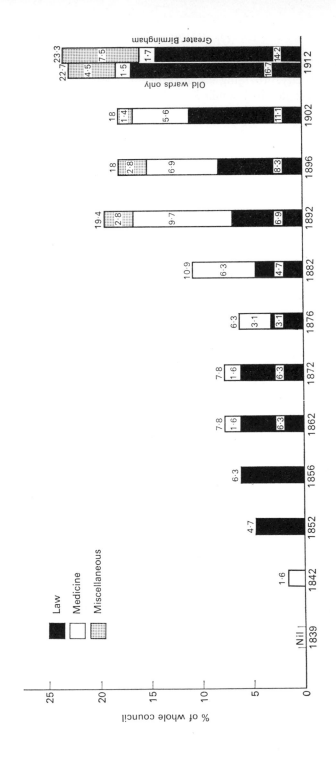

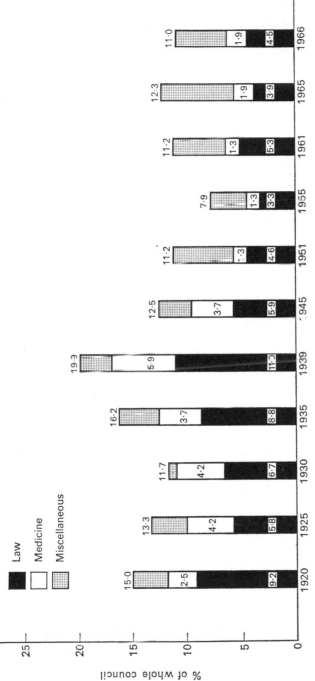

The figures for the years 1920–66 are drawn from Table 3.2 in D. S. Morris and K. Newton, 'The Occupational Composition of Party Groups on Birmingham Council, 1920–1966', Unpublished Discussion Paper, Series F. No. 3 (January 1969), University of Birmingham, Faculty of Commerce and Social Science. I am grateful to the authors for permission to use their figures. For these post-1920 columns the category 'Miscellaneous' counts surveyors and accountants only, the category 'Law' counts only solicitors. Dr. Newton assures me that the difference that this makes is minimal since the other occupations were hardly represented at all.

FIG. 2. *Birmingham Town Council 1839–1966: the professions*

not usually been of comparable standing. Such men as Sir Thomas and Ernest Martineau, G. J. Johnson, C. G. Beale and Arthur Godlee belonged to the economic and social elite as much as did the large businessmen whose relatives they often were.[8] This applies much less to those newly recruited in 1912. Nor is that the only reason for thinking that something new was starting, not unlike the generational change of the seventies. In numerical terms the rising trend continued. But within two or three years of the creation of Greater Birmingham many of those recruited in the eighties and nineties had retired. By 1914, even if we count Ernest Martineau, whose membership was temporarily interrupted by war service, there were only three lawyers left who had begun their municipal career before 1911.

We know enough about the composition of the Birmingham City Council in the years since the First World War to compare the situation in 1912 in this respect with what came after. Since 1925 members of the professions which provided the figures for the pre-1914 statistics have normally furnished a much smaller proportion of the Council. The exceptions are the sample years 1935 and 1939, when recruitment reached proportions not unlike those experienced before the War. It is not difficult to see that the general contrast between the two periods has to do with the numerical growth of the Labour Party on the City Council. Between the wars the Labour benches hardly contained any professional men; since 1945 they have contained a considerably lower proportion than the Conservative benches. Taking the non-Labour part of the Council only, we find that in six out of the ten sample years between 1925 and 1966 the proportion of professional men is well up to the percentages for the period 1892–1912 ⟨figure 4⟩. We must conclude therefore that the decline in the professional element on the Council is due partly to party political changes, but not entirely so. They do not account for the marked fluctuations of the figures for the non-Labour members. Far from being a horizontal line, the graph plotting the non-Labour figures dips sharply for the 1920s and again for the 1950s. For that an explanation is more likely to be found in terms of the relative attractiveness of the Council to other elements within the non-Labour spectrum during those decades. But this is speculation.

Such extensions of the pre-war figures are illuminating, provided that one remembers the pitfalls of comparison over long periods of time.

---

[8] Sir Thomas Martineau, Ernest Martineau and C. G. Beale belonged to the social set of Chamberlains, Nettlefolds and Kenricks. Arthur Godlee was a nephew of Lord Lister; Walter Barrow was related to the Cadburys.

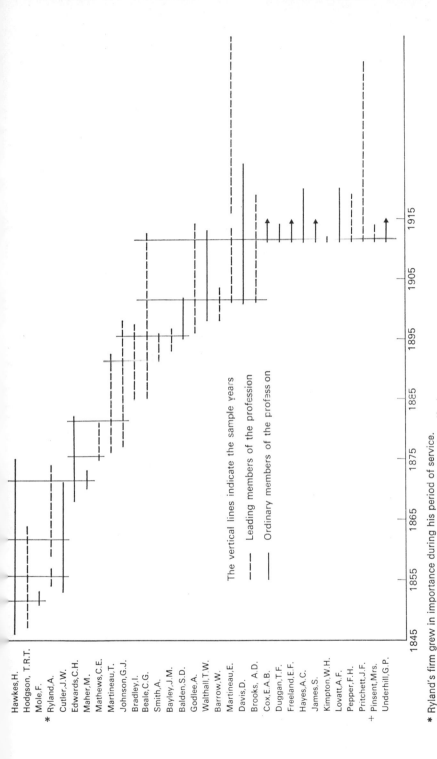

* Ryland's firm grew in importance during his period of service.
† Mrs. Pinsent was the wife of a prominent barrister, but not herself a lawyer.

FIG. 3. *Lawyers on the Birmingham Town Council: length of service*

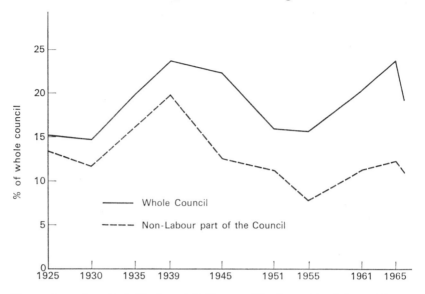

Figures drawn from D. S. Morris and K. Newton, 'The Occupational Composition of Party Groups on Birmingham Council, 1920-1966', Discussion Paper Series F3.

FIG. 4. *Birmingham 1925–66 : the professions as a percentage of the whole City Council and of the non-Labour part of it*

For a study that did justice to the years since 1920, without concerning itself with such long-range comparison, other and less rigorous definitions of the professions would probably be appropriate. Messrs. Morris and Newton by including bank managers, statisticians, scientists and company secretaries in the definition for their own forthcoming study have smoothed out the fluctuations that appear so striking in figure 4.

More straightforward than such comparisons between professional men as such is to focus on what has happened to medicine and the law, the two groups that between them comprised the bulk of professional men on the Council before 1914. The figures are to be found in figure 2, pp. 44-5.

The case of medicine is surprising. In 1912 it looked as if the involvement of the medical profession in elected municipal service, an involvement which dated from the mid-1870s, had practically come to an end. The inter-war figures show that this was not the case. Between 1925 and 1945 there were never less than five medical men on the City Council and in 1939 there were eight. It is only in the years since the Second

World War and the introduction of a national health service that doctors have contracted out of the City Council. 1912 and to some extent 1920 now appear as a freak and demand an explanation more historical than those that automatically come to mind in the 1970s.

Little needs to be said about solicitors, in addition to what has already been noticed about the impact of Labour on the occupational composition of the Council. Although their share of the Council fell after the Second World War to levels below those established by 1892, they continued to be the most important single group of professional men. Their share of the non-Labour part of the Council remained much as it was between 1892 and 1902, although it never again touched the phenomenally high percentage seen in 1912 ⟨table 6 and figure 2⟩.

TABLE 6. *Solicitors as a percentage of the non-Labour part of the Birmingham City Council 1925–66*

	No.	Percentage	Total
1925	7	6·7	105
1930	8	9·1	88
1935	12	10·9	110
1939	13	11·4	114
1946	7	10·4	67
1951	6	6·4	94
1955	4	5·7	70
1961	6	8·1	74
1965	5	6·9	72
1966	5	6·3	79

Figures drawn from D. S. Morris and K. Newton, Discussion Paper F.3.

To judge from the Greater Birmingham Council of 1912, the occupation whose presence on the Council was most affected by the incorporation of areas with their own distinctive pattern of local politics and representation, was the building trade. Like the drink trade it was one that tended to be fairly prominent on town councils in the nineteenth century. In Exeter municipal politics were dominated for twenty years after 1848 by a Conservative party boss, Henry Hooper, who was a builder. Nine per cent of all Exeter City Council members serving between 1868 and 1877 were builders, and even in the period 1837–46 they had accounted for 6·6 per cent. They made up 8·3 per cent of the Council in 1867–8, 6·3 per cent in 1870–71 and 5·8 per cent in 1913–14.

In Newcastle-under-Lyme between 1872 and 1899, 9·5 per cent of all successful municipal candidates were builders. Liverpool is another town in which builders and timber merchants operated as an important group in municipal politics, particularly in mid-century. In 1856 the Liverpool Town Council contained ten builders and timber merchants, i.e. 15·6 per cent of its total membership.[9]

There was nothing like this in Birmingham. In the 1850s and '60s there had been a brickmaker and a small house decorator. A dealer in building material in the 1870s comes rather nearer to that mixture of expertise and self-interest that one associates elsewhere with the local builders prominent in municipal affairs. It is their absence in Birmingham that calls for comment, rather than their presence elsewhere in the West Midlands. After the incorporation of Aston and Yardley three building contractors were elected to the Birmingham Council of 1912. Two had been on the Yardley District Council; the other on the Aston Borough Council. From then onwards the presence of builders on the Council became a regular feature of Birmingham municipal life.

TABLE 7. *Builders on Birmingham City Council 1912–66*

1912 No. %	1920 No. %	1930 No. %	1938 No. %	1950 No. %	1960 No. %	1966 No. %
3 2·5	2 1·7	4 3·4	5 3·7	6 3·9	6 3·9	6 3·9

Figures for 1920-66 drawn from D. S. Morris and K. Newton, 'Profile of a Local Political Elite: Businessmen as Community Decision Makers in Britain 1838-1966', *The New Atlantis*, I.2 (1970), 117-19.

However, we need to bear in mind that their presence has acquired a significance since the First World War, and even more so since the Second, which it did not have before. Once it had been merely municipal contracts that were at stake and this became a matter of sectional as well as personal interest in the 1890s and 1900s when the direct employment of labour for municipal work in place of private contractors became an issue of municipal politics. In the 1920s that issue shaded into the bigger question of whether the housing of the working classes should be provided by the Corporation or the speculative builder. Since the Second World War the systematic application of town and country planning procedures has drawn developers into the Council whose planning decisions largely determine the price of land. The same thing has happened to estate agents. Such recent trends, however, presuppose the

[9] R. Newton, Appendix I; F. Bealey, p. 66; B. D. White, p. 88.

existence of modern planning powers, they do not affect the picture in the period under review. Although auctioneers and house agents provided a sprinkling of Birmingham councillors in the early-Victorian period and again from 1882 to 1912,[10] their presence did not have the significance that it had acquired by the 1960s when eight estate agents sat on the 1966 Council, together with six builders and three other persons chiefly concerned with property development.[11] Between them they made up 11 per cent of the whole Council or more than one-fifth of those on the Conservative benches.

The Council of 1912 contained five full-time trade-union officials, more than ever before both in absolute and in relative terms. By contrast the representation of manual workers as such is not noticeably higher than before. If we add the two categories together we have nine councillors in 1912, or 7·5 per cent of the Council, compared with five councillors in 1892, or 6·9 per cent. As table 8 indicates, the presence of working men, whether full-time union organisers or not, dates to all intents and purposes from the 1892 sample. In the following twenty years the percentage fluctuated, but it appears to have risen by no more than 0·6 per cent. This, however, is an occasion where the boundary extension masks the real change that occurred. In the area of the pre-1911 city the percentage was 10·8 per cent, which shows a much more substantial rise.

Four of the trade-union officials represented working-class wards in the north-eastern part of the pre-1911 city—Duddeston, Washwood Heath and particularly Saltley, where the municipal gas works and sewage works were sited.[12] They belonged to one or other of the unions

[10]	1839	1842	1852	1856-76	1882	1892
	2(3·1%)	2(3·1%)	2(3·1%)	Nil	2(3·1%)	2(2·8%)

1896	1902	1912 old wards	1912 whole city
2(2·8%)	4(5·6%)	3(4·5%)	4(3·3%)

[11] This was a fairly recent development. In 1950 there had been only two estate agents, in 1930 one and in 1920 none. D. S. Morris and K. Newton, *The New Atlantis*, p. 117.

[12] John Beard, clr. Saltley 1911–20, Organiser of the Workers Union, the militant union for the unskilled, I.L.P. member and before 1909 Secretary of the Birmingham I.L.P. Federation. See Richard Hyman, *The Workers Union* (1971); Birmingham I.L.P. Federation Minute Book 1909–1914, Birmingham Corporation Social Science Library.

Joseph Gregory, clr. Saltley 1911–18, ald. 1918–32, Organiser of the Amalgamated Society of Gas, Municipal and General Workers.

Eldred Hallas, clr. Duddeston and Nechells 1911–19, Labour M.P. Duddeston 1918–22. National Union of General and Municipal Workers.

Henry Simpson, clr. Washwood Heath 1911–20, General Secretary of the Amalgamated Society of Gas, Municipal and General Workers.

TABLE 8. *Trade union officials and manual workers on the Birmingham City Council 1882–1966*

Date	1882		1892		1896		1902		1912 Old city		1912 New city		1920		1925		1930	
	No.	%	No.	%	No.	%	No.	%	No.	%	No.	%	No.	%	No.	%	No.	%
T.U. officials	1	1·6	1	1·4	1	1·4	2	2·8	5	7·7	5	4·2	7	5·8	4	3·3	11	9·2
Foremen and skilled	—		4	5·6	3	4·2	2	2·8	2	3·0	4	3·3	12	10	7	5·8	5	4·2
Unskilled and semi-skilled	—		—		—		—		—		—		—		—		—	
Total	1	1·6	5	6·9	4	5·6	4	5·6	7	10·8	9	7·5	19	15·8	11	9·1	16	13·4

Date	1935		1939		1945		1951		1955		1961		1965		1966	
	No.	%	No.	%	No.	%	No.	%	No.	%	No.	%	No.	%	No.	%
T.U. officials	4	2·9	3	2·2	7	5·1	4	2·6	6	3·9	2	1·3	1	0·6	2	1·3
Foremen and skilled	4	2·9	5	3·7	15	11·0	7	4·6	17	11·2	17	11·2	21	13·5	17	11·0
Unskilled and semi-skilled	—		—		2	1·5	3	1·9	4	2·6	3	1·9	2	1·3	5	3·2
Total	8	5·9	8	5·9	24	17·6	14	9·2	27	17·8	22	14·5	22	14·5	24	15·5

Figures for 1920-66 drawn from table 34 in D. S. Morris and K. Newton, 'The Occupational Composition of Party Groups on Birmingham Council, 1920-1966', Discussion Paper, Series F3 (January, 1969).

organising municipal workers. Two of them had taken a prominent part in the agitation against conditions at the Corporation gas works in 1889, which led to the formation of the Amalgamated Society of Gas-workers.[13] Three of them were sponsored by the Birmingham and District Labour Representation Council, the local manifestation of the Labour Party. Eldred Hallas of the National Union of General and Municipal Workers had stood as an independent, and although he was invited after his election to join the Labour Party, he seems to have refused.[14] The fifth trade-union official belonged to a different world. He sat for a central ward and had been a councillor intermittently since 1889. The secretary of the Birmingham Tinplate Operative Workers, a union for skilled men, he had been a pillar of the Birmingham Trade Council since the 1880s and Liberal-Labour candidate for East Birmingham at the general election of 1900. He was still a Liberal in 1912.[15]

J. W. Kneeshaw has been returned in table 8 merely as a skilled manual worker, so as not to create a separate category for one person. But as the paid organiser of the I.L.P. he was not so different from the trade-union officials.[16] None of the other three manual workers were Labour Party supporters. Two of them had previously served on local authorities in the newly incorporated areas and the third had been a member of the Birmingham Council since 1894. In spite of their different political allegiances they had much in common and were good examples of the public-spirited men who gave their time to the voluntary associations of the town.[17]

In looking at the representation of the working class, we have already touched on the somewhat different question of the representation of the Labour Party. Birmingham was not a fertile area for the idea of independent Labour representation. The Unionist Party with its Chamberlainite traditions on the one hand, and a Liberal opposition,

[13] 'Trade Unionism, its Progress in Birmingham V', *Birmingham Evening Dispatch*, 30 January 1908.
[14] Birmingham and District Labour Representation Council, 10th and 11th Annual Reports, January 1912, March 1913.
[15] J. V. Stephens, clr. St. Thomas's 1889–1907, St. Bartholomew's 1911–20, School Board 1887–90. See John Corbett, *Birmingham Trade Coucnil 1866–1966* (1966); 'Trade Unionism, Its Progress in Birmingham II', *Birmingham Evening Dispatch*, 9 January 1908.
[16] J. W. Kneeshaw, clr. Rotton Park 1911–19. For his activities see I. L. P. Kings Heath Branch Minute Book 1906–19, Birmingham Corporation Social Science Library.
[17] John Edwards, Handsworth U.D.C. 1896–1911, clr. Soho 1911–13, engineers pattern maker, Conservative.
John Fryer, Kings Norton and Northfield U.D.C. 1905–11, clr. Kings Norton 1911–31, ald. 1941–43, foreman packing-case maker, Liberal.
Alfred Jephcott, clr. Bordesley 1894–1911, Small Heath 1911–12, ald. 1912–32, School Board 1891–96, M.P. Yardley 1918–27, foreman engineering mechanic, Liberal Unionist, President Birmingham Trades Council 1887, 1899.

unsullied for a quarter-century by the compromises and disillusionment that comes with power, still made between them a powerful appeal to most sections of the community. The Labour Representation Council had had four members on the City Council in 1904 but by November 1907 there were none. It was not until the elections of November 1911 that the wheel of fortune turned and five of its candidates were elected. Beard, Gregory and Simpson, the three trade-union officials, and Kneeshaw, the I.L.P. organiser, have already been mentioned. The remaining member, George Shann, was a lecturer at Birmingham University.[18]

In history the choice of a period determines the perspective, and a project that ends in 1914 does not provide a good perspective for a study of the working-class presence on town councils. For the years 1892–1912 are merely the beginning and are better understood in relation to what followed than what went before. The same is true of the Town Council service of trade-union officials. Changes in the strength of both these groups are naturally more close linked in the twentieth century to the fluctuating electoral fortunes of the Birmingham Labour Party than those in any occupational group had been linked to the electoral fortunes of political parties in nineteenth-century Birmingham. Any treatment of changes in the occupational structure of councils in the twentieth century is therefore obliged to pay far closer attention to party-political fluctuations than is necessary for the period 1838–1912.

The presence of manual workers and of salaried trade-union officials is indeed linked to the fortunes of the Labour Party. But this does not mean that after 1912 the history of both groups follows the same pattern. Table 7 shows that this is not so. The working-class presence on the Birmingham Council had its ups and downs—a sharp increase to 1892 followed by a slight downward drift to 1912, a sharp increase in 1920 followed by another downward drift in the inter-war years, a further sharp rise in 1945 followed by an upward trend thereafter. But the pattern for trade union officials is rather different. The solitary presence first of W. J. Davis,[19] then of J. V. Stevens, was a prelude to the rise from 1902 to 1920. An even higher peak was reached in 1930 and thereafter we find little but downward drift. The Labour triumph of 1945

[18] George Shann, Kings Norton U.D.C. 1904–11, clr. Selly Oak 1911–16, ald. 1916–19. Lecturer in economics and industrial subjects, he was associated with the Workers Union. the I.L.P. and the W.E.A.

[19] For W. J. Davis, General Secretary of the National Society of Amalgamated Brassworkers, first historian of the T.U.C., clr. Nechells ward and member of the Birmingham School Board, see W. A. Dalley, *The Life Story of W. J. Davis*, J.P. (Birmingham, 1914).

was no more than a fluctuation in the trend. By 1966 there were only two trade union officials; in 1965 there had been one. The 1960s are like no other period as much as the 1890s, except that they show the end instead of the beginning of a curve. The Labour party may be strong in the Birmingham Council chamber, but trade union officials have left city government to others. Like other executive officers of large organisations they have found it difficult to fit into their routine. It may be guessed that they have also found it less necessary than in days before collective bargaining was firmly established in local government.

TABLE 9. *Turnover of members of the Birmingham Town Council*

(a) Those with 10 years' service and multiples of ten as a percentage of the possible total:

Council of	10 years	20 years	30 years	40 years	50 years
1852	25	—	—	—	—
1862	27	9	—	—	—
1872	36	14	3	—	—
1882	42	11	5	—	—
1892	44	20	3	2	—
1902	43	19	8	2	2
1912	36	11	3	2	—

(b) Those with 15 years' service as a percentage of the possible total:

Council of	15 years
1852	14
1856	14
1872	19
1876	23
1892	27
1896	25
1912	18

It is at first sight surprising that the figures for 1882 and 1902 in the 10 years column should be so much higher than those given in E. S. Griffith, *The Modern Development of City Government* (1927), II, appendix N for 1885 and 1900. Griffith gives 34·3 per cent (22) for 1885 and 36·3 per cent (24) for 1900. My own cards confirm the figures for 1885 and the absolute total of 24 for November 1900. Strangely enough, the absolute total for November 1899 was 28 and for November 1901 it was 31, a reminder of the hazards of sampling from single years. Unfortunately by working out the percentage from a possible total of 66 instead of 64, which is the correct figure, Griffith magnifies the difference between the two sets of figures. Bearing in mind that the Council in November 1891 had been enlarged to 72, the true comparison in percentages over these three consecutive years is 43·8 per cent (November 1899), 37·5 per cent (November 1900), 43·1 per cent (November 1901).

55

When we look back to 1838 from the vantage point of 1914 and seek the outstanding feature in the changing occupational and social composition of the Birmingham Council, the answer is clear. It is the marked change that came about between 1862 and 1882, which determined the nature of the Council almost to the end of the period. The changes that occurred in the mid-1850s or after 1896 are slight by comparison. The relative number of large and of small businessmen, the fate of the drink trade, the pattern of recruitment from the professions in general and from lawyers and doctors in particular, have all pointed to the same conclusion. The figures for the replacement of old Council members by new also indicate the 1870s as a time of political convulsion and as the beginning of a period of stability.

From these tables we can see that significantly more of those recruited between 1862 and 1882 than in any other decade gave twenty years

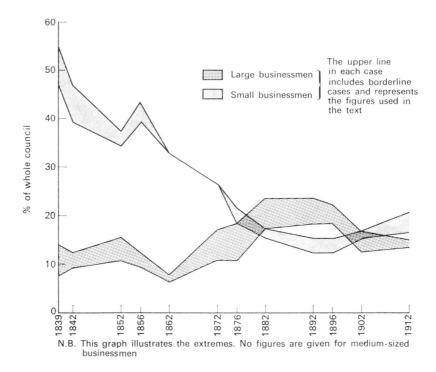

N.B. This graph illustrates the extremes. No figures are given for medium-sized businessmen

FIG. 5. *Large and small businessmen on the Birmingham Town Council 1839–1912*

service on the Council and that the other measures point to the same conclusion.

That is as far as statistics can take us. To understand why these changes occurred, what those involved in them thought they were doing, and what effect they had on the government of the town, demands a detailed study of those years. That is what the next section provides. It is a case-study of a movement for municipal reform.

Part II
The Municipal Gospel

I

The Influence of George Dawson

The events in the municipal history of Birmingham to which we now turn can be regarded from several points of view.

In one sense they involved the recruitment to the service of the Corporation of a significant proportion of the social and economic elite of the town—large businessmen and leading professional men—and the establishment of a tradition of municipal service among this section of the community which survived into the next generation. This is the aspect which emerges prominently from the statistical evidence presented in Part 1.

They were also regarded as the reform of municipal administration by the bolder and more efficient use of the Corporation's financial resources. The new recruits from big business set the stamp of their experience on the administration of the town. Of the tradesmen and small manufacturers, whom they replaced in the control of municipal affairs, it has been justly said the 'in their private businesses they were not accustomed to deal with big transactions and high figures, so that spending large sums of money, if proposed, filled the brewer, the baker, and the candlestick maker with alarm.'[1] Of course there was more to the new methods than the mere willingness to spend money, for as we shall see the new policy makers were no less obliged than their predecessors to operate within the limitations set by a ratepayers' franchise. But it is the way in which they did so that marks the difference. In 1874 Joseph Chamberlain, then mayor, proposed that the Corporation should at one bold stroke enlarge its financial resources by buying out both the local gas companies. In a brilliant speech he explained the negotiations into which he had entered. He calculated the savings that would be made by the merger of the two firms, the additional savings that would result from the Corporation's ability to borrow at 4 per cent instead of the

[1] T. Anderton, *A Tale of One City* (Birmingham, 1900), p. 6.

7 per cent that public companies had to pay, and also pointed out that unlike the company the Corporation paid no income tax. On the strength of this, he argued, they could afford to treat the shareholders generously and still make a profit of at least £14,800, less transfer fees and sinking fund, even in their first year. The Council voted in favour of the proposals but during the debate William Brinsley, successful grocer and one of the leaders of the older Economist party, explained that

> 'the only thing that enabled him to vote for the resolution was the knowledge that it would have to be submitted to the ratepayers, and it was for them to decide whether they would have the Works or not.'[2]

If he could not assess the financial basis of the proposals, what could a ratepayers' meeting do?

Thirdly, and most significantly, in Birmingham there emerged in these years a new way of thinking about the nature and function of a municipal corporation. Just as the administrative changes are best understood in the light of the recruitment of a different and abler kind of councillor, so that recruitment must in turn be seen in the light of the new theory. It was this that provided men, who had not previously been associated with municipal politics, with the incentive for service on the Town Council. It was also this that gave to what happened in Birmingham in those years an importance that extended far beyond the town. By the 1880s the characteristic features of the Birmingham doctrine had become widely accepted in England. This success was due not only to the vigour of its exponents and the subsequent fame achieved by Joseph Chamberlain in national politics. Above all it was due to the fact that in the 1860s and early 1870s the Birmingham men had been quick to recognise the changes that were coming over England, and to draw out their consequences in ways that were to be of significance for the country as a whole.

This was an achievement of the creative imagination. It is often ascribed to Joseph Chamberlain, who became the leader of the movement and the most prominent exponent of the Birmingham municipal doctrine. But Chamberlain was not its originator. The creator of the municipal doctrine, the prophet of the new movement, was George Dawson, public lecturer and heterodox preacher, one of the most

---

[2] *Short History of the Passing of the Birmingham (Corporation) Gas Act and Birmingham (Corporation) Water Act with the Speeches of the Mayor (Joseph Chamberlain)* (Birmingham 1875), p. 28; *D.P.* 25.3.1874, p. 6.

colourful figures of mid-Victorian Birmingham. To understand the springs of the new movement, we need to understand his mind and the relationship between him and his disciples.

George Dawson was born in London in 1821, where his father, a devout Baptist, kept a private school. There he was educated, before spending a few months at Aberdeen University. At the age of seventeen he decided to enter the Baptist ministry, and thereupon went to Glasgow University to take a degree in the Humanities.[3] There he steeped himself in the latest literary and philosophical ideas, and throughout his life his perspective was mainly derived from the literary prophets of his youth and early manhood—Emerson, Carlyle, and the German Romantics and Idealists.[4] For the next two and a half years he taught in his father's school, and took occasional preaching engagements. Then in December 1843 he became pastor of a small Baptist church in Rickmansworth, and in October 1844 moved to Mount Zion Chapel in Birmingham.

For a Baptist minister of his time Dawson's education had been unconventional. His better educated colleagues had normally spent three years at one of the Baptist or Independent colleges, dividing their time between a general education and a theological grounding in the standard works of the accepted orthodoxy. They knew a great deal about the orthodox Evangelical scheme of doctrine, and this normally determined their mental perspective. From an established stronghold they regarded the new critical and philosophical ideas either anxiously or defiantly as an enemy at the gate. In addition a host of less educated ministers owed to Mutual Improvement societies and preaching classes all the doctrinal grounding that they had.

The church to which Dawson came was in some difficulties.[5] The huge octagonal structure in Graham Street, capable of holding 2,500 persons, had been erected in 1824 as a piece of private speculation. The present Baptist church was formed in 1831 and moved into the building. Its pastor, James Hoby, was a gentleman of independent means who expected no stipend. There seems to have been little zeal or foresight, and when he retired in 1844 the church, already in financial difficulties, began to look for a successor. Dawson was their second choice. He

[3] W. Wright Wilson, *The Life of George Dawson* (Birmingham, 1905).
[4] He became friend and travel companion to both Emerson and Carlyle. Article, 'George Dawson', *D.N.B.* XIV.
[5] J. M. Gwynne Owen, *The Chronicles of our Church* (Birmingham, 1902), pp. 7 ff.

preached for a few Sundays, as was customary, and was then offered the post.

The church elders had hoped to find someone who would bring new life to the church, but what they got was more than they had bargained for. Dawson was then an athletic young man of twenty-three, with long, black, curly hair and clothes of a most unclerical cut.[6] Nor was his unconventionality confined to his appearance. Having escaped the atmosphere of the theological seminary, he brought to his prayers, reading and preaching a straightforward and intelligent freshness. It was this that had commended him to the members of Mount Zion Church and it proved attractive to many others in the town. They flocked to hear the new man in large numbers, not once but repeatedly, and in many cases became pew-holders. Dawson's preaching was deliberately un-Evangelical, and he especially attracted those who had little or no sympathy with the Evangelical creed, to which Mount Zion was formally committed. Most conspicuous among the new adherents were those from the two old-established Unitarian congregations in the centre of the town.[7] Dawson's impact on the Unitarian New Meeting in Moor Street can be followed in the reminiscences of T. H. Ryland. Its minister was learned but dull and his flock was soon going curiously to hear the new man in Graham Street.

> 'To say that we were delighted is nothing. After the dry bones and thrashed out chaff we had so long been fed on, it was indeed a feast. On leaving, we encountered Robert Martineau; he was enchanted . . . I can hear him now exclaiming, "Oh! Will, this is the preaching I have longed for all my life!" '[8]

Their loyalty kept them in Moor Street in the mornings, their interest drew them to Graham Street at night, until the minister openly rebuked Dawson's admirers from the pulpit and provoked a breach.[9] That sermon added many pew-holders to Mount Zion Chapel.

As was only natural, the original Baptist element soon grew anxious at the changes that were coming over their church. The bright financial prospect could not compensate them for the threat to their beliefs. Dawson had at no time displayed any sympathy with Evangelical

---

[6] Wright Wilson, *Life of George Dawson*, p. 3; T. H. Ryland, *Reminiscences*, ed. W. H. Ryland (Birmingham, 1904), p. 134.

[7] The Old Meeting, Old Meeting Street, and the New Meeting, Moor Street.

[8] T. H. Ryland, *Reminiscences*, pp. 137–8. The Martineaus were like the Rylands one of the leading Unitarian families in England.

[9] 'The veriest babes in grace would have known better!', Ryland, p. 139.

orthodoxy, and conscious of an admiring following he began to show ever less consideration for the feelings of the orthodox. One doctrine after another was subjected to attack. The atmosphere in the church became increasingly tense, and Dawson's decision to admit those who were not full church members to the Communion precipitated the final rupture. This was a definite breach of the church's articles of trust, and therefore presented a clear-cut issue.[10] In December 1845 Dawson announced that he would retire from the ministry in mid-summer of the following year. It looked at first as if his followers might eject the orthodox from their building, for the mortgage holder, a fervent admirer of Dawson, threatened to foreclose and hand the chapel over for his use. But other Baptist churches in Birmingham came to the rescue, and with the help of contributions from London, Bristol, Manchester and Liverpool raised £2,094 to pay off the debt. The orthodox remnant was left in possession of the chapel, but the twenty-one months that had begun with such promise left them decimated and financially ruined. They ceased for the moment to be an independent church, and were only saved from complete extinction by twenty experienced men and women who migrated from another church to swell their numbers and provide an element of strength.[11]

From these facts it must be assumed that the most vigorous members of the old church as well as the newcomers of the previous few months followed Dawson into the wilderness. They decided to found a church of their own and chose a central site in Edward Street. The new building was formally opened on 8 August 1847, and called the Church of the Saviour.[12]

Assured of an eager following and generous financial support Dawson was now free to express his own ideas. In contrast to the usual practice, the new church was to have no credal basis for membership at all. The old doctrinal statements were becoming an embarrassment to many ministers and some laity and an occasion of disunion and suspicion between them and their less informed congregations. It was a situation, of which R. W. Dale has left a sensitive description in an article which he wrote on Dawson shortly after the latter's death.

[10] This was a contentious matter at the time among Particular Baptists, leading to secessions in several places all over the country. See W. T. Whiteley, *The Baptists of North West England* (1913), pp. 187–8, 341; A. J. Klaiber, *The Story of the Suffolk Baptists* (1931), pp. 121 ff, 137; George Gould, *The Baptists in Norwich and Open Communion* (1860), *passim*.

[11] Gwynne Owen, *Chronicles*, pp. 23–30.

[12] *The Pilot*, 17.1.1846, *Dawson Collection*, XVIII, 1, Birmingham Public Reference Library; 'The Church of the Saviour, its History, Principles and Work', in *Church of the Saviour's Teachers' Magazine*, *Dawson Collection*, X, 6 ff.

'When he began to preach, the theological systems of Nonconformist churches were beginning to show signs of decay. Calvinism
in its severe and strict form, which had been the theory of orthodox
Nonconformists up to the middle or close of the last century, had
already almost disappeared. It had been melted down into what
used to be called Moderate Calvinism, a system which had neither
the logic of the older theory to satisfy the understanding, nor its
tremendous solemnity and awfulness to command the fear and
wonder of the heart. The traditional theory of the atonement was
beginning to give way. . ... There was a great deal of uneasiness
even among those who most firmly held the substance of the
Evangelical truth. They felt that the forms in which the truth had
been stated were no longer tenable; they were quietly and timidly
revising their definitions and re-examining their theories. They
were using old language, for as yet they had no other language to
use; but they were more or less distinctly conscious—even some
of the most Evangelical of them—that they were not using the old
language in the old sense.'[13]

This process had still a long way to go and with creeds in such a state
they were of little value as bonds of church union. But in 1846 this was
still far from obvious. It was one of Dawson's characteristics to be
sensitive to currents which were ultimately to affect large sections of
the religious world.

He turned for his doctrine of the Church to the teaching of James
Martineau, who was then just beginning to make a name for himself.[14]
Martineau attacked the notion that Scripture was the depository of
revealed truth whose divine origin had been authenticated by miracles.
This had been generally accepted doctrine among English Unitarians
since Belsham and Priestley, and indeed since Locke. He substituted for
it a doctrine of progressive revelation, mediated through the natural
faculties of men. In a sense he was reacting to the pressure of German
biblical criticism, but what was basic for Martineau was his abandonment of Belsham's and Priestley's necessitarian philosophy in favour of
that German idealism, which Dawson had also accepted. When Dawson
was drafting his Church Principles, which were largely a corollary of

---

[13] R. W. Dale, 'George Dawson: Politician, Lecturer and Preacher', *Nineteenth Century*,
II (August 1877), 53.
[14] On Martineau see H. McLachlan, *The Unitarian Movement in the Religious Life of
England* (1934), pp. 63–7; 'Unitarianism' in *Hasting's Encyclopaedia of Religion and Ethics*
(1921); J. E. Carpenter, *James Martineau, Theologian and Teacher* (1905).

these views, the theological controversy started by Martineau was raging among the Unitarians. Not until 1857 with Martineau's appointment to both the Chairs of Religious Philosophy and of Mental and Moral Philosophy—a distinction whose validity he denied—did the new theology triumph at New College, Manchester, the chief Unitarian seat of learning. Dawson himself repeatedly denied that either he or his church were Unitarian, but did so on grounds which only strengthen the supposition of Martineau's decisive influence. For Martineau also looked on 'Unitarian' as a sect-label with which he would not burden what he called free Catholic churches, and accused the Unitarians of having degenerated into 'a sect enslaved in the letter of Scripture and tradition'.[15] In January 1846, just when he was drawing up his Church Principles, Dawson was asked to preach in Martineau's chapel in Liverpool, and was afterwards introduced to a large party invited to meet him at Martineau's house.[16]

The members of the Church of the Saviour accordingly declared that

'They unite for the study of Christian truth under the instruction of a Teacher, whom they do not regard as the "retained advocate of certain doctrines, and therefore bound to publish and support them", but as one whose duty it is to aid them in their studies, by giving them the benefit of his earnest inquiry into the truth of God.

They unite in the bonds of charity, as Students, with a feeling that each man has much to learn, and perchance much to unlearn: their bond is prospective rather than retrospective—a common spirit rather than a common "belief" or "creed".

They unite to do good to others . . .'[17]

But it must be added that the most important fact about the Church of the Saviour was both simpler and less permanent than any new principles of church union. The church was above all else George Dawson's. For thirty years his personality gave it a richness and a vigour above any other institution in Birmingham.

Birmingham knew him as a lecturer with a national reputation, and large audiences heard him at the Midland Institute on literary and biographical subjects. It knew him as a platform or after-dinner speaker; it even knew him for short spells as a newspaper editor. But nothing

---

[15] Quoted in J. E. Carpenter, *Martineau*, p. 364.
[16] J. Drummond and C. B. Upton, *Life and Letters of James Martineau* (1902), I, 129.
[17] The Church Principles, Nos. 2, 3 and 4. Extract from the Minutes of the Proceedings of the Congregation, March 1846, published for general circulation, 1850. *Dawson Collection*, X, 64.

gave him the scope that was provided by his congregation. Regularly for thirty years he spoke to a body which included some of the most intelligent men in Birmingham. Many of them became disciples and adopted his views as their own. Indeed they came to understand him as his occasional hearers hardly could. Never one to qualify the statement of the moment, Dawson easily laid himself open to misunderstanding by those who were not familiar with his ways. R. W. Dale, who knew him in all his roles, was convinced that 'his large resources were more richly illustrated in his sermons than either in his lectures or his speeches.'[18] He broke through the formalism of a Sunday service by the freshness of his approach. He never sermonised, he never declaimed. Even in church he was conversational, and his speaking was 'the conversation of a brilliant man speaking to his friends from a platform'.

He was a born talker, 'the greatest talker in England', as Charles Kingsley called him. Had he lived a century later, he would have been a great broadcaster. Then he made a reputation for himself wherever people came together to listen to the spoken word, especially in church and in evening institutes. From 1845 onwards he travelled regularly throughout the country, lecturing in the towns. When he died, *The Spectator* called him 'a kind of literary middleman between writers like Carlyle and Ruskin and those ordinary English manufacturers, or merchants, or tradesmen, who like thought but like it well illustrated', and added that 'it would be well if every great town in England had such another literary middleman to keep it familiar with the best thinkers of the day.'[19]

Dawson's success was due not merely to 'the sparkling sentence, the cutting antithesis and the flowing speech', for which he was remembered in Leamington.[20] Behind his verbal facility lay an exceptional clarity and intensity of perception, and his frequent descriptions of human behaviour were vivid and uncomfortably to the point.

'Quickly descending from generalities to the particular, he would talk to his congregation about Avery's scales, and about yard measures, about tea and sugar, about adulterated mustard and about butter half of which was fat, about stock-taking and long credit; about dressing shop-windows; about all the details of the

---

[18] R. W. Dale, 'George Dawson', *Nineteenth Century*, II, 48.
[19] R. W. Dale, 'Memorial Sermon on George Dawson', *D.P.* 9.12.1876; A. W. W. Dale, 'George Dawson', in *Nine Famous Birmingham Men*, ed. J. H. Muirhead (Birmingham, 1909), p. 90; *Spectator*, 2.12.1876.
[20] Tom Burgess, editor of *The Leamington Spa Courier*, in Wright Wilson, *op. cit.*, p. 157.

doings of a scoundrel who had been tried a day or two before for his transactions in connection with a fraudulent joint-stock company; about dress and jewelry; about dinners and evening parties; about all the follies and sins and vanities of the day. This made his sermons effective. Men of business knew what he meant when he talked about honest trading. Women knew what he meant when he talked about simplicity of living. Masters and servants, parents and children all had their turn, and could hardly miss the intentions of his lessons.'[21]

Only a man of his charm could so persistently touch on the follies of his hearers without turning them away. But his humour, his versatility of mood, and the amazing hold that he exerted on his audience sweetened the pill without making it innocuous.

His gifts were those of a talker, not of a writer. When transposed on to the printed page, most of the spell is lost. The praise of men as discriminating as Kingsley, Dale and Johnson is difficult to square with the flat impression made by the surviving sermons, prayers and lectures. It is reassuring that his contemporaries had found the same. A journalist, who for a time had been Dawson's amanuensis, complained in 1898:

'There are still extant somewhere two or three volumes of his printed lectures, sermons and prayers, but they convey no more idea of the mental magic of the man than a child's description could give you of the differential calculus.'[22]

Dawson himself was not responsible for their publication, nor even committed them to paper. He was always reluctant to use a pen. He thought too rapidly and spontaneously to leave himself time to write, and when he spoke only the best stenographer could keep up with the unexpectedness of his turns of speech.[23]

It was this that largely accounts for his failure as a newspaper editor on at least two occasions. The medium did not suit him. At his second attempt he used to dictate his leading articles, not in their finished form, but as long talks as he walked up and down the room. A journalist-amanuensis then condensed and recast as much of this as possible in article form.[24] For in cold print the diffuseness of his mind was cruelly apparent. He never appealed to those who looked for logical construction.

[21] R. W. Dale, 'George Dawson', *Nineteenth Century*, II, 49.
[22] D. C. Murray in Wright Wilson, *Life of George Dawson*, appendix, pp. 211–12.
[23] Wright Wilson, *Life of George Dawson*, pp. 159–60.
[24] D. C. Murray in Wright Wilson, *Life of George Dawson*, appendix, p. 213.

Such men complained that they could not tell what he believed, and that his lectures lacked all shape.

> 'The entire address, harangue, or oration, consisting of a multitude of things—good, bad and indifferent—strung together as girls thread beads, and boys put buttons on a string,'

wrote a hostile newspaper, and even a friendly critic complained:

> 'You bring your subject to an apparent conclusion with a most admirable passage, and then, instead of leaving us charmed and—greatest triumph of all—longing for more, you rush back again into the middle of your subject, repeating allusion after allusion, and spoiling each of six perorations by making them tumble over each other.'[25]

But such criticism was the exception. Most comments testified to his power as a speaker and the delight with which the audience responded to his personality.

As for Dawson himself, his diffuseness never troubled him, and he seems to have made no effort to correct it. Men found him inspiring and that was what he wanted. For whether he lectured or preached his purpose was always moral and practical. He concentrated 'on what he considered to be the main point of every question. And this main point was always that view of the subject which concerned human life and conduct.'[26]

This preoccupation with conduct throws some light on Dawson's relation to the Evangelicalism, against which he had rebelled. Like other and more distinguished figures he took with him into the rebel camp much of his former equipment. His rebellion was that of one half of the Evangelical heritage against the other.

In the generation of Wilberforce and Hannah More, the generation in which Evangelicalism set its mark firmly on English society, it was characterised as much by its insistence on conduct as on justification by faith. It has even been suggested, not implausibly, that what made Evangelicalism for the first time socially acceptable during the French Revolutionary war and after was its vigorous moralising at a time when it was widely feared that the mutual bonds of social obligation were being loosened.[27] With a creed in which the doctrine of free grace

---

[25] Quoted in R. W. Dale, 'George Dawson', *Nineteenth Century*, II, 57.
[26] G. J. Johnson in Wright Wilson, *Life of George Dawson*, p. 172.
[27] Maurice Quinlan, Victorian Prelude (New York, 1941), pp. 96–100; V. G. Kiernan, 'Evangelicalism and the French Revolution', *Past and Present*, No. 1 (1952), 44–55.

played so conspicuous a part, there was always the danger of antinomianism. But it was a danger, which Wilberforce's generation resisted vigorously. His own book, *A Practical View of the Prevailing Religious System of Professed Christians in the Higher and Middle Classes in this Country contrasted with Real Christianity*, was a model of the way in which the doctrine of free grace could be logically and intimately linked to a strong 'practical' preoccupation. It was one of its merits, in the eyes of his favourite preacher, the Rev. Thomas Scott, that

> 'it is especially calculated to show those their mistake, who preach evangelical doctrines without a due exhibition of their practical effects.'[28]

The book became a best-seller, and did more than any other to mould the religious thinking of the next twenty years.

But the marriage of doctrine and conduct, which had been achieved in the second generation of the Revival, frequently broke down in the third. This is well demonstrated in the Evangelical manual, which held among early Victorian Dissenters an influential place comparable to that once occupied by Wilberforce's *Practical View*. The *Anxious Inquirer after Salvation Directed and Encouraged* was written by John Angell James, Congregational minister at Carr's Lane, Birmingham. First published in 1834, by 1858 it had sold more than half a million copies, without taking American editions into account.[29]

The centre of Wilberforce's doctrinal presentation had been the knowledge of the living Christ. The centre of Angell James' was the doctrine of justification by faith, presented in such a way as to make any connection with matters of conduct and disposition exceedingly tenuous. *The Anxious Inquirer* was typical of its school in being at pains to demonstrate the difference between justification and sanctification, without troubling to explain their connection. Right conduct and disposition were usually thought of in these circles as a matter of gratitude, an extra that the fully fledged Christian threw in out of the fullness of his heart. Although it was common to speak of righteous living as *evidence* of a saving faith, such talk brought its own peculiar difficulties. It accorded ill with the strongly urged tenet that assurance of salvation lay entirely in God's faithfulness to His promises.

It was symptomatic of this situation that in *The Anxious Inquirer* the chapter on repentance, although full of good advice, was noticeably

[28] Quoted in Thomas Price, 'Memoir of William Wilberforce', p. 59, appended to William Wilberforce, *A Practical View* (1834 edition).
[29] R. W. Dale, ed., *Life and Letters of John Angell James* (1861), p. 308.

disconnected from the main argument of the book. What is more, whereas Wilberforce had dealt with Christian living in such a way as to include the doctrine of justification, James was unable to direct the anxious inquirer to his salvation in such a way as to include Christian living. When nineteen years later he published a sequel entitled *Christian Progress*, its opening chapter demonstrated the need for progress by arguments derived from Scriptural injunctions and from the implications of such Scriptural metaphors as race, life and path. There was no attempt to trace any connection with what Evangelicals called the Gospel, or the scheme of salvation.[30]

None of this meant that there were not many people in the circles of early Victorian Evangelical Dissent who lived saintly lives, conquered their self-will and did their duty to their neighbour as they understood it. It is not necessary for teaching and preaching to be coherent in order to be effective. On the contrary, the logic of a doctrine is not one of the important factors behind any strong moral revival. But there was a marked insensitivity to changing situations, largely, it may be suspected, because there was little concern with the situation as such, with the temporal setting. When right conduct was valued primarily as evidence of spiritual grace, the least debatable evidence, the one that all would unquestionably recognise as such, was the most desirable.

In consequence those who were primarily interested in the scheme of salvation clung to conservative moral types, while those, like Dawson, whose primary loyalty lay with the moral reform aspect of the joint heritage, were driven to protest against a preoccupation with doctrine which seemed to them largely irrelevant. To Dawson 'the practical side of truth was like the practical side of sunshine.' It did not make any difference whether one knew the theory.[31] The fact that the doctrine was in any case under intellectual attack was an additional reason for thorough-going pragmatism.

Such pragmatism brought liberation from religious cant. Dawson's moral teaching firmly emphasised effectiveness in contrast to good intentions. Here his shrewd understanding of human nature and powers of detailed observation stood him in good stead. His conversational style was the instrument for descending quickly from the general principle to the particular local application. R. W. Dale, who learnt much from this side of Dawson's work has given a detailed description of it.

[30] J. Angell James, *Christian Progress: A Sequel to the Anxious Inquirer after Salvation Directed and Encouraged* (1853), chapter I.
[31] Wright Wilson, *Life of George Dawson*, pp. 180–1.

'The strength of his moral teaching was largely derived from the firmness of his own conviction that the laws which govern human life are not to be evaded . . . that we must obey them or else suffer the consequence of our disobedience. He insisted . . . that the facts of the physical and moral universe have a stern reality; and that if we refuse to learn and to recognise the facts, the best intentions are unavailing. The iron girder must be strong enough to bear the weight that is put upon it, or else it will give way—no matter whether the girder is meant to support the roof of a railway station, or the floor of a church or the gallery of a theatre.'[32]

Dale was referring to the 1850s, but Dawson's preoccupation with the effectiveness of good conduct runs as a major theme throughout his career. When in 1866 an epidemic of the cattle-plague broke out and the Archbishop of Canterbury called for a day of humiliation and fasting, Dawson took the opportunity to re-assert 'the glorious uniformity of cause and consequence'.

'There is a great charm to me to think that I cannot escape the evil unless I find out the cause.
Learn that piety will not save you from the results of stupidness; and that if you pray to God and make no bread, you are likely to pray to God and go without; and that if you pray to God and eat too much you are likely to damage your digestion. We must understand God's laws and obey them.'[33]

It is perhaps because his teaching focused on the idea of effective moral action that the Church never became to him more than an instrument for something else, and not necessarily the best instrument in all cases. There is no indication that he himself felt or encouraged others to feel any loyalty to the Church in its own right. It was with 'the world —by which I mean all people who do not call themselves the Church' that he identified himself.[34] His relationship to the Church of the Saviour makes sense only if we take seriously both his repeated repudiation, on both counts, of the title 'Dissenting Minister', and the description of himself as a teacher instructing his congregation, which he had written into the Church Principles. The interior of the building had

[32] R. W. Dale, 'George Dawson', *Nineteenth Century*, II, 49–50.
[33] George Dawson, 'On Humiliation and Fast-Days' in *Sermons on Disputed Points and Special Occasions*, ed. Mrs. George Dawson (Birmingham, 1878), p. 14.
[34] Speech at the first Annual General Meeting of the National Education League, *D.P.*, 13.10.1869. Also in *Dawson Collection*, XV, 190.

been modelled on a lecture theatre in the University of London, with benches instead of pews and a platform to take the place of the pulpit, which in 1846 was elsewhere still the most important piece of chapel furniture.[35] From this platform Dawson preached twice each Sunday and led the services, but his frequent lecture tours and the fact that after 1858 his daughter's health caused him to live a considerable distance from Birmingham severely limited any additional ministry to the church.[36] When he died suddenly in December 1876, the church was doomed to gradual extinction, unless the congregation could find another teacher of his talent. They never did. A marble bust of Dawson looked coldly down upon the efforts of three successors, and in 1895 the building was sold cheaply to the Primitive Methodists.[37]

Untroubled by the doubts which beset those who wrestled with the problem of the place of the Church in a changing world, Dawson knew where his allegiance lay. Early in life he had come under the spell of idealistic nationalism. He had been a founding member of the Society of the Friends of Italy, and responsible for the first public meeting held in England on behalf of the Hungarian nationalists. He had met Kossuth and persuaded him to visit Birmingham, and after 1848 made it a rule to offer Christmas hospitality to some of the nationalist exiles.[38] It was to the nation as the community transcending all divisions that he had given his allegiance.

Quite early in his ministry he had taken the doctrines of idealistic nationalism and given them a local twist.[39] The more he understood the key role which the borough and its municipal corporation could play in all efforts for the practical improvements on which he had set his heart, the more he came to regard the town as the local manifestation of the nation, like it comprehending all divisions and charged with an idealistic task. In each case he exalted the comprehensive community over against individualism on the one hand, and sectarianism on the other. He proclaimed both 'the doctrine of the family life of the nation',[40] and also

---

[35] 'The Church of the Saviour, its History, Principles and Work', *Dawson Collection*, X, 9–10.
[36] Wright Wilson, *op. cit.*, pp. 82–4; *D.P.* 15.10.1895 for his refusal to fulfil pastoral functions.
[37] *Dawson Collection*, X, 549–62.
[38] Wright Wilson, *Life of George Dawson*, pp. 110, 113; 'Obituary', *D.P.*, 1.12.1876.
[39] R. W. Dale, 'George Dawson', *Nineteenth Century*, II, 46.
[40] Speech at the first Annual General Meeting of the National Education League, *D.P.*, 13.10.1869.

'that a great town exists to discharge towards the people of that town the duties that a great nation exists to discharge towards the people of that nation.'[41]

Throughout the 1860s he consistently proclaimed this double message —both

'the sublimer creed of this and the next generation . . . that the whole nation was one family acting for itself and for every member through its own agency, righteously elected and religiously obeyed,'

and

'that a town is a solemn organism through which should flow, and in which should be shaped all the highest, loftiest and truest ends of man's moral nature.'[42]

Nor did he stop there. The community of town and nation was not merely a family or an organism, powerful metaphors though these were. It was also the new Church. Speaking in 1861 at the opening of the first public library in Birmingham, he put it thus:

'It was the tendency of old associations, old corporations, old churches and the like, to go to ruin and to serve no longer the objects which in bygone days they were established for . . . But while the old guilds and old corporations had declined, we had found a new plan of forming ourselves together more in accordance with the thought and feeling of the time, and capable of bringing about a better union of classes; and he regarded the movement just inaugurated as the largest and widest Church ever established, and he had taken more interest in it than perhaps in any other Church; for there could not be anything more valuable than men finding rallying points at which they might forget sectarianism and political economy, which they did not half understand, and find a brotherhood removed from the endless grovellings, and the bickerings— which he detested more than the grovelling—that surrounded us. This then was the new corporation, the new Church, in which they might meet until they came into union again—a Church in which

[41] George Dawson, *Inaugural Address at the Opening of the Free Reference Library, 26 October 1866* (Birmingham, 1866), p. 23.
[42] Speech at the luncheon following the stone-laying of the undenominational schools in All Saints ward, *D.P.*, 4.9.1869, p. 8, *Inaugural Address*, p. 23.

there was no bond, nor text, nor articles—a large Church, one of the greatest institutions yet established.'[43]

What Dawson was doing is plain to see. Mazzini with his Jansenist background had drawn on religious concepts to proclaim a doctrine of nationalism which benefited from the emotional and mystical associations of the terms in which it was expressed. The Protestant Radicals whom he met in England had been led by his imagery to transfer their abundant religious fervour to the cause of national liberation abroad. Dawson was a disciple who had caught not the doctrine only but the method. Prompted by the administrative circumstances of England, he saw the town as Mazzini saw the nation, and with the same result. The Protestant Radicals of Birmingham were led by his imagery to see their municipal institutions in the light shed by the Church and the Gospel.

'He who wants to persuade should put his trust not in the right argument but in the right word.'[44] That was the lesson which Dawson had learnt, and not from Mazzini alone. He never ceased to acknowledge his debt to Carlyle who had exercised a major influence both on his thought and on his style.[45] Dawson's speech at the opening of the Free Reference Library in 1866 was the finest example of his skill. His imagery invested both the occasion and the library with an aura that lifted it free from all association with an undignified third-rate town council. By the municipal reformers it was always considered the finest expression of their ideal.

Neither Dawson nor his followers would have regarded his views on the nature of municipal life as merely of limited application. Yet it is significant that the statements from which they are drawn were all made in connection with ventures for the extension of popular education, whether the opening of a public library or the establishment of schools for the working classes.

Dawson's habit of saying one thing at a time, and of saying it as if it were the only thing that mattered, probably contributed to the formulation of the new municipal ideal.[46] In this respect his influence was so great because like him his followers were deeply concerned for the

---

[43] *Dawson Collection*, XV, 29.

[44] Joseph Conrad, *A Personal Record* (Uniform ed., 1923), p. 13.

[45] R. W. Dale, 'George Dawson', *Nineteenth Century*, II, 47. For a parallel analysis of Carlyle's method, see John Holloway, *The Victorian Sage: Studies in Argument* (1953), chapter 2 *passim*, but especially pp. 44–6 on the gospel of work.

[46] R. W. Dale drew attention to this habit of Dawson's in his article. *Nineteenth Century*, II, 57.

spread of education among the people. In the 1860s they were catching a glimpse of the significant role that municipal institutions could play in this process. It is striking how his teaching on the dignity of municipal government came to be more widely accepted as it became apparent that local authorities, having begun by providing libraries and museums, were to assume responsibility for the creation of a whole network of schools.

Dawson's influence can be traced first among those who were closest to him. In 1852 the first but unsuccessful initiative for the adoption of the Public Libraries Act came from ten men, of whom eight, including Dawson himself, were members of the Church of the Saviour.[47] Between 1859 and 1860 it was a founder-member of the church, E. C. Osborne, who took the matter up again and brought it to a successful conclusion. Robert Wright, to whom the passing of the Improvement Act of 1861 was mainly due, was another member and a close friend of Dawson.[48] During the course of the bitter controversy, which broke out over that Bill, first in the Council, then in the town at large, a group of men decided to launch a humorous paper, *The Town Crier*. Its object was subsequently described by one of the founders:

> 'It was felt that there were certain things, and perhaps certain people, who could be best assailed and suppressed by ridicule . . . It only dealt with public affairs and with men in their public capacity. Indeed, I may say that all the men connected with *The Town Crier* at its starting were interested in the good government and progress of the town and they used the influence of the paper for the purpose of removing stumbling-blocks and putting incompetent and pretentious persons out of the way.'[49]

The claim is borne out by an examination of the paper. Its particular target was petty and undignified conduct on the part of councillors, and it must have played a considerable part in the moulding of public opinion during the next fifteen years. Of the seven men who were anonymously responsible for that venture, four were members of the Church of the Saviour and closely associated with Dawson.[50] A fifth, Sebastian Evans,

---

[47] *Birmingham Mercury*, 23.4.1852.
[48] Wright Wilson, *Life of George Dawson*, p. 61. For the 1861 Improvement Act see above, p. 34.
[49] T. Anderton, *Tale of One City*, pp. 133–4.
[50] Samuel Timmins, G. J. Johnson, William Harris and J. H. Chamberlain (no relation of Joseph Chamberlain).

4

was a friend and a member of the Shakespeare Club over which Dawson presided.[51]

The Town Crier did not rest content with criticism of actual shortcomings or with demands for greater decorum. It laid the blame for what was going wrong squarely on the shoulders of those substantial ratepayers who agreed with it in deploring the ignorance and incapacity of Birmingham's public men. It sketched an imaginary ratepayer of this sort, Gideon Bagsworth, in a choleric fit over the latest news from the Town Council, and commented:

> 'Here is Bagsworth, with every qualification requisite for a Town Councillor, shrewd, honest, liberal, energetic, and persevering, ready in word and deed, with a decent balance at his bankers and sufficient leisure on his hands, who resolutely and persistently refuses to mix himself up in any way with local politics, though he could command a majority in at least half a dozen wards if he chose to try. Gideon is strongly possessed with the notion that everything local and provincial is of necessity vulgar, and that to become a Town Councillor is nothing less than to undergo a voluntary degradation. He really in his heart believes that his dignity as a gentleman would be compromised by fulfilling his duties as a citizen. To this disgraceful prejudice, mingled it may be with a fastidiousness born of nobler feelings, Gideon adds an enormous dead weight of indolence in all matters unconnected with his own particular business, or his own domestic life, and more than all, he "devotes" himself to these two objects with a perfect fanaticism, a fanaticism which he only does not recognise as pure selfishness, because it is sufficiently expansive to include wife and family. When he has subscribed to those institutions which other Bagsworths subscribe to, he considers that he has amply fulfilled the duties of citizenship, and that he is thereby exempted from any obligation to take the slightest real personal interest in the well-being of the town in which he lives, moves, and makes his money.'[52]

This was the message which *The Town Crier* put forward from the first year of its publication. It may be described as the policy of the Dawson group. By the later sixties its characteristic double attack, both on the quality of the Council and on the public spirit of its critics, could at

[51] Wright Wilson, *Life of George Dawson*, p. 209. The remaining two, Tom Anderton and J. Thackray Bunce, were journalists. Bunce was editor of the influential Liberal papers, *The Birmingham Daily Post* and *The Birmingham Journal*.
[52] *The Town Crier*, November 1861, p. 14.

times be found on the lips of others not immediately connected with their circle. In October 1866 Charles Vince, Baptist minister of Mount Zion, Graham Street, made a pertinent reference to it at the Mayor's luncheon itself.[53] Bunce was also using the editorial columns of his papers for the same purpose. In 1867 he commented in the *Birmingham Journal* on recent irregularities at the municipal elections:

> 'If on the occurrence of a vacancy, some gentleman holding a leading position in the town could be induced to come forward, there would be little danger of two candidates, each imperfectly qualified, having to struggle for victory by making use of illegal practices.'[54]

Yet in the end the policy of the Dawson group was not to be achieved by the Bagsworths of this world, men exclusively devoted to their business and their family and satisfied with financial subscriptions to the conventional institutions. It was to be achieved by men, most of whom were already deeply committed to other public causes.

[53] *D.P.*, 27.10.1866, p. 3.
[54] *B.J.*, 9.11.1867, p. 6.

2

The Education of the People

Between 1867 and 1873 the question how best to provide schools for the working classes became a major preoccupation in the public life of Birmingham, and this was particularly true of the years 1869 and 1870. This chapter will explain the effect of these educational preoccupations in channelling political energy into municipal service, and to some extent even in shaping the alignments of municipal politics.

In those years so crucial in the history of the Corporation, municipal politics were closely intertwined with the struggle over the making and implementation of the 1870 Education Act. It is no accident that the leaders of the National Education League, that great but largely unsuccessful pressure group on the stage of national politics, were also the leaders of the Birmingham municipal reform movement. But for this interest in popular education few of them would have become town councillors. This is paradoxical since the body that provided the schools was not the Town Council at all but the totally separate School Board. But men's actions are governed by what they think will happen, even if history proves them wrong. The history of the making of the 1870 Education Act and its implementation, complex as it is, has never been written though much has been written about it. This is not the occasion for such a study in the round, but we shall need to refer to that history where it throws light on the making of the Birmingham municipal reform movement.

To men campaigning for the provision of schools, unfettered by consideration for the vested interests of churches, George Dawson's views on the civilising mission of municipal authorities went to the heart of the matter. The municipal teaching of the Dawson circle, as expounded in *The Town Crier* and elsewhere, gained converts in direct proportion to the growth of interest in the provision of popular education from the rates. How closely these two matters are connected is shown in the case of William Harris, the first of the group associated with *The Town Crier* to turn precept into practice. He entered the Town Council in November 1865 and remained until November 1871, when illness forced him to retire.

No one else touches this story at so many important points as he. An architect and surveyor, he was a founder-member of the Church of the Saviour. In 1867, after the passing of the Reform Act, it was he who suggested the reorganisation of the Birmingham Liberal Association on a representative basis, and he was successively its Honorary Secretary, Vice-President and President. His were also the ideas behind the creation of the National Federation of Liberal Associations in 1877 and he became Chairman of its General Committee.[1] In the conflicts which rent the Town Council between 1866 and 1871, and which are discussed in chapter 3, Harris worked closely with Thomas Avery. A strong advocate of the establishment of a joint drainage board for the Tame and Rea valleys, he became Clerk to the Board on its creation in 1877 and served it for over thirty years.[2]

Above all he was a persistent advocate of a national system of elementary education. In 1850 he had been Honorary Secretary to the short-lived Birmingham branch of the National Public School Association, which agitated for the public provision of schools on an uncompromisingly secular basis.[3] He never swerved from his conviction that it was essential for representative institutions to obtain adequate funds for purposes of education. In 1865 his hopes were fixed on the ample endowments of the Birmingham Free Grammar School. A Royal Commission was investigating the use made of endowments of this sort, and a local association had sprung up to wrest the control of the school from the small group of Church of England Tories who composed its governing board. Like some other members of the association Harris wanted the Town Council to acquire a controlling voice on the board and use its funds for purposes of elementary education.[4] His election speech struck

---

[1] Wright Wilson, *op. cit.*, p. 61; *B.J.*, 5.10.1867; J. L. Garvin, *Life of Joseph Chamberlain*, I (1932), 261; Obituary in *Birmingham Mail*, 25.3.1911. He was the author of a *History of the Radical Party in Parliament* (1885).

[2] *W.P.*, 25.1.1908; obituary in *Birmingham Dispatch*, 25.3.1911.

[3] Birmingham and District Branch of the National Public School Association, *Report for 1851*.

[4] *Report to the Grammar School Association by the Committee appointed on the 11 November 1864* (Birmingham, 1865); *Reform of King Edward School. Deputation to the Governors*, reprinted from the *D.P.*, 14.10.1865. The three-cornered struggle between the governors, the Association and the Town Council, and their relation to the Royal Commission on Endowed Schools can be followed step by step in the *Birmingham Collection*. It spanned the years 1864–78.

a note not usually heard at ward meetings, expressing a hope that the Council would soon 'acquire the power of increasing the educational institutions' in the town.[5] But nothing came of this for the moment.

In 1865 Harris's accession was an isolated case but from the perspective of a few years later he was a significant precursor. After 1867 we find a number of able recruits to municipal politics, 'belonging indeed to precisely the class of burgesses most desirable to the Council', to quote the words used of Joseph Chamberlain, who seem to have been brought there by their interest in the extension of popular education. Their accession was crucial. Having entered under what proved to have been a misapprehension, they stayed on, dealing with the pressing tasks with which the Corporation was faced at the time, and thereby raising considerably the ability and general tone of the Council.

It all began in March 1867 with the creation of the Birmingham Education Society. The idea came from Manchester, whose Education Aid Society had been founded in 1864 and whose secretary was invited to explain its object at a private meeting in George Dixon's house.[6] Dixon, a wealthy and philanthropic merchant with political ambitions, was himself a recent recruit to the Town Council and mayor for the year. He became President of the new Society, whose object was 'the advancement of Education in Birmingham and the immediate neighbourhood', and whose methods were modelled on those of Manchester.[7] It was recruited from those actively interested in popular education. This meant those whose sphere of work lay mainly in the philanthropy of the churches or of a few paternalistic firms. Of the thirty men, who composed its officers and committee in 1867, eleven were clergy. The great majority of the nineteen laymen were prominent in the churches, while several were associated with the philanthropic industrial schools in Penn Street and Gem Street.[8] At the time not more than five were members of the Town Council but several were to be drawn by their work for the Society into the orbit of municipal politics.

[5] *D.P.*, 20.10.1865, p. 4.
[6] S. E. Maltby, *Manchester and the Movement for National Elementary Education 1800–1870* (Manchester, 1918), pp. 95–6; *D.P.*, 14.2.1867.
[7] 1. By collecting and disseminating information on the subject generally.
　2. By taking steps for obtaining local rating powers on behalf of Education.
　3. By securing Educational provisions in any legislative measure for the regulation of labour.
　4. By paying all or part of the school fees for the Education of children, whose parents or guardians cannot pay such fees themselves.
　5. By raising and distributing funds for or towards the enlargment, the building and the maintenance of schools.
Birmingham Education Society, 'Rules and Objects', in *Annual Report* (1868), p. 1.
[8] *Annual Report* (1968), for list of officers and committee.

The Honorary Secretary, Jesse Collings, was a relative newcomer to the town. Owner of an ironmonger's business, he was a Unitarian from Devon but since 1864 a member of Dawson's church. In Exeter he had taught in a ragged school and had also taken the lead in the founding of an industrial school. It was he who had persuaded Dixon to take the initiative in founding an education society on the Manchester model.[9]

Joseph Chamberlain, head of the commercial side of Nettlefold and Chamberlain, the large firm of screw-manufacturers, was a member of the committee. Of old Unitarian stock he had come to Birmingham in 1854, where he soon became prominent in the Unitarian Church of the Messiah. He was Warden from 1860–62, almost continuously on the Vestry Committee from 1863–71, and, until October 1867, on the Committee of the Sunday schools. After 1865 he taught only intermittently on Sundays, but appears to have helped regularly with evening classes which the Sunday school teachers conducted from 1862–6.[10] The meeting which publicly launched the Education Society on 13 March 1867 made such an impression on a group of those connected with the Church of the Messiah Sunday Schools, that they decided to start day-schools for boys and girls in the Sunday school buildings, which stood empty during the week. Joseph Chamberlain was Treasurer of the new venture.[11] His 'blazing interest in popular education', to use his biographer's phrase, showed itself also in his connection with the Working Men's Institute at the Smethwick branch of the firm. He had suggested it, acted as its treasurer, and occasionally taught French there. He started its debating club and frequently chaired the readings on Monday nights. Apart from this educational work he had taken little part in the public life of the town. The local debating society appreciated his talent, and he was respected enough in philanthropic circles to succeed Dixon in 1867 as chairman for a recently established charitable fund.[12] But it was the Birmingham Education Society that drew him from church and works into municipal and ultimately into national politics.

The Birmingham Society was fortunate to have the earlier experience of Manchester to draw on. In 1865 the Manchester philanthropists had

[9] Jesse Collings and J. L. Green, *Life of the Right Honourable Jesse Collings* (1920); N. Murrell Marris, *Joseph Chamberlain, the Man and the Statesman* (1900), p. 74.
[10] Records of the New Meeting and Church of the Messiah, Birmingham. Minutes of Church General Meetings; Minutes of the Vestry Committee; Minutes of the Sunday School Committee; Minutes of the Sunday School Teachers' Society, 6.10.1862; Annual Report for 1866.
[11] Minutes of the Day School Committee, 10.7.1867; Minutes of the Vestry Committee, 24.4.1867; Minutes of the Church General Meeting, 28.4.1867.
[12] J. L. Garvin, *Joseph Chamberlain*, I, 66; N. Murrell Marris, *Joseph Chamberlain*, pp. 47 ff; *D.P.*, 3.1.1867.

still been optimistic about the ease with which the condition of the uneducated masses might be improved. By 1866 they had discovered that 'no private or voluntary effort can reach the depth of this evil.' Only compulsion could obtain school attendance in view of the 'lamentable indifference on the part of the parents', and only a public rate would suffice to deal with the financial problem. The Birmingham men did not accept all these conclusions ready made. They rejected a resolution in favour of compulsory school attendance. But they accepted the policy of obtaining local rating powers.[13]

That policy was then being embodied in an Education Bill, inspired by the experience of Manchester, which H. A. Bruce introduced into the House of Commons on 5 April.[14] The Bill permitted the levying of local rates for education, and laid down that in corporate towns the management of the funds should be in the hands of a committee elected by the Town Council. It must have seemed obvious that once schools were to be provided from the rates their administration would rest directly or indirectly with the Town Council. In support of the policy of the Manchester Bill and of the Education Society Dixon moved a resolution in the Birmingham Town Council 'that corporate bodies should be empowered to levy rates for educational purposes'.[15]

It was no accident that, when Dixon became M.P. for the borough and retired from municipal politics in February 1868, he was replaced by Jesse Collings. Two months before another committee member of the Education Society had joined the Town Council, George Baker, a life-long teacher at the Quaker adult school.[16]

In the mean time the passing of the unexpectedly sweeping Reform Act in August 1867 had given the nation a jolt, and the following twelve months were to witness a rapid movement of public opinion both in Birmingham and in the country as a whole. To the Congregationalists and their Board of Education it offered the pretext for withdrawal from an untenable position. In October 1867, its chairman, Edward Baines, the leader of those who had since 1843 condemned all government support of education, recommended the acceptance of Treasury grants in future. The Baptists, as usual, followed suit.[17] The following month

---

[13] Manchester and Salford Education Aid Society, *First* and *Second Annual Reports*, 1865, 1866, in S. E. Maltby, *Manchester*, pp. 97–9; *D.P.*, 23.2.1867, 6.3.1867.

[14] S. E. Maltby, *Manchester*, p. 107.

[15] *D.P.*, 5.6.1867; *B.C.P.*, 4.6.1867.

[16] *B.C.P.*, 10.3.1868; *D.P.*, 9.12.1867.

[17] For the policy of the Congregationalists on education see Albert Peel, *These Hundred Years. A History of the Congregational Union of England and Wales 1831–1931* (1931), chapter X.

Robert Lowe, the bitter opponent of the Reform Bill, captured the popular imagination with a speech at Edinburgh in which he had urged the need 'to compel our future masters to learn their letters'.[18]

When educationalists from all over the country met in Manchester in January 1868 they were almost unanimously in favour of the compulsory provision of schools in places where accommodation was deficient. It was felt that public opinion had progressed so rapidly that a permissive Bill would be almost laughed out of the House. The previous year's Bill was consequently re-introduced with clauses which made the levying of a rate compulsory where there was inadequate school provision. Even the Conservative government, which had killed Earl Russell's Resolutions on National Education only the previous autumn without even a division, now felt obliged to make a gesture. It introduced an Education Bill of its own into the House of Lords only a week after the first reading of the Manchester Bill in the Commons, but withdrew it on the first opportunity. When the impending dissolution of Parliament forced the withdrawal of the Manchester Bill in June 1868, it was certain that the next government would have to introduce a measure of its own, and carry it through.[19]

In Birmingham local factors were superimposed on the national movement of opinion. The Birmingham Education Society rapidly learned from its own experience the lessons which Manchester had already mastered. A survey of the educational requirements of the town revealed the unexpectedly large dimensions of the problem, while another disillusioned the inhabitants with the quality of many of the so-called schools that existed.[20] Financial difficulties quickly strengthened the conviction that a philanthropic society could be no more than a stop-gap in this field. The Education Society had set out boldly by paying the school pence of 5,000 poor children; by July 1868 it was forced to cut the number down to 2,000, and the future looked bleak. The provision of an undenominational school depleted another fund, which was never again to be filled.[21] In a sense the achievements of the Society had been considerable. It had aroused a strong concern for the education of the working classes in Birmingham and had led so rapidly to a maturing of views that by the beginning of 1869 it was already out of

[18] A. P. Martin, *Life of Lord Sherbrook* (1893), II, 330.

[19] *P.P.* 1867–8 (64) ii, pp. 359 ff. especially clauses 14–18; S. E. Maltby, *Manchester*, pp. 107–9.

[20] Birmingham Education Society. *First Annual Report* (1868). This gloomy picture was subsequently borne out by an official inquiry set up in 1869. *Reports on Schools for the Poorer Classes in Birmingham etc.*, (1870) (91) liv, 265.

[21] Birmingham Education Society. *First Annual Report* (1868), *Second Annual Report* (1869).

date. From the first it had been a union for immediate purposes between men with differing loyalties. They had been able to agree sufficiently to demand local rating powers, but beyond that step lay major divergences. Only by creating two separate funds and allowing subscribers to allocate their money either to denominational or undenominational schools had it been possible to found the society at all. It was bound to fall apart as soon as issues of national policy arose.

None knew this better than its Secretary. In 1868 Jesse Collings had produced a pamphlet on the American School system, in which he advocated 'the immediate formation of a Society, national in its name and constitution, refusing all compromise, but adopting as its platform —national, secular (or unsectarian) education, compulsory as to rating and attendance, with State aid and inspection, and local management.' The society was to be modelled on the Anti-Corn Law League, then regarded as the prototype for successful agitation. It was to produce publications and send out lecturers, to found local branches controlled from central headquarters, and thereby to 'give direction and voice to the fresh and ever increasing interest felt by the people in this matter'. He hoped that 'it would effectively prevent the passing of any half measure; and more important still, it would put in open opposition those who now join the education movement, either to retard it, or to direct it into some narrow and inefficient channel.'[22]

This return to the uncompromising line of the National Public School Association of 1850 appealed to the temper of many of the Birmingham educationalists and the outcome was the formation of the National Education League. Its manifesto appeared in February 1869 and before the first public meeting was held in October it had recruited 2,500 adherents.[23]

---

[22] Jesse Collings, *An Outline of the American School System with Remarks on the Establishment of Common Schools in England* (1868), pp. 47–8. Collings was heavily indebted to the *Report of the R.C. on Endowed Schools* for his information. *P.P.* 1867–8 [3966], xxviii.

[23] *Object:*
'The establishment of a system which shall secure the education of every child in the country.
Means:
1. Local authorities shall be compelled by law to see that sufficient school accommodation is provided for every child in their district.
2. The cost of founding and maintaining such schools as may be required shall be provided out of local rates, supplemented by Government grants.
3. All schools aided by local rates shall be under the management of local authorities, and subject to Government inspection.
4. All schools aided by local rates shall be unsectarian.
5. To all schools aided by local rates admission shall be free.
6. School accommodation being provided, the State, or the local authorities, shall have power to compel the attendance of children of suitable age not otherwise receiving education.'
Francis Adams, *History of the Elementary School Contest in England* (1882), p. 198.

The officers of the League were almost all former members of the Birmingham Education Society. Dixon was chairman, but so taken up with Parliamentary duties that the effective lead fell to the acting chairman, Joseph Chamberlain. Collings was secretary, F. R. Martineau responsible for local organisations all over the country, Harris chairman of the Parliamentary committee, Bunce of the publishing committee. Most impressive was a guarantee fund towards which twelve men from Birmingham alone had promised £1,000 each. £3,000 of it were contributed by partners of Nettlefold and Chamberlain. By the following February, 113 branches of the League had been founded, and between 100 and 200 public meetings held all over the country.[24]

Whatever their differences, there was one point on which the new Liberal Government, the League, and the Manchester Bill committee were agreed: local school rates necessarily implied management by elected local authorities. In the corporate towns this meant in 1869, as it had done in 1867, a body selected by the Town Council. Only the National Education Union, founded in August 1869 for the defence of the denominational control of education, denied this premiss. It was therefore those who moved from the Education Society to the League, and not those who moved to the Union, on whom the Town Council exerted an attraction. In November 1869 Collings was joined in the Council Chamber by Joseph Chamberlain, and the deputation that asked him to stand for election was headed by Harris, his colleague in the League, and at the same time pledged to the programme of *The Town Crier* and deeply involved in the faction fighting on the Council.[25] December saw the accession of James Deykin, a League member, who was soon to become Chamberlain's lieutenant in municipal politics and unofficial whip of the party that was being formed.[26] By the end of 1869 the League had eleven prominent representatives on the Town Council.

The long awaited government Bill was published on 17 February 1870. On the question of school management it proposed that:

1. The country be divided into School Districts formed from municipal boroughs and civil parishes.

[24] Francis Adams, *Elementary School Contest*, pp. 204–6; *National Education League Monthly Paper*, January 1870.

[25] George Titterton and Others, 'Recollections of Joseph Chamberlain', *The Searchlight of Greater Birmingham*, 13.11.1913, p. 23.

[26] 'List of Members made up to the 14 September 1869', in *Collection of Circulars etc. relating to the National Education League*, p. 11. *Birmingham Collection;* 'Our Representatives XVI', *B.M.N.*, 12.4.1875. Apart from the reference to Deykin's role in this well-informed article, written from within the movement, I have found no surviving clues to his role as whip.

2. The Government take powers for ascertaining the deficiency of school accommodation.

3. The religious denominations then have a year's grace, in which to supply this deficiency.

4. On the failure of the donominations, School Boards be elected, with powers of rating for the purpose of establishing schools.

5. In municipal boroughs the School Board be elected by the Town Council, in parishes by the vestry.[27]

The Bill did not satisfy the League, but the clause that gave the election of school boards in boroughs to the town councils was cordially approved. It was not due to the League that it never reached the Statute Book. The initiative for its amendment came from Sir Charles Dilke, who had resigned the previous month from the chairmanship of its London Branch on finding himself at loggerheads with the leaders. It was therefore as a guerilla-fighter on the left that he rose in the House on 4 July to propose 'that School Boards should in all cases be elected by the ratepayers'. He added that 'the amendment was not looked on with favour either by the League or the Union; but it had been frequently commended by meetings out-of-doors.'[28] The amendment was defeated by only five votes, but it had been strongly opposed by Dixon and several other M.P.s from large towns. For one thing they disliked the turbulence of a double set of contested elections in the wards. For another it was suggested from many sides that town councils would select a better class of men than the ratepayers, to whom it was too easy to appeal with cries of mere economy. But particularly interesting was an argument put forward by the member for Sunderland, and taken up with approval by several speakers, including both Dixon and W. E. Forster, the minister responsible for the measure. He argued

> 'that the effect of imposing this duty on the Town Councils would be to raise the tone and character of these municipal bodies throughout the country; it would give them something more than matters of police to think of.'

Forster had explained during the debate that the point involved in Dilke's amendment 'was not one upon which the government would

---

[27] *P.P.* 1870, [33], 505. Schedule I, clauses 8, 9, 10, 28. Clause 28 became clause 27 when the Bill was next amended.

[28] Stephen Gwynn and Gertrude Tuckwell, *The Life of the Right Honourable Sir Charles W. Dilke* (1918), I, 97; *Verbatim Report of the Debate in Parliament during the Progress of the Elementary Education Bill, 1870. Prepared under the Direction of the National Education Union* (1870), p. 365.

wish to resist very strenuously any decided view of the committee', and when he was subsequently led to introduce election by the ratepayers both for country parishes and for the metropolitan area, he 'did not see how one rule was to be laid down for London, and another for the large towns of the country'. The principle of direct election was therefore adopted for all areas. To the end Dixon and Muntz, the two members for Birmingham, fought for its rejection. They presumably knew the feeling in Birmingham on the point. But the argument for uniformity was such that on the 19 July the government amendment was carried by 273 to 57.[29]

In consequence of that vote the Birmingham leaders of the Education League, instead of organising the new school system from an entrenched position on the Town Council, had to contest the first School Board election in December 1870. Unfortunately for them they did not foresee the effect of the system of cumulative voting, introduced by the Education Act. By putting too many candidates in the field they scattered the votes of their supporters. Only six of them were elected, in opposition to nine supporters of denominational schools—eight Churchmen and one Roman Catholic. Of the four town councillors among the candidates, Chamberlain was the only one to get in.[20]

The others threw themselves into what educational work the Council could provide. Collings, as well as Chamberlain, sat on the free library committee under the chairmanship of Harris, whom he succeeded in 1871. He also served on the industrial school committee with such allies as Arthur Ryland and George Baker.

The development of industrial schools had run parallel to that of elementary day schools. They were first founded by private philanthropists in the 1840s, for the reclamation of the children of the 'dangerous and perishing classes'. 1849 saw the establishment of one in Gem Street, Birmingham, founded and managed entirely by a group of Churchmen, on the initiative of the Reverend and Honourable Grantham Yorke, Vicar of St. Philip's Church. The Industrial Schools Act of 1857 introduced a system of licensing by the Committee of the Privy Council on Education. It also permitted magistrates to send children, brought before them on a charge of vagrancy, to certified industrial schools.

In 1861 a further Act transferred the power of licensing to the Home

[29] *Verbatim Report*, pp. 377, 494–5. They were supported by Mundella, M.P. for Sheffield and National Education League Council member. Bright, the third M.P. for Birmingham, was ill and unable to attend.
[30] Francis Adams, *Elementary School Contest*, pp. 249–50.

Office. Children who were found begging, or who had committed a punishable offence, or were beyond the control of their parents could now be committed to an industrial school. For all but the last category the Treasury now provided a capitation grant, and this support from public funds led to the foundation of many more schools. In Exeter Jesse Collings took the initiative; in Birmingham Penn Street Ragged School was turned into a certified industrial school. In contrast to Gem Street, the moving spirits here were Nonconformists, and it resembled a school of the British and Foreign Schools Society in its approach to institutional religion. Like a British School it offered a basis for co-operation with those Churchmen who did not wish to tie education exclusively to the Established Church. The most important of these associated with the Penn Street school was T. C. S. Kynnersley, the stipendiary magistrate.

The next piece of legislation followed in 1866. Although only permissive and not mandatory, it provided for these schools what the Education Act of 1870 was to do for elementary schools in general. Prison authorities, i.e. in boroughs the municipal corporation, could use the rates both to support existing industrial schools or to establish new ones under their own management. The Act was passed in August; in December Kynnersley was urging the Birmingham Town Council to take action. He was supported by Alderman Arthur Ryland, connected with the Penn Street school, and by Alderman Charles Sturge, co-founder and life-long manager of a reformatory school in Worcestershire. In January 1868 the Council decided to start a municipal industrial school of their own.[31]

In addition to this work for public libraries and industrial schools the chiefs of the National Education League found scope for their fighting qualities on a committee of the Council set up in November 1869 to conduct its vendetta with the governors of the Free Grammar School. Members included Chamberlain, Collings, Harris and Baker. Its object, to obtain control of the town's leading school and its subsidiary branches, was a final manifestation of the older Radicalism, which from 1830–51 had inspired the offensive against every form of 'self-elected' authority. Like so much else at the time it was deeply impregnated with the antagonism between Church and Dissent. An echo from the past,

[31] 20 & 21 Vic. c. 48, clauses 3, 6; 24 & 25 Vic. c. 113, clauses 4, 9, 17; 29 & 30 Vic. c. 118, clause 12; R. and F. Davenport-Hill, *Life of Matthew Davenport-Hill, Recorder of Birmingham* (1878), pp. 151–75, 308; *B.G.*, 12.12.1866; *B.C.P.*, 11.12.1866, 9.4.1867, 25.6.1867, 9.11.1867, 7.1.1868, 9.11.1868; Stephen Hobhouse, *Joseph Sturge: his Life and Work* (1919), pp. 176–7.

it appealed strongly to both the older and the newer Radical group on the Council. Fighting in alliance with the Grammar School Association, whose interests were wider and whose attitude less rigid, the Council gained a partial victory in 1878, when it was given the right to appoint eight of the twenty-one governors.[32]

The cause of education did not, however, absorb them exclusively. Once on the Council they were quickly caught up in the other tasks that faced that body, as we shall see in chapter 3, and in the conflicts by which these were accompanied.

But before turning to other matters, we shall do well to spell out the significance of these events for the recruitment to the Town Council.

2 THE TRANSFER OF RESPONSIBILITY FOR EDUCATION

It made no difference whether a man's interest lay chiefly in the provision of free libraries for adults, or an adequate system of elementary schools for children, or in the special disciplinary education intended for the children of the criminal classes. His expectations centred on the work of public authorities, permissive as this largely was and hence dependent on the vision and initiative of its members. George Dawson's municipal ideal had been largely formed with reference to the provision of popular education. His teaching was the theoretical response, just as the recruitment of the new type of councillor was the practical response to one and the same historical situation.

To say merely that local government authorities were assuming the provision of popular education does not adequately describe the situation. It is true, of course, and the implication of this fact alone for the reform of local government had been succinctly stated by Matthew Arnold in 1867:

> 'What is the capital difficulty in the way of getting them [the working classes] public schools?' he had written. 'It is this: that the public school for the people must rest upon the municipal organisation of the country. In France, Germany, Italy, Switzerland, the public elementary school has, and exists by having the commune and the municipal government of the commune, as its foundations, and it could not exist without them. But we in England have our municipal organisation still to get; the country districts, with us, have at

---

[32] *Scheme for the Management of the Grammar School of King Edward VI in Birmingham etc. Approved by Order in Council, 1878. With Index* (1878).

present only the feudal and ecclesiastical organisation of the Middle Ages, or of France before the Revolution. This is what the people who talk so glibly about obligatory instruction, and the Conscience Clause, and our present abundant supply of schools, never think of. The real preliminary to an effective system of popular education is, in fact, to provide the country with an effective municipal organisation: and here, then, is at the outset an illustration of what I have said, that modern societies need a civic organisation which is modern.'[33]

This is excellent, but there is more to be said, because there was more at stake than the provision of an institutional framework. Nowhere is this more apparent than in the municipal boroughs, the sole areas in England and Wales where this framework was already in existence.

The public authorities were not assuming functions which had never been carried out before. The teaching of the common people had from time immemorial been the recognised sphere of the churches and of their ancillary organisations, and in attempting to fulfil that function they had drawn on the service of their members freely given. These had not needed to make any distinction between their educational work and other kinds of practical Christian devotion. On the contrary, there had been a tendency, natural enough and historically well founded, to regard the provision of even the rudimentary skills as part of the work of the Church in proclaiming the gospel. Now secular public authorities were assuming the provision of education because the churches could no longer perform this traditional function in a manner adequate to the needs of the society. Between 1810 and 1867 they had made a formidable effort to measure up to the constantly increasing task which they had assumed. The importance of the years 1867–70 lay in the nationwide discovery that despite Treasury support they had failed. Whatever recognition might be extended to their past achievement, in future public authorities would alone be adequate to the needs as they were now defined. Implicit in the direct assumption by those authorities of provisions for popular education was therefore the transfer to them of one of the Church's oldest functions. The great tenderness shown by the Act of 1870 towards the existing Church-schools merely served to delay among many members of the Established Church an understanding of

---

[33] Matthew Arnold, 'Report on Schools and Universities on the Continent, submitted to the Royal Commission on Endowed Schools', published separately as *Schools and Universities on the Continent* (1868), p. 274.

what was implied. The weaker financial position of the Dissenters, due to their smaller resources and to their refusal in many cases to accept Treasury grants, made them quicker to see what was at stake.

When a change of this sort occurs, it is not confined merely to a transfer of the function itself. Feelings and ideas with which it had been closely associated were also torn from their former context, and they influenced the new setting in which the work of education was in future carried on. For one thing, the personal service which loyal church members had in the past brought to educational work was to be diverted to the public authorities. But these authorities gained more than that service. They profited from the sense of mission which had been a major factor in keeping up the flow of recruits to support educational work. Moreover, concepts drawn from the language of the Christian Church now enriched the carefully circumscribed terms in which the role of mere boards and corporations had customarily been conceived, not least by Liberals. Local government had fallen heir to no meagre heritage.

We have noticed already in the case of Jesse Collings and of Joseph Chamberlain how a long-standing concern for education had been transferred to a new environment to be translated into a zeal for municipal service. In this respect as in so many others they were representative Dissenters. Indeed there was much in the corporate life of the most prominent Dissenting churches of the town which was capable of responding to the appeal implicit in the altered circumstances.

(a) *The Church of the Saviour and the Unitarians*

The most prominent of the Birmingham Dissenting churches, and also the most significant for the municipal reform movement, has been mentioned already. It was the Church of the Saviour. Even in the 1850s it had provided the Town Council with some of its more pertinacious fighters for the cause of good government.[34] The recruitment of Harris in 1865 and Collings in 1868 was followed by two less prominent members in 1871,[35] and in 1875 and 1877 by that of two well-known public

[34] Arthur Ryland in 1854, Robert Wright in 1858. See above, p. 34.
[35] William Shammon, clr. and ald. 1871–94. Whip manufacturer and saddler's ironmonger, a medium-sized business of standing.
Robert Mann, Sunday School teacher for over twenty years, ex-Chartist and member of the Reform League, ex-secretary of a trade union and president of the Master Builders' Association. He tried repeatedly to enter the Council between 1869 and 1871, but having succeeded was forced to retire in 1872 on becoming legally disqualified.

figures in the town, both of them prominent solicitors.[36] Six of these eight showed quite exceptional interest in educational work, and the same can be said of their church. Its elementary schools were the best in the town. There were also evening classes and a vigorous Sunday school.[37] The church was conspicuous for its interest in the public libraries of the town, which owed their existence to the initiative of its members and attracted a long line of benefactors and administrators from among them. For thirty-one of its first thirty-three years, the free library committee was under the chairmanship of a member of the church,[38] and others served it in a co-opted capacity.[39]

Almost as important was the Church of the Messiah, as the congregation of the Unitarian New Meeting called their brand new Gothic church in 1862. Joseph Chamberlain's educational work had begun in its Sunday school, out of which grew the Church of the Messiah day schools in 1867. The group which founded it provided four other town councillors in addition to Joseph Chamberlain: his brother-in-law, William Kenrick,[40] his younger brother, Arthur Chamberlain,[41] R.F. Martineau,[42] and a younger man C. G. Beale.[43] Richard Chamberlain,[44] whose municipal career was to be almost as distinguished as that of his brother, belonged essentially to the same set. The direct influence of Joseph Chamberlain on them all was of course enormous, but like him they had been drawn from those active in the educational work of the Church of the Messiah.

The treatment of its day school by this church clearly demonstrates

[36] C. E. Mathews, clr. Edgebaston 1875–81 in succession to Jesse Collings. 1864 Founder of the Grammar School Association, 1878 governor of the school and chairman of the School Committee; 1869 Chairman of the Parliamentary Committee, National Education League, whose headquarters were at his office; 1871 appointed solicitor to Birmingham School Board; 1891 appointed Clerk of the Peace to the Corporation. He was at various times president of the Birmingham Law Society, the Society of Notaries for England and Wales and the Society of Clerks of the Peace.

G. J. Johnson, co-opted member Free Library Committee 1866–77, clr. and ald. 1877–98, 1857–62 professor of Law, Queen's College, Birmingham; 1865 Committee member, Birmingham Liberal Association; 1869 Provisional Committee, National Education League; 1874 governor of the grammar school.

[37] *Report on Schools for the Poorer Classes in Birmingham etc.*, P.P 1870 (91) liv; *Dawson Collection*, X, 298 ff. It was here that W. J. Davis was educated. W. A. Dalley, *The Life Story of W. J. Davis, J.P.* (Birmingham, 1914), pp. 12–15.

[38] E. C. Osborne 1860–65, 1866–8; William Harris 1868–71; Jesse Collings 1871–8, 1879–80; G. J. Johnson 1880–93.

[39] E.g. Samuel Timmins, J. A. Langford, H. S. Pearson.

[40] Clr. and ald. 1870–1914.

[41] Clr. 1872–5.

[42] Clr. and ald. 1874–1909. He belonged to the Old Meeting, but was connected with the Church of the Messiah Sunday schools.

[43] Clr. and ald. 1885–1912.

[44] Clr. and ald. 1874–86.

how Dissenters considered the Education Act to have transferred the work of education from church to local government. Two months after the election of the first Birmingham School Board on which the 'undenominational' party was in a minority, the managers of the local Nonconformist day schools met to decide on a concerted policy. Since the formation of the Birmingham School Board 'relieves the religious congregations of the town from the responsibility which has hitherto rested upon them with regard to the elementary education of the people', they agreed on the terms on which school buildings should be offered to the Board. There was to be a merely nominal rent for a limited period but 'religious teaching therein shall be confined to the reading of the Bible without note or comment'.[45] The Church of the Messiah accordingly decided to offer the school to the School Board on these terms, and to close it down if, as was very likely, the restrictions on the religious teaching were rejected. This is in fact what happened.[46]

At the same time the minister of the church was advocating the establishment of a home mission with the money previously spent on the schools. As soon as the schools were closed he wrote to the vestry committee:

> 'The argument we have so strongly urged upon the nation has been, that if the State provided for secular education, the energies of a Christian Church could be more thoroughly devoted to its own noble work; and I feel exceedingly anxious that the Church of the Messiah should practically confirm this position and show that the abandonment of secular teaching means the enlargement of its spiritual and moral influence.'[47]

The home mission was not the only continuation of the day schools. The interest in educational work was still intense, and in October 1871 night classes were re-started for those age groups, from thirteen to eighteen, untouched by the Education Act. They too were discontinued in 1879 once the School Board had opened its own night school in the district.[48]

[45] *D.P.*, 8.2.1871, p. 8; Central Nonconformist Committee, *Occasional Papers*, No. 1 (July 1871).
[46] Records of the Church of the Messiah. Day School Committee Minutes, 26.4.1871, 14.5.1871; Vestry Committee Minutes, 5.5.1871, 13.10.1871; Church General Meeting Minutes, 16.1.1872. In 1873 after the School Board had been captured by the party of the National Education League the offer of the premises was renewed on roughly similar terms and accepted. The Church of the Saviour had followed the same policy but decided to keep their schools open until 1874, when the School Board took over.
[47] Records of the Church of the Messiah. Church General Meetings Minutes, 16.1.1872; Vestry Committee Minutes, 24.4.1872.
[48] Records of the Church of the Messiah. Sunday School Committee Minutes, 6.10.1871, 29.9.1873, 30.8.1879.

None of the other Unitarian churches were as influential in the municipal reform movement as the Church of the Messiah. But Henry Payton, who entered the Town Council in 1871 and became a supporter of Avery and Chamberlain, had for years been active in the educational work at Newhall Hill Unitarian Church, was a subscriber to the undenominational fund of the Birmingham Education Society, and subsequently a member of the League.[49]

The other large Unitarian congregation, the Old Meeting, was in the early years of the Reform movement more remarkable for the older type of town councillor than the new.[50] Only after 1874, when Chamberlain's influence had made itself felt, did it provide the new type of member in any numbers.[51]

After his arrival in Birmingham in 1869 the leading Unitarian minister in the town was undoubtedly H. W. Crosskey of the Church of the Messiah. An early disciple of James Martineau, his theological position was very similar to Dawson's. So was his attitude to municipal government. Coming relatively late on the scene his role is that of the disciple, but the tone is the same. Here is a passage from the funeral sermon on a church member who had given thirty-eight years unbroken service on the Town Council.

> 'Among all the various methods of divine service, the service of a great town is one of the most honourable and in these modern days, is of increasing importance and worth.'[52]

Such a use of the phrase 'divine service' might have come from Dawson himself. If anything, Crosskey's language exceeded that of the earlier exponents of the new idealism. The quiet irony in Dale's voice is unmistakable when he wrote after Crosskey's death: 'to Dr. Crosskey the atmosphere that he found among his immediate friends was exhilarating—almost intoxicating.' Dale's picture of the

> 'adventurous orator who (at Ward Meetings) would excite his audience by dwelling on the glories of Florence and of the other cities of Italy in the middle ages, and suggest that Birmingham too might become the home of a noble literature and art,'

is almost certainly drawn from Crosskey.[53]

---

[49] Clr. 1871–88.

[50] Sadler and Biggs among others. See below pp. 104, 136–37.

[51] R. F. Martineau 1874, Felix Hadley 1875, Thomas Martineau 1876.

[52] H. W. Crosskey, *A Citizen of no Mean City. Discourse in Memory of Alderman Thomas Phillips* (Birmingham, 1876), p. 5.

[53] R. A. Armstrong, *Henry William Crosskey, His Life and Work* (Birmingham, 1895), pp. 251, 249. See also Crosskey's comparison of the future Birmingham with Athens in H. W. Crosskey, 'A Plea for a Midland University', *Proc. B'ham. Phil. Soc.*, V, 2, 255.

While the Unitarian minister was imitating Dawson's characteristic approach to the nature and scope of public authorities, the leading Unitarian layman testified to the impression made on him by *The Town Crier's* plea for service on the Council. 'Long before I had any idea of being a member of the Corporation', said Joseph Chamberlain in 1874, when he was Mayor, 'much less filling my present position, I always protested against any depreciation of municipal work and those who performed it. . . . I have always thought that those who professed to think themselves above such work were infinitely beneath it.'[54]

(b) *Congregationalists and Baptists*

The case of the Unitarians and the quasi-Unitarians is straightforward. The reaction of the Congregationalists and Baptists to the transfer of educational work from churches to public authority is less so. There were five Congregationalist or Baptist congregations who supported flourishing day schools in the town.[55] They should have been at least as susceptible to the process whereby personal service and the sense of obligation to render it was focused on the public authorities as were the others. But they were not. None of the five leading Baptist churches contributed a single member to the new movement on the Town Council. Prior to November 1873[56] the Congregationalists contributed only Josiah Derrington. Derrington was a leading member of the United Kingdom Alliance, the Prohibitionist body, at whose request he successfully contested the representation of Duddeston-cum-Nechells in 1870 with one of the local brewers. Once on the Council he made strong claims of independence from either party and although his votes were normally given to the new policy, the reforming *Birmingham Morning News* complained in 1875 of 'the crotchety manner in which he frequently votes'. He was obviously a case in his own right.[57]

The difference between the municipal recruitment from the two sets of Dissenters is too great to be mere chance. It is improbable that between 1865 and 1873 all the suitable Congregationalists and Baptists were too busy to take up municipal service, whereas by a fortunate coincidence, at least nine Unitarians and members of the Church of the

[54] C. W. Boyd, ed., *Mr. Chamberlain's Speeches* (1914), I, 49.

[55] *Congregational churches:* Carr's Lane; Ebenezer, Steelhouse Lane; Legge Street Chapel. *Baptist churches:* Wycliffe Chapel, Heneage Street Chapel. See *Report on Schools for the Poorer Classes in Birmingham etc.*, pp. 26 ff.

[56] Not counting Thomas Avery, a member of Carr's Lane Congregational church. His candidature in 1862 could have had no connection with the subsequent developments that are the subject of this chapter.

[57] 'Our Representatives XVII', *B.M.N.*, 19.4.1875.

Saviour had found themselves with time to spare. Nor can it have been a matter of class. The average wealth of the Unitarians and the members of Dawson's congregation was probably greater than that of the Congregationalists, and certainly than that of the Baptists. But there were many members of either who would easily have compared with the large businessmen of Unitarian background from whom the new movement was being recruited. The Congregational Church in Francis Road, Edgbaston, was overwhelmingly recruited from such men, yet from 1863 until at least 1881 not a single member sat on the Town Council.[58]

The explanation is more likely to be found elsewhere. Except for the period from about April 1867 to June 1870, the pull of the Town Council on those concerned for elementary education—as distinct from library provision or industrial schools—was indirect, mediated through the prophetic role of George Dawson. The *direct* appeal once the Education Bill had been amended was rather to the School Board. That Board consisted, however, of only fifteen members, compared with the Town Council's sixty-four. The clergy were not debarred from membership, as they were from membership of the Council, and since they were widely known in the town and well versed both in educational matters and in the denominational issues which had been raised by the Forster Act, they were naturally regarded as particularly eligible. Of the fifteen Liberal candidates in the School Board election of 1870, six were clergymen, and of these three were elected. When allowance had been made for the representation of Churchmen, Unitarians and Quakers, there was little room for Evangelical Dissenting laymen among the group and of these only J. S. Wright was actually elected.[59] It is typical that of the five laymen who were defeated, the one Unitarian and the two Quakers were already on the Town Council, the two Baptists were not.[60] The Birmingham School Board therefore gave little scope to the ordinary church member's sense of mission. Moreover being a single-purpose authority, it did not easily lead its members from their educational interests to a wider view of the role of public authorities in the life of the nation.[61]

These considerations indicate the great importance of George Dawson's prophetic role in any explanation of the movement before 1873.

[58] Edgbaston Congregational Chapel, Francis Rd., *Annual Reports* for list of church members.
[59] For J. S. Wright's role see below, pp. 100–103.
[60] One of them, William Radford, became a councillor in the 1880s.
[61] It was otherwise in London. Before the creation of the London County Council in 1888 the School Board, as the only directly elected authority for the metropolis, became a focus for whatever civic aspirations there were.

The appeal which his idealisation of municipal authorities made to his own congregation and to the Unitarians has already become apparent. But his influence was bound to be less among orthodox Evangelical Dissenters. His biting attacks on their creed put them off, and the unfavourable contrasts he was apt to make between the ideal municipality and the 'grovelling and bickering sects' would not have helped. All those characteristics of Dawson's which appealed so strongly to the heterodox must have put a barrier between him and orthodox Evangelical Dissent.

Had they been able to disregard his unpalatable way of putting it, they would have seen that what Dawson had to say about the public life of the town was relevant to all its citizens. It was the achievement of R. W. Dale, minister of Carr's Lane Congregational Church, to have understood this and to have set himself the task of re-interpreting Dawson's teaching in terms that were acceptable to Evangelical Dissent. His efforts bore no fruit until November 1873, when Robert Arculus, a lay preacher connected with Dale's church and a close acquaintance, successfully stood for St. Martin's Ward. The real harvest of Evangelical Dissenters was not reaped until public opinion in Birmingham entered a new phase in 1874, and it became plain how great a work the Corporation was taking on for the improvement of the conditions of life among the poor.

It therefore looks as if the transfer of responsibility for popular education, which goes far to explain the action of the Unitarians and members of the Church of the Saviour, made little immediate impact on Evangelical Dissent. That may not have been true in the long run but after 1873 it is impossible to isolate this consideration from other more powerful preoccupations.

(c) *The People's Chapel*

There was apparently one exception to what has been said about Evangelical Dissenters. The People's Chapel, Hockley, was the home of a Baptist church, but it was exposed to such singular influences as to demand separate treatment.

It was founded in 1848 by forty men and women from Arthur O'Neill's Christian Chartist Church in Newhall Street. O'Neill's congregation were small men of the artisan-type from which the Birmingham Chartists had been mainly recruited, and the forty who separated in the year of the final Chartist fiasco were no exception. They left Newhall Street to set up a church whose policy would mirror their own strong democratic

views. They charged no pew-rents and did without a professional minister.[62]

This group of obscure Radical artisans is not the most obvious recruiting ground for the new municipal movement, which however democratic its rhetoric was distinctly patrician in most of its personnel.[63] But among them one had risen to wealth and position in the town. In 1836, at the age of fourteen, John Skirrow Wright had entered the works of George Smith, a button manufacturer. He became a commercial traveller and finally a partner. The firm prospered and Wright became by Birmingham standards a large employer and a man of commercial influence. After 1868 he was president of the Birmingham Chamber of Commerce which he had helped to found, and at the time of his death in 1880 was a director of Lloyd's Bank.[64]

His loyalty to the People's Chapel was unaffected by his success. He built himself a house in Handsworth, the suburb from which Hockley was most accessible, and devoted himself to the work of the church. Although he ceased to be a regular preacher after about 1865, the chief burden of the educational work rested on his shoulders and that of his family. Superintendent of the Sunday school until his death, after 1862 he also organised evening classes for about 150 youths. These were customary activities, but for a church which in 1864 had only seventy-three members the People's Chapel showed great vigour. Its premises sheltered the first off-shoot from the Quakers' Severn Street adult school. Wright, who had sponsored it, and his sons were among the teachers.[65]

Although Wright's interest in every form of popular education is not in doubt,[66] it is more likely that his attention was drawn to the Town Council in another connection. A keen Radical politician all his life, he took an interest in every form of popular election. In time he became something of a local boss in the poor district of north Birmingham in which his works and his church were situated. In 1867 he had engineered

[62] *The People's Chapel, Great King Street, Birmingham, 1848–1948. Centenary Souvenir* (Birmingham, 1948), pp. 3–5.

[63] 'He is a thorough Radical, brimful of the doctrine of equality and thoroughly believing that one man is quite as good as another, if not a trifle better', wrote an anonymous journalist of R. F. Martineau, thereby hitting off very neatly the special brand of Radical egalitarianism professed by the Unitarian patricians of Edgbaston. 'Our Representatives XVIII', *B.M.N.*, 26.4.1875.

[64] Eliezer Edwards, *J. S. Wright M.P., a Memorial Tribute* (Birmingham, 1880).

[65] Records of the People's Chapel. Church Minutes, 26.10.1862, 22.3.1863. For the number of church members see *Report as passed at the Social Meeting*, 5.1.1864. They did not have the resources for a day school.

[66] 1869–77 Executive Committee, National Education League; 1870–80 Birmingham School Board.

an electoral coup against the Board of Guardians, which he had accused of incompetence. The equal if not greater incompetence of the newly composed Board[67] throws a suggestive light on the very different course that events were to take in the Town Council. In 1870 when the new recruits were accusing the dominant group on the Town Council of extravagance and incompetence, and the passionate scenes enacted in the Council chamber were being reported in detail in the press, Wright may have decided to replace the members for his own district by better men. That district consisted of Hampton Ward, in which the People's Chapel was situated, and St. George's Ward on the other side of Great Hampton Row, where his works were found. In 1870, Dr. Alfred Barratt, one of the few professional men to live in this poor district, had entered the Council for Hampton Ward. Wright knew him through the Liberal Association. There is no way of telling whether he had had a hand in this, but the next year the initiative was undoubtedly his. He persuaded one of his church, James Whateley, a pearl-button worker in a Hockley street near his own button works, to oppose Naish, the sitting member, whom he publicly arraigned for incompetence. Naish had been elected at the height of the Allday regime and had represented Hampton Ward for fifteen years, but he lost his seat.[68] Whateley was one of that type of 'Labour' councillor with a small-chapel and temperance background, who made their appearance in Birmingham municipal politics from the 1880s onwards and whom the People's Chapel was eminently qualified to produce. In the eighties and nineties it produced several of them. Whateley's debut a decade earlier was due entirely to J. S. Wright's political patronage.

Much the same can be said of the next candidate whom Wright chose to complete the task of cleaning out the ward. Again he showed no interest in the patricians of Edgbaston, although he knew them through his political work,[69] but picked a North Birmingham man. The new councillor, William Cook, was a pin manufacturer in Princip Street; a small man just risen into the master class who proudly retained his membership of the Amalgamated Society of Engineers for the rest of his life.[70]

[67] See *P.P.* 1870 (464) lviii, 1, for its prolonged dispute with the Poor Law Board over an increase in staff.

[68] *D.P.*, 25.10.1871–2.11.1871.

[69] He was chairman of the Birmingham Liberal Association 1868–80. Elected M.P. for Nottingham in 1880, he died before he could take his seat.

[70] Clr. and ald. 1872–1908; Chairman Health Committee 1784–1908; Liberal M.P. East Birmingham 1885–6; president, Birmingham Liberal Association 1889–1902; knighted 1906. For his active connection with the Quaker adult school from 1865 to at least 1891 see below, p. 152. This connection is of more significance for his public service than his attendance at Perry Barr Wesleyan Chapel. He was the only Wesleyan prominently connected with the municipal reform movement within the period 1865–77 covered by this case study.

This was a remarkable performance on Wright's part since he was not stepping into a political vacuum. It involved the utter rout of William Brinsley, the heir to Allday's electoral influence, whose political connections, while extending over most of the borough, were especially strong in Hampton Ward, for which he was the presiding alderman. It may be suspected that that fact provided an extra incentive to Wright, for no one could have been personally more offensive to the Baptist Total Abstainer than the beery alderman and his cronies.[71]

There are also traces of Wright's hand in the politics of the neighbouring St. George's Ward. He never entered the Town Council himself but his son Frank did in 1874, when the rush of Evangelical Dissenting lay preachers for seats on the Council had begun. When he died, the local press compared the loss to the town with that suffered through Dawson's death four years earlier. However in the perspective of the municipal reform movement Wright's place was without parallel. It derived from his association with one of the congregations in the poorer parts of the town, an association so close as to make him impervious to the normal effects of suburban living.

In 1863 R. W. Dale had reminded the wealthy Congregationalists, worshipping in their recently erected suburban church, that it was from among them

> 'that there ought to rise up those who shall be qualified to engage personally in zealous Christian labour among the crowded streets and courts where the working people live, from whom they derive their wealth.'

And he added,

> 'It is one of the gravest facts in connection with the future social conditions of this country, that the separation seems to become wider every day between the poor and the rich. . . . In our manufacturing districts, we have streets upon streets of working people, covering immense areas, in which no professional men, except the doctor and the minister of religion, are ever seen.'[72]

In this respect Birmingham was better placed than some other cities. In Edgbaston it had a wealthy residential district which was not only

---

[71] For Brinsley, see below p. 137. For the temperance factor in the reform movement see pp. 149–53.
[72] Obituary notices in *The Dart*, 17.4.1880, p. 9; *Birmingham Mail*, 9.4.1880; R. W. Dale, 'The Suburban Pastor', in *Discourses delivered upon Special Occasions* (1866), pp. 339–40.

within the borough boundary, but comparatively near to the town centre. This was a most important fact for its development.

On the other hand, Wright's experience with the Board of Guardians suggests the inadequacy of a political activism that thought in terms of 'throwing the devils out'. Both the positive administrative programme and the positive ideology of the Birmingham municipal movement were forged by other brains than his.

3
The Administration Reformed

I THE NEW PARTY

This chapter deals with the administrative aspect of the reform movement and shows the impact of the new recruitment on the well-being of the inhabitants of the town. To understand the position of the Council and the challenges, which the new men had to face there, we must turn back to the early 1860s.

It took two years of bitter conflict before Birmingham obtained its Improvement Act in 1861. Although the Economists were defeated over this issue and their leader, Joseph Allday, withdrew from political affairs, power largely remained with his political heirs. Of these the most important were a grocer, William Brinsley, and a hinge manufacturer, Thomas Sadler, drawn from the middle ranks of the Birmingham metal trades. Sadler was the abler of the two, and in so far as anyone was capable of exercising a controlling influence in the Council chamber, it was he. He was a bad man to have for an enemy, resentful if worsted, unmeasured in his invective and unscrupulous in the manner in which he pursued his vendettas.[1] Brinsley, whose personality is described in more detail in chapter 4, was more colourful and likeable.

The atmosphere that reigned in the Council chamber and the ward meetings did little to encourage the participation of men who held leading positions in the social and economic life of the town. But every now and then such a man did join the Council. One of them was Thomas Avery of W. and T. Avery, the scale-makers, and he proved himself capable of leading an opposition in the Council.

[1] The comments on him in 'Our Representatives XI', *B.M.N.*, 8.3.1875, although from a hostile source, are borne out by his conduct during the previous years, as it can be followed in the newspaper reports of the town council debates. 'What a d——d shame it is that our time should be taken up and wasted by having to discuss the spiteful nonsense of such a cad as Sadler', wrote Chamberlain in 1873. Joseph Chamberlain to J. T. Bunce, 14 July 1873, Chlain. MSS., JC 5/8.

Avery, a Congregationalist in religion and a Conservative in politics, had retired from business at an early age and been elected to the Town Council in 1862. But it was only in 1865 that he became at all prominent. He struck up a partnership with another substantial businessman, William Holliday, who, although first recruited to the Council in the false dawn of the early 1850s, had recently returned to it. For the next five years these two became the champions of a new emphasis on efficiency and economy. For the older party were Economists only in their reluctance to undertake bold and far-reaching ventures. In effect their administration was both inefficient and extravagant.

Between 1865 and 1870 it looked as if there would be an improvement in the quality of administration without any change in the policy of strict economy, which was making Birmingham one of the more backward boroughs in England.

The first thing that Avery and Holliday attempted, in their distrust of those who controlled council policy, was to restrict the borrowing powers of the Corporation. Under the Birmingham Improvement Acts of 1851 and 1861 the Corporation was not permitted to raise additional loans without the prior consent of the ratepayers. But loans under the 1860 Municipal Corporation Mortgages Act required nothing more than the consent of the Treasury. The attraction of the Act was considerable. By charging the interest to the Borough rate, it by-passed the preferential treatment which canal and railway companies enjoyed in the assessment of the street improvement rate.[2] But to anyone bent on preventing extravagance, the most striking aspect of the Act was that it prevented the minority on the Council from appealing to the ratepayers for support. When therefore in 1865 the Council proposed to apply under the 1860 Act for a loan to be used for street widening, Avery and Holliday became spokesmen for a determined opposition. There was a strong feeling in the town that the Council was under a moral, and possibly even a legal obligation to follow the procedure of the local Act, a feeling with which the canal and railway interests were only too glad to identify themselves. The intervention of the Treasury was inconclusive, and in August 1866 Avery and Holliday figured prominently among those who filed a lawsuit against the Corporation. The controlling group on the Council were enraged at this 'treason'. Sadler, the chairman of the public works committee, poured a torrent of abuse on the two renegades. A weak mayor was quite unable to control the debate, which rapidly came to

[2] J. T. Bunce, *History of the Corporation of Birmingham*, (Birmingham, 1885), II pp. 23–4.

resemble a bear-garden. Avery would have resigned, had he not been locked in a room by his friend Dale until he changed his mind.[3]

Even before this storm had passed Avery had taken action to cut out financial waste. Elected chairman of the finance committee after the discovery of a fraud he reorganised the system of accounts to prevent its recurrence, and reduced the cost of loans. Two years later he terminated expensive law-suits that had been allowed to drag on for years.[4]

Here were the signs of a new efficiency to give substance to the cry for economy. But economy it remained. Avery's record in these years is that of an opponent of the provision of public services. In 1865 when the Corporation was skimping all its most important functions, he argued that municipal expenditure was so rapidly outstripping the economic progress of the town, that all public works should 'either be suspended altogether or proceeded with more slowly and deliberately'.[5] This was almost the standard reaction of any mid-century critic of his local authority, and it was an attitude not quickly discarded. In 1867 he was cautioning the Council against losing further money on the provision of public bath-houses, and in 1868 when he was mayor he denied in the face of shocking reports from eye-witnesses that the sanitary supervision of the town was inadequate. In the same year he and his more consistent supporters voted with the extreme wing of the old Economists to prevent the expenditure of £350 on road construction.[6]

Yet in spite of this alignment an occasional success can be recorded for those who looked less coldly on the provision of public amenities. In 1860, the year in which the Ratepayers' Protection Society was being undermined by the efforts of Robert Wright, the town had adopted Ewart's Public Libraries and Museums Act (1855), which added to the rates by a penny in the £. The creation of public lending libraries continued slowly throughout the sixties, and a central reference library was opened in 1866.[7] But when it was suggested in 1863 that the Corporation should purchase Aston Park with its Jacobean Hall and save it from being sold for building plots, the Council refused. Most reluctantly, and under great pressure from the town and even from beyond, the Council

[3] *D.P.*, 30.1.1867, 6.2.1867, 3.4.1867, 10.4.1867; *W.P.*, 24.1.1894.

[4] *B.C.P.*, 12.2.1867, 19.2.1867, 7.5.1867, 25.1.1870, 26.4.1870; *D.P.*, 20.2.1867, p. 4.

[5] Thomas Avery, 'The Municipal Expenditure of the Borough of Birmingham. Paper read at the Meeting of the British Association held in Birmingham, September 1865', in British Association for the Advancement of Science, *Report of the 35th Meeting* (1866), p. 140.

[6] *D.P.*, 12.6.1867, 5.10.1868; *B.C.P.*, 16.6.1868.

[7] An attempt to obtain the adoption of an earlier Public Libraries and Museums Act had been defeated in 1852. J. T. Bunce, *Corporation of Birmingham*, II, 207–15.

yielded in the following year, when £7,000 was raised by private individuals towards the cost. Among those who provided this inducement only two were Council members.[8] This was indeed the very kind of venture upon which neither the old Economists nor the new were willing to embark.

Avery's was the decisive attitude for the group who gradually formed themselves around him.[9] Like him they were dissatisfied with the administration and concerned at the financial recklessness of the older leaders. Not all were equally extreme in their distrust of new municipal responsibilities, but in these years they were still finding their bearings and on the whole took their cue from him. Towards the end there were signs that he had begun to take new factors into account,[10] but the impetus that wrought a fundamental change of policy came from outside the Council. It was the impact of hard facts, backed by the sanction of the courts, that forced the new Economists into the mould for which Birmingham was subsequently to be known.

2 THE SEWAGE PROBLEM

These facts were first drawn to the attention of the Council on 5 July 1870, when it was informed that the town clerk had been served with notice of two legal actions. Sir Charles Adderley was applying for a renewal and extension of the injunction, granted to him in 1858, to restrain the corporation from fouling the River Tame. Secondly, a number of residents at Gravelly Hill, the district near the sewer outlet, were asking for an injunction against the nuisance committed in that area. After vainly protesting since 1864 they had finally lost patience.[11]

On more than one occasion in the past the twin problems of drainage and sewerage had produced crisis and change in municipal affairs. When following the Improvement Act of 1861 the drainage system was steadily extended, difficulties were bound to occur sooner or later. For an adequate system of house and street drainage with an outlet at Saltley for the whole town served merely to concentrate the problem of pollution. It relieved the ditches and canals of the borough at the expense of the River Tame. But Birmingham, an inland town with two small streams passing through it, could not permanently discharge its ever-increasing

---

[8] Bunce, *Corporation of Birmingham*, II, 199–200; *B.C.P.*, 12.1.1864.
[9] Holliday retired in November 1868.
[10] See below, p. 121, for his initiative in the attempt to purchase the waterworks.
[11] *B.C.P.*, 5.7.1870. Bunce, *Corporation of Birmingham*, II, 126 for a detailed treatment of the events described below.

sewage in the simple manner that was open to estuary towns like Liver-pool. Had Birmingham been the only place to attempt it, it would have been insufferable, but the Black Country communities helped to make the situation worse. In any comparison between the administration of large towns in the nineteenth century access to the sea is an important factor to be considered. After 1857, Liverpool could take drastic steps towards the general adoption of water closets, whereas fifteen years later Birmingham was to think seriously of penalising the owners of water closets by a special tax. Again Manchester with access to larger and more numerous rivers could continue until 1894 to pour its untreated sewage into the water courses.[12] The technical implications of such delay, and the saving of money spent in pioneering experiments, were enormous.

For Birmingham after 1858 the real sewage problem started at the place where more fortunately situated towns ceased to think about it—the outfall of the main sewer. Under legal pressure its filtration works were enlarged in 1860,[13] but the state of technical knowledge was still most rudimentary, and the quantities discharged increased from year to year. For ten years Adderley, himself keenly interested in questions of local government,[14] encouraged the Council to improve their works at Saltley and held his hand, while the river continued to stink and dead fish floated past Hams Hall.

If filtration helped to assuage Sir Charles Adderley, it left the Public Works Committee with vast quantities of sewage sludge spread out to dry near the outlet, of which a mere fraction was occasionally removed by farmers. This was the nuisance of which the inhabitants of Gravelly Hill complained. The amount of land at the disposal of the public works committee was quite inadequate, and had been covered four feet deep with sludge when the Sewage Utilization Act of 1865 empowered muni-cipal corporations to acquire tracts of land outside their boundaries.[15]

Birmingham immediately launched its first experiments at sewage farming. The description of the farm in 1871 bore eloquent witness to the incompetence of the public works committee. The land was quite

[12] B. D. White, *A History of the Corporation of Liverpool 1835–1914* (Liverpool, 1951), p. 50; A. Redford and I. S. Russell, *The History of Local Government in Manchester*, II (1940), chapter XXVII.
[13] Bunce, *Corporation of Birmingham*, II, 128.
[14] He was president of the Board of Health in the Derby government of 1858–9, chairman of the Royal Commission on the Sanitary Laws 1869–71 and president of the National Association for the Promotion of Social Science in 1878.
[15] 28 & 29 Vic. c. 75. It had been drafted on the initiative of Birmingham Corporation, which was desperate. See also Report of Public Works Committee, *B.C.P.*, 24.3.1871.

unsuitable for the purpose and had never been properly drained. It had had sewage applied to it in such excessive quantities that it was no better than a sodden morass.[16]

In 1870 'that never failing specific, a Chancery injunction' put an end to the Council's leisurely maladministration.[17] With the threat of sequestration hanging over it, it was forced to take hurried and drastic action. But the public works committee, the principal spending committee of the Council by reason of its responsibility for drainage, paving and street widening, had been for years the target of attack by the new Economists. Changes in its membership had come to be interpreted as censures on the competence of the member concerned, so that its composition had become peculiarly rigid. Nothing short of a reversal of the political balance on the Council would produce any significant change.[18]

Avery therefore tried to have the whole matter referred to a more widely based committee of enquiry, but without success. The public works committee proposed a large-scale irrigation scheme, and after further investigation reported in favour of the compulsory purchase of 23,000 acres in the Tame valley. Such a staggering proposal made some of the more independent members of the Council pause. To surround Hams Hall entirely with sewage fields seemed hardly the best way of meeting Sir Charles Adderley's objections. The upshot of a month's debate was the appointment, after all, of a special sewage enquiry committee. But so bitter had the conflict been that Avery's original plan for a broadly based membership was even less feasible than four months before. A sarcastic challenge, never seriously meant, led to the appointment of a committee composed entirely and deliberately of the leading figures in the opposition group with Avery in the chair. Only Joseph Chamberlain excused himself from serving on it, pleading that he was fully occupied elsewhere.

This appointment forms a watershed in the history of the Corporation. Power had come to Avery after six years' persistence in the face of insult and discouragement, and to his supporters. His pace was

---

[16] Report of the Sewage Committee, *B.C.P.*, 5.12.1871 qd. in Bunce, *op. cit.*, II, 133.
[17] The phrase is from the wittiest and, save for the writing of the Webbs, the best informed work on English local government in the nineteenth century, no less valuable for being fictitious, *The Natural History of Local Boards, or Local Government as it is* (1888), p. 140.
[18] 'While changes might be made on other committees they should have the aurora borealis and lunar rainbows at noon, if they moved into another sphere of usefulness the sacred Sadler or any of his friends.' Debate on the unsuccessful attempt to place Avery on the public works committee, *D.P.*, 10.11.1870.

5

dictated for him by the threat of sequestration, and he was drawn for the first time into large expenditure and bold experiments.

The actual problems of sewage disposal were too great to be solved easily. Detailed enquiry convinced the committee that in the rudimentary stage of technical knowledge which then existed it was essential to reduce the problem at the outfall to more manageable proportions.[19] When planned in the fifties the sewers had been designed to carry off no more than the town's waste water, and the committee therefore recommended the exclusion of all obnoxious elements. Close on 14,000 open middens, draining into the sewers, were to be gradually removed. Between them they covered an area of about $13\frac{1}{2}$ acres, a vast pestiferous lake in the heart of the town. The refuse from slaughter-houses, cattle market, urinals, cow-houses, stables and certain acid-using manufactories was also to be excluded.

That left the excreta of 325,000 people to be disposed of. For this purpose the use of pans of standard pattern, which could be covered with a lid and removed on carts at weekly intervals, was decided upon. The committee had even proposed a tax on water closets, the one device that could not be disconnected from the sewers, but Parliament would not hear of such a thing. Fortunately their number was relatively small. Although it was ultimately recognised that water-borne sewerage was the only satisfactory system, the primitive pan-system made it possible to escape all legal penalties and to reduce the problem at the outflow to proportions which allowed the necessary freedom for experiments.

Yet the plans for these experiments, moderate compared with the 23,000 acre scheme, were still too much for the landowners along the Tame. Their opposition killed its land-purchase bill, and forced the Council back to crude methods of precipitation and filtration. The sludge was dug into the soil,[20] while the liquid passed through such land as was available before entering the Tame. Further and larger tanks were installed and some additional land was purchased, and by March 1875, in spite of great initial difficulties, the Council had satisfied the Court of Chancery that no further nuisance existed.[21]

The technical work of the sewage committee continued to perplex its members. Their attempt to exclude the excreta from the sewers was severely condemned in 1876 by the select committee on town sewage, who reviewed the whole sorry tale of too little and too late in a very

[19] *B.C.P.*, 3.10.1871.
[20] The original intention had been to employ a steam-plough, but the plough kept on foundering in the mire, and men with spades had to be employed instead.
[21] Report of Sewage Committee, *B.C.P.*, 30.3.1875.

critical spirit.[22] But after 1873 the political struggles over it were past. The committee had been accepted as one of the regular organs of administration, carrying out its task with the full approval of the Council. The centre of interest in town council politics had moved elsewhere.

3 THE HEALTH OF THE BOROUGH

By 1875 the centre of interest had shifted to the subject of sanitary inspection, where events followed a very similar pattern. Once again the complaisance of the old Town Council, which had been proof against the criticisms of a minority, had to yield to compulsion from beyond the borough before a reforming policy became possible.

In the 1860s it was becoming normal to appoint medical officers of health in large towns. The precedent had been set far back in the 1840s by Liverpool and the City of London, and in 1858 the Local Government Act gave a general sanction for such an optional appointment. Glasgow and Leeds made theirs in 1863, Manchester in 1868. Even small places like Oldbury in the Black Country followed suit.[23] In Birmingham a minority supported by *The Birmingham Daily Post* began to press for such an appointment repeatedly from 1864.[24]

The Council had appointed a borough analyst in 1861 to examine drugs and food submitted by doubtful purchasers upon the payment of a fee. Other small duties were added in the course of the next few years. He could be consulted by the inspector of nuisances and this created a widespread impression that the town had secured all the benefits of a local medical officer of health without any of the expense. It was a misunderstanding, for the borough analyst possessed none of the powers of initiative, which a medical officer would have had. As long as the sanitary work of the Corporation was at the discretion of a mere inspector of nuisances, it was confined to lime-washing and the removal of the worst filth accumulating in the ashpits, conventional measures that had become acceptable even to the slowest minds.[25]

Despite the insistence of a minority, local public opinion was oddly complaisant about the health of the borough. Birmingham had been regarded for a long time as an exceptionally healthy town, and it was

---

[22] Report, S.C. on Town Sewage, *P.P.*, 1876 [C. 410] xxvii, pp. xxxii, lix.
[23] J. B. Russell, *The Evolution of the Function of Public Health Administration, as illustrated by the Sanitary History of Glasgow* (Glasgow, 1893), p. 29; Redford and Russell, *Local Government in Manchester*, II, 277; *B.J.*, 4.8.1866, p. 6.
[24] There had been isolated petitions before dating back to 1853. Bunce, II, 96; *D.P.*, 14.2.1865, p. 3; *B.J.*, 25.5.1866, 4.8.1866; *D.P.*, 19.11.1867, 27.11.1867; *B.J.*, 3.10.1868; *D.P.*, 24.4.1872.
[25] *B.C.P.*, 5.2.1861, 16.5.1865; *B.J.*, 26.5.1866.

noted how favourably it compared in the Registrar-General's statistics with other cities in the kingdom. Its annual death-rate was rarely bettered by more than two or three comparable centres of population, and the tables which gave this information received great publicity in the town. They led to a widespread belief that Birmingham was as healthy as a large town could be. Its immunity from cholera epidemics removed the greatest single factor making for public health reform elsewhere.

The reasons for this favourable state were largely topographical. Its distance from the sea-ports made Birmingham less vulnerable to attacks from the epidemics that periodically swept across the European continent. Drainage was greatly facilitated by the sloping and undulating surface and by the sandy or gravelly soil, which allowed the water to percolate rapidly to the red sandstone below. Although all the industrial towns of the nineteenth century were, by later standards, badly overcrowded, Birmingham's expansion was not hindered by any geographical features, so that the density of population was relatively low. Not being an old town there were not the large old houses available for subdivision into tenements, which formed the worst slums of Liverpool or Glasgow. When population began to increase fast new accommodation had to be provided, and two-storey buildings arranged around court-yards became the typical housing pattern. They were lower than tenement houses and so admitted more light and air to the courts and alleys. The soil on which they stood has not yet been soaked in the refuse of previous generations, and the structures themselves were new and took a while before falling into really hopeless dilapidation. Attic and cellar dwellings, the cause of much sanitary trouble in Liverpool and Manchester, were unknown. The total effect had been to postpone the time when slum dwellings became a major menace to public health.[26]

These factors had tended to delay the realisation in Birmingham of what administrative measures were required for the health of a modern town. 'Nature, geography and soil had done a great deal for the health of Birmingham and . . . the governmental authorities of the town had done very little,' as a belated convert put it in 1872.[27] Advocates of a more vigorous sanitary policy were met with evidence furnished by the comparative statistics. The lack of uniformity, which characterised local administration in England, meant that the best work was frequently done

[26] Paper read by Dr. Alfred Hill at the Birmingham Sanitary Conference, *D.P.* 15.1.1875; Conrad Gill and Asa Briggs, *History of Birmingham* (1952), I, 121.
[27] Thomas Avery speaking to the Town Council, *D.P.*, 20.11.1872, p. 6.

in the worst places, while in less unsatisfactory districts the stimulus to action was lacking. This gave the administrative measures that were taken the character of first-aid work, and did little to raise the general standard of health expected from a town. Places like Birmingham were able to treat their favourable topographical conditions as a substitute for administrative action, instead of making them a springboard to a higher standard. This fact makes the study of administrative history a treacherous pointer to any general picture of social conditions. It makes Liverpool better known as the home of the most determined public health administration in the 1840s than as the town that even twenty years later still had the highest death-rate of any city in the kingdom.

Unfortunately the satisfaction with the health of Birmingham was not even based on realities. It was largely due to naïve reliance on statistics which lumped together the wealthier suburbs with the overcrowded quarters in the centre of the town. But the inhabitants of the courts and alleys in the Lower Priory, where the annual death-rate in 1873–5 averaged 62·5 per thousand, could draw scant comfort from the fact that in the borough as a whole it did not exceed 25·97.[28]

The mischief that these statistics did was shown in 1868 when the National Association for the Promotion of Social Science held its conference in Birmingham for the second time. After visiting some of the worst districts off Snow Hill, the editor of *The Builder* reported to the Health Section of the Conference that

> 'In more than three-fourths of the district he found houses tumbling down, no floors, no windows; floors torn up, pavements retaining decaying matter, and of a character always to retain it; an utter want of closet accommodation . . . In No. 5 Court Brick-Kiln St. the neighbouring cess-pool of the Court was some 3 feet higher than the pavement of the court; and the consequence was that the filth was constantly oozing through and spreading over the floor of the court. The first woman he enquired of had three children living and she praised the locality as being very healthy. Then he elicited from her that she had five children dead.'

His description was confirmed by other members. The mayor, who that year happened to be Avery, had not been present on either occasion but attended the following session to say that

---

[28] Figures drawn from Bunce, *Corporation of Birmingham*, II, 116–17.

'He should regret if our visitors left the town with an impression that some of the statements that they had heard conveyed an accurate description of the condition of the health of Birmingham, as compared with other large towns in the kingdom.'[29]

He went on to quote statistics to show that for thirteen successive weeks that summer the death-rate in Birmingham had been less than in any other large town. Soon afterwards the Town Council confirmed after a debate that the existing arrangements for inspection were adequate.

Only when the Public Health Act of 1872 made the appointment of a medical officer compulsory for even the smallest rural district did the corporation of the third-biggest English borough reluctantly step into line. The Local Government Board offered to pay half the salary on condition that it should approve the appointment, but the Council refused, ostensibly to 'retain intact their power over the appointment, salaries and duties of their own Officers.'[30] However, it was apparent that the appointment was being made with bad grace and that the Council was afraid of being pushed into undertaking more than they wanted. In 1875, when they had become committed to energetic sanitary reform the contribution was at last accepted.[31]

Important as was the appointment of a medical officer, it was made doubly so by the election of a substantially different sanitary committee after the electoral landslide of 1873. The majority of the old personnel, and especially the chairman William Rolason, had so firmly identified themselves with the old order that their replacement was inevitable. The new chairman, Dr. Alfred Barratt, had been one of the original members of the sewage enquiry committee and among the avant-garde of the victorious party. He was succeeded in the following year by William Cook, who for thirty-four years was to be the driving force behind the sanitary policy of the reformed Town Council.

The new committee found itself at once with a serious smallpox epidemic on its hands. It acted as energetically as the public would permit, but found itself frustrated on the most important measure, the establishment of an isolation hospital. The only accommodation available was the fever ward of the workhouse with all the stigma of pauperism that was attached to it. Public opinion was agreed on the need for larger and different accommodation, but every locality felt that the hospital ought to be at the other end of the town. Finally the committee, by now

[29] *D.P.*, 2.10.1868, 5.10.1868.
[30] Report of Sanitary Committee, *B.C.P.*, 19.11.1872.
[31] *B.C.P.*, 27.7.1875.

the most hated body in Birmingham, much against their will took over the workhouse fever ward after all. Fortunately it was detached from the actual workhouse buildings, though on the same premises. The paupers on the one side and the inmates of the lunatic asylum on the other were the only people whose protests might safely be ignored.[32]

Such unpopularity was less damaging than it would have been earlier, for public health had become for the first time a subject of widespread and urgent interest in the town. Such was the regular effect of epidemics, but the town was also sharing in a national movement of opinion. The Royal Sanitary Commission of 1869–71 had been appointed at the request of professional and specialist bodies to examine anomalies of which they, but few others, were conscious. When it presented its report in the spring of 1871, 'popular knowledge of the subject had advanced so much . . . that some of the most necessary recommendations . . . may have seemed to come at last as mere matters of course.'[33] The report of the Commission in turn served to attract public interest, and at least seven important health measures were placed on the statute book between 1871 and 1875. When Joseph Chamberlain organised a sanitary conference in January 1875, he found the attendance so much in excess of expectation that he had to apologise for the inadequate arrangements.[34]

There followed a spate of regulations, as the Sanitary Committee seized on any available powers old or new. The enormous extent of the problem was revealed by a detailed survey undertaken in the winter of 1874–5. This drew attention to faulty house construction as a danger to public health.[35] Building bye-laws, familiar in other towns, were unknown in Birmingham.[36] They were provisionally drawn up in December 1874, but shelved after a meeting between Chamberlain and a body of property owners. This was not entirely the result of sinister opposition, for stringent bye-laws tended to produce a shortage of cheap houses and the subsequent overcrowding of existing accommodation. But the answer to such objections lay in policies far more radical than

---

[32] Bunce, *Corporation of Birmingham*, II, 102.
[33] Sir John Simon, *English Sanitary Institutions*, 2nd ed. (1897), p. 327. See also Royston Lambert, *Sir John Simon 1816–1904 and English Social Administration* (1963), chapter 21.
[34] *D.P.*, 15.1.1875, pp. 6–7.
[35] Borough of Birmingham, *Statutory Powers possessed by the Town Council relative to Sanitary Matters* (Birmingham, 1875); Report of Sanitary Committee, *B.C.P.*, 26.2.1875. There were 39,259 back-to-back houses; 19,502 others also had defective ventilation.
[36] Liverpool and Sheffield had passed such bye-laws in 1864. By 1874 the list included Manchester, Salford, Birkenhead, Bristol and the neighbouring district of Balsall Heath. B. D. White, *Corporation of Liverpool*, p. 61; Mary Walton, *Sheffield, its Story and its Achievements* (1948), p. 214; Information given at the Birmingham Sanitary Conference, *D.P.*, 15.1.1875.

anyone who was willing to countenance in the 1870s. For the moment the choice was between bye-laws or none. In March 1876 at the height of his power Chamberlain broke the deadlock and pushed them through the Council 'in the teeth of Harris and *The Birmingham Daily Post* and all the timid ones'. Thereafter builders had to comply with certain minimum standards for ventilation, the thickness of walls and the safety of chimneys.[37]

The number of sanitary inspectors was also increased from twelve to thirty-eight and a system of regular inspection introduced for those houses that had been identified as most in need of surveillance. It is a measure of the backwardness of Birmingham's administration that even then the proportion of inspectors to population was lower than in Manchester, and only slightly higher than in Leeds and Bristol.[38]

Such a policy cost more money. At the same time the sewage committee was spending large sums, and the public works committee was under pressure to pave streets and footpaths that had been too long neglected. In the mid-fifties, the sudden increase in the activities of the Council had led to a financial crisis, activities which were as well-intentioned and necessary as these now were. In 1873 there were signs that the sequence might be repeated. It is true that the Public Health Act of 1872 gave unlimited rating powers for just these purposes, so that no financial problem existed in law. But in Birmingham the Improvement Rate had never exceeded 2s. in the £, and it was thought politically inexpedient to increase it without the consent of the ratepayers. In March 1874 the town rejected the proposal by an overwhelming vote.[39]

In any case even those who wished to put up the rates knew that this did not really meet their needs. A determined attack on the neglected state of the town called for resources independent of the rates, if it was not to throw power back into the hands of their opponents. At least this was the lesson that the reformers drew from comparisons with Liverpool and Manchester. Liverpool could subsidise street maintenance and improvement from a corporate estate, such as Birmingham did not possess. Manchester derived additional income from the profits of the gas works.[40] Here lay a possible solution to the financial impasse of Birmingham.

[37] *D.P.*, 12.12.1874; Borough of Birmingham, *Bye-Laws for regulating the Construction of New Streets and New Buildings* (Birmingham, 1876); Joseph Chamberlain to Jesse Collings, 12 March 1876, Chlain. MSS., JC 5/16.
[38] Report of Sanitary Committee, *B.C.P.*, 26.2.1875.
[39] *D.P.*, 31.3.1874.
[40] B. D. White, *Corporation of Liverpool*, pp. 104–5, 111–12, 183–5; Redford and Russell, *History of Local Government in Manchester*, I (1939), 264.

4 GAS

Manchester was unusual in that the gas works had been built in the first place by the Manchester street commissioners as long ago as 1817. She was the pioneer in the public ownership of gas works and for seven years no other place followed suit. But by 1870 there were forty-nine municipal gas undertakings in England and Wales alone and most of these the result of buying out a private company.[41] Some purchases had recently occurred in towns, like Glasgow (1869) and Leeds (1870), whose example was obviously relevant. Such transactions required the consent of Parliament and the drift of parliamentary opinion was strongly in favour of municipal purchase. The Public Health Act of 1875 was soon to permit urban authorities to buy gas companies by mutual agreement subject only to the consent of the Local Government Board.

The reasons for this favourable parliamentary opinion were two-fold. In the first place, it had been discovered that in the provision of gas competition was positively harmful. The duplication of gas mains resulted in greater leakage and in the constant breaking up of the road surface, as service pipes were changed from one set of mains to the other. In any case, it was never long before the competing companies arrived at an understanding. By 1850 competition had practically ceased outside London. But if commercial companies enjoyed a territorial monopoly, how could they be prevented from abusing their position? Parliament's answer was to limit their dividend in the expectation that, once the maximum was reached, profits would be applied to a reduction of the price. These expectations were seldom fulfilled. It was too easy to issue new shares instead. Glasgow's experience illustrated the inadequacy both of competition and of limiting dividends. In 1869 a Parliamentary committee advised the Corporation to purchase the existing companies.

Buying out the local gas works was therefore a common enough step. But whether it happened or not depended on local circumstances. There was no pressure from outside. What were these circumstances in Birmingham?

The town was supplied by two companies. The Birmingham Gas Light and Coke Company, founded in 1819, had a share capital of £300,000 in 1874. The Birmingham and Staffordshire Gas Light Company, founded in 1825, was the larger of the two with a share capital of £607,900. Its area of distribution overlapped the borough on

[41] For these two paragraphs see Herman Finer, *Municipal Trading* (1941), pp. 45–9.

all sides.[42] The Town Council which was responsible for street lighting was the largest customer for gas and its normal attitude towards the companies was a mixture of distrust and aggressiveness. In 1864 to the disgust of the new Economists £6,523 had been spent opposing two local gas Bills before Parliament.[43] In spite of its distrust of the companies the Town Council had never seriously considered buying them out prior to 1873 when Joseph Chamberlain suggested it. It must be pointed out that the interests of the gas companies were most inadequately represented on the Council. Of the nineteen directors only one was a councillor or alderman. Although the final agreement whereby the Corporation bought out the companies in 1875 was satisfactory to all parties, it had not been arrived at without an element of pressure,[44] and may well never have proceeded so far had the composition of the Council been radically different.

Chamberlain was convinced that the solution to the Council's financial straits lay in the ownership of the gas works. Even before he knew that he would be mayor in November he had approached the Gas Light and Coke Company.[45] His election assured the Council for the first time of his sustained attention to their affairs. No one could have been better suited to negotiate with the companies. A firm believer in the virtues of amalgamation and rationalisation, he had in recent years as head of the commercial side of Nettlefold and Chamberlain successfully conducted several negotiations which had given his firm a quasi-monopoly position in the industry.[46]

The time was favourable because the Birmingham company had just decided to extend their works and to ask Parliament for additional borrowing powers. As usual they were nervously hoping to be spared an expensive parliamentary contest with the Corporation, although past

[42] Bunce, *Corporation of Birmingham*, II, 341–6; *B.C.P.*, 24.3.1874.
[43] *B.C.P.*, 30.8.1864, 7.2.1865.
[44] Note also Chamberlain's comment to the ratepayers, 'Out of the 64 members of the Town Council there were only three or four who had any shares in these undertakings.' *D.P.*, 14.4.1874, p. 5. For the pressure, see the speeches of the directors, *D.P.*, 25.3.1874, pp. 6–7.
[45] On this point the evidence is conflicting. The chairman of the Birmingham Company definitely mentioned September and had no motive for pushing the date forward. Chamberlain, speaking to the Council, said 'very shortly after accepting my present office'. He may not have wanted it to be generally known that he had already taken such an unauthorised step as a mere councillor. *D.P.*, 25.3.1874; Borough of Birmingham, *Short History of the Passing of the Birmingham (Corporation) Gas Act and Birmingham (Corporation) Water Act with the speeches of the Mayor (Joseph Chamberlain)*, (Birmingham, 1875), p. 12. [To be cited as *Short History*.]
[46] S. Timmins, (ed.), *Resources, Products and Industrial History of Birmingham and the Midland Hardware District* (Birmingham, 1866), pp. 604–9; N. Murrell Marris, *Joseph Chamberlain*, pp. 37–43.

experience held out little hope. By 13 January 1874, the mayor's enquiries had progressed far enough for him to unfold his scheme to the Council, and to persuade them to accept it in principle. By 24 March 1874, complete agreement had been reached. While the directors of the two companies explained to their respective shareholders what a good bargain they had made, Chamberlain expounded the financial details to the Council.[47]

Chamberlain's main argument was based on the financial advantage to be gained. It was not hard to convince the Council that they needed an income greater than the rates would yield. They had recently had to countermand an increase in the town clerk's salary, which was overdue but which had raised a storm of protest in the town. They needed money for roads, for sewage disposal and for sanitary inspectors, and were not sanguine that the impending ratepayers' poll would sanction even a 3d. increase in the rates. Chamberlain reminded them that they had just resolved on the establishment of a municipal fire-brigade, and 'every day new duties are being imposed upon the Corporation'. He then proceeded to a brilliant demonstration of the profits that could be expected from the deal. The amalgamation of the companies would save the future duplication of gas mains, with its consequent effect on leakage, it would lead to a reduction of staff and of administrative overheads. Directors' fees would be abolished, and there were ingenious savings on income tax. But above all, the Corporation could borrow money at 4 per cent instead of the 7 per cent which public companies had to pay, and this promised an enormous future saving. The Town Council listened awe-struck as he juggled with figures and promised them a profit of at least £14,800, less transfer fees and sinking fund, even in the first year. In fourteen years' time he confidently expected a profit of £50,000 per annum 'without in the slightest degree increasing the cost of gas to the consumer more than would have been the case had not the Corporation taken the concern'. Small wonder that the Council approved the terms that very day by 46:1.

Quite apart from financial profit it was felt strongly by those who were hoping to improve the quality of pavements that 'it is intolerable that streets, for which we are responsible, should be liable to be torn up at any moment at the pleasure of a private company'.

To Chamberlain and those who thought like him, the scheme was not only a matter of utility. In addition there were principles at stake.

[47] *D.P.*, 25.3.1874, pp. 6–7; *Short History*, pp. 1–29.

'In the first place I distinctly hold that all monopolies which are sustained in any way by the State ought to be in the hands of the representatives of the people—by the representative authority should they be administered, and to them should their profits go, and not to private speculators. In the second place I am inclined to increase the duties and responsibilities of the local authority, in whom I have myself so great a confidence, and I will do everything in my power to constitute these local authorities real local Parliaments, supreme in their special jurisdiction.'

In Chamberlain's view monopoly achieved by the methods of private enterprise was different from monopoly conferred by public authority. The former was the reward of efficiency, the latter a perversion of the function of the State. Such monopolies were only fit to be held in trust, and to a Radical a reliable trustee meant a representative authority. The second principle is even more significant from our point of view. Such a declaration of faith was to be heard not once but often in the coming months. Other corporations had purchased gas works before Birmingham did so. Under Chamberlain Birmingham made the transaction into the symbol of a new faith. The cumulative effect of these arguments was overwhelming. The opposition in the town was overborne, and the hostile second thoughts of the old Economists were disregarded.[48] Even the opposition of the local boards whose districts were supplied by the Birmingham and Staffordshire Company served but to reveal the incompetence of its personnel and to demonstrate Chamberlain's goodwill towards them, as themselves 'public and equally representative bodies'. On 2 August 1875, the Birmingham (Corporation) Gas Act received the royal assent. Contrary to precedent the Mayor was appointed chairman of the gas committee, so strongly was it felt that the success of the new venture was in a special sense his responsibility. The main burden of the Parliamentary work had been his and he now threw himself into the congenial task of business organisation. Characteristically, the committee immediately arranged to take over the companies four months before the prescribed date.[49]

Financially, the undertaking fulfilled every expectation. Chamberlain's business acumen had saved the Corporation from the extravagantly high price paid by Glasgow, and from the purchase of worn-out equipment like that in Leeds.[50] In 1876, £30,000 could already be

[48] Vote and Council debate, *B.C.P.*, 8.12.1874, *D.P.*, 9.12.1874.
[49] *Short History*, pp. 32–48; Report of the Gas Committee, *B.C.P.*, 5.10.1875.
[50] *Short History*, p. 19. See also Sir Joseph Heron's evidence before the Select Committee of the House of Commons on the Birmingham Corporation Gas Bill, 1874 [101].

transferred to the Borough Improvement Fund, and by 1884 it had reached a total of £241,965, while the price of gas had been reduced by about 30 per cent.[51] Nor were such direct transfers the only way in which the gas profits benefited the town. In 1876 the gas committee laid out a recreation ground on some spare land next to their works in one of the worst parts of the town. In 1880 the Council wished to provide suitable accommodation for the works of art presented to the town at various times. Short of going to Parliament for special powers there were no funds available for building, but the gas committee stepped into the breach. They paid for the erection of a large building on a central site, moved their offices into the ground floor, and allowed the rest to be used as a municipal museum and art gallery.[52]

5 WATER

Whereas the purchase of the gas works had scarcely been considered before 1873, that of the water works had been almost continually in men's minds since 1869. In Birmingham, as in Parliament, the argument for the public control of water had come first. As early as 1851 the Birmingham Improvement Act had contained a clause which provided that the Corporation might purchase the undertaking of the Water Works Company by agreement or, failing that, by recourse to compulsory arbitration. It had been when trying to put this policy into practice in 1854 that the Council had felt the first wave of the ratepayers' reaction. After the draft Bill had to be put aside in December 1854 nothing more was heard of the matter until 1869 when Avery took it up. The *Report of the Royal Commission on Water Supply* (1869) had convinced him that the power of life and death, as he called it, ought not to be left in commercial hands. He was, however, stimied by the public works committee. Although there was an enquiry and an approach to the Company whose directors had no wish to sell, the matter petered out for lack of vigour. The Council was almost unanimous that it would have been a good thing to do, but as there was no Court injunction to lend a spur to action no one could muster the force needed to overcome inertia.[53]

It should not be inferred that the Birmingham Water Works Company was a bad one. On the contrary it was exceptionally good. The town

[51] Bunce, *Corporation of Birmingham*, II, 393.
[52] Joseph Chamberlain to Jesse Collings, 26 May 1876. Chlain. MSS., JC 5/16; Bunce, *Corporation of Birmingham*, II, 237–43.
[53] Bunce, *Corporation of Birmingham*, II, 401–6; D.P., 24.11.1869, 15.11.1869; Thomas Avery, *The Corporation of Birmingham and the Water Supply of the Town* (Birmingham, 1869); R. Rawlinson, *Birmingham Water Supply. Report on the Public and Domestic Supply of Water to Birmingham* (Birmingham, 1871); *Short History*, pp. 60–61.

was not easy to supply on account of its location, yet the Company's water was considered satisfactory and the whole of the district had enjoyed a constant supply since 1853, earlier than most towns. Nor were its charges illiberal. The Company could not be blamed for levying its maximum water rate in the poorest districts where the cost of repairs and of collection was great.[54] It had to be run on commercial principles, and the result was that between one-third and one-quarter of the inhabitants drew their water from local surface wells.[55] To do so cost them nothing in money, but the price in human life was great, for the well-water was almost without exception seriously contaminated. The real problem was to find a method of making it no longer worth anyone's while to use these wells instead of piped water. The solution had been found long ago in Manchester, where the Corporation levied two compulsory water rates: a public rate on all property, and a domestic rate on all dwelling houses. Since even the poorest had to pay for the piped water in any case, there was no temptation not to take it. But such compulsion could be employed only by the Corporation, and this was the main reason for Avery's initiative in 1869, as for Chamberlain's in 1874. It is a commentary on the apathy of the Birmingham Council and the complacency in the town in general that the damning facts about the wells had been publicised by the borough analyst in 1868, and repeated by Avery a year later, and still no action taken.[56] The Corporation could have proceeded in one of two ways to deal with the threat posed by these wells. It could have levied a compulsory rate, if it had acquired the water works, or it could have applied for powers to close them. By 1874, the first year of active sanitary measures under a reformed committee, the latter course was under consideration. However, to do so would provide the Company with additional customers from 24,000 houses. If the Corporation still hoped to buy out the Company one day, there was everything to be said for doing so before its value was enormously increased by the Council's own action.[57]

This last point was the only new argument when Chamberlain raised the matter again in December 1874. His really important contribution

[54] Bunce, *op. cit.*, II, 396, 400; T. Avery, *Water Supply*, 15; *D.P.*, 27.10.1875, p. 6.
[55] Borough surveyor's estimate. *House of Commons Select Committee on Birmingham (Corporation) Water Bill, Minutes of evidence* Q.804. *P.P.* 1875 [138].
[56] *R.C. on Water Supply. Minutes of evidence*, QQ.7277–88, 7314–15; *P.P.* 1868–9[4169–I] xxxiii; Avery, *Water Supply*, pp. 10, 14, 18–20; *House of Commons Select Committee on Birmingham (Corporation) Water Bill, Minutes of evidence* QQ.358–61; 1875 [138]; Alfred Hill, *What is the Relation of Water Supply in Large Towns to the Health of the Inhabitants?* (Birmingham, 1868).
[57] *Short History*, pp. 61–2.

lay elsewhere, in his skill and his determination not to be thwarted. This time he had a more difficult task than in the case of gas. The Birmingham Gas Light and Coke Company had been in a weak position on account of its urgent need for additional capital, and the Birmingham and Staffordshire Gas Light Company had preferred to come into line rather than to be left to compete with the Corporation. The Water Works Company was financially impregnable, and had no intention of selling.

The wisdom of starting with the gas works, even though there had been less popular demand for it, now became apparent. The success of these negotiations had built up a momentum of public opinion impatiently looking to the acquisition of the water works, and had aligned the town solidly behind Chamberlain's policy. What is more, the epidemic of 1874 had made the town acutely conscious of the urgency of sanitary action, a consciousness which Chamberlain did everything to foster. The Council was unanimous; no one demanded a ratepayers' poll, and the only opposition came from the Company itself. Before Parliament the Corporation argued that the powers of purchase granted in 1851 were still valid, and after a critical time in the House of Lords the Birmingham (Corporation) Water Act was passed on 2 August 1875.[58]

An agreement was with difficulty arrived at over the price and the transfer took place on 1 January 1876, four months after that of the gas works. The new water committee, with Avery as its chairman, did not set out to make a profit, although it did make a small one from the first, and it coped adequately with the rapidly rising demand for water which resulted from its policy. At the same time, the Health Committee enforced the closing of the contaminated wells.[59]

Quite apart from the direct benefits that the acquisition of these two undertakings brought to the town, it set the seal on the revolution in the Council's policy. It would not have been as easy to return to the old ways of small-scale enterprise as it had been in 1855. Between the 'sagacious audacity' which marked the Council's action over gas and water and the endless fumbling over the disposal of sewage lay a mere four to five years, but the gulf was immense. The contrast was striking even when compared with 1872-3.

When Chamberlain was elected in November 1873 he brought a new interpretation to the mayor's role. His predecessors, including Avery,

[58] Bunce, *Corporation of Birmingham*, II, 407–14.
[59] C. E. Mathews, *The Water Supply of Birmingham* (Birmingham, 1886), p. 26; Bunce, *Corporation of Birmingham*, II, 105 for numbers of wells closed annually 1876–84.

had regarded themselves as presiding officers temporarily inhibited from taking the initiative even on the committees of which they had previously been chairmen. It was rare for them to take a leading part in debate. In contrast, Chamberlain used the office and the access it gave him to all committees as a vantage point from which to overhaul the whole administration. Every department benefited from his advice. Moreover he initiated the major policies and conducted them personally at every stage. In addition to the gas and water schemes he was negotiating, vainly as it proved, for the acquisition of a park. When the baths and parks committee submitted a report in August 1875, it was the mayor, not the chairman, who introduced it.[60] The crowning triumph for the Reformers came in March 1876 when they confounded their critics by actually reducing the rates. 'This is a smasher for our opponents and is as good as three years' lease of power', wrote Chamberlain to his friend Jesse Collings. 'I had to use my despotic authority a little in arranging these estimates and took the matter out of the Finance Committee for the purpose.'[61]

Prior to November 1873 he had been too preoccupied with the School Board and the Education League to do more than take an occasional part in debate. Now all his briskness was turned upon the Council. He began his year of office by rebuking members for unpunctuality, and the speed with which he despatched business was a new experience for the Council. Occasionally he used this briskness and the increasing personal ascendancy which he acquired in order to out-manoeuvre the slower members of the Council, and people 'found themselves giving their votes at the very moment they had intended to make a speech or move an amendment'.[62] The difficult problem of the building bye-laws was a case in point.

> 'I took the matter in hand myself, explained the position of affairs to the council and begged them to pass the Bye-laws without discussion of the details. This they did like trumps as they are, and the whole set was printed and approved before the opposition had time to turn round and while they were arranging for interminable criticism and hostility. Deykin says the resolution was carried by a majority of 47, 46 of whom voted against their consciences. I don't

[60] 'Joseph Chamberlain', *Central Literary Magazine*, XXI (1913–14), 302; *D.P.*, 5.8.1875. He continued to talk to property owners about the needs for parks and recreation grounds and obtained at least two gifts. Joseph Chamberlain to Jesse Collings, 26 May and 6 June 1876, Chlain. MSS., JC 5/16.
[61] Joseph Chamberlain to Jesse Collings, 12 March 1876, Chlain. MSS., JC 5/16.
[62] *D.P.*, 26.11.1873, p. 6; 'Our Representatives V', *B.M.N.*, 14.1.1875.

care about their consciences—we have got the bye-laws and mean to work them.'[63]

This letter gives the inside view of the matter. A year earlier an outside observer, remembering how he had made his reputation as a violent partisan, thought him 'impartial to a degree that twelve months ago his opponents would hardly have given him credit for'.[64] In November 1875, he was elected to a third year of office, for there was still one undertaking to be launched.

6 THE IMPROVEMENT SCHEME

The last municipal venture with which Chamberlain was associated before he resigned the mayor's office to enter Parliament was a scheme of town improvement.[65]

No more than in the case of gas and water was Birmingham the innovator in this field. That credit goes to Glasgow, and on a smaller scale to Edinburgh, where just such a scheme combining slum clearance with town improvement had been initiated in 1866.[66] These towns suffered from slum conditions far worse than anything in Birmingham. Their pioneering action was prompted by their exceptionally grave problems, in much the same way as had the early action of Liverpool in the field of public health.

The work in Glasgow served as the model for the Artisans' and Labourers' Dwellings Act of 1875. It also greatly impressed Joseph Chamberlain who was determined to make use of the 1875 Act at the earliest moment. While it was still passing through Parliament he was in consultation with its author, Richard Cross the Conservative Home Secretary, with a view to making it serviceable for use in Birmingham. He regarded it as the most Radical measure of the last twenty years, because it disallowed the customary compensation for compulsory sale. 'For the first time the claims of large communities had been recognised as superior to . . . the sacred rights of property.'[67] On the passing of the

---

[63] Joseph Chamberlain to Jesse Collings, 12 March 1876, Chlain. MSS., JC 5/16.

[64] 'Our Representatives V', *B.M.N.*, 14.1.1875.

[65] Borough of Birmingham. *Artisans' and Labourers' Dwellings Improvement Act. Proceedings on the Adoption by the Council of a Scheme for the Improvement of the Borough, with the Speeches of the Mayor (Joseph Chamberlain) and the Chairman of the Improvement Committee (Clr. White)* (Birmingham, 1875). [To be cited as *Proc. Improvement Act.*] The details of the Improvement Scheme have been presented in Bunce, *op. cit.*, II, chapter 14; C. A. Vince, *History of the Corporation of Birmingham*, III (Birmingham, 1902) chapter 16; Gill and Briggs, *op. cit.*, II, pp. 77 ff.

[66] C. M. Allan, 'The Genesis of British Urban Redevelopment with Special Reference to Glasgow', *Econ. Hist. Rev.*, 2nd Ser., XVIII, 3 (1965), 598–613.

[67] *Proc. Improvement Act*, p. 19; *D.P.*, 25.11.1875, p. 8.

Act an improvement committee was appointed by the Birmingham Town Council, and on 6 October 1875 the first version of the scheme was presented for approval. It was repeatedly modified as time went on.

In the improvement scheme the three outstanding developments that marked the municipal history of those years were brought together, and found their most ambitious expression.

The first of these was the awakening concern for the sanitary conditions of the town. One half of the scheme consisted of a formidable piece of slum clearance. The condition of the area scheduled for demolition was enough to rouse the compassion and the indignation of all who would take the trouble to visit it—acre after acre of 'dreary desolation' in the very heart of the town 'completely given over to misery and squalor', privies oozing through damp walls into the sitting room, ceilings falling on the children's bed, snow water flowing down the stairs, and falling tiles and chimney-pots driving people in terror from their beds. Here was the nemesis of earlier jerry-building. 'If it were possible with safety to the lives of the inhabitants', added Councillor White at the end of his pitiful catalogue, 'the very best and cheapest thing to do would be to burn it clean down.' Its average death-rate was more than twice that of Edgbaston, and even that did not represent the full facts of the case.

> 'People are too poor, too wretched in St. Mary's Ward even to die there. Many of them die in the hospital, more of them in the workhouse, and some of them in the gaol.'[68]

The proposal to clear an area such as this made an immediate appeal. It arose directly from the survey which the reformed sanitary committee had presented in February 1875, and which had come as a salutary shock to public opinion in the town. The discoveries of the sewage enquiry committee, the appointment of a medical officer, the reform of the sanitary committee and the attack on the pestilential surface wells had contributed their share to the conception of this first deliberate piece of slum clearance. Previous removals of derelict property had been the incidental result of railway building. Now, at the same time as it laid down building regulations for the future, the Corporation made itself responsible for the wreckage from the past. The speech in which William White, chairman of the committee, introduced the scheme was entirely devoted to this sanitary aspect. White was a Quaker philanthropist with a life-time spent in work among the poor. 'The simplicity of purpose'

[68] *Ibid.*, pp. 12–13, 21.

which pervaded his presentation appealed very powerfully to the newly awakened conscience on public health in Birmingham.

It was left to Chamberlain to show that the proposed scheme was not entirely a matter of slum clearance. On the contrary, almost half of it was an ambitious piece of town improvement. The choice of a central area made it possible to combine town improvement with slum clearance, but there was a large area scheduled where demolition could not have been justified on sanitary grounds. Yet, whether slum or not, the centre of Birmingham was an overgrown village, a mean huddle of streets and courts. Two shopping streets, Bull Street and New Street, pushed their separate way through the congestion, but the town, as Chamberlain put it, was in danger of being choked by its own prosperity. On sanitary grounds a wide street was to be driven through the slum clearance area from the Aston Road to Bull Street. Had it terminated there, Bull Street might well have become impassable. But by continuing it so as to link up finally with New Street it would help to solve the traffic problem of the town. The plan to pierce the solid mass of houses west of Bull Street, sound though they were in construction, was not totally without value as a measure of public health. It allowed more light and air into the unhealthy district. But it was freely admitted that the reasons for the New Street scheme (as it was called) were primarily of another sort. It was a bold attempt to improve the amenities of the town. Threatening the shopkeepers of Bull Street with a vision of pavements too crowded for anyone to want to buy there, Chamberlain dangled before them the prizes to be gained by the creation of a fine shopping centre in the district. Were they not losing potential customers to Liverpool or even Leamington and Cheltenham, because 'there is no town in the kingdom of such magnitude which has so poor a show of retail shops to make to the stranger who comes to it?'

The inspiration for the New Street scheme was a vision of a better and a different kind of city.

'I have always held that Birmingham ought to be the metropolis of the Midland Counties. To it should come all the principal retail trade of those counties... I am sure that every penny which can be spent in Birmingham, to change what has hitherto been a straggling village with little of beauty to delight the eye and very little to interest the mind, into what a large town should be, will be spent not only to the advantage of the shop-keepers, but of the whole town.'[69]

[69] *Ibid.*, p. 30. In 1911 despite the Improvement Scheme the central office and shopping district was still the smallest of any large town in England. J. H. Muirhead, ed., *Birmingham Institutions* (Birmingham, 1911), p. 51.

The new street was intended for shops of a good quality, which would incidentally increase the rateable value of the district. It was to set an example of dignity worthy of the place. The thought was similar to that with which a few months later Chamberlain as chairman of the School Board argued for the erection of schools, 'fitting and congruous to the noble purpose which [they] are destined to serve'.[70]

It is touching to find that the example of Paris was never far from the minds of the reformers as they planned their improvement scheme. Chamberlain liked to describe the new street as a 'boulevard'. White spoke of 'the leafy verdure' to be seen in Paris, 'its healthy look, and its broad streets and boulevards, and charming flowery open spaces in every direction'.[71]

Additional to considerations of public health and corporate pride and welding them into a single scheme, was the third great development of these years—the business ability which had been put at the service of the Corporation. The negotiations over the compulsory purchases were handled with great skill. On one occasion an agent for one of the owners accepted £51,000 after he had asked £75,000 and been offered £50,000. 'That is the right way to split a difference!' crowed Chamberlain.[72] On its own the cost of the slum clearance would have been prohibitive but the creation of new amenities saved at least £50,000 through increases in the value of the land acquired. Nowhere was this business ability seen to better advantage than in the way in which a scheme intended to promote the health and amenities of the town was also turned into a successful piece of financial speculation. By purchasing property compulsorily and only leasing it out for seventy-five years the improvement committee ensured that the Corporation of Birmingham would one day be among the richest property owners in the land.[73]

Once again, as in the case of gas and water, the initiative had been Joseph Chamberlain's. Once again, however, the originating thought had not been his. Morley was right in thinking that 'Chamberlain did not originate new political ideas, nor launch political projects that nobody had ever heard of before', but that his contribution lay in the force of his personality. Without him the plan would have been still-born. When the scheme was first shown to some members of the Council in

[70] Joseph Chamberlain, *Six Years of Educational Work in Birmingham. An Address delivered to the Birmingham School Board* (Birmingham, 1875), p. 12.
[71] *Proc. Improvement Scheme*, p. 17.
[72] Joseph Chamberlain to Jesse Collings, 12 March 1876. Chlain. MSS., JC 5/16.
[73] Joseph Chamberlain, *The Progress of the Birmingham Improvement Scheme* (Birmingham, 1878), p. 24.

1873, 'it was thought . . . so gigantic and its difficulties so great that it was not thought advisable to bring it either before the Public Works Committee or the Council.'[74] In Chamberlain the Birmingham Town Council possessed a man capable of taking up ideas of that stature. He was an example of the great entrepreneur in the public service. But the business ability which marked the administration of those years was not merely the personal genius of one man. When he went into national politics, others were left to carry on. The whole policy was feasible only because the Council was able to draw on the business talent in the town.

In the improvement scheme we can trace the influence of the boom, which was affecting the national economy from 1870–76 and particularly that of Birmingham.[75] Surprisingly enough this cannot be said of the earlier measures. Oblivious of their great prosperity the burgesses had even in 1874 re-affirmed their determination to keep the rates down, and the earlier reforms had been either legally inescapable or financially profitable. Although the purchase of the gas- and water-works had involved the Corporation in long-term indebtedness, the liabilities were so well covered by profits as to be impervious to changes in the economic climate. But the improvement scheme involved the Corporation in a different kind of long-term indebtedness, and promised to put a considerable burden on the rates. Its financial success was to depend largely on the ease with which shop-sites along the new thoroughfare could be let once the ground had been cleared. In 1876 it was taken for granted that this would pose no problem. However, demand was bound to fluctuate with the economic climate, and a reluctance to take up new sites was to cause a serious set-back to the scheme in the 1880s.[76]

The dash of recklessness which characterised the scheme was not induced entirely by the boom, for it appeared in other contexts than the assessment of economic risk. When Chamberlain sketched the housing provision 'that the Committee would probably make . . . for the poor', lodging-houses, flats and houses of different sizes and suited to persons of different means, he was allowing his imagination to run away with him.[77] The speech was to lead to embarrassed denials at a later date, to disappointed hopes and a long-delayed search for a housing policy more positive than the mere demolition of slums.

[74] John Morley, *Recollections* (1917), I, 147; Speech by Ambrose Biggs, mayor in 1873, *D.P.*, 7.10.1875, p. 6.
[75] G. C. Allen, *Industrial Development of Birmingham and the Black Country 1860–1927* (1929), p. 197.
[76] Gill and Briggs, *History of Birmingham*, II, 80–81.
[77] *Proc. Improvement Scheme*, p. 25.

Yet the imagination, which had for once outstripped the facts, was itself an integral part of the story. In the improvement scheme the vision of the ideal city impinged directly on the administrative policy of the Town Council. Something like this had happened in the founding of the chain of public libraries and many lesser examples can be found.[78] Its fullest impact was, however, indirect. Without it the unprecedented flow of talent into municipal service, the pivot on which all the administrative changes turned, would not have taken place.

[78] The newly found pride, which called the new thoroughfare Corporation Street, led the Council in 1876 on Chamberlain's suggestion to sponsor a history of the Corporation. Bunce's two-volume work, to be continued later into several more volumes by Vince and others, was the result. For Chamberlain's initiative in this matter see Joseph Chamberlain to J. T. Bunce, 27 March 1878, Chlain. MSS., JC 5/8.

4

The Liberal Association

A prominent part was played in the reform of municipal politics by the intervention of the Birmingham Liberal Association, an intervention which was at the time unique. The annual contests proved of benefit to the Association, for they kept it active and efficient in the intervals between parliamentary elections. But this was not the reason for its interventions in municipal politics. Indeed from both the municipal and the national party point of view its action appeared highly paradoxical. It has been said that the caucus was the result of the revival of civic spirit and its purpose being civic betterment.[1] But this is to read history backwards. The Birmingham Liberal Association was caught up in the movement for civic betterment and became its instrument, but it was founded in 1865 and reorganised in 1867 entirely for purposes of national politics.

It was founded in February 1865, a few months before the general election,

> 'To maintain the Liberal representation of the borough.
> To assist in obtaining the return of Liberal members for the county.
> To promote the adoption of Liberal principles in the Government of the country.'[2]

As the first two objects indicate, it was essentially an election committee put on a permanent basis. But the third object connects its ancestry with organisations such as the Birmingham Reform Association of 1858.[3] Its committee included the more influential Liberals in Birmingham, such as would normally have appeared on an election committee, and it kept up an uneasy relationship with the democratic Reform League, the

---

[1] F. H. Herrick, 'The Origins of the National Liberal Federation', *Jl. of Modern History*, XVII, 2 (June 1945), 120.
[2] *B.J.*, 18.2.1865, p. 6.
[3] See J. A. Langford, *Modern Birmingham and its Institutions* (1877), II, 24–8.

officers of whose Birmingham branch would, it was hoped, be *ex officio* members of the committee.[4]

The borough members were returned unopposed in 1865 and, although the Association concentrated all its resources on north Warwickshire, its candidate was soundly defeated. Thereafter the Association organised meetings in favour of Parliamentary reform. In 1867 there was a bye-election in the borough, and George Dixon as President of the Association, snatched the Liberal nomination almost before most people knew what was happening. His election campaign against a popular Liberal-Conservative added to the excitement over the Reform Bills and kept the Association prominent and active. It was Birmingham's first contested election since 1859 and it did much to stimulate political interest and to create a consciousness of party allegiance in the wards. So far the Association had no permanent organisation at ward level, but the bye-election was hardly over when it was suggested that the canvassing books be kept permanently up to date so as not to waste the work that had gone into the recent contest.[5] Nothing came of this idea for the moment. However after the passing of the Reform Act William Harris recognised the importance of extending the organisation downwards. There was a general reason in the great increase of the electorate whose allegiance had to be retained. There was a particular reason in clause 9 of the Act, which gave three members to Birmingham, Manchester, Liverpool and Leeds, although each voter was to have but two votes.[6] This attempt to secure the representation of minorities, although it appealed to John Stuart Mill, roused the indignation of less sophisticated Radicals. Bright complained that in crucial party voting the arrangement would leave the large towns with no more than a single effective vote,[7] and his supporters in Birmingham were determined to keep the Conservatives out. This could be done if the Liberal voters distributed their votes evenly over the three candidates, an operation impossible without organisation at ward level.

It was now that Harris provided what had been a normal body, consisting of a committee and a subscribing membership, with a new structure which was to be widely imitated elsewhere during the course of the next ten years. It was based on permanent ward committees, linked to

---

[4] *B.J.*, 18.2.1865, p. 6. See also T. R. Tholfsen, 'The Origins of the Birmingham Caucus', *Historical Jl.*, II, 2 (1959), 161–84.

[5] Letter by Thomas Mollard, *D.P.*, 8.8.1867.

[6] Clause 10 gave the City of London 4 members on the same principle, Clause 7 of the Scottish Reform Act gave Glasgow also 3 members on the same principle.

[7] *Hansard*, CLXXXIX, 1131 (8 August 1867).

and represented upon a general committee, and a smaller executive committee. The new constitution was officially adopted on 4 October 1867.[8] The membership fee was fixed at 1s. per annum, but subsequently even this small sum ceased to be obligatory and mere 'adherence to the objects and organisations of the Association' became a sufficient qualification.[9]

The establishment of permanent ward committees was a significant innovation, but in view of the great increase in the electorate it followed logically from the steps already taken. Prior to 1865 the Liberal borough election committee used to spring up when needed and be dissolved again. In that year it was given a continuous existence. But in large boroughs Parliamentary elections had also been fought by means of election committees at the ward level. In Birmingham this practice dated from 1841.[10] By 1867 when ward committees became permanent they had been known intermittently for close on a generation.

This establishment of a political organisation in the wards proved unintentionally to be of great importance for municipal politics, since that was the level on which it was conducted. The Liberal Association had become a potential instrument for intervening in town council elections, but for a while not much happened. It became the custom for men to stand with the support of the local ward committee, but this did not mean that the initiative came from the Association, nor that the Association's resources were mobilised on their behalf.

Two things changed this situation and harnessed the new organisation to municipal politics. One was the personal antagonism felt by members of the party towards certain leading figures in the other camp; the other the success of the National Education League in capturing the Liberal Association for its own purposes.

At the general election of 1868 the Association had triumphed. All three Liberal candidates were elected, but their defeated 'Constitutionalist' opponents, Sampson Lloyd and Sebastian Evans, were both local men and remained the leading figures in the Conservative camp. Party passion had run high; there had been violent meetings when none of the speakers could make themselves heard, and when in 1870 Evans decided to stand for the Town Council the leaders of the Liberal Association were roused. The same canvassers were used as in the general election

[8] *B.J.*, 5.10.1867. Constitution printed in Langford, *Modern Birmingham*, II, 362–3.
[9] Birmingham Liberal Association, *Constitution* (1875).
[10] Resolution at a meeting of electors held in the Birmingham Public Office, 14.6.1841. *A.G.*, 21.6.1841, p. 3.

and a prominent part in the campaign was played by Joseph Chamberlain who had absolutely no connection with the ward.[11] The Association kept Evans out, not only once but permanently. Nothing but party passion could account for such inconsistency on the part of those who professed their concern for the standards of the Town Council and were appealing to citizens of education and public standing to serve on it. Evans had both. A friend of George Dawson, he had been a co-founder of *The Town Crier*, and his resentment was understandable.

This was an isolated case and no further intervention took place for another two years. When it came, personal antagonism though strongly present was swallowed up in the general party battle over educational policy. That this battle should have been fought with the resources of the Liberal Association was due to the success with which the Association had been captured by the National Education League. It had always been the intention of the League to convert the Liberal Party to its policy, an object which its leaders considered that they had achieved on the parliamentary level by 1876.[12] They worked for it also at the constituency level, and wherever a branch was formed it sought to capture the Liberal organisation. It was due to the success of these tactics in many of the boroughs that it was possible to dissolve the League in January 1877 and transfer its remaining activities to the Liberal Associations, soon to be united in a National Federation under the former leaders of the League.[13] Naturally this policy had been particularly easy to carry out in Birmingham. There was some opposition in October 1870 when the Association decided to intervene in the impending School Board elections. Alderman Hawkes, who was among those to protest, had been its President from 1867–8 and had only resigned to become the election agent for the Liberal candidates. But he was outvoted, and fifteen candidates were adopted, all of whom were prominent members of the League. By the time of the next School Board election, in 1873, events had moved so rapidly that Hawkes himself proposed the resolution 'that this meeting pledges itself to support the Liberal candidates'.[14]

The defeat of nine of its candidates in the 1870 School Board elections condemned the League to three years spent obstructing the policy of a majority intent on subsidising Church schools out of rates. Defeated on the School Board they rallied their supporters on the Town Council, and

[11] *D.P.*, 19.10.1870, p. 8; 'Our Representatives XVII', *B.M.N.*, 19.4.1875.
[12] F. Adams, *Elementary School Conflict*, pp. 321–2.
[13] F. H. Herrick, *Jl. Mod. Hist.*, XVII, 2, 125–8.
[14] 'Our Representatives VII', *B.M.N.*, 8.2.1875; *D.P.*, 11.11.1870, 13.11.1870; *W.P.* 11.10.1873, p. 6.

in February 1872 the Council refused to carry out its legal duty of levying the school rate demanded by the Board. Rather than provoke a conflict the Board yielded, but the issue had been merely postponed to the next year.[15] It is easy to understand why the Conservative supporters of Church schools made a furious attempt to change the composition of the Council at the following municipal elections.[16] They made it a party matter, as it had indeed become, and in their attack on Liberal supporters of the League drew additional strength from the unpopularity of the Liberal government's recent Licensing Act.[17] They put up candidates in several wards, but threw their greatest forces against such hated figures of educational politics as Chamberlain and Schnadhorst, Secretary of the sectarian Central Nonconformist Committee.[18]

The Association rallied as one body and fought in the wards, suffering defeat only over Schnadhorst. In the following March the general committee decided on Chamberlain's suggestion 'that in consequence of recent action by the Tory party in Birmingham in reference to municipal elections, the Liberal Association should in future take part in such elections, and that whenever a Liberal candidate is opposed by a Tory candidate, the support of the Association should be given to the Liberal.'[19]

Yet there is a paradox here. The Association had entered municipal politics in order to drive off the Conservatives, but it soon assumed quite another function as well. The battle-cry continued to be, 'Down with the Tories!', but the foes that were left slain on the field were also those thoroughly orthodox Liberals who were opposed to the new municipal policy.

The conflict over municipal policy and personnel had been complicated by issues which strictly speaking had nothing to do with it. It had been possible from the beginning to describe it roughly in class terms, but in a council that was predominantly Liberal-Radical it had not been possible to describe it in party-political terms. The older members of the Council had always stressed their Radical anti-oligarchical traditions. It was a Conservative complaint in 1867 that 'the key to the door of the Town Council was to profess to be a Radical'.[20] No difference of party

[15] *B.C.P.*, 6.2.1872; *D.P.*, 7.2.1872; *W.P.*, 11.10.1873, p. 6; *B.C.P.*, 11.2.1873; *D.P.*, 12.2.1873. In 1873 the Board took the matter before the Courts.
[16] For a statement of their view, see the letter of the Rev. F. S. Dale, their leader on the School Board. *D.P.*, 16.9.1872, p. 5 also *D.P.*, 11.9.1872, p. 4.
[17] 35 & 36 Vic. cap. 94. Clause 24 gave optional powers to the magistrates to enforce the earlier closing of public houses. The issue was quite irrelevant to municipal politics.
[18] Schnadhorst became secretary of the Liberal Association in the following year, and of the National Federation of Liberal Associations in 1877. He had only been a clr. for a few days, having won a bye-election on 18 October. *D.P.*, 19.10.1872, p. 5; 2.11.1872, p. 5.
[19] *D.P.*, 26.3.1873, p. 5. R. A. Armstrong, *Henry William Crosskey*, p. 259.
[20] *D.P.*, 29.10.1867.

label separated Sadler from Harris, and the few Conservatives, of whom Avery was one, were equally to be found on either side. But the factors which brought the chief protagonists of the Education League into the Town Council, where their ability gave them a prominent position, introduced organisations and attitudes of mind that had not been there before. They largely created an identity of personnel in the leadership of the new municipal policy and of the educational policy. They were responsible for keeping out Conservative supporters of the new line, and as Chamberlain rather than Avery came to take the lead, it became increasingly difficult for Conservative councillors to support the municipal policy of the group. Avery always continued to do so, but he was not an active party man, and his own Nonconformity made him sympathetic towards men with whose policy he disagreed. But John Lowe, a leading Birmingham Conservative who had been on most topics a supporter of the Avery–Chamberlain policy well into 1871, became ever more estranged from the municipal reformers. By 1874 he had definitely changed sides, was opposing the purchase of the gas works, and retired from the Council in 1875.[21]

Lowe's case is an illustration of the forces that were creating an alliance between the Radicals of the old Economist party and the Conservatives, however 'progressive' their municipal views. In each case the Chamberlain group was fighting the enemies that they had made. To oppose Chamberlain, as the Conservatives did, was almost necessarily to take up an attitude of disapproval towards the policies that he advocated, and to become acceptable allies for Sadler's group.

These developments came to a head in the November elections of 1873, which were fought over the choice of a mayor for the coming year, an issue never before debated in the wards. It was a matter that had always been arranged behind the scenes and formally voted upon at the first meeting of the newly elected Council. In recent years the recruitment of wealthy men with greater ability and dignity in public business had led to their rapid elevation, to the frustration of men with greater seniority. The election of Dixon in 1866, of Avery in 1867, and of G. B. Lloyd in 1870 had each produced complaints against the practice of picking gentlemen with money and by-passing long-standing members.[22] After the expiration of Lloyd's term it had been tacitly decided to give the leaders of the older party a turn. Sadler made a good mayor in 1871–2 and was followed by Biggs, who had for years been chairman

---

[21] *B.C.P.*, 6.7.1871, 24.3.1874; *D.P.*, 25.3.1874.
[22] *D.P.*, 10.11.1866, 16.7.1876, 10.11.1870.

of the much-contested public works committee. Even there he had allowed his committee to be run by Sadler and during his term as mayor his weakness was disastrous. He lost complete control of council meetings, and there were scenes reminiscent of the worst days.[23]

After Sadler and Biggs, William Brinsley, the remaining member of the triumvirate, confidently expected to have his turn. But that was too much to swallow for most of the Council. Brinsley was a grocer who had invested his profits in small houses in the poorer parts of the town, of which he owned fifty-eight in 1859–61 and about 200 by 1871. A model of regularity in his attendance at council and committee meetings, he lived entirely for municipal politics, much as Allday had done, and retired from them only in 1901 at the age of seventy-nine. His great influence in the wards was based on the good-fellowship of the public house and had only recently begun to be challenged. He was, without doubt, one of the picturesque characters of Birmingham public life. Unpolished in his manner, erratic in his grammar and pronunciation, there was hardly a local vulgarism that he did not habitually employ. But the richest coin came from his own mint. 'This 'ere institooshun as is now defunking', a phrase with which he enlivened a creditors' meeting after a bank-failure, was still gratefully remembered ten years later.[24] His tactlessness could attain heroic proportions.

As soon as it became known that his friends seriously intended to propose Brinsley as mayor, others tried in vain to secure a widely acceptable candidate. When a conflict appeared inevitable, they turned to Chamberlain. He had been a mere four years on the Council and his other duties had made his attendance very irregular. But he had acquired an outstanding position in the town by his work on the School Board and the League, and this was held to justify the choice. Once again the educational interests, which dominated the public life of the town, had a decisive influence on the development of municipal government.

In the subsequent elections, which were fought in all the wards as an issue between the supporters and opponents of Chamberlain, the Liberal Association intervened with every weapon, including a newspaper of its own.[25] The pro-Chamberlain candidates were everywhere adopted by the ward committees, either against Conservatives or against Liberals who were then accused of endangering party unity on the brink

[23] E.g. *D.P.*, 17.6.1873, 6.8.1873.
[24] Rate books 1859, 1861; *D.P.*, 27.10.1871, p. 5; 14.8.1906 (obituary); 'Our Representatives XII', *B.M.N.*, 15.3.1875.
[25] *The Liberal*, started 26 September 1873. Also *Nechells Ward Liberal Association Ward Paper*, No. I (1 September 1873).

of the School Board elections, due the following month. On the whole its propaganda tried as much as possible to exaggerate the Tory element in the opposition, but the Conservative *Daily Gazette* distinguished between six wards, where the contest was between Liberal and Conservative, and four, where it was between two kinds of Liberals.[26]

This hard-fought election was decisive. Chamberlain became mayor, and the 1874 election was merely a ratification of his gas purchase scheme. In 1874 and 1875 strong supporters, including his brother Richard and personal friends like R. F. Martineau and C. E. Mathews, had little difficulty in being elected for wards to whom they were entirely unknown. Nomination by ward committees was the rule and leading figures in the Association could be relied upon to intervene. Behind the scenes these leading figures were active in the work of recruitment. In 1875 we can catch a glimpse of Chamberlain and Bunce, the highly influential editor of the Liberal *Daily Post*, calling on a prominent physician to ask him to stand, while Schnadhorst, the secretary of the Association was recruiting a wholesale confectioner for another ward.[27] The hold of the Liberal Association on municipal politics was assured.

This was the pattern that soon after was being held up for imitation to Liberals in other towns. The new structure, which was widely adopted by Liberals in the aftermath of the 1874 election and by Conservatives after 1880, by providing permanent organisation on a ward basis lent itself to intervention in municipal elections. The advantages of these annual contests served in turn as an inducement for intervention of this kind, even where the rather special circumstances that had first led to it in Birmingham did not exist.[28] 'Municipal elections in politics are the equivalent of Autumn manoeuvres in military affairs; they are the best means we possess of keeping our fighting forces in the highest efficiency', wrote a Parliamentary candidate to the president of the Wolverhampton Conservative Association in 1912. He in turn drew the logical conclusion and laid down the principle that 'the policy of contesting Municipal Seats has to be considered purely with relation to the effect that may be produced on our Parliamentary prospects and nothing else.'[29] This was not quite what the Birmingham municipal reformers had intended.

---

[26] Contrast *The Liberal*, No. I. 26.9.1873, *D.P.* for October 1873 with *D.G.*, 3.11.1873, p. 5.
[27] Joseph Chamberlain to Jesse Collings, 12 September 1875, Chlain. MSS., JC 5/16.
[28] Records that have survived for the years 1882–8 show that the management committee of the Liberal Association had regular discussions in preparation for the municipal elections. They normally left the process of selecting candidates to the ward committees but were required to approve their choice. Birmingham Liberal Association, Management Committee Minutes 1882–8; Finance Committee Minutes 1883–8.
[29] Quoted in G. W. Jones, *Borough Politics*, pp. 46–7.

5
Social Improvement

I THE PHYSICAL ENVIRONMENT

It is a paradox that a municipal reform movement, whose administrative achievements lay mostly in the improvement of the physical environment, should have sprung in the first instance from a concern for popular education. But the evidence is too strong to be denied. Not until 1874 was it at all widely realised in the town that the conditions under which the poor lived posed a major challenge to the Corporation.

The reasons for this complacency have already been described. Much of it was due to an easy reliance on misleading appearances which a closer acquaintance with the worst quarters of the town would have dispelled. It is relevant that at that time slum visiting was usually left to salaried domestic missioners and Bible women, while the educational work of a church was often done by members of its leading families. There was a minority group in the town, mainly doctors, who had long pressed for reforms in public health administration. But unlike the educationalists they confined themselves to fruitless petitions to the Town Council and to occasional letters to the press. Very different was the position of those who had entered the Town Council between 1867 and 1870 in pursuit of their educational concern. They had to deal with the problems of town sewerage by the sheer compulsion of a suit in Chancery. Then followed the statutory appointment of a medical officer of health and the sharp reminder provided by the smallpox epidemic. By the beginning of 1874 public health had become a matter of concern to the town and not least to those who had been obliged to cope with the successive emergencies which had confronted the Council.

During the course of his first two years as mayor, Joseph Chamberlain took the opportunity afforded by his official presence at functions of every sort to create a strong public opinion in support of the schemes that he was preparing. The following passages from three speeches of this kind given between November 1874 and January 1875, suggest that for him personally and for the town in general the interest in public health sprang directly from an earlier concern with the education of the poor. Both drew strength from their close association with the moral and philanthropic work of the churches.

'My favourite town . . . is not perfect, and the question to which I am specially devoting my attention, during the present year [water-supply] is one so closely allied to the one we have been considering to-night, that I believe Mr. Gooch was right in connecting the two. How can we educate the children of the town when after keeping them in school for a few hours, we send them for the rest of the night to houses where the education they receive is of the worst possible kind, where anything like decency and honesty, and morality is almost impossible.'[1]

'You must have found that your educational and other work is hindered by the obstacles which the existing sanitary condition of the town interposes. It seems to me that education must be a perfect farce when the instruction at the school is contradicted by the experience of the home. It seems to me absurd to preach morality to people who are herded together in conditions in which common decency is impossible. It seems to me ridiculous to talk of temperance to men who have every reason to leave their homes, and are driven thereby to the public house. It seems to me monstrous to preach thrift to those whose whole lives are wasted in a perpetual struggle with disease and death.'[2]

'What folly it is to talk about the moral and intellectual elevation of the masses when the conditions of life are such as to render elevation impossible! What can the schoolmaster or the minister of religion do, when the influences of home undo all he does? We find bad air, polluted water, crowded and filthy homes, and ill-ventilated courts everywhere prevailing in the midst of our boasted wealth, luxury and civilisation. A paternal government provides for our criminals in gaol 1000 cu. ft. of air as a minimum; and those criminals, after their confinement is terminated, go back to their homes

[1] Reply to a Vote of Thanks for presiding at a Lecture on 'School Children and Their Homes', at the Howard St. Institute, 19.11.1874. C. W. Boyd, ed., *Speeches*, I, 51. Ephraim Gooch was clr. for All Saints Ward 1866–75. A supporter of Brinsley and Sadler, but a member of the Birmingham Education Society and interested in the provision of schools.
[2] Speech at the Annual General Meeting of Severn St. Adult School, 30.11.1874. C. W. Boyd, ed., *Speeches*, I, 55. Boyd's editorial note at the head of the speech is incorrect.

1 The centre of Birmingham from the south-east about 1886: the Town Hall and the Council House are represented on the skyline.

2 The front page of *The Town Crier*, the satirical champion of the Dawson group and the enemy of municipal incompetence. It was founded in 1861 as a twopenny monthly, became a weekly at the end of 1889, and ceased publication in 1903.

No. 4.—Vol. II.]   [TWOPENCE.

THE

TOWN CRIER:

Or, Jacob's   Belles Lettres.

"Parcere Subjectis   "Ridentem Dicere
et Debellare Superbos."   Verum Quid Vetat?"
—VIRGIL.   —HORACE.

"Hear the Cryer!
What the devil art thou?
One that will play the devil, sir, with you!"
KING JOHN, ii. 1.

BIRMINGHAM, OCTOBER, 1862.

The Right of Translation and Contradiction will be enforced by Jacob's "Staff."

SOLD BY W. WILLEY, AND ALL NEWSVENDORS,
FOR THE PROPRIETORS.

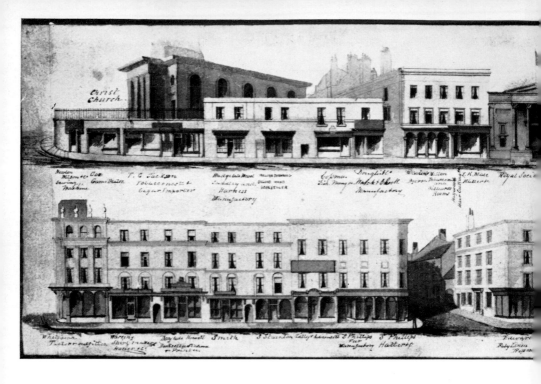

The two aspects of the Improvement Scheme:

4 (*right*) **Slum clearance.** No. 6 Court off Thomas Street about 1875. (*Photo: James Burgoyne*)

5 (*far right*) **Town improvement.** Nos. 13–16 Union Street, as they appeared about 1875 before being demolished. (*Photo: James Burgoyne*)

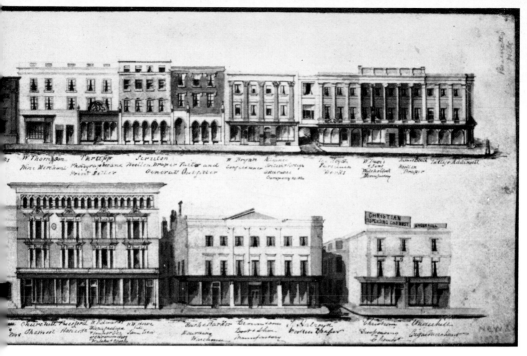

3 The north side of New Street between Paradise Street and the future junction with Corporation Street, as it appeared in 1873. Apart from a firm of solicitors and the Royal Society of Artists, the street was occupied entirely by petty tradesmen and manufacturers. From a contemporary drawing.

ALDERMAN AVERY
[AND A VERY GOOD ALDERMAN TOO]

6 & 7 'To the Sewerage Farm'. Thomas Avery (1813–1914) *left*, as seen by *The Dart*, 18 November 1876. His high-wheeled carriage (a double-bodied phaeton), harnessed to a pair of exceptionally fine horses, made him a conspicuous figure in the town. *Below left* as he appeared in a photograph of the period from the Whitlock Collection.

8 (*below*) William White (1820–1900) during his office as mayor in 1883. He came to Birmingham from Reading in 1848. A Quaker and temperance advocate, he was elected to the Council in 1873 and was chairman of the Improvement Committee for five years. He remained an alderman from 1882 to his death. From *The Birmingham Graphic*, 28 February 1883.

9 (*right*) Joseph Chamberlain (1836–1914) as mayor, about 1874. He was three times mayor and became M.P. for Birmingham (subsequently Birmingham West) from 1876 until his death. This portrait of the thirty-seven year old mayor gives little hint as yet of the over-carefully dressed, monocled public figure whose picture became familiar in the 1880s and 1890s. From a photograph among the Chamberlain Papers in the Library of the University of Birmingham.

10 (*below*) 'Grand Transformation Scene— a Vision of the Future'. Joseph Chamberlain as the pantomime fairy, banishing the slums and other evils of 'Old Brum' and conjuring up a millenial vision of the New Birmingham. The promise included, among other urbanities, a 'Boulevard de Chamberlain'. From *The Dart*, 23 December 1876.

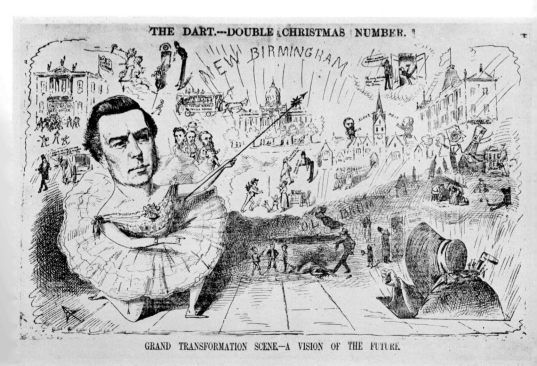

GRAND TRANSFORMATION SCENE—A VISION OF THE FUTURE.

11 (*above left*) George Dawson (1821–76), from a drawing made towards the end of his life. He was born in London and came to Birmingham as a Baptist preacher in 1844, becoming minister of the Church of the Saviour when it was founded in 1847.

12 (*above right*) Robert William Dale (1829–95), from an undated photograph in the Whitlock Collection but probably taken about 1890. He was born in London and came to Birmingham as a theological student in 1847, becoming pastor at Carr's Lane Chapel in 1854. An admirer of Dawson and supporter of Chamberlain, he became the leading educationist of the town and also served on the Royal Commission on Elementary Education in 1885.

13 (*left*) William Brinsley (1822–1906), grocer, property-owner, and devotee of municipal politics, as he was in mid-career as a councillor during the 1880s. He did not leave the Council until 1901. (*Photo: John Collier*)

14 Enthusiasm for the Improvement Scheme turned sour during the depression of the early 1880s, especially as the estimates were being exceeded. Chamberlain, shown here putting on the screw, had been one of the principals in the firm of Nettlefold & Chamberlain, wood-screw manufacturers, before he retired from business in 1874 to devote himself entirely to politics. From *The Dart*, 21 April 1882.

15 (*below*) 'The Battle of the Wards'. Chamberlain and his supporters hold the municipal heights in the electoral battle of 1878. The cartoonist is George H. Bernasconi, who came to Birmingham from London in 1866 and earned a big local reputation for drawings of this kind. From *The Dart*, 26 October 1878.

16 Corporation Street in process of being developed, about 1883, showing the intersection with Bull Street.

17 Chamberlain Square in the late-1880s, looking down Edmund Street, showing the City Museum and Art Gallery (beneath the clock tower), the side of the Council House, and the back of the Town Hall. The centerpiece is a monument to Chamberlain erected in the form of a fountain in 1880. The canopied statue is of George Dawson put up the following year; it replaces one which had caused general dissatisfaction. The other is of Sir Josiah Mason, founder of Mason College, the parent body of the present University of Birmingham.

in which 300, 200, and 100 cubic feet of air is the maximum. Even the air they have is contaminated by unmentionable impurities and filth. Hardly a gleam of sunshine ever comes into the dark and dreary courts, which exist in the centre of all large cities. The dead and living lie together in the same room for days; all reverence is blotted out from the minds of the people subjected to such conditions: as for common decency, it is an empty name; it is obliterated from the category of virtues.'[3]

This evidence supports the view that the glorification of public authorities, which characterised the Birmingham municipal reform movement, was the consequence of assuming functions intimately connected with the traditional work of the churches. George Dawson's speeches in the 1860s had stemmed from a concern for popular education. Those in which Chamberlain now took up Dawson's theme were deliberately designed to awaken the churches to the implications for them of the Corporation's sanitary work.

In October 1874 he spoke at the Annual Meeting of Hurst Street Chapel, a former Unitarian mission in a very neglected part of the town. Gently disposing of the common opinion that drunkenness was the fundamental cause of all the misery and vice in Birmingham, he indicated the two causes which had impressed themselves on him:

'In the first place . . . the gross ignorance of the masses: and in the second place, the horrible shameful homes in which many of the poor are forced to live.'

After arguing at length for the abolition of school fees, he turned to his second point with the following words:

'As to the condition of many of the houses of the poorer classes in the town, we talk about missions to the poor; but I think the men who preach Christianity to the poor must feel themselves powerless in the presence of the conditions in which the poor have to live. How can we tell a man to be good and decent and moral when we find him living in a place that is not fit for a beast to live in, much less a human being. The fact is that in our missions we begin at the wrong end; we attempt to apply remedies to diseases which ought never to exist in the social state at all. What we ought to do is to prevent the disease and then we shall not want the remedy.'

[3] Opening Address to the Sanitary Conference called in Birmingham, 13.1.1875, C. W. Boyd, ed., *Speeches*, I, 63–4.

6

What moral did he draw from this? That the work of the Corporation would help to make that of the Church possible? Not at all. It was rather the Corporation

> 'engaged in a great struggle to promote the welfare, health and happiness of the population over which it rules whose labours are supplemented by the individual efforts of such institutions as this.'[4]

The same language was used to the teachers of the Severn Street adult school, the most outstanding of the moral and educational religious agencies in Birmingham.

> 'I hold it to be one of the duties as well as one of the pleasures of my office to give whatever sanction that office can give . . . to institutions like this, which is supplementing the work of the municipal authorities, which is paving the way for the good government of the town, and doing all in its power to promote the welfare and happiness of all our citizens.'[5]

The adult school had been founded to supplement Bull Street Quaker meeting, not the Corporation, in promoting the welfare and happiness of the inhabitants of Birmingham. But how natural and reasonable the transposition could appear in 1874!

We know that these were no isolated instances. Early in 1876 Chamberlain was attending ward meetings for what he called 'a preachment on the duties and work of the Council' and commented on the favourable reception he received.[6]

It was not necessary to share Chamberlain's view of the churches as somewhat less effective prototypes of the Corporation—a view so characteristic of heterodox Dissent—to be impressed by the intimate bearing of the Town Council's new activities on the moral and philanthropic work of the churches in their domestic missions, Sunday schools and similar agencies. The relevance was clearer and more impressive than it had ever been before 1874. Strictly speaking this was not another instance of the transfer of functions previously undertaken by the churches. But the new work of prevention and reclamation on which the Corporation had embarked, while it supplemented the philanthropic

---

[4] Speech at the Annual Meeting of Hurst Street Chapel, Birmingham, 12.10.1874. C. W. Boyd, ed., *Speeches*, I, 45, 42.

[5] Its official title was Severn Street first-day school, the Quaker equivalent to a Sunday school. It is being called by its conventional name throughout this work to prevent any confusion with a day school. Boyd, ed., *Speeches*, I, 52.

[6] Joseph Chamberlain to Jesse Collings, 13 February and 12 March 1876, Chlain. MSS., JC 5/16.

work of the churches, also dwarfed it by comparison. 'All private effort, all individual philanthropy', as Chamberlain said to the Town Council, 'sinks into insignificance compared with the organised power of a great representative assembly like this.'[7]

Where Sunday schools had insisted on personal cleanliness, the Corporation was to inspect the conditions of dwellings and lay on a regular supply of pure water. Where home missions had provided comforts for the sick and encouraged the formation of provident societies, the Corporation was filling the open middens, which bred disease, and providing a fever hospital to check infection. Where the churches rescued a few from drunkenness, the Corporation was imposing building regulations and clearing whole slums to remove the conditions which made drunkenness endemic. What were the gifts of clothes and money distributed by home missioners and Bible women compared to the new conditions of life which the Corporation was intending to bestow on the poor? Is it surprising that those deeply involved in the moral and philanthropic work of the churches, not least those connected with the poorer districts like Frank Wright and Robert Arculus, answered the call of the Town Council? Is it surprising that, like the educational enthusiasts from the Unitarian churches before them, they felt themselves to be performing a religious duty? Finally, can it be wondered at that even orthodox Evangelical Dissenters began to regard public authorities with sentiments akin to those traditionally bestowed on churches?

The recruitment of Arculus in November 1873 began the accession of Evangelical Dissenters to the reforming party on the Town Council. By July 1874 when the far-reaching nature of the Corporation's plans had become apparent, the municipal reformers were joined by an outstanding member of the Congregational Church in Steelhouse Lane. Samuel Edwards, a life-long Sunday school teacher and Honorary secretary of the Birmingham Sunday School Union, had been 'many times previously solicited unsuccessfully to enter the Council'.[8] Now, at last, he agreed and never abandoned municipal work until he died in 1920.

The previous March had seen the accession of another Nonconformist. Arthur Holden's 'real taste lay in the direction of philosophical study and quiet country life', but his idealism drove him nevertheless to become a representative of the squalid ward in which his factory was situated.[9] In November 1874 followed the election of Frank Wright of

[7] Speech to Town Council on his third election as mayor, *D.P.*, 10.11.1875, p. 6.
[8] 'Our Representatives XVIII', *B.M.N.*, 26.4.1875.
[9] *Central Literary Magazine*, XXI, 160.

the People's Chapel and Richard Kneebone, a Nonconformist whose church it has not been possible to trace. George Marris's candidature in March 1875 was as significant as that of Samuel Edwards. A deacon at Carr's Lane, the leading Congregational church in Birmingham, he was responsible for much of its educational and philanthropic work. 'A man of business, accustomed to large transactions, with ability enough . . . to give him five years' start of many of his fellow-members', he had been 'urgently entreated' by Avery two or three years before to join the Council. He had then considered his time too valuable, but now on his own admission he was standing for election 'under the influence of a sanitary impulse'.[10] Essentially of the same type were the brothers Hart, elected in November 1875 and November 1876, who were lay preachers in the United Methodist Free Church.

These men were deeply involved in the work of the church with which they were connected. Soon after the end of his term of office Chamberlain claimed that

> 'If a man has leisure, and wants occupation, his taste must be difficult indeed if he cannot find some congenial employment in connection with the multifarious duties of the Town Council of Birmingham. . . . If he is a philanthropist, where else can he expect to be influential in saving the lives of thousands of persons and in bringing health to tens of thousands of homes?'[11]

These men were not in want of occupation, but as philanthropists their action acknowledged the justice of his claim.

2 THE ROLE OF THE QUAKERS

Among the philanthropists of Birmingham few were held in such high esteem as the Quakers, and Chamberlain's arguments would have appealed to them greatly. In March 1869 *The Town Crier* had observed that

> 'If every Quaker in Birmingham were to leave it a month hence, their departure would hardly affect the public life of the town. Yet their loss would be keenly felt and a multitude of the poor would suffer from their absence, for they are great in all charitable works, self-denying, and are ever ready to help the distressed.'[12]

[10] *D.P.*, 25.2.1875, p. 8, 2.3.1875, p. 8, 4.3.1875, p. 8; 'Our Representatives XVIII', *B.M.N.*, 26.4.75.
[11] Speech at a dinner given in his honour, 9.11.1876. C. W. Boyd, ed., *Speeches*, I, 72–3.
[12] 'Our Social Life', *The Town Crier*, March 1869, p. 3.

Ten years later this was no longer true. From 1878–82 the Town Council contained as many as nine Quaker members, and in subsequent years Quakers continued to be well to the fore. Their contribution to public life was disproportionate to their numbers, even making allowance for the high proportion of wealthy and educated men among them. But something else had changed. In 1869 the distinction between public life and philanthropic works had meant something; in 1879 it no longer did. The Quakers were still great in all charitable works, but among these were now numbered service on the improvement committee, the baths and parks, the lunatic asylum and industrial school committees of the Town Council. With the addition of the health committee, these could well be called the philanthropic agencies of the Council. They were also those on which the Quakers served longest and in greatest numbers.[13] This kind of work made an obvious appeal to them. But the timing of the Quaker recruitment was different from that of orthodox Evangelical Dissent. As close-knit a community of families as the Unitarians, as susceptible to the call of education as to that of other aspects of philanthropy, they experienced the pull of the Town Council in their own way.

Between 1866 and 1873 the number of Quakers on the Town Council increased from two to seven. Since the Quaker community had not provided a single new recruit to the Council for twenty-three years this was quite a change. The new wave began with two candidatures in 1866, those of George Braithwaite Lloyd and George Baker. Lloyd was a close friend of Arthur Ryland, one of Dawson's disciples on the Town Council. He had just retired from the family bank and had no business commitments more pressing than a directorship of the Midland Railway Company, when Ryland asked him to stand for a vacant seat on the Council. He was an abler man than the majority of his colleagues in 1866 and behaved with more decorum, but he was no reformer. In later years he was treated with goodwill by the Chamberlain party but never became a close collaborator. He disapproved of their private meetings to plan party tactics and consistently refused to attend.[14]

George Baker was much more of a political figure. A committee

---

[13] See H. M. Bailey, *The Contribution of Quakers to some aspects of local government in Birmingham, 1828-1902*, unpublished M.A. dissertation, University Birmingham, 1952 p. 242.

[14] *B.G.*, 25.5.1880; clr. 1866–1871, ald. 1871–1902, died 1903. 'Alderman Lloyd, being possessed of a cautious rather than a venturesome and aggressive disposition, always regarded it as somewhat of an irony that he should have been so intimately associated with the most progressive municipal corporation, the most aggressive railway company, and the most expansive banking concern in the Midlands.' *D.P.*, 9.2.1903.

member of the Liberal Association and a leading Liberal on the Board of Guardians, of which he was soon to become chairman, Baker stood in November for the same ward for which his fellow-Quaker had been elected seven months before. He was sponsored by a group of councillors and residents in opposition to the sitting member, whose conduct on the Council had given strong offence, but failed to dislodge him. When the chief organiser of the attempted coup retired the following year from the representation of another ward, he arranged for Baker to succeed him without much trouble.[15]

Hardly had he entered municipal politics when he found himself caught up by the same interests as Collings and Chamberlain who soon joined him. Keenly interested in popular education, he became a committee member of the Birmingham Education Society in 1868, a member of the Provisional Committee of the National Education League in 1869, and an unsuccessful candidate for the Birmingham School Board in November 1870. Moving in these circles and sharing their interests he must have felt that the service of the borough had been unduly neglected by the cultured and well-intentioned members of his own religious community. His municipal service as Avery's lieutenant would have convinced him of the need to improve the personnel of the Council. In 1875 someone exceptionally well informed on the inner history of the Liberal group wrote of him:

> 'He is one of the knot of men who have changed the composition of the Council. He has helped to weed out undesirable members and to send in their stead gentlemen with some qualifications and abilities for government. In this he has, thanks to his own energy and zeal and the co-operation of his friends, been eminently successful.'[16]

(a) *The Severn Street adult school*

One place where his friends were to be found was the adult school in Severn Street, conducted on Sunday mornings by members of the Bull Street Quaker Meeting. It was from its teachers, rather than from the Bull Street Meeting as such, that the Quaker town councillors were recruited.[17] The school was free from those characteristics of

[15] *D.P.*, 27.10.1866–2.11.1866; *B.G.*, 9.12.1867, p. 8.
[16] 'Our Representatives XIV', *B.M.N.*, 29.3.1875.
[17] George Braithwaite Lloyd (1866), George Baker (1867), Richard Cadbury Barrow (1871), John Edward Baker (1872), William White (1873), George Cadbury (1878), Richard Tangye (1878), Francis Corder Clayton (1882). For the remainder of this section where no specific references are given the authority is William White, *The Story of the Severn Street and Priory First-Day Schools, Birmingham* (Birmingham, 1895), and S. Price, *Severn Street Christian Society, a Short Sketch, 1873–1907* (Birmingham, 1907).

mid-Victorian Quakerism, which would have been distinctly hostile to the spirit of the municipal reform movement.[18] It was not the sort of institution to have been deliberately founded by the typical Quakers at that time, but owed almost everything to outside pressure and the initiative of one or two exceptional individuals.

It had begun as a Sunday school for older boys in 1845, but the boys dropped off and adults began to come in ever-growing numbers, so that in a short time the schools were completely and unexpectedly transformed. By force of circumstances the young Quaker teachers were led away from the normal religious work of their community into the heart of the social problems of the town.

In the mid-fifties the pupils were once again responsible for changing the character of the school. They had learnt to read and write, but instead of leaving, as was expected, they set up as pupil-teachers for the benefit of the many illiterates who would otherwise have been turned away. This made for a great increase in numbers.[19] It also meant that the now literate pupils were able to move towards a proper liberal education. But for this, the school and its later branches would never have achieved the incalculable influence among the working classes in Birmingham for which it was renowned. Moreover it enabled the Quakers to reach a stratum of the population which would otherwise have remained inaccessible to them. William White, the outstanding figure among the senior teachers, commented on the unique influence that the elementary teachers exercised:

'Very many men who have been introduced into our school have begun by sitting with these elementary teachers who would never have ventured in the first place to sit with someone whom they would suppose to be a little above them in social position, because there is really in some of these people a preparatory process necessary. They have to be brought into contact by degrees with the

---

[18] Rufus M. Jones, *The Later Periods of Quakerism* (1921), vol. II for a description of the attitude of mid-Victorian Quakers to politics. Also Elizabeth Isichei, *Victorian Quakers* (1970), which appeared after the completion of this chapter.

[19] The following table of the increase in numbers conveys some idea of the growing influence of the schools in the life of the town:

	Men	Women
1855	422	224
1865	789	318
1875	1738	535
1885	3082	798
1895	3396	968

Taken for the third quarter of the year. White, *Severn Street*, p. 124.

aristocracy of the working men, with whom they feel as far distant as we should with the great ones of the West End here.'[20]

This comment is a reminder of the degree to which the work of Severn Street was shaped by the class structure of the town. The slight graduations whereby the employer of fifty men shaded into the small sub-contractor, and he again via the under-cutting garret-master down to the unskilled labourer, had given Birmingham a social climate in marked contrast to some other parts of the country. On the one hand, it was favourable to the reclamation of the slum population. On the other, by giving the well-to-do employer ample contact with an energetic and superior type of 'working man', it encouraged the optimistic Radicalism which distinguished Birmingham from the days of Attwood to those of Joseph Chamberlain.[21]

There was less in the social or political atmosphere to encourage ideas of class-war or class-domination than in highly polarised communities. Even when the rank and file of Birmingham Chartists broke in 1839 with their middle-class leaders, ideas of class co-operation had been kept alive. They found their spokesman in Joseph Sturge, the founder of the Severn Street school. Sturge was an exceptional Quaker, not least in his manifold political activities and in the strong brand of Radicalism which he professed.[22] His powerful influence and the social climate of Birmingham gave to a section of the Birmingham Quakers a Radical tinge, which was in marked contrast to the Whiggism of the majority of Quaker communities at the time. It found a perfect expression in the adoption of Bright as M.P. for the borough in 1857. The Severn Street adult school was permeated by the same social philosophy. The Radicalism of its founder and his disciples gave it much of its distinctive atmosphere of brotherliness. It was one of the first examples of a courteous egalitarianism, in striking contrast to the patronising benevolence normal in its day.

Almost from the first, the school had taken on a momentum that was all its own. The Bull Street congregation watched with embarrassment the strange offspring of their philanthropy. When the school retained its literate pupils it acquired a strong corporate life. Under the

---

[20] William White, 'The Development of the Sunday School System in the Direction of Adult Instruction'. Paper read at the Autumnal Convention of the Sunday School Union, 1886, pp. 9–10.

[21] See footnote 20, p. 23.

[22] For Sturge's sponsorship of the Complete Suffrage Movement in 1842, see R. Tholfson, 'The Origins of the Birmingham Caucus', *Historical Jl.*, II, 2 (1959), 161–84. There is a *Life* of Sturge by Stephen Hobhouse (1919).

circumstances it could not fail to have a religious influence on the pupils, the great majority of whom had no connection with any place of worship. They were encouraged to join churches near their home, but many preferred to remain in the fellowship of the school. In response to a strong demand some of the teachers had begun to conduct Sunday worship on modified Quaker lines. The men who attended were 'too near Friends to go elsewhere', but Bull Street Meeting was loath to recognise the new congregation as a Quaker meeting. In 1873 a visiting American minister, Robert W. Douglas, saw the similarity of these Sunday services to his own missionary work in the U.S.A. Since English Quakers were too conservative to incorporate their converts into their own system, he urged them to provide them at least with some form of corporate membership. The outcome was the Severn Street Christian Society, a rudimentary organisation on Quaker lines, but not officially linked with the Society of Friends. It grew rapidly, started its own children's Sunday schools and spread into the suburbs, thereby duplicating the Quaker organisation. Still the parent body was too embarrassed to rise to the occasion. Not until the 1890s, when the adult school movement had spread all over the country and the character of English Quakerism began to change, were the first attempts made to welcome those who had been influenced by the adult schools into the Society of Friends. The move came thirty years too late and met with little success.

(b) *The battle against drink*

It was from this background with its mixture of individual initiative and official timidity that George Baker and his friends were drawn into the Town Council. Although none of the others were as closely involved in the educational controversies as he, all were committed to the cause of popular education. There was much in Dawson's teaching that must have appealed to them, not least what he and his disciples had to say on the dignity proper to municipal government.

Like the patrician Unitarians, or indeed the cultured Tories who sat on the governing body of the Free Grammar School, they resented the low tone of those who claimed to be the official representatives of the borough. Since the middle fifties the public house had been the main power in municipal politics, and to the large number of publicans on the Council must be added the larger number of their regular customers. The Quakers objected to the manners of the public house in the Council chamber not a whit less for objecting on principle to public houses as such. The prominent role of the Quakers in the English temperance movement of the nineteenth century is well documented. Brian Harrison's recent study lists 273 leaders of the teetotal cause between 1833 and 1872 whose religion he has been able to trace. Twenty-four per cent were Quakers. Particularly close were the links with the United Kingdom Alliance, the political arm of the movement which advocated local political action to curb the sale of drink. Among the 124 people who subscribed £5 or over to the Alliance in 1868–9 and whose religion could be discovered, fifty-three were Quakers.[23] What is true of Quakers in general is particularly true of the Birmingham Quakers associated with the Severn Street adult school. That local power should be in the hands of publicans and regular frequenters of their houses was to them as objectionable as were the manners of the Mayor and Corporation.

When considerations of dignity and temperance merged so closely they made a powerful appeal to a considerable section of citizens, among whom the Quakers were merely the most prominent. It is doubtful whether but for this fact so much would have been heard of the dignity of public life, as distinct from its duties and responsibilities. It soon became a commonplace to identify the political habits and presuppositions that had passed away by 1876 with the public house, *The Woodman* in Easy Row, which had been the favourite haunt of Brinsley, Sadler, Biggs, Cornforth and others.[24] 'The Woodman regime' is a phrase that occurs repeatedly in historical accounts of this era of Birmingham history. Popular myth identified the crucial turning point in the history of the municipal reform movement not with anything that occurred in the Council or in the ward elections, but with a public meeting held some time in 1873. Here is a relatively restrained account of the event:

> 'It was the custom in those days for several prominent members of the Town Council to meet at the "Woodman" a well-known tavern in the town, and to discuss Council business in a kind of informal caucus . . . The habit was, to say the least, undignified, and was strongly resented by those of the new school. Direct protest, of course, would have done more harm than good; but at last the opportunity came. It was at the time when the country rose in arms to support Mr. Plimsoll's demand that the Government should take action against unseaworthy ships. A town's meeting

---

[23] Brian Harrison, *Drink and the Victorians* (1971), pp. 165–6, 226.
[24] For a list of the habitués of *The Woodman* at this time, see *Birmingham Daily Mail*, 4.12.1909 (obituary of Ald. Ambrose Biggs). The house was closed in 1965 and the whole area has since been demolished in the course of the city's redevelopment.

was held at Birmingham, presided over by the Mayor. Mr. Vince, the Minister of Graham Street Chapel, was one of the speakers; a man of genial humour who always fought smiling. In his speech he reminded the meeting that the sailor's whole life was bounded by his ship. The ship was the sailor's home, and at the same time his prison, from week to week and from month to month. It was his Free Library and his Art Gallery; 'and if, Mr. Mayor', he continued, 'he wants to spend an hour in the parlour of the *Woodman*, the ship must be his *Woodman* too'. The Mayor of the day was generally understood to be one of the most regular frequenters of the tavern in question, and the sally was received with tumultuous laughter. Then suddenly the laughter stopped; the audience saw the reproof veiled in the jest, and with one impulse they began to applaud, steadily—one might almost say seriously—for several minutes. The significance of the demonstration was clear—the town had set up a new standard of dignity for its public men.'[25]

'There was nothing against the house', as the same writer explained on another occasion. 'It was not a drunken *Woodman*, or a dissolute *Woodman;* but it was a beery and a gin-and-watery *Woodman.*'[26]

This sums up to perfection all that offended the respectability of Edgbaston and roused the temperance advocates in a score of chapels to the fight. It may be of interest to see how the same house appeared through the eyes of a sympathetic customer one spring night in 1856:

'The room on this occasion was nearly full; Walsh occupied the principal seat. Not far from him was the versatile, erudite, somewhat dogmatic, but always courteous and polite, John Cornforth. There too was Ambrose Biggs, who since, as Mayor, so fully justified the choice the Corporation made when they elected him to be their head.[27] Nearly opposite was seen the gentlemanlike figure of poor Joseph Collins, whose untimely death a few years later created an intense sorrow in the minds of all who knew him. The worthy host, Jem Onions, occupied his usual seat. At a short distance was seen the upright figure and full round face of genial, but somewhat fussy George Tye, his countenance beaming with good nature, and his eye bright with the light of poetic and artistic intelligence.'[28]

[25] A. W. W. Dale, *Life of R. W. Dale* (1899), pp. 403–4.
[26] A. W. W. Dale, 'George Dawson' in J. H. Muirhead (ed.), *Nine Famous Birmingham Men* (1909), p. 104.
[27] Compare the different judgment on pp. 136–7.
[28] Eliezer Edwards, *Personal Recollections of Birmingham and Birmingham Men* (1877), p. 72.

To defeat such men, not least to debar the worthy host of similar or less respectable houses from local political power, appeared a most desirable object to members of the United Kingdom Alliance, both Quakers and others. It had brought the Congregationalist Josiah Derrington into local politics in 1870, and was a major consideration in the two most spectacular contests of the campaign of 1873, which put Chamberlain firmly into power. Eighteen months later the victory of William White was still remembered as 'one of the greatest ever achieved in our town in the cause of progress and reform'.

> 'Mr. Michael Maher's seat in St. Mary's Ward might indeed have been deemed impregnable. The solicitor to the licensed victuallers, the prominent Roman Catholic with hereditary claims on the burgesses, might surely have been deemed safe against any ordinary opposition, but it was no ordinary candidate that was now in the field. "Who is Mr. William White?" the St. Mary's burgesses might have asked not unreasonably, and from every quarter of the town there flocked into the ward an army of unpaid canvassers, each eager to do a little to repay his benefactor, by testifying who he was and what he had done.'[29]

In such a fashion was the most unpolitical of Quaker philanthropists launched on a public career which lasted until his death. He had before him the example of several colleagues at Severn Street, and particularly of William Cook, his pupil and class secretary, who had been elected the previous year.[30] But for White, president of the Birmingham Band of Hope Union, perhaps the greatest inducement of all was the prospect of driving out the well-known champion of the liquor trade.

Scarcely second to the contest in St. Mary's, and strictly parallel in kind, was that in St. Martin's Ward against Wadhams, the president of the Licensed Victuallers Defence League and a town councillor of many years' standing. The reformers' candidate, Robert Arculus, was a lay preacher in charge of a mission chapel in the ward, a branch of Carr's Lane church. Since he was also a glass manufacturer and treasurer of the local Y.M.C.A., it is not surprising that he had previously taken almost no part in public affairs. He was close to Dale and the first of the Evangelical Dissenters to go on the Town Council in support of the reform movement. What must have weighed with him strongly in a decision

[29] 'Our Representative XVIII', *B.M.N.*, 26.4.1875.
[30] See above, p. 101.

which contributed to his early death,[31] was the knowledge that only his reputation in the ward would suffice to snuff out Birmingham's leading publican for ever.

The candidature of John Edward Baker also showed signs of temperance considerations, nor were they altogether absent from that of his brother.[32] But by 1878 when George Cadbury stood for Rotton Park and 'beer could be had as freely as rain-water' the boot was on the other foot. For on this occasion it was Cadbury's reputation as an extreme prohibitionist that brought the publicans into the fray.[33]

In the particular situation of Birmingham hostility to the public house easily became hostility to the group who dominated municipal affairs. It linked up with a demand for 'a new standard of dignity for its public men', which was partly an assertion of the nobility and dignity of public life and partly a call for the services of 'men of the highest ability and culture'. In consequence the *Woodman* regime was replaced by one whose leading members met in the library of Southbourne, Chamberlain's house in Edgbaston. Instead of sipping gin and water they formed part of what Chamberlain called his 'tobacco parliament'.[34] From one point of view the difference between the sawdust of the *Woodman* and the carpets of Southbourne seems trivial; but in terms of the class location of municipal politics the shift was momentous.

This link between temperance politics and the recruitment of a different social class of councillors was not fortuitous, but neither was the connection necessary and inevitable in mid-Victorian provincial England. It is a fact that temperance politics frequently became a prominent feature of municipal life in the 1870s. But they did not have the same consequences everywhere. In Leeds we shall find them associated with a style of administration that had more in common with Brinsley than with Chamberlain. Quaker temperance advocates, however fastidious in their own conduct, found their allies there among men for whom hostility to the public house did not imply a rejection of the manners of the tap-room.

[31] He died of a stroke on 15 November 1875. He had recently been intending to give up some of his public duties, *D.P.*, 16.11.1875.

[32] For J. E. Baker, *D.P.*, 14.9.1872, p. 8, 17.9.1872, p. 5. For George Baker, *D.P.*, 9.12.1867, p. 8.

[33] A. G. Gardiner, *Life of George Cadbury* (1923), pp. 67–9.

[34] J. L. Garvin, *Life of Joseph Chamberlain*, (1932), I 177–8.

6

The Contribution of R. W. Dale

I HIS THOUGHT

It has been pointed out in a previous chapter that there was a time-lag between the heterodox Dissenters' concern for municipal service and that of their Evangelical fellows. This is not strange for Dawson was peculiarly unsuited to be the teacher of orthodox Evangelical Dissent. Yet in time they came to adopt the views of which he had been the first exponent. The new functions assumed by the Corporation after 1873 contributed to this development. So did Chamberlain's attempt to bring home the implications of them to the town in general and the churches in particular. But the foundations had been laid by the work of R. W. Dale, minister of the Congregational church at Carr's Lane.

Dale had himself come under Dawson's influence at the most impressionable stage of his life and was therefore peculiarly well fitted to act as the mediator of what Dawson had to teach. While a student at Spring Hill College, he had attended the Church of the Saviour for two years at least once, if not twice, every Sunday. For four more years he went to hear Dawson as often as his own preaching engagements permitted, and only broke off the connection in June 1853, when he left college to settle at Carr's Lane.[1] The thought and personality of George Dawson made a deep impression on him. His biographer found that almost every letter that survived from 1847–9 contained a reference to Dawson's teaching. An article written in 1877 shows how vivid his recollection, particularly of the ethical sermons, still was after thirty years.[2] What attracted him was the originality of Dawson's thought and manner.

The college authorities were disturbed, as well they might be. He would not have been the first promising student training for the Congregational ministry to have run onto the rocks of heterodoxy. But they

[1] A. W. W. Dale, *Life of R. W. Dale* (1899), pp. 50–51.
[2] R. W. Dale, 'George Dawson', *Nineteenth Century*, II (August 1877), pp. 44–61.

were too wise to make an issue of it, and their judgment was rewarded. For the cast of Dale's mind was such that he could not long remain content with the woolliness of thought that, for all its shrewdness, lay behind Dawson's attractive preaching. Dawson was 'a creature of intimations', Dale a solid and logical thinker who won the gold medal for philosophy at London University. 'Massive' was the word applied to his mind repeatedly on later occasions.[3] Herein lay his second qualification as Dawson's interpreter to the Evangelical churches. For he was incapable of becoming a mere echo. He would have to think Dawson's message out anew for himself.

The chief lesson that he had learnt from his attendance at the Church of the Saviour was the importance of insisting with clarity and vigour on the everyday duties of life. Dawson's talent for presenting moral teaching in practical terms filled the young man with admiration and occasionally with despair. Although his own natural tendency was towards abstract ideas, he disciplined himself deliberately to emulate what he rightly considered the most conspicuous merit of Dawson's preaching. In the first flush of his ministry he had given full rein to his love of doctrine, but as he became more familiar with the needs of his congregation moral teaching came to occupy an equally conspicuous place. The discovery that his hearers were disposed to resent a sermon 'on weights and measures', as they described it, roused his concern and his fighting spirit. Quite in Dawson's vein he complained

> 'that an undue emphasis is laid upon the worth of religious emotion, and that the sacredness of the practical duties of life is depreciated.'[4]

This new stage in his development as a religious teacher dated from the summer of 1860. He now began to work at the lessons learnt from the effortless excellence of George Dawson. To descend quickly from the general to the particular required not only a quick eye for the world in which he moved. It required also a knowledge of practical life as it was lived by the laymen of his congregation, such as does not easily come to a minister. He would have liked occasionally to have given up his pulpit to a solicitor, banker or merchant who could have spoken with the

---

[3] D. C. Murray in appendix to Wright Wilson, *Dawson*, p. 214; J. G. Rogers, *Memorial Sermon preached in Carr's Lane Chapel on the occasion of the death of Dr. R. W. Dale* (1895), p. 10; H. F. Keep, 'Dale of Birmingham', in *Transactions of the Congregational Historical Society*, X (1929), p. 248.

[4] 'Morality and Religion'. Sermon preached on the 13.8.1865, R. W. Dale, *Discourses Delivered on Special Occasions* (1866), p. 41.

authority that only experience can command. But the custom of the churches was against it, nor would it have been easy to find suitable men.[5] He therefore set out to study systematically the inner working of the shop, the office and the factory, and acquired a knowledge of affairs that often astonished those who met him. It was typical of him that on his return from a visit to Australia he published his impressions in five articles in which a formidable range of knowledge was deployed. He had consulted not only the denominational, criminal and educational statistics, but the distribution of population, of climate and fertility, detailed agricultural statistics of many kinds, the output of coal, tin and copper mines, the comparative import of wool from Australia and the Argentine and the prices paid on the London market. He quoted the interest paid on the capital of Australian railway companies and other investment figures, the maximum size of land holdings and the tonnage of vessels using the different Australian ports. In addition he had gone through the reports of several important royal commissions on the economic potentialities of the colonies.[6]

During the first half of the 1860s he applied in his own way the lessons that he had learnt as a student from Dawson. He warned young men against establishing themselves in independent business on insufficient capital. To the steady trickle of bankruptcies among his church members he reacted by setting up an eleventh commandment: 'Thou shalt make a balance sheet.' At a time when limited liability companies were springing up as the result of the Act of 1862 he directed some trenchant remarks from the pulpit of Carr's Lane, and in print, against

> 'country clergymen and devout widows who are shocked when they see three or four commercial travellers playing Poker or Nap in a railway carriage for coppers [but] are bribed by a promise of 10 or 15 per cent to risk half their capital in all kinds of insane adventures.
> 'What can they know of the real character of some of the schemes in which they take shares? It may be perfectly safe for men who live among merchants, railway people, and stockbrokers, and who find the *Economist* newspaper light and pleasant reading, to invest . . . in London land schemes which are to pay 25 per cent, and in companies for running steam boats on the Danube; but what right have

[5] 'Morality and Religion', R. W. Dale, *Discourses on Special Occasions*, p. 45. A. W. W. Dale, *Life*, p. 144, for comment.
[6] R. W. Dale, 'Impressions of Australia', *Contemporary Review*, LIV–LV (November 1888–April 1889).

most of us to touch things of this kind? . . . We might just as well stake our money at *rouge-et-noire* in a saloon at Baden-Baden.'[7]

While insisting on 'the use of the understanding in keeping God's law', his strongest words were reserved for the sins of omission. He saw that the moral ideal of the Evangelical churches had become seriously perverted and enfeebled by a superficial view of what was meant by worldliness. This had led religious men to abstain altogether from some matters of importance, while making them insensitive to the proper distinction between right and wrong in those pursuits which they considered lawful.[8] Few things, he felt, had suffered more from this false distinction than the political life of the nation. As a student he had already been keen on national politics, and he set out to dispel the timid prejudices on this subject that were common among Evangelicals of his day.[9]

When he visited America in 1877 he was appalled to find a state of affairs far worse than anything he had known in England even at the start of his ministry—the rogues doing public work in order to make money, and the honest men neglecting it in order to save money. 'Judged by the laws of public morality, there is not much to choose between them.' To the theological students of Yale he spoke with some warmth on this vice of the churches:

'For men to claim the right to neglect their duties to the State on the grounds of their piety, while they insist on the State protecting their homes, protecting their property, and protecting from disturbance even their religious meetings in which this exquisitely delicate and valetudinarian spirituality is developed, is gross unrighteousness.'[10]

The interesting thing about his speeches and sermons in the early 1860s is that they contain no reference to the claims of municipal politics, even where this would have been appropriate. This omission suggests that his mind was not yet working along those lines.

The duty to serve the community on the Town Council had become a familiar theme in Dawson's immediate circle by 1861, but the earliest

[7] R. W. Dale, 'Impressions of Australia V', *Contemporary Review*, LV (April 1889), 579; 'The Use of the Understanding in keeping God's Law', R. W. Dale, *Week-Day Sermons* (1867), pp. 19–20.
[8] 'Amusements', R. W. Dale, *Week-Day Sermons*, pp. 183 ff.
[9] R. W. Dale, *Churchmen and Dissenters. A Lecture delivered in the Town Hall, Birmingham* (1862), pp. 22–3; also *D.P.*, 30.1.1864, p. 3.
[10] R. W. Dale, 'Impressions of America II', *Nineteenth Century*, III (April 1878), p. 767; R. W. Dale, *Nine Lectures on Preaching* (1877), p. 258.

evidence from Dale is a sermon published in April 1867 and presumably delivered not long before. This makes it about contemporary with his conversion to a belief in the need for rate-provided schools controlled by elected local authorities.[11] The sermon largely followed the lines of one delivered in 1863,[12] but when he spoke of the obligations incumbent on prosperous men he struck a note not found before:

> 'They ought to feel "called of God" to act as "Guardians of the Poor." They ought to work on the Committees of Hospitals. They ought to be Aldermen and Town Councillors. They ought to give their time as well as their money to whatever improvements are intended to develop the intelligence of the community. They ought to be reformers of local abuses. They ought to see to it that the towns and parishes in which they live are well drained, well lighted, and well paved; that there are good schools for every class of the population; that there are harmless public amusements; that all parochial and municipal affairs are conducted honourably and equitably. In nearly every part of the country I hear that prosperous manufacturers and merchants leaving public duties in the hands of men of lower position and culture than themselves. They shrink from the roughness of local elections, and from the alleged coarseness of language and manners of the actual leaders of local parties. But this is to forget that self-denial must be endured in the discharge of nearly every duty. And if they were more active and energetic, the power which is now in inferior hands would be their own. Even the mob prefer a gentleman to a blackguard in the long run. When the prosperous people of a free nation cease to take an active interest in the public life of the towns and cities in which they live, the political greatness and stability of their country are exposed to the most serious dangers.'[13]

The call to municipal reform had reached the Evangelical Dissenters. It was another six eventful years before they answered it.

When considering the municipal reform movement in Birmingham it is important to distinguish between feelings on the one hand and doctrine on the other. The assumption by public authorities of functions once associated with the churches had focused a marked sense of religious

---

[11] A. W. W. Dale, *Life*, p. 268.
[12] R. W. Dale, 'The Suburban Pastor', *Discourses on Special Occasions*, p. 338.
[13] 'The Perils and Uses of Rich Men', R. W. Dale, *Week-Day Sermons*, pp. 175–6.

obligation on the Town Council. This had been given intellectual expression by a doctrine about the nature of local authorities, which represented them as the modern equivalent of churches. The doctrine had been the creation of the heterodox Dissenters and in particular of George Dawson. As the last quotation shows, Dale shared the sense of religious obligation. But he rejected the doctrine. Another man might have been satisfied merely to preach the duty of municipal service. While tacitly rejecting Dawson's doctrine, he need not have replaced it by another more in keeping with orthodox Christianity. But to Dale such eclecticism was impossible for two reasons. In the first place he was too much of a theologian not to want to relate all aspects of his thought to the central doctrines of the Faith. Secondly to have done so would have implied tacit assent to Dawson's view of the Church. In that case he might never have captured the ear of his denomination, or else have become a disintegrating force whose destructiveness was in proportion to the influence that he acquired. For both these reasons Dale was driven to become the exponent of an alternative doctrine which was neither degrading to the new role of the State nor destructive of the Church. The process by which he did this must now be examined.

Dale's admiration for George Dawson's freshness and moral insight was always tempered with a regret that he had 'not more of the old Evangelical doctrine'. For the lack of this, he felt, no genius, however fresh, could ever compensate.[14] He knew that much of Dawson's scorn for the decaying structure of Calvinist theology, whose phrases were still in use although few believed them as they had once been believed, was justified. He was convinced of the need to re-examine old doctrines. While hardly out of college he had preached on the Epistle to the Romans and caused consternation by his rejection of Calvinist dogmas.[15] In 1866–7 appeared his first articles on the doctrine of the Atonement and his lectures on the same subject were published in 1875.[16] They represented his most important contribution to the theological reconstruction which he declared to be the great need of the day.

'The Protestant attempt to recast theological thought in scholastic forms has broken down . . . .. The elaborate and stately system of theological belief which had been created by the theologians of the

[14] A. W. W. Dale, *Life*, p. 53.
[15] *Life*, pp. 109–15.
[16] R. W. Dale, 'The Moral Theory of the Atonement', *British Quarterly Review*, 44 (October 1866); 'The Expiatory Theory of the Atonement', *Ibid.*, 46 (October 1867); R. W. Dale, *The Atonement* (1875).

Reformed Church, has been sinking into decay for two centuries. And, as yet, no other organised theological system has taken its place.

That seems to be a great evil. For it shows that we have no intellectual expression of the contents of faith which satisfies us . . .. While the intellect has no part, or very little part, in the religious life, the religious life will never have in it the elements of enduring vigour. The work of reconstruction must, I think, be done piece by piece. We may be satisfied if in a generation we make one or two great doctrines clearer and are able to define them with more precision. . . .

A strong intellectual conception of the great truths of the Christian faith is a real aid to moral and religious vigor. Where thought is vague, character is likely to be feeble.'[17]

In their analysis of the contemporary religious situation, Dawson and Dale were in fundamental agreement. It was in their reaction to it that the deep difference showed. Dawson's close friend G. J. Johnson accurately interpreted his views when he wrote:

'The objection generally made to Mr. Dawson's doctrinal teaching was that it did not embody itself in any set of propositions, or, as it has been since expressed, that it was concerned with the production of pictures, not of maps. Had the objection been put to him in that form he would most probably have answered that for practical conduct a map was not requisite. . . .

What is wanted from the preacher is not a map but motive-power, and this (he could have truly said) I do my best to supply. And as for making maps, it is not my fault that the science of the nineteenth century has produced the same effect on the theological maps of the sixteenth as did the discovery of America on the maps of the fifteenth century. These discoveries have advanced sufficiently far to enable me to pronounce your old map erroneous and incomplete, and yet not far enough to enable me to construct a perfectly accurate new one.'[18]

[17] 'The Ministry Required by the Age' (November 1890), R. W. Dale, *Fellowship with Christ and other Discourses* (1891), pp. 263–6. He had expressed similar views throughout his ministry, e.g. 'Genius the Gift of God', (April 1864), R. W. Dale, *Discourses on Special Occasions*, pp. 277–8; 'The Work of the Ministry in a Period of Theological Decay and Reconstruction' (June 1880); *The Evangelical Revival and Other Sermons* (1880), especially pp. 274–5.
[18] G. J. Johnson in Wright Wilson, *Dawson*, pp. 183–4.

There was much sense in this view. But when it is placed alongside Dale's reaction to the same dilemma we can see why Dale felt that Dawson 'disparaged the functions of the intellect in relation to religious truth'.[19]

> 'The old maps of the country may be more or less inaccurate; they may have become untrustworthy; but this is generally acknowledged and nothing is to be gained by further attacks on them; give us another map that shall more truly represent the outlines of the coast, the lie of the mountains, the course of the rivers; if you can only give us a fairly accurate map of a single district, this will be more to the purpose than your demonstration of the untrustworthiness of the old maps of the continent.'[20]

While therefore he learnt much from Dawson's moral preaching, the difference between the two became increasingly marked. His first volume of moral sermons, published in 1867, showed all Dawson's preference for a morality that was positive and would lead to action rather than abstention, his delight in robustness and his repugnance for the neutral tints of character. These qualities were to remain with him all his life. But what he aimed at in the years that followed and increasingly achieved was to expound as concretely as possible the implications to be drawn for conduct from the central doctrines of the Christian faith.[21] He set out to show 'the sacredness of what is called secular business' and to present 'a new and Christian conception of the industrial and commercial pursuits of mankind'.[22] The most mature of this collection of moral sermons, *The Laws of Christ for Common Life* (1884), was devoted entirely to this task, from the sermon 'Every-Day Business a Divine Calling' with which it opened, to 'An Ethical Revival' with which it closed. Right at the heart of it was to be found his exposition of political and municipal duty.

> 'I sometimes think that municipalities can do more for the people than Parliament. Their powers will probably be enlarged; but under the powers which they possess already they can greatly diminish the amount of sickness in the community, and can prolong human life. They can prevent—they have prevented—tens of

---

[19] R. W. Dale, 'George Dawson', *Nineteenth Century*, II, 56.
[20] 'The Ministry Required by the Age', R. W. Dale, *Fellowship with Christ*, pp. 255–6.
[21] See the sermons of 1879 especially 'Morality and the Evangelical Faith' in R. W. Dale, *The Evangelical Revival and Other Sermons* (1880).
[22] R. W. Dale, *The Evangelical Revival*, pp. 37–8.

thousands of children from becoming orphans. They can do very much to improve those miserable homes which are fatal not only to health, but to decency and morality. They can give to the poor the enjoyment of pleasant parks and gardens, and the intellectual cultivation and refinement of public libraries and galleries of art. They can redress in many ways the inequalities of human conditions. The gracious words of Christ, 'Inasmuch as ye did it unto one of these my brethren, even these least, ye did it unto Me.' will be addressed not only to those who with their own hands fed the hungry, and clothed the naked, and cared for the sick, but to those who supported a municipal policy which lessened the miseries of the wretched, and added brightness to the lives of the desolate. And the terrible rebuke, "Inasmuch as ye did it not unto one of these least, ye did it not unto Me." will condemn the selfishness of those who refused to make municipal government the instrument of a policy of justice and humanity.

'If years ago, the Christian people of the metropolis had insisted on having an effective system of municipal government and had worked its powers vigorously, the "Bitter Cry of Outcast London" need never have been heard. Now that the cry has come to them the churches will never be able to remedy the evil apart from the action of municipal authorities. Medicine, and not the gospel only, is necessary to cure the sick. Municipal action, not the gospel only, is necessary to improve the homes of the poor.'[23]

The sermon from which this extract is taken contained the most thorough exposition of his doctrine of the State. He set out to interpret Romans, chapter XIII, in terms suited to the new role of government.

'Civil authority—this is the main point I want to assert—is a Divine institution. The man who holds municipal or political office is a "minister of God". One man may, therefore, have just as real a Divine vocation to become a town councillor or a Member of Parliament, as another to become a missionary to the heathen. In either case it is a man's peril that he is "disobedient to the heavenly vision". The Divine right of Kings was a base corruption of a most noble truth; so was the fanatical dream about "the reign of the saints". We shall never approach to the Christian ideal of civil

---

[23] 'Political and Municipal Duty', R. W. Dale, *The Laws of Christ for Common Life* (1884), pp. 198–200. *The Bitter Cry of Outcast London* was the arresting title of an anonymous pamphlet published by the London Congregational Union in 1883 which drew attention to the housing conditions of East London, and created no small stir.

society, until all who hold municipal, judicial, and political offices, recognise the social and political order of the nation as a Divine institution, and discharge their official duties as ministers of God.'[24]

It will be seen from this that Dale no less than Dawson was emphasising the religious character of the State. Wherein lay the difference between the two? It lay in what he had to say about the character of the Church. Like most Nonconformists of his generation Dale had originally been forced to think about the nature of the Church by the challenge contained in the teaching of the Oxford Movement. In 1866 his ideas still followed the lines suggested by that controversy.[25] But after 1870 he very carefully re-examined his views on the subject in a very different context. His son has pointed out that he habitually reacted to the stimulus of his intellectual environment[26] and it may be assumed that one of the main reasons for this new departure was provided by the events which form the theme of this study.

The challenge, as he now saw it, came not from the pretensions of High Churchmen but from the ecclesiastical modesty of those concerned with social reform. Was a Christian church to be truly understood by the 'Christian work' that it did? Dale answered on a level higher than that to which Evangelical Nonconformists were then accustomed. He insited that 'the Church is not an artificial Society or voluntary Club', 'distinguished from the Royal Institution, or the College of Surgeons, or the Association for the Promotion of Social Science, or a Freemason's Lodge, only by its greater antiquity, and the superior importance of the objects for which it is maintained.' 'The Church is always a society of men who have received the Holy Ghost, and entered into the Kingdom of Heaven.' 'It is the organic realisation of the supernatural oneness of those who have been made "partakers of the Divine nature", and of the kinship of the sons of God.'[27]

There could be no firmer rejection of everything for which Dawson had stood in Birmingham since he had promulgated his Church Principles in 1846. At the same time Dale was accepting everything that

[24] *Ibid.*, p. 193.
[25] 'Anglicanism and Romanism', *British Quarterly Review*, 43 (April 1866). It was occasioned by the controversy over Pusey's *Eirenicon* (1865).
[26] A. W. W. Dale, *Life*, p. 200.
[27] 'The Idea of the Church in Relation to Modern Congregationalism', in H. R. Reynolds, ed., *Ecclesia. A Second Series of Essays on Theological and Ecclesiastical Questions* (1871), reprinted in R. W. Dale, *Essays and Addresses*, (1899), pp. 153, 123, 122, 153. Contrast this with a typical statement of the time: 'The Congregational Church is nothing more than as association of persons for spiritual objects'. W. M. Fawcett and others, *The Congregational Polity: Religious Republics* (1869), p. 1, quoted in J. W. Grant, *Free Churchmanship in England 1870–1940* (1955).

Dawson had ever taught about the family life of the nation. But for him the rejection of exaggerated individualist theories had implications for the *Church* as well as for the *State*. On no account would he allow the new emphasis on the positive role of the State to lead to a denigration of the Church. He saw the danger which the Church incurred by clinging to emasculated individualist conceptions and warned against it. If men, he wrote, 'cannot find a home—a real home—in a true Church, they will enter a false Church rather than be without any home at all'.[28] This was a reference to Roman Catholicism but the warning applied no less to the collectivist religion of the State, whose shape was then but as a small cloud on the horizon.

2 HIS INFLUENCE

There is a final question to be asked about Dale. How great was his actual influence on the public life of Birmingham?

As a platform speaker his popularity was second only to that of Bright. He had all the vigour and stamina needed for the crowded and often turbulent political meetings that characterised the borough. Opposition never disconcerted him as it did Dawson. His son's description here is admirable.

> 'The vigour with which he pulled off his overcoat as he rose to speak was a sure sign of what was coming; and when both political parties were present in force, he ploughed along through the storm with the steady rush of an Atlantic liner as it shoulders its way through blustering seas.'[29]

There was nothing clerical about his costume or his manner. He had discarded the white tie early in the sixties and grown not merely a beard but, after some hesitation, a moustache; this at a time when a moustache was still thought to impart 'an air of levity and worldliness'. His character was not easily judged from his appearance. Large in build with a swarthy complexion, he looked like a prosperous merchant or manufacturer. 'Robust' was one of his favourite words, and it well described a quality in him which was much appreciated. 'What a splendid fellow Dale is', P. H. Muntz had said to Bright during the election campaign of 1874, 'he always reminds me of the Church Militant'. Bright quoted

---

[28] 'The Evangelical Revival', R. W. Dale, *The Evangelical Revival and other Sermons*, p. 33.
[29] A. W. W. Dale, *Life*, p. 404.

the remark shortly afterwards in public, and the crowd roared its appreciation.[30]

He could always be relied on for the work of local politics and his membership of almost every political and quasi-political body, with the exception of the Town Council from which he was debarred, attests the extent of his influence. The power of his example in this respect was very great because it was so patently not accompanied by neglect of his primary duties or a shallow religious life. His example affected many who were incapable of responding to the quality of his intellect.

In 1871, when he was thinking of leaving Carr's Lane for a London chapel, the utmost concern was felt by 'all who cared for the intellectual, moral and political life of Birmingham'. Official resolutions were passed and a letter by a selected number of the town's leading men urged him on public grounds to remain.[31]

A tribute to his hold on the town came from so different a person as Cardinal Newman. It must be added that Dale was not equally enthusiastic about Newman's incarceration of himself in the Oratory at Edgbaston.[32] More important, in view of the peculiar religious composition of the town, were the cordial relations which existed between him and the leaders of heterodox Dissent.[33] The deep divergence in their creed was not allowed to endanger their co-operation in public work, and the oft-predicted split within the Radical camp between Dale and J. S. Wright on the one hand, and Chamberlain, Collings and Harris on the other, never occurred. When division came in 1886 it ran along altogether different lines. For Dale it signalised the time to withdraw from political life.

It was Chamberlain and his Unitarian friends in Parliament and in the National Liberal Federation who in the long run exercised the major control over the political developments that sprang from the Birmingham municipal reform movement. Dale had had his moments of influence,[34] but he was not in a position to make himself really effective in politics. He had deliberately refused to consider a seat in Parliament. The House of Commons he felt to be incompatible with the pastorate, and for him there could be no question of abandoning his work as a Christian minister.[35]

[30] A. W. W. Dale, *Life*, p. 203; *B.G.*, 14.3.1895 (obituary); 'Our Representatives XX', *B.M.N.*, 31.5.1875.
[31] A. W. W. Dale, *Life*, pp. 300–301.
[32] *Life*, pp. 209, 532.
[33] See the comment in 'Our Representatives XX', *B.M.N.*, 31.5.1875.
[34] E.g. over the leadership of the Liberal Party in 1875. A. W. W. Dale, *Life*, pp. 297–9.
[35] *Life*, pp. 295–6.

The power of his example did much for the municipal reform movement. But his own distinctive contribution was largely an intellectual one. His actions could be misunderstood, and wrongly imitated if the grounds on which he took them were not appreciated. Since all his important teaching was given in the pulpit, even if it soon found its way into print, his pulpit influence is of some importance. Here the standard which he set himself was uncompromisingly high, and so was the standard required from his audience. The sermons, especially the important ones, were closely knit arguments, and much of their importance lay in their sense of balance. Dale was continually asking himself how effective he was as a teacher, but he was hardly the best judge. The most reliable evidence comes from a Methodist who observed the life of Carr's Lane closely over an extended period. He wrote of his first visit:

'The sermon betrayed most of the features which I found from repeated visits were Dr. Dale's characteristics. First of all it required every scrap of knowledge and intelligence I possessed to grasp his meaning and follow the stringent, unpicturesque logic. I was convinced then, as I was upon dozens of later visits, that to hundreds of his hearers he must have been largely unintelligible, and that he influenced them, as he undoubtedly did influence them, rather by the fine rhetorical splendour of his discourse, and the sense of intellectual and spiritual mastery, together with the intense atmosphere of moral integrity with which he impregnated the very building, than by the exact truth that the sermon dealt with. This of course does not apply to many who have been reared under him and had caught by long experience the dominating notes of his theology.'[36]

The negative part of this judgment was undoubtedly accurate in many cases. The writer was also correct to draw attention to the influence of his personality in filling the gap. 'Ah me', said an old woman of sixty-five, 'I cannot understand his sermons but his prayers do me so much good that I always come.'[37] His public prayers were in fact widely appreciated.

More important to this study is his influence among the substantial members of the congregation who were reared under him. They appear to have caught the dominant features of his theology, although even

[36] W. S. King, ' "Dale of Birmingham", a Remembrance and an Estimate', *British Monthly* (February 1904), p. 127.
[37] A. W. W. Dale, *Life*, pp. 644, 592.

they complained at times about the hardness of his preaching. He certainly demanded a congregation of trained hearers but the notable thing was that he seems to have obtained it.[38] To this judgment the delay before his people took up the public service which he was commending to their conscience provides no objection. Such work took time, no less for Dawson than for Dale. When the Evangelical Dissenters did take up municipal service they did not talk as Dawson and Chamberlain were talking about the Church. That must be accounted some measure of Dale's success.

Something more than this may be said of his work among the young members of the Church. From 1865–9 he took a class of about seventy to eighty young people in theological subjects, and from this there developed in the latter year a young men's Bible class under a certain Henry Hindmarsh. For thirty years this class enjoyed a strong corporate life. Its meetings were followed by informal discussions over tea on social and political themes, and a remarkable proportion of its members proceeded to positions of influence in civic life. It was the beginning of a strong tradition of enlightened work among young people with an emphasis on public service which continued to characterise the church well after Hindmarsh's death.[39] Dale himself was very close to the group, who called him 'The Headmaster'. At least one of them applied to him in subsequent years the lines of Matthew Arnold:

> 'Therefore to thee it was given
> Many to save with thyself;
> And, at the end of thy day,
> O faithful shepherd! to come,
> Bringing thy sheep in thy hand.'[40]

Over the other Evangelical Dissenting ministers in the town his influence was immense. He attached great importance to contact between them, and was partly responsible for instituting regular meetings. Through his published sermons, he was a model for many.[41] Among them, only Charles Vince, the Baptist minister of Mount Zion Chapel, Graham Street, held a position in the public life of the town at all comparable to Dale's. But despite popular tradition to the contrary

---

[38] R. F. Horton, 'Robert William Dale', *Contemporary Review*, LXXV (1899), 39.
[39] A. H. Driver, *Carr's Lane 1748–1948* (1948), pp. 65–6.
[40] From 'Rugby Chapel'. W. S. King, 'Dale of Birmingham', *British Monthly* (February 1904), pp. 131–2; H. F. Keep, 'Dale of Birmingham' in *Transactions of the Congregational Historical Society*, X (1929), 249.
[41] A. W. W. Dale, *Life*, p. 205.

Vince's contribution to the municipal reform movement was not great. His speech at the mayor's luncheon in 1866 has been mentioned, but one searches the volume of his sermons, published in 1875 when the municipal reform movement was at its height, in vain for a single relevant reference.[42] His public work focused rather on the School Board, the National Education League and the Central Nonconformist Committee, the Nonconformist educational pressure group. He was in general a conventional Radical of the Dissenting sort, keen on Disestablishment and on humanitarian causes.[43] Like the rest of the Liberal Association he was drawn into municipal politics, but when he spoke in support of Chamberlain in 1872, he mentioned that this was 'the first municipal election in which he had ever taken a public part'.[44]

When Vince died suddenly in October 1874, shortly after the triumph of the Chamberlain group with which he had been politically associated, his part in the struggle was generously magnified in memorial sermons and obituaries. His funeral was a great public display of respect. But those best qualified to judge did not claim an outstanding place for him in the municipal reform movement. The legend that associates him prominently with the municipal transformation springs from less reliable sources, or from men whose memory had to reach back a long way. He was a successful pastor, but his church provided no recruits to the reforming party on the Council either before 1873 or after.

Dale's distinctive contribution to the municipal reform movement was, as has been said already, an intellectual one. While others cared deeply for the town and saw the process of secularisation as a liberation from the limitations and vices of churchiness, Dale cared also for the Church. What others saw as mere secularisation, and welcomed or abhorred accordingly, he saw as a rediscovery of the function of the Church. The great importance of religious idealism in the creation of that modern phenomenon, collectivism, and of totalitarianism its more unrestrained and logical offspring, is plain to those who study its history. To that process the vision of George Dawson and the driving force of Joseph Chamberlain contributed, and in its history the municipal reform movement associated with their names rightly has its place. But the limitations of collectivism have become more apparent with every further

---

[42] Charles Vince, *The Unchanging Saviour, and other Sermons* (1875). The same is true of the sermons preserved in the *Birmingham Collection*, Public Reference Library, Birmingham.

[43] See his lecture on the Disestablishment of the Irish Church, *D.P.*, 10.12.1867. He spoke in 1873 in support of Plimsoll's agitation against unseaworthy ships, and was a Guardian of the Poor until 1870.

[44] *D.P.*, 19.10.1872, p. 6.

success. To anyone who does not wish to see all life subordinated to technical efficiency and the glorification of the State, the balanced attitude of Dale may appeal more than that of Dawson or Chamberlain. They were capable of seeing only one thing at a time; he saw all that they could see and more.[45]

[45] A good example of his concern with the functions of institutions in changing historical circumstances is his lecture, *Liberalism* (Birmingham, 1878), delivered to the Birmingham Junior Liberal Association.

7

Perspectives

The scope and character of English local government in the period under review made it highly desirable that able and public-spirited men should serve on the elected town councils. Yet the job was unpaid, increasingly time-consuming and accompanied in the case of councillors by the obligation to submit regularly to re-election. Basically there were two reasons why men served on a town council: for what it did and for what it was.

For some the functions carried out by the council were important enough to outweigh the inconvenience of being a councillor. There were indeed some vested interests in the town who were almost bound to be attracted to the council—market traders if it controlled the market, merchants and shippers if it controlled the docks, small house property owners with an interest in the action of the sanitary inspector or the medical officer, publicans who wished to keep an eye on the watch committee, tradesmen with an interest in contracts. The dangers to the public well-being if these were the only concerns represented on the town council are obvious.

The second reason always present was and is the social attraction of the council. The town hall was the best club in Barking in the early 1960s, and in other areas too to judge from the evidence to the Maud committee.[1] Such considerations were at least as important in the nineteenth century. Nor was this the only way in which the council exerted a social attraction. For some the status conferred by the ceremonial aspect of an alderman's and particularly a mayor's position was an inducement. But above all there was the complex set of considerations implied in the existence of a tradition of council service among a certain section of local society. Where this existed it made nomination to the

---

[1] Anthony M. Rees and Trevor Smith, *Town Councillors, a Study of Barking* (Acton Society Trust, 1964), p. 79; *Maud Committee*, V, chapter 3, para. 80, on p. 337 below.

council into a symbol of membership of and acceptance by the group in question. It was social tradition of this kind that had ensured the willingness of country gentlemen to serve on the committee of quarter session, at least as much as the power that this conferred. In towns in which a similar unbroken tradition existed among the leading inhabitants the recruitment of talent presented fewer problems. But the same process could operate the other way once town council service came to be conventionally associated with other sections of the community, as it had in Birmingham and in not a few other towns that experienced a ratepayers' reaction.[2]

This is the problem to which the Birmingham municipal reformers had found an answer. They had done so by emphasising function, and it is in their new and enhanced understanding of the proper functions of municipal government that their importance lay.

'Whatever the defects of the present governing body, I defy you to make a better one for the place except by gradually increasing its functions and responsibilities and so raising its tone', wrote Chamberlain in 1877 to John Morley, who had deplored the state of the publican–controlled town council of Hanley in the Potteries.[3] In appealing to his own fellow citizens three years before, he had stated the grounds for such an enlargement of the corporation's functions, as well as the consequences that should follow for themselves:

> 'There is no nobler sphere for those who have not the opportunity of engaging in imperial politics than to take part in municipal work, to the wise conduct of which they owe the welfare, the health, the comfort, and the lives of 400,000 people.'[4]

By placing the functions of municipal government in such a perspective, they raised it above the plane on which town councils were regarded primarily as the stamping ground of corrupt vested interests. Such notions may have been dispelled in Birmingham but were common enough in Liberal-Radical circles elsewhere, as Chamberlain discovered on entering Parliament. 'I am perfectly sickened with the observations of our so-called Radicals on the subject—Cowen, Eustace Smith and

---

[2] It was the ability to ward off such a movement that explains the long continuity of town council service by the upper classes in Leicester. See my 'Finance and Politics in Urban Local Government in England 1835–1900', *Histl Jl.*, VI (1963), 218–19.

[3] Joseph Chamberlain to John Morley, 13 January 1877, Chlain. MSS., JC 5/54/151.

[4] Proposing the Toast of the Corporation, 17 October 1874, C. W. Boyd, ed., *Speeches*, I, 49.

others, who talk in Lowe's strain of the corruption of Local Government.'[5]

His own answer to such talk was the one he had learnt from *The Town Crier*, and he drove it home on all possible occasions with the missionary zeal of someone who knew he had a prejudice to overcome:

> 'If we are to do anything radical in the way of sanitary reform, it must be by means of our local governing bodies. It is only through them that we can act upon the population in this matter. It seems to me therefore suicidal to bring into contempt, and to depreciate the only machinery by which we can efficiently secure our needs.'[6]

When he presented £1,000 to the art gallery for the improvement of its collection of industrial design, his letter began, 'I am anxious to show in some practical way my confidence in our municipal institutions.'[7]

Thus it cannot be stressed too much that the Birmingham municipal reform movement was more than a successful attempt to provide a rather backward borough with necessary municipal services. The crucial innovation was a new vision of the function and nature of the corporation. Because it was this, it was also the recruitment to the Town Council of the social and economic elite of the town whose abilities made the actual administrative improvements possible.

The previous chapters have explained the reasons for the high emotional charge and for the sense that great principles were at stake, which is so striking a feature of Birmingham municipal politics in this era. The eclipse of Avery by Chamberlain as leader of the new municipal party was due not least to their very different style. Chamberlain knew what Avery was temperamentally incapable of apprehending, that the reform movement was a moral crusade. Two sudden deaths, Charles Vince's in 1874 and George Dawson's in 1876, quickly provided it with its canonised saints. At the climax of success the funeral processions winding through the streets and the fulsome appreciations of their work gave solemnity to the cause which they had supported. Moreover in Chamberlain the movement possessed a figure of outstanding administrative

---

[5] Joseph Chamberlain to Jesse Collings, 14 February 1877, Chlain. MSS., JC 5/16. He was trying to obtain support for a Bill to give local authorities power to municipalise the trade in alcoholic drink as they had done the trade in gas.

[6] Opening Address to the Sanitary Conference called in Birmingham, 13 January 1875, C. W. Boyd, ed., *Speeches*, I, 59.

[7] Joseph Chamberlain to Jesse Collings, Chairman of the Free Library Committee, 26 April 1876, Chlain. MSS., JC 5/16. See above, p. 120, for the same point made in connection with the purchase of the gas works two years before.

and political gifts. His initiative gave an air of dramatic suddenness to the administrative changes. His use of an efficient political machine, working in a highly charged atmosphere, gave an air of equally dramatic suddenness to the parallel political changes. Such is the stuff of which great traditions are made.

Once the breakthrough had been achieved the social forces that had once worked against the recruitment of the social and economic elite now operated equally effectively in its favour. The tradition of municipal service was effectively preserved into the twentieth century among the large business and professional strata of Birmingham society despite the tendencies that in England as a whole pulled such men the other way, towards the metropolis, into the county and into professional and industrial organisations on a national scale. In the transmission of the tradition the close-knit network of families that made up the Unitarian and the Quaker communities of the town was particularly effective. As late as 1914 these groups were still recognised as the opinion leaders in this respect, so that 'public opinion throughout the city has accepted their attitude and their standards very much as its own'.[8]

There can be no doubt about the importance of what was being said and done in Birmingham during these years for the subsequent developments in the country at large. Its approach towards the nature of local government and the problem of recruitment became the orthodox view and attempts to imitate its characteristics were common. In their different ways both book II and book III demonstrate how powerful its influence was.

Nor was the influence of the Birmingham municipal reform movement limited to what we now think of as the history of local government. The experience of these years was seminal for Chamberlain's approach to politics, and when he transferred to the national stage soon after he took the preconceptions of the Birmingham reform movement with him. Asa Briggs has drawn attention to the effect of this on his approach to the problems of Ireland and of South Africa.[9] But much more direct was the way in which the municipal reform movement shaped his contribution to domestic policies. When he set out to impart a collectivist emphasis to Liberal Radicalism in the 1880s, he repeated in a national setting the very arguments which he had expounded in his years as municipal reformer:

[8] Norman Chamberlain, 'Municipal Government in Birmingham', *Political Quarterly*, I (February 1914), 93.
[9] Gill and Briggs, *History of Birmingham*, II, 87–8.

7

'There are always one million, or very nearly a million, of persons in receipt of parish relief. There are more than one million others on the verge of pauperism, who, in times of depression like these, and at any moment of bad trade, are subject to the most desperate privations. The whole class of agricultural labourers of this country is never able to do more than make both ends meet, and they have to look forward in the time of illness or on the approach of old age to the workhouse as the one inevitable refuge against starvation. Tens of thousands of households do not know the luxury of milk. Children are stunted in their growth and dulled in their intellects for want of proper nourishment and proper food, and the houses of the poor are so scanty and insufficient that grievous immorality prevails, which seldom comes to the surface, but which is known to all those who move among the poor. The ordinary conditions of life among a large proportion of the population are such that common decency is absolutely impossible . . . .'

'Private charity is powerless, religious organisation can do nothing to remedy the evils which are so deep-seated in our social system . . . .'

'I venture to say that it is only the community acting as a whole that can possibly deal with evils so deep-seated as those to which I have referred . . . . It is our business to extend its functions and to see in what way its operations can be usefully enlarged.'

'Let me take one single illustration. I venture to say that of all the legislation which this generation or century has seen, the most important, the most far-reaching, and the most beneficial is the socialistic organisation of State education . . . . On all points I say that it remains by far the most thoroughly satisfactory and creditable piece of legislation to which we can lay claim. Is it surprising that we who look forward to the future should desire to give further application to the principles which are embodied in the Education Act? For my part I am convinced that the most fruitful field before reformers at the present time is to be found in an extension of the functions and authority of local government. Local government is near the people. Local government will bring you into contact with the masses. By its means you will be able to increase their comforts, to secure their health, to multiply the luxuries which they may enjoy in common, to carry out a vast co-operative system for mutual aid and support, to lessen the inequalities of our social system, and to raise the standard of all classes in the community. I believe that in this way you may help to equalise to a great extent the condition of men, and to limit the extremes which now form so great a blot on our social system.'[10]

This passage, so prophetic of the domestic history of the following eighty years, is a mirror in which the shape of the municipal reform movement in Birmingham can be plainly seen. It is in this way, as a form of collectivism, that the Birmingham movement of the early seventies lies at the root of the major developments in modern British history.

This was possible because none of the principal factors that contributed to its birth were peculiar to Birmingham. Its educational deficiencies were those of all large towns, and in all of them led to the establishment of school boards under the Elementary Education Act. Action by municipal corporations was also needed everywhere to deal with crowded urban conditions. The social work of the churches, upon which these factors acted, was similarly found in all towns.

And yet there were good reasons why the new development first found its full expression in Birmingham. Chief among these was the fact that the town was the stronghold of the National Education League, the body that stood for no compromise on the issue of public responsibility for education. For the supporters of the League there was no longer any room for schools not fully controlled by elected local authorities. Manchester, the centre of the National Education Union to safeguard the interests of denominational schools, or Liverpool with its large Roman Catholic population, reacted differently to the school deficiency revealed in the later 1860s. To the members of the Established Church, and to Roman Catholics and many Wesleyan Methodists who thought like them, the challenge of the Education Act of 1870 did not appear the same as to the Protestant Dissenters. The heterodox, and after 1867, the orthodox Dissenters had put their hopes in the creation of local public authorities. These were the instruments through which they were anxious to work, and the means on which they had set their hopes. Not so the Established Church. Since it controlled the great majority of schools in the country, most churchmen closely connected with these schools were more concerned to preserve as much of the old ways as possible than to discuss the logic of the new structures being created. It may be argued that in the long run the position of the Established Church was not to be fundamentally different from that of the Nonconformists. But the change came slowly during the course of the twentieth century,

[10] 'State Socialism and the Moderate Liberals', 28 April 1885, C. W. Boyd, ed., *Speeches*, I, 163–5.

whereas to Nonconformists it came all at once and acted as a catalyst. To Roman Catholics it has not yet come even now.

Both in the National Education League and in the municipal reform movement the pacemakers were not so much the orthodox Evangelical Dissenters but the Unitarians, quasi-Unitarians and Quakers. By comparison with other large towns these groups formed an exceptionally high proportion of the religious spectrum in Birmingham. Appendix III shows the comparative strength of religious denominations in the eight largest English provincial towns. The 4·9 per cent given for Unitarians and Quakers does not include the Church of the Saviour, which features among the isolated congregations whose contribution to the total was also exceptionally large. Of course in all towns the figures for Unitarians and Quakers are small in relation to other bodies. But it is well known that the social and economic position occupied by these groups lent them a weight quite disproportionate to their numbers. They were the leaven and in Birmingham the leaven were plentiful and worked the dough with the results that we have seen.

BOOK II

LEEDS

Part I

The Composition of the Council
1835–1888

I

1835–1852

In 1831 Leeds, with 123,393 inhabitants, ranked immediately after Birmingham, with 146,986, as the fourth largest English provincial town.[1] It had been a municipal borough since the seventeenth century. The grant of a charter of incorporation in 1626 had given a small group of woollen merchants exporting overseas the right to control the market, the standard of quality and other aspects of the trade. From that date until the early nineteenth century Leeds was dominated economically, socially, and politically by this oligarchy of merchants. They were wealthy men charging apprenticeship fees of £300 and over, and were closely connected with the local landed gentry, from whose younger sons they were in part recruited and with whom they inter-married. The most successful in turn became gentry or even peers. They furnish a classic instance of that co-operation between landed and mercantile wealth on which eighteenth-century English society rested.[2]

The prosperity of eighteenth-century Leeds had been due to its function as a marketing centre for much of the West Riding. It depended on

[1] They were exceeded in size by Manchester with Salford (227,808) and Liverpool (189,241). Also in the United Kingdom by Glasgow (202,426) and Edinburgh (161,909). The population of London was 1,471,941.

[2] James Wardell, *Municipal History of the Borough of Leeds* (1846). Also R. G. Wilson, *Gentlemen Merchants. The Merchant Community in Leeds 1700–1830* (Manchester, 1971) which is the basis for much of the next six paragraphs. I am grateful to Dr. Wilson for permission to consult the Ph.D. thesis on which his book is based, while my own work was still in its early stages. The reformed Corporation of Leeds still awaits its historian. There is Jean Toft, 'Public Health in Leeds in the Nineteenth Century. A Study in the Growth of Local Government Responsibility, 1815–1880', unpublished M.A. thesis, Manchester University, 1966 and an essay on the building of the Leeds town hall in Asa Briggs, *Victorian Cities* (1963). The history of the town as such is almost as neglected. The nearest approach to such a history is *Leeds and its History* (Leeds, 1926), a series of articles originally published in *The Yorkshire Post*. For studies of Leeds politics see below. R. J. Morris, 'The Social, Political and Institutional Structure of the Leeds Business and Manufacturing Community 1830–1851', unpublished Oxford D.Phil. thesis 1971 was completed too late for me to be able to use it for this study. The general economic history of the town is dealt with in three excellent articles by W. G. Rimmer in *Thoresby Society Publications*, L, 113 (1967).

179

the improved navigation of the rivers Aire and Calder, which linked the town to the North Sea ports. Industrially Leeds was the centre of the finishing trades for woollen cloth which was generally manufactured in the surrounding district and sold in the two cloth halls of the town. In addition the economy displayed the great diversity of trades normally found in a prosperous regional centre.[3]

Between 1806 and 1835 the merchant oligarchy of Leeds came under both economic and political pressure. They lost their hold over the worsted industry of the Bradford-Halifax-Huddersfield region as that industry became mechanised and a new class of large manufacturers took over the marketing of their own wares. Moreover, as the older channels of trade with Europe dried up and markets in other parts of the world had to be found, new men found an opportunity to break in. But the work of pioneering was hard, the returns less certain, and the life less gentlemanly than in the past. Since the status and financial rewards of lawyers and doctors were rising at the same time, the sons of merchants were more frequently apprenticed to the professions than had been the case before.

The Corporation, recruited by co-option, was in 1835 still predominantly composed of cloth merchants, wool staplers and professional men. Out of thirty-eight members there were twenty cloth merchants and wool staplers (including one linen merchant), four bankers, four professional men and one gentleman, comprising over 75 per cent of the total. Those admitted since 1827 showed, however, that the Corporation had begun to open its ranks to the owners of wealth created in newer ways. They included two flax spinners (the factory industry *par excellence* in Leeds), an ironfounder, a dyer, a timber merchant and a glass merchant. ⟨*See* tables 10 and 11.⟩

Until 1819 the Corporation had had a complete political hold over the town. It had controlled the Vestry, Improvement Commission, and the Workhouse Board which administered the Poor Law. But by 1822 the members of the Corporation had lost control over every one of these bodies.[4] In 1835 they lost their hold on the Corporation itself as a result of the first elections under the Municipal Corporations Act. They lost it to the Reforming party led by Edward Baines, editor of *The Leeds Mercury*, who had created a new kind of power in Leeds, the power of opinion and of open debate.

---

[3] W. G. Rimmer, 'The Industrial Profile of Leeds, 1740-1840', *Thoresby Society Publications*, L, 113 (1967).
[4] S. and B. Webb, *The Parish and the County* (1906), pp. 94-8 for details.

Unlike that of Nottingham for instance, the Corporation of Leeds had been a Tory body exclusively composed of members of the Established Church. During the ascendancy of the younger Pitt at Westminster it had been in close accord with Henry Lascelles, follower of Pitt and M.P. for Yorkshire, and with the dominant opinion in the county. But the Whig cause, which had once been so strong in Yorkshire, was never entirely crushed. 1801 saw *The Leeds Mercury* launched as a Whig paper. It gained rapidly in influence during two stormy county-elections in 1806 and 1807 when the Whigs triumphed. But the Corporation of Leeds retained its close identification with the Tory cause. When in 1832 Leeds became a Parliamentary borough, the return of two Liberals marked yet another set-back for the Tories and the Corporation. The final blow came in 1835. The new Town Council of forty-eight councillors and sixteen aldermen contained fifty-one Liberals and thirteen Conservatives. Only six of these had been members of the old Corporation. It was a defeat, not an abdication. Among the unsuccessful candidates were another eight of the former rulers of the town.

The continuity between the old and the new would have been even less but for the willingness of the victors to acknowledge the eminent position which some of their opponents occupied in the town. Four aldermanic places were given to Conservatives, two from outside the Council. One of these was Henry Hall, grand old man of Leeds, twenty years a member of the old Corporation, who had refused all invitations to contest a ward. It was a gesture of generosity on the part of the Liberals, but also of political principle. For years they had attacked the old Corporation for its rigid exclusion of political opponents, and during the election campaign *The Leeds Mercury* had advocated a mixed corporation of all parties as the ideal.[5] However, the gesture was almost unique in nineteenth-century Leeds municipal politics, and the principle did not long survive the first flush of victory. By 1838, when the Conservatives were winning elections in the wards, the Liberal majority refused to re-elect the Conservative aldermen, and thereafter the majority party consistently monopolised the aldermanic bench.[6]

If we look more closely at the first municipal election we shall find that of the nine Conservative councillors, five came from Mill Hill, three

[5] *L.M.*, 21.11.1835. For Henry Hall see R. V. Taylor, *Biographia Leodiensis* (Leeds, 1865), pp. 474–7.
[6] There were only two short-lived exceptions, the election of Henry Hall in 1841, which was a piece of political mismanagement and reversed the following November, and the election of a Conservative alderman in June 1846 who lasted until November 1847.

from Headingley and one from Kirkgate. The borough had been divided into twelve wards, of which four returned six councillors each and the remainder three each ⟨*see* map 3⟩.[7] Mill Hill, the wealthy central ward of the town containing far and away the largest number of ratepayers assessed at over £40 per annum, had originally returned three men from each party. But in the bye-election caused by the aldermanic vacancies the Conservatives gained another two seats. The Kirkgate seat was also won in the bye-election.

Headlingley was the only ward which the Liberals did not contest. There was to be no contested election until 1843 and no Liberal councillor returned until 1844. It was very much a special case. The borough of Leeds covered a very extensive area, 32 square miles compared with the 13 square miles of Birmingham in 1838. It was identical with the parish of Leeds, which like most parishes in the North of England, where the population in the middle ages had been sparse, covered great tracts of country. Much of this was in 1835 still agricultural land thinly dotted with hamlets. Headingley ward, north of the river Aire, and Bramley ward south of it, were to all intents and purposes still extensive rural constituencies, much larger than the wards that covered the more central parts of the borough. The hamlets in Bramley ward were settlements of out-workers who voted Liberal. Headingley ward contained three small hamlets, of which Headingley itself was the largest, but held no more than 340 ratepayers in 1835. The ward contained 785 ratepayers altogether. Both the principal landowners, Lord Cardigan and the Beckett family, the Leeds bankers, were strong Conservatives, and left no room for an effective opposition. In 1835 the ward returned Thomas Beckett together with Griffith Wright, gentleman, and scion of a merchant family, who owned the Tory paper, *The Leeds Intelligencer*. After 1836, Lord Cardigan's agent, who lived in Headingley Hall, was for many years a councillor for the ward. It was the continued migration of wealthy men to Headingley that gradually created an effective Liberal presence there.[8]

It would be a mistake to identify the leadership of the reforming party in Leeds with the new manufacturers. Of the eleven men who provided the capital for *The Leeds Mercury* in 1801 no more than two were manufacturers. Six were cloth merchants and the rest were a physician, a spirit merchant and a gentleman. But seven of them were

[7] The double wards were Mill Hill, West, Holbeck and Bramley. The ward boundaries were to be revised in 1881 and sixteen wards created with three councillors each.

[8] J. Mayhall, *Annals and History of Leeds* (Leeds, 1878); *L.M.*, 2.11.1839, p. 6, 6.11.1841, p. 4; Municipal Corporation Boundaries (England and Wales).

Dissenters, and all of them supporters of Walter Fawkes of Farnley, the 'independent Whig' who was to contest the county in 1806.[9] Much the same is true of the leaders of the Reform agitation in the town from 1806–32. They included members of important merchant houses and leading professional men, as well as manufacturers.[10] The two flax spinners among the leaders of the Reformers can be balanced by two flax spinners on the old Corporation. Between them they owned the largest factories in Leeds. What distinguished them from each other was that the two Reformers, like the vast majority of the party leadership, were Dissenters. The political divisions of the 1830s were the result of genuine disagreement about the nature of authority. To this disagreement the distinction between a Churchman and a Dissenter was of some relevance in Leeds; that between a merchant and a manufacturer was not.

If we examine the overwhelmingly Liberal Council of 1836, we shall find the numerical strength of the traditional occupations greater than ever, although in view of the increase in the total numbers the percentage showed a drop.

TABLE 10. *Leeds Corporation 1835–6: traditional occupations*

	Old Corporation 1835 Tory	New Corporation 1836 Liberal, Tory, Total		
Cloth or linen merchants, wool staplers	16	13	2	15
Cloth merchants-cum-manufacturers	4	7	1	8
Bankers	4	2	3	5
Lawyers	1	2	0	2
Doctors	3	2	1	3
Gentlemen	1	0	1	1
Totals	29	26	8	34

The occupations which had already been accepted by the Tory oligarchy between 1827 and 1835 are shown on table 11. They too are now more strongly represented than before.

[9] The list of names is given in Edward Baines, *Life of Edward Baines* (1851), p. 47. For religious affiliations see Donald Read, *Press and People* (1961), p. 76, for political affiliations see Wilson, *Gentlemen Merchants*, p. 176.

[10] Names cited in Baines, *Life* and in A. S. Turberville and F. Beckwith, 'Leeds and parliamentary reform 1820–1832', *Thoresby Miscellany*, XII (1954).

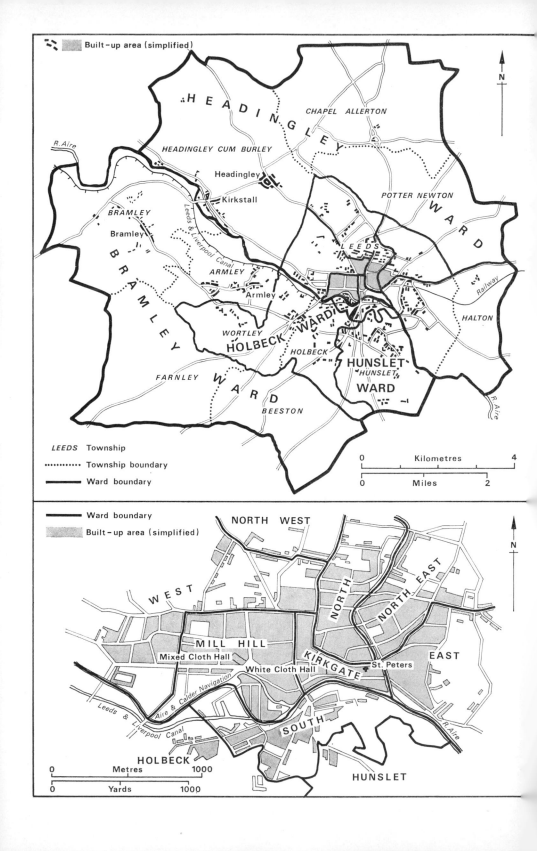

Built-up area (simplified)

LEEDS Township
·········· Township boundary
▬▬▬▬ Ward boundary

0 —————— Kilometres —————— 4
0 —————— Miles —————— 2

Ward boundary
Built-up area (simplified)

NORTH WEST

WEST

NORTH

NORTH EAST

MILL HILL

Mixed Cloth Hall

White Cloth Hall

KIRKGATE

St. Peters

EAST

SOUTH

HOLBECK

HUNSLET

Leeds & Liverpool Canal

Aire & Calder Navigation

R. Aire

0 —————— Metres —————— 1000
0 —————— Yards —————— 1000

TABLE 11. *Leeds Corporation 1835–6 : occupations admitted between 1827 and 1835*

	Old Corporation 1835 Tory	New Corporation 1836 Liberal, Tory, Total		
Flax or silk spinners	2	4	0	4
Dyers	1	1	2	3
Glass or timber merchants	2	0	2	2
Ironfounders or machine makers	1	3	0	3
Totals	6	8	4	12

Curiously enough on the 1836 Council it was among the relatively recently accepted occupations, not the traditional ones, that the Tories represented the higher proportion of the total. Between them the two groups of occupations accounted for close on three-quarters of the first elected Council. The rest was made up of seven manufacturers in the modern sense, three handicraft manufacturers of the older sort, four malsters or brewers, one corn-miller, one tobacco manufacturer, one wholesale grocer and one wine and spirit merchant.[11]

The old Corporation had been controlled by leading merchants and professional men with an admixture of outstanding manufacturers. Although the door had now been opened more widely, the same was still true of the new. The more we concentrate on those who actually provided the leadership, the more striking the parallel becomes. It is as if the opposing team had gone in to play. The rival merchants, the rival bankers, lawyers and doctors, even the rival flax spinners, are now in charge. In 1833 *The Leeds Mercury* had proclaimed its confidence that under a representative regime 'men of character and station would be sought for'. It rejected with contempt and every appearance of justice the claim of the Conservatives to monopolise 'all the respectability of the place'.[12] The really striking change that had taken place in the

[11] The wine and spirit merchant might have been included in table 10 since there was also one on the old Corporation. But I am not convinced that the two cases are parallel. William Osburn, corporation assistant, i.e. clr., 1830–35, inherited his father's business as wholesale wine and spirit merchant and ran it for a while. But he was really a scholarly gentleman of means, an Egyptologist and in his earlier years tutor to the sons of the nobility. *L.M.*, 27.2.1875; *Y.P.*, 1.3.1875.

[12] *L.M.*, 20.4.1833; 23.1.1836.

MAP 3. (opposite) *Borough of Leeds 1835.*
    Source: P.P., 1837 (238), xxvii.

composition of the Council, apart from its party complexion, was not occupational, it was religious. According to the *Mercury*, out of the first fifty-one men elected no more than twenty were Churchmen.[13] Even more remarkable is the fact that during the next twelve years the town had only two mayors who were Churchmen.[14]

Although not a difference in occupation, the contrast between the membership of the old Corporation and that of the new was, however, far from negligible. The difference in religious composition implied other differences too. For those in the upper ranks of society in the eighteenth century the pressure to conform in matters of religion was immense and in the long run few prominent families resisted it. Those who had made their fortune within the last generation or two might be either Churchmen or Dissenters, but the oldest families of Leeds, who had often been Dissenters in the later seventeenth century, were with but one exception Churchmen by 1800. Although there were not a few men among the Tories on the old Corporation whose fortunes had been made since 1780, there were others whose families had belonged to the oligarchy for much longer. The Dissenting heads of the Reforming party had all risen to wealth in the previous half-century. The conclusion to be drawn is not that manufacturers were Reformers or even that more recently established merchants were, but that the Reformers, dissenters as they were both in religion and politics, numbered none of the oldest merchant dynasties among their ranks. In this sense continuity was broken and the oldest families dislodged from their position of pre-eminence.

When we turn from the composition of the new body to its functions, we must remember that municipal reform was primarily meant to change the basis of authority, and only to a very limited extent to change the functions of corporations.[15] As in Birmingham, so in Leeds, the improvement commissioners remained in existence and continued to be

---

[13] *L.M.*, 2.1.1836. The bye-election to fill vacancies caused by promotion to aldermen had at that date not taken place; hence the incomplete total.

[14] But in 1836 the mayor's office had first been offered to and refused by Thomas Benyon, then by William Williams Brown. It was then offered to George Goodman, a Baptist, who accepted. Brown was Church of England. Benyon had been a Unitarian but gave up his seat at the Mill Hill Unitarian Church in 1834. Fraser lists him as Church of England on evidence drawn from the years after 1835. R. V. Taylor, *Biographia Leodiensis* 462; Mill Hill Pew Rent Book; Derek Fraser, 'Politics in Leeds 1830–52', unpublished Ph.D. thesis, School of History University of Leeds, 1969, p. 207, footnote 1.

[15] The Municipal Corporations Act of 1835 enabled but did not oblige such bodies as improvement commissioners to transfer their powers to the Municipal Corporation. Advantage was taken of this in only two boroughs prior to 1845, Newcastle-upon-Tyne and Manchester. See *Webb Loc. Gov. Col.*, volume 66, 'Memorandum on the Local Acts of Rating Authorities 1836–1900', p. 2.

responsible for the main environmental services. Street lighting, scavenging, the control over obstructions and nuisances, the licensing of hackney carriages and the control of the market all came within their domain, although their authority extended only over a fraction of the borough, i.e. the township of Leeds. Before the establishment of a waterworks company in 1837 they had also been responsible for the supply of water. The Act of 1835 imposed only one new function on the Corporation, the provision of a police force.

The Council chose its ablest and most respected member, Alderman Tottie, to be chairman of the statutory watch committee. There was at the time no public police office in Leeds and no watchmen provided during the day, although some form of night watch existed. The other issue that faced the Council almost immediately was the state of the gaol. The same wave of investigation into the working of institutions, which had led to the reform of municipal corporations, had also shown up the inadequacies of corporation gaols and caused them to be placed under the supervision of the Home Office.[16] In January 1836 the Home Office wrote to the Council, pointed out the deficiencies of the gaol and asked it to provide a new one.[17] By the end of the year prisoners sentenced in Leeds were being sent to the county gaol at Wakefield. Unless the borough was prepared to see the abolition of its quarter sessions this could only be a temporary solution. The retention of the quarter sessions in the town was a matter both of status and convenience, yet only in 1842 did the Council finally commit itself to the expense of a new building. So little did they anticipate the rate of future change that less than ten years later the new structure was already too small.[18]

Both the police force and the gaol cost money and the Corporation finances called for early attention. Tottie became chairman of the finance committee. A borough treasurer was also appointed, but since this was an honorary post held by the manager of the Leeds Banking Company who was in no way involved in such matters as the drawing up of estimates, the Council was relying heavily on Tottie's skill.[19] The financial position was obscure, since one of the last acts of the old Corporation had been to dispose of all its funds to the local charitable institutions. The Council claimed a right to the property of its predecessor, took the matter to court and in 1840 finally won its case. This dispute

[16] Second Report House of Lords Committee on the State of the Gaols P.P., 1835 (439) xi; Prisons Act 1835, 3 B 4 William IV, c. 38.
[17] *L.M.*, 23.1.1836.
[18] MSS. Corporation Reports 1836–1842; 1851, Corporation Archives, Leeds Civic Hall.
[19] *L.M.*, 16.1.1836.

did at least inject a genuinely municipal issue into the party conflict, which on account of the highly charged political situation inevitably dominated municipal politics. The £6,500 that were recovered were, however, not enough to put Leeds into the rank of wealthy corporations. There was no corporate estate, no fat dock dues as in some of the ports, and the income from the cloth halls was insignificant. There was never any chance of avoiding a borough rate, as Newcastle and Swansea did for many years,[20] or of cushioning the ratepayers from the impact of increased expenditure. In these respects there was little difference between Birmingham and Leeds. A borough rate and a watch rate totalling 9¾d. in the £ had been levied straightaway in 1836, 'swingeing rates' as the opposition dubbed them, and in 1841 they rose to 11¾d.[21]

The most surprising initiative taken in these early years was a statistical investigation into the social, moral, and educational state of the borough. The Council incurred an expenditure of £320 in 1837–8 and the results were communicated to the Statistical Society of London in 1839.[22] Copies were sent to the mayors of other towns with a recommendation for similar inquiries. Unlike the other activities this was neither imposed on the Corporation from outside nor to be understood in terms of the party struggles within the town. The initiative had come from the two medical men on the Liberal side of the Council, James Williamson and Robert Baker, particularly from the latter. Baker was, next to Tottie, the most active and to the historian the most interesting of the new Council. His role as an investigator of the social conditions of Leeds had begun during the cholera epidemic of 1832. He was then a town surgeon, i.e. a surgeon to the Poor Law authority, 'an ordeal all the medical men in the town go through as a high road to better practice'[23] and when cholera appeared on Tyneside, he travelled there to study it. It was not long before he had an opportunity to do the same in Leeds. A temporary board of health was set up, as in most towns affected by the epidemic, which fought the hitherto unknown disease by means of whitewash and scavenging carts. These boards were disbanded again at the end of the epidemic, and in most places there was little reflection

---

[20] The borough rate was a rate for general purposes and should be distinguished from such things as improvement rates levied for specific purposes sanctioned by a special statute. For Newcastle see *Operation of Small Tenement Rating Act 1850, Sel. Cttee. HL. mins. of ev.* QQ. 1705–6; *P.P.*, 1859 Session 2 (56) vii, 269. For Swansea, Glyn Roberts, *The Municipal Development of the Borough of Swansea to 1900* (1940), pp. 47–8.
[21] Council Minute Books IV & V, Corporation Archives.
[22] *Jl. Statistical Society of London*, II (1839–40), 397–424.
[23] Quoted in W. R. Lee, 'Robert Baker' *Brit. Jl. of Industrial Medicine*, XXI (1964), 85–93, 167–79 which gives biographical details.

on the causes of the new disease. Not so in Leeds. In January 1833 Baker published a report on the causes and circumstances of the epidemic, accompanied by a remarkable map which plotted the areas in which the highest number of outbreaks had occurred.[24] He in no way anticipated Dr. John Snow's discovery more than twenty years later that the cause of the infection lay in the drinking water. The factors that stood out from the cholera map of 1833 and the conclusions to which medical opinion was led by it are best described in the words of a resolution signed in January 1833 by eight physicians and thirty-eight surgeons at a public meeting organised by Baker:

'We whose names are undersigned are of the opinion that the streets in which malignant cholera prevailed most severely were those in which the drainage was most imperfect, and that the state of general health of the inhabitants would be greatly improved, and the probability of a future visitation from such malignant epidemics diminished by a general and efficient system of drainage, sewerage and paving, and the enforcing of better regulations as to the cleanliness of the streets.'[25]

Ten years later such opinions were commonplace; they were not so in 1833. The Leeds Improvement Commission did not have the necessary powers, and before it was dissolved, the local Board of Health sent a request to the Home Secretary for general legislation on the subject, but nothing more was done at either the national or the local level.

The reformed Town Council gave Baker and Williamson an opportunity to return to the subject. The wider scope of their inquiries compared with those of 1832 had been suggested to Baker by his new experiences and preoccupations as a factory inspector. Their investigations should be seen in conjunction with the founding of the Leeds Statistical Society in 1838. It was the local manifestation of a more widespread interest in exact social investigation, which had led to the founding of the Manchester Statistical Society in 1833 and of the London Society in the following year. It found expression in the inquiries of royal commissions and select committees and was in turn stimulated by

---

[24] Robert Baker, *Report of the Leeds Board of Health* (Leeds, 1833). There were 702 deaths in Leeds. Baker himself caught the disease from his patients, and it so unnerved him that he gave up general practice and became a factory surgeon. In 1834 he was appointed a factory inspector under the Factory Act of 1833, the only one among them with a medical training. W. R. Lee, 'Robert Baker'.

[25] *L.M.*, January 1833, in *Leeds and its History*, p. 104.

them.[26] It was, however, the interest of an enlightened minority, the beginning of that 'impact of the educated intelligence on the amorphous greedy fabric of the new civilisation' to which G. M. Young has so eloquently referred.[27] What is remarkable is that in the Leeds Town Council it found a majority willing to support it out of public funds. The Conservatives protested at the waste of money and at the 'inquisitorial nature' of a survey that asked householders the number of their children who had died. 'It was contrary to the feelings of Englishmen that their family affairs should be dragged unnecessarily before the public' complained Dr. Adam Hunter, a Conservative councillor.[28] But for the moment his more radically inclined colleagues had the ear of the Council. These included the most important members of it, those leading citizens who had become borough magistrates in 1837 and were thereby *ex-officio* members of the Street Commission. For it was the Improvement Commission that was strategically placed to take note of these matters, and it was here that the initiative was taken that ultimately led to the important Leeds Improvement Act of 1842.

The Leeds Improvement Commission consisted of the borough magistrates and nineteen members annually elected by the vestry.[29] The elected commissioners tended to deal with the routine work, but whenever the magistrates thought that important matters were at stake, they descended in strength and easily carried the meeting with them. It was at one such meeting in December 1840, called on Dr. Williamson's initiative, that the commissioners decided to ask the Home Secretary for legislation that would enable populous places to provide adequate drainage of the streets. The Home Secretary passed the matter to the Privy Council and both pointed out that they had no competence to deal with such a subject, whereupon the Commission began to take a close interest in three Bills then before Parliament, dealing respectively with drainage, street improvement and building regulation. The details of the measures were so far from their liking that after appointing a committee to petition against them, they considered whether to introduce a Bill of their own. At a sparsely attended vestry meeting in June 1841 they obtained authority to do so.[30] The men principally behind these

[26] Baker was to write the *Report on the Town of Leeds*, appended to Edwin Chadwick's *Report on the Sanitary Condition of the Labouring Poor* (1842). The job had originally been offered to Williamson.

[27] G. M. Young, *Victorian England. Portrait of an Age* (1936), p. 42.

[28] *L.M.* 2.11.1839.

[29] The borough magistrates succeeded to the right enjoyed before 1835 by the mayor and aldermen. L.I.C. *Proceedings*, 7.2.1838. Corporation Archives.

[30] L.I.C. *Proceedings*, December 1840–June 1841; *L.M.*, 5.6.1841, p. 5.

moves were Baker, Williamson and Edward Baines junior, the Liberal M.P. for the borough.[31] The magistrates authorised their clerk to help with the drafting of the measure, but even so the Commission proved a slow and incompetent body for the task. After Baker had persuaded the Town Council to stake out a claim in the preparation of the Bill, a joint committee of six commissioners, six J.P.s and six town councillors was set up, which fell increasingly under the domination of Baker and Baines. In January 1842 the Leeds vestry came under Chartist control, who elected their own men as commissioners, but nothing could now stop the momentum that had been built up in the other two bodies. The Chartist commissioners were dragged along, protesting against the expense involved, and at a chaotic vestry meeting, prolonged for several days, the projected bill was destroyed clause by clause at the behest of Joshua Hobson, publisher of the Chartist paper *The Northern Star*. It made no difference to the outcome, except that the Commission, having lost its mandate, was obliged to withdraw from the prosecution of the Bill. It became the sole responsibility of the magistrates and the Town Council, who could snap their fingers at Chartist resolutions, and the extensive new powers were consequently vested in the Corporation. By capturing the Commission the Chartists had destroyed it. They boycotted its final meeting at which, with Baines in the chair, it handed over its duties to the Town Council 'in a manner the most courteous'.[32]

If, therefore, we are interested not in constitutional reconstruction but in the acquisition of a wide range of new administrative functions, the crucial date in the history of the municipal corporation was not 1835 but 1842. Anticipating by nine years the similar developments in Birmingham, the Corporation of Leeds became the authority for most of the environmental services in the town.[33] The Leeds Improvement Act of 1842 was indeed a remarkable legislative achievement. It granted powers for the paving and drainage of the borough, for controlling the width of streets and the standard of housing, for scavenging and the cleansing of footpaths, for the control of nuisances and the suppression of vice. It enabled the Corporation to provide a town hall, public

---

[31] Speeches at vestry meeting 16.2.1842 in *L.M.*, 19.2.1842; L.I.C. *Proceedings passim*.

[32] The claim of the magistrates to share in the administration was rejected by Parliament. L.I.C. *Proceedings*, August 1841–August 1842; *L.M.*, 16.4.1842, 23.4.1842, 30.4.1842, 6.8.1842.

[33] Apart from the two towns mentioned on p. 7, footnote 3, who had availed themselves of the Municipal Corporation Act of 1835, only Stockport had anticipated Leeds in entrusting its reformed Corporation with improvement powers under a local Act. *Webb Loc. Gov. Col.*, volume 66, 'Memorandum on the Local Acts of Rating Authorities 1836–1900', p. 2.

conveniences as well as public clocks; to light the streets; to extend the market and to prevent the sale of unwholesome food. This is to mention only a few of its 391 clauses, which together covered a range of subjects such as would normally have been presented in eight separate Bills. It is a measure of the acumen of those in control of the town's affairs that this consolidation of clauses into one Bill saved the town something between £1,000 and £2,000 in parliamentary costs.[34] The Leeds Act ranks with the Liverpool Improvement Act of the same year as one of the pioneering measures in the history of public health in England. Twenty-nine years later the contrast between the comprehensive ideas embodied in the Act and what had actually been achieved was still great enough to cause comment when a government inspector surveyed the state of the town.[35]

What kind of council was it that took on the new duties, lying as they did at the heart of the question not merely of health but of survival for the 150,000 inhabitants of Leeds? The most striking contrast between the Town Council in January 1836 and its successor in January 1842 was in party composition. By March 1841 the number of Conservatives had risen from a baker's dozen to thirty-two, exactly half the Council, and this despite the loss of their four aldermen in 1838.

In October Dr. Williamson's aldermanic seat was unexpectedly declared vacant since he had recently moved to Brighton. The Conservatives obtained it on a snatch-vote for Henry Hall who had been an alderman until 1838, and so for a brief moment captured the majority. This was very different from the humiliating defeats they had suffered in the first municipal elections. It was a critical moment for the Liberal party in the town whose share of the Council had been reduced at every single municipal election since January 1836. At the Parliamentary election in July 1841 William Beckett, the Conservative, had come top of the poll. But the Conservative triumph was to be short-lived at least in municipal affairs. The November ward elections restored a safe majority to the Liberals and thereafter the Conservative tide ebbed steadily away. There was to be no further threat to the Liberal domination until the early 1870s.

Our second sample catches the Conservative rally only just past its peak, the proportions being thirty-nine Liberals to twenty-five Conservatives. How far had the considerable turn-over in personnel implicit in

[34] 5 & 6 Vict. c. 104; MSS. Reports, Leeds Improvement Act, 3.8.1842.
[35] J. N. Radcliffe, *The Sanitary State of Leeds with particular Reference to Diarrhoea and Fever. Report made to the Local Government Board* (1871), p. 4.

this fact altered the social composition of the Council? The most relevant occupations are listed on table 12, side by side with those already cited on tables 10 and 11.

The number of cloth merchants (worsted as well as woollen) and woolstaplers was two more than in 1836. (Sixteen in 1835, fifteen in 1836, it was seventeen in 1842.) Seven of these had been on the Council already in 1836. Of the nine newcomers three Liberals belonged to houses which were large and easily comparable with the earlier recruits. Not enough is known of the remaining six (three Liberals and three Conservatives) on which to base an equally firm statement. In addition to the merchants *tout pur* the three merchant/manufacturers also definitely belonged to large well-established firms. Next comes a group of six textile manufacturers without any claim to be merchants, two less than in 1836. Two of these were large flax spinners, Henry Cowper Marshall, partner in the largest industrial establishment in Leeds, employing 31,000 spindles and J. R. Atkinson of Hives and Atkinson, employing 18,000 spindles and 923 hands.[36] One was a very large woollen manufacturer.[37] The remaining three were not in the same bracket; one can be identified as a much smaller flax spinner with a labour force of fifty hands.[38] This was small for a flax spinner, but it was not despicable by the standards of the Leeds economy as such. Thus in the major section of the economy, that of textiles, the fifteen merchants still greatly outnumbered the six manufacturers and three merchant/manufacturers. Taking the figures another way, the firms that were undoubtedly large numbered sixteen compared with eight which were either definitely of medium size or on which the information is inconclusive.

There were slightly more professional men than before. The table shows the number of lawyers unchanged at two and the increase in the number of doctors from three to four. Lord Cardigan's agent at Headingley Hall, who was a land surveyor, also belongs to the professional group making a total of seven, or 10·9 per cent of the Council. On the other hand the bankers have withdrawn. They had never formed a very large group, being four in 1835 and five in 1836, and their disappearance

---

[36] Marshall MSS. Brotherton Library, Leeds, MS. 200/15/42, List of Leeds Spinners and Spindles 1837–1841. For a discussion of the Leeds flax-spinning industry see W. G. Rimmer, *Marshalls of Leeds, Flax-Spinners, 1788–1886* (1960).

[37] Obadiah Willans, on the Council since 1836. He was already employing 473 hands in 1833 and using steam engines totalling 70 h.p. He was the largest woollen manufacturer in Leeds listed in the survey made by the Royal Commission on the Employment of Children, *Supplementary Report, P.P.*, 1834, xx, 795.

[38] Martin Cawood, Conservative clr. 1840–43. See Marshall MSS., *List of Leeds Spinners and Spindles*.

TABLE 12. *Leeds Town Council 1835–52: selected occupations*

	1835 C.	1836 L.	C.	Total	1842 L.	C.	Total	1852 L.	C.	Total
Woollen or worsted cloth merchants or wool staplers	16*	13	12	15	13	3	16	10	0	10†
Cloth merchant/ manufacturers	4	7	1	8	1	2	3	1‡	0	1
Flax and silk spinner	2	4	0	4	1	2	3	1	0	1
Wool textile manufacturers incl. carpets	0	3	1	4	1	2	3	2	1	3§
Gentlemen	1	0	1	1	0	2	2‖			0
Bankers	4	2	3	5			0			0
Lawyers	1	2	0	2	2	0	2	1	3	4
Doctors	3	2	1	3	2	2	4			0
Other profession	0			0	0	1	1	0	1	1
Ironmasters or machine makers	1	3	0	3	3	3	6	4¶	1	5
Bootmaker**	0	1	0	1			0	1	0	1
Tanner or currier	0			0	0	2††	2	1	0	1
Retailers of all kinds‡‡	0	1	0	1	2	2	4	8	1	9
Retailers of food	0		1§§	1	1	1	2	6‖‖	0	6

* Included one linen merchant.
† Included one carpet merchant.
‡ Small.
§ None of these was large.
‖ One of these is doubtful.
¶ Included one small millwright.

** Bootmakers were small.
†† One large and one small.
‡‡ Each of these includes one hatter.
§§ This grocer is probably a wholesaler not a retailer.
‖‖ Three of these were Chartists.

might be no more than a coincidence of individual decisions. It marks practically the end of the long connection between the local bankers and the Town Council.[39] Otherwise the most striking change was the

[39] The one exception was Henry Oxley, partner in William Williams Brown & Co. He was a Liberal alderman between the 1850s and 1870s, and appears in the samples for 1862 and 1872. Significantly, he had never been a clr. having 'strong objections to going through the turmoil of a contested election'. Obituary notice, *Y.P.*, 22.2.1890.

increased representation of the newer industries. The number of iron-masters and machine-makers rose from three to six.[40] Leather, the other industry rising to great importance, had been represented in 1836 only by a small shoemaker from Bramley, the outer township in which this had become the chief occupation. In 1842 a large tanner and a very much smaller currier mark the beginning of a representation of these economically important but stream-polluting processes. It was to continue throughout the rest of the century.[41]

One result of the Conservative revival in the late 1830s was a return of men who had been members of the old Corporation. Thirteen of the original thirty-eight served at some time or other on the reformed Corporation. However, the frustration of being excluded from all share of power and the hazards of contested elections meant that few of them stayed long, especially once the hopes of a Conservative-controlled council waned rapidly in the early eighteen-forties.

To sum up therefore, in January 1842 the leading occupations of Leeds were still strongly represented on the Corporation. Taking all the industries together there were twenty-four men whose business could be considered large or medium-large by the standards of the Leeds economy in 1842. Together with seven professional men and two gentlemen this gives just over 50 per cent of the Council. The figure is approximate for the judgment of size lacks precision. But the contrast with Birmingham is large enough for the point to be worth making. Despite considerable political changes the occupational structure of the Council had changed little.

This was no longer so ten years later. Table 12 shows the contrast. By 1852 the cloth-merchants and woolstaplers were down to nine (plus one carpet merchant). There was only one flax spinner and the other textile manufacturers are definitely not large. Nor is the decline in the number of substantial men engaged in textiles balanced by an increase in substantial men engaged in the newer industries. The significant change had occurred among the small retailers, especially those dealing in food. These men, who formed a substantial section of the Leeds

---

[40] The ironmaster was Thomas Butler of the Kirkstall forge. Machine maker was an occupation in which small men predominated, but the ones on the Town Council were at the large end of the scale. They included Peter Fairbairn, Liberal clr. 1836–42, 1854–9, who was employing 550 hands and £50,000 of capital in 1841. *First Report, S.C. on Exportation of Machinery, Minutes of Evidence*, p. 208; *P.P.*, 1841, vii, 201. See also *Appendix to Second Report*, p. 105; *P.P.*, 1841, vii, 400.

[41] For the Leeds leather industry and its place in the local economy see W. G. Rimmer, 'The Leeds Leather Industry in the Nineteenth Century', *Thoresby Society Publications*, XLVI (1961), pp. 119–64. The tanner referred to was Richard Nickols, Conservative, of the Joppa Tannery. In the 1830s a few large works like the Joppa Tannery were 'like a huge mountain overshadowing a number of small factories'. *Leather Trades Review*, 14.1.1896, quoted in Rimmer's article p. 140.

economy, had previously been markedly under-represented on the Town Council with its high proportion of social and economic leaders. But in 1852 there were two butchers, two grocers and two coffee-house keepers among the councillors, a total of six food retailers compared with two in 1842, and none before.[42] There is a similar progression if retailers of all kinds are taken. Taking together all those who can be reasonably identified as really small businessmen, we find their number increased from seven in 1842 to twenty-four in 1852, i.e. from 10·9 per cent to 37·4 per cent of the whole Council.

Politically and administratively the early years of the decade between the samples of 1842 and 1852 were dominated by economic crisis and the impact of Chartism on local politics, a harsh climate that was fatal to the promise inherent in the great Improvement Act. That Act had provided Leeds with the powers to create a healthier urban environment and had vested them in the Town Council. Robert Baker became chairman of the new streets committee and for a few months his energy carried all before him. But not for long. No worse moment could have been chosen to launch a programme of expenditure than the economic depression of 1842. By December 1842 an agitation had been started in Baker's own ward, which called upon him to resign. In March 1843 there were meetings in six of the wards to petition the Council against the expenditure involved in carrying out the new duties under the Improvement Act. This pressure immediately affected the decisions of the Council, as the streets committee found to its cost. Already in December 1842, when asked to spend £250 on obtaining accurate levels for the town from the Ordnance Survey for the drawing up of a drainage plan, members replied that the Council had already spent £650 on various maps and plans and refused the request. In February 1843 there had been a bitter struggle over the adoption of an improvement scheme which would have cost £700. The ward meetings put an end to that idea and it was defeated in early April. Thereafter there was little momentum left. Baker himself was about to leave Leeds and in September a meeting to organise a presentation to him in recognition of his services to the town was vetoed. It was clear that he would not have been re-elected had he not retired in November.[43]

---

[42] Food retailers, as here enumerated, do not include corn-millers. There was one corn-miller in 1836, 1852, and 1862, none in any other samples. Nor are publicans being included, unless the latter are also grocers or tea-dealers. They are not important on the Council at this stage and will be discussed below.

[43] *L.M.*, 3.12.1842, 10.12.1842, 11 March–8 April 1843; Minutes, Leeds Improvement Act, 14.2.1842, 8.2.1843, 22.2.1843, 5.4.1843. I am indebted to Derek Fraser, 'Politics in Leeds 1830–1852', p. 416, footnote 1, for the reference to the presentation to Baker.

Politically the most important development was that the Reforming party, which had been forged in the struggles of 1830–35, broke apart. November 1842 saw the first electoral effort of a Complete Suffrage party, which condemned those whom it described as Whigs and appealed for Tory support.[44] It returned eight of its candidates at the municipal election and with probably a touch of exaggeration claimed twenty-two supporters on the Council including three aldermen. In municipal matters this Radical group attacked both the 'oppressiveness' and the 'extravagance' of the local authorities. To carry economy into every department of the public expenditure, to pay off unnecessary officers and police, to cut down salaries, and to 'endeavour to reduce the cost of public prosecution' were its avowed aims.[45] One of the unsuccessful candidates, Joshua Hobson, publisher and editor of the *Northern Star*, had stood explicitly as a Chartist, and he was elected in 1843 when he tried again. He was the first of a group of Chartist councillors who were successful at the polls between 1843 and 1853.[46] But they shaded fairly easily into others who called themselves Radicals or Liberals and there was no consistency in the nomenclature used at the time. They were all opposed to the more moderate Liberals, and electoral contests between the two factions were not uncommon.

This political movement does much to explain the greater proportion of small men, especially of the shopkeeper type, to be found in the 1852 sample. Because they had to occupy premises of at least £30 rateable value or else own property worth £1,000, even the Chartist councillors could not be proletarians. The occupations listed in table 13 are a reminder of the appeal that Chartism made in Leeds to the small tradesman:

The demand for maximum economy which featured so prominently in Radical municipal politics is understandable in view of the bad state of trade in the early 1840s, but it proved fatal to the hopes of the sanitary reformers. In 1842 the Council had instructed Captain Vetch R.E. to devise a comprehensive scheme of drainage for the town. The plans

---

[44] Such a move had had its attraction for a section of working-class Radicals in Leeds since the early 1830s. See Asa Briggs, 'The Background to the Parliamentary Reform Movement in three English Cities, 1830–32', *Cambridge Hist. Jl.*, X (1952). The details of Radical politics in these years are given in Dr. Fraser's thesis.

[45] *Leeds Times*, 5.11.1842.

[46] After the Chartist success in capturing the Improvement Commission and the subsequent disappearance of that body it was a natural step to seek election on the Town Council. They also elected the churchwardens of the parish church in April 1842 and for the next three years. See J. F. C. Harrison, 'Chartism in Leeds', in Asa Briggs, ed., *Chartist Studies* (1959).

TABLE 13. *Chartist town councillors in Leeds*

Name	Date of election as Chartist		Ward	Occupation
Hobson, Joshua	1843,	1846	Holbeck	Printer, editor of the *Northern Star*
Jackson, John	1843		Holbeck	Corn miller
*Robson, George	1844,	1847	West	Butcher
Brook, William	1844,	1847	Holbeck	Tobacconist and tea dealer. Later acquired a small nailmaking business
White, Thomas	1845		North West	Draper, retired
Gaunt, George	1847		Holbeck	Painter
*Barker, Joseph	1848		Bramley	Printer
*Barker, Benjamin	1849		Holbeck	Woollen manufacturer
*Waring, George	1849		Bramley	Boot and shoemaker
Lees, Dr. F. R.	1850		Holbeck	Temperance lecturer
*†Carter, R. M.	1850,	1853‡	Holbeck	Coal merchant
*Parker, William	1851		Hunslet	Coffee-house keeper
Scholey, Thomas	1852		West	Cardmaker
Williamson, John	1853		Hunslet	Grocer

* In 1852 sample.
† In 1856 sample.
‡ He continued as councillor for Holbeck standing as a Radical. See below, pp. 204 fn. 3, 215-17 for his subsequent career.

Source. Taken with additions from Harrison in *Chartist Studies*, pp. 86-93. For his comments on the social composition of Leeds Chartism see *ibid.,* p. 72.

that he submitted for a main sewer running along each bank of the river with an outfall below the level of the town were rejected in 1844. There was no sense of urgency and no concern about the sewage in the river. 'The refuse of the dye-houses mingling with the water of the river . . . stop the progress of the decomposition', explained one councillor in a letter to the press the following year. The *Report* of the Royal Commission on the Health of Towns in 1845 did, however, have some effect on public opinion. There were public meetings and petitions. The Borough Surveyor was therefore instructed to prepare a scheme to drain at least a portion of the town. A long controversy followed over the merits of the rival plans, and under the influence of public discussion a more sympathetic opinion began to emerge in the Council. The Chartists abandoned their opposition in 1846, seeing 'more economy in paying for sewerage than sickness'. The Corporation obtained additional powers by another Improvement Act in 1848, but although there was much talk there was still no action taken. It was the cholera epidemic of 1849 that finally overcame all hesitations. The decision to undertake the drainage of the town was made in September 1849 and the work began in 1850.[47] By 1855 15¾ miles of sewer had been constructed on a plan that was a modification of that suggested by Vetch. The 1850s saw a limited improvement in the local death-rate and thereby reversed a dangerous trend. But as in other towns a progressive reduction of the death-rate did not occur until the late 1870s.[48]

In its outlines this clash over sanitary expenditure displays familiar features: the conjunction of popular radicalism with economy, and the determination not to let the town's masters have their way at the expense of the 'people' but to call them to account and cashier them if need be. In Leeds the clash occurred earlier than in most towns but then the town had been in the vanguard of the sanitary movement.

More idiosyncratic was the other political upheaval of the 1840s which had a marked effect on the personnel of the Council. In 1847 the Liberal party in Leeds tore itself apart, one half supporting, the other vehemently opposing the Liberal government's policy on education.[49] The government had decided to increase the grant to be paid to schools controlled by religious bodies and to place the management of the denominational schools on a mutually acceptable basis. This revived the objections to State subsidies for education that had been felt by an important section of Protestant Dissenters ever since they had clashed with the Conservative government in 1843. The most ardent champion of this voluntarist position was Edward Baines junior, deputy editor of *The Leeds Mercury* and a great figure in the Leeds Liberal party.[50] But Baines had never acquired the pre-eminent position once enjoyed by his father, and in this matter in particular he could not hope to carry the whole of the local party with him against the Liberal government of Lord John Russell. The party was deeply divided when Parliament was dissolved and a

[47] Corporation Report Books, and Minute Books, Leeds Improvement Act; *L.M.*, 13.6.1846, 18.6.1846. See also Jean Toft, 'Public Health in Leeds in the Nineteenth Century.'
[48] Average annual death-rate 1848–54 (excluding deaths from cholera during 1849 epidemic) 31·16 per thousand; 1854–58 27·18 per thousand. This improvement was in line with that recorded in other large towns. Dr. Greenhow, 'Survey of Diarrhoeal Diseases' in *Second Report of the Medical Officer of the Privy Council; P.P.*, 1860, xxix.
[49] This crisis is treated most fully in Fraser, 'Politics in Leeds, 1830–1852' from which the information in this paragraph is largely drawn.
[50] See Edward Baines, *Letters to the Rt. Hon. Lord John Russell, First Lord of the Treasury, on State Education* (1846) for the fullest exposition of his position. See also Charles Birchenough, *History of Elementary Education in England and Wales from 1801 to the Present Day*, 3rd. ed. (1938).

general election announced. On the one side were most of the Evangelical Dissenters, on the other were the Unitarians, the Church of England and Roman Catholics. The election could not have come at a worse moment. The voluntarists put up Joseph Sturge, the Birmingham Quaker, as their candidate, the pro-Russell Liberals chose J. G. Marshall, the ex-Unitarian local flax spinner. Neither section would support the other's candidate, and the supporters of Marshall helped to put Beckett, the Conservative, at the top of the poll. Sturge came third.

The election was in July. By November the wounds had not yet healed and the Bainesite majority on the Town Council took their revenge on the aldermen due for re-election. Hamar Stansfeld, chairman of Marshall's election committee, and Darnton Lupton, a member of the committee, lost their seats. Both were Unitarians and in the first rank of Leeds cloth merchants. Alderman Tottie, the Unitarian solicitor, had also been on Marshall's committee. Despite his distinguished service he only just scraped in and thereupon resigned. All three had been on the reformed Town Council from the first, and had been very prominent in the conduct of its affairs. Another veteran, William Pawson, cloth merchant and manufacturer, was also defeated, even though he had been a supporter of Sturge.[51] Two more of Marshall's supporters among the long-standing aldermen resigned in 1850. By January 1852, only four members of the original Council still survived. This compares with nine for almost the same period in Birmingham.

The treatment of the distinguished aldermen probably did little *pour encourager les autres*. At the time of the next municipal election Baines was writing in the *Mercury* that

> 'the higher classes of our townsmen as a body have not only withdrawn from offering themselves as willing candidates for the honours of the Council but have in many cases repeatedly rejected the solicitations of their fellow townsmen to be put in nomination. In some instances they have even manifested a contemptuous sneering indifference to the constituted authorities.'

A week before the editor of the *Intelligencer* had said much the same.[52]

Dr. Fraser has drawn attention to another indicator of the declining social standing of the Council, the degree of overlap with the bench of magistrates. Appointments to the bench were made from among the

---

[51] Pawson's defeat is mysterious, so is the re-election of J. D. Luccock, another supporter of Marshall.

[52] *L.M.*, 21.10.1848; *L.I.*, 14.10.1848, both quoted in Fraser, 'Politics in Leeds 1830–1852', p. 453.

leading citizens of the town. They occurred in 1836, 1842 and 1848 and always reflected the political colour of the government of the day. Because of the way in which municipal elections in Leeds ran parallel to the trend of national politics these political appointments also mirrored the party composition of the Council. His calculation of changes in the proportion of J.P.s who were on the Council at about the time of their appointment are therefore not vitiated to any significant extent by a party bias. Table 14 shows how great the contrast was in this respect between the period 1836–42 and the end of the 1840s.

TABLE 14. *Leeds magistrates bench and Town Council 1836–48: overlap of membership within a year or two of appointment**

		Magistrates		Those also on
	Liberal	Conservative	Total	Town Council
Appointed 1836	19	3	22	15
Appointed 1842	0	9	9	8
Whole Commission 1848	20	9	29	7

* Drawn from information in Fraser, pp. 452-4. I am grateful to Dr. Fraser for allowing me to use these figures.

2

1852–1888

There is not much to be said about the composition of the Council in 1856 or 1862. It has been impossible to discover enough about the majority of firms whose owners make up these mid-century samples to distinguish with any certainty between large, medium and small. All that can be done is to note the occupational composition, adding any more discriminating comments on the few occasions where the evidence is available.

In these respects there is little change. Table 15 shows that the pattern established in 1852 largely persisted through the next decade. It is not until 1872 that we find important breaks in continuity. The number of textile merchants, which had dropped so sharply in 1852, remained much the same. The number of professional men was also largely unchanged. Fewer lawyers in 1862 were balanced by the fleeting reappearance of three doctors. The large businessmen from the metal industry were mainly machine makers. The leather industry produced only one large businessman on the Council in 1856 and 1862.[1] There is a temporary drop in the number of retailers, which is mainly due to the food retailers who had made such a sudden appearance on the Council in 1852. There seems to have been a very rapid turnover among these shopkeeper councillors. Several of those listed by J. F. C. Harrison in his study of Chartists had already left the Council by the time of the 1852 sample. None of those caught in 1852 were still on the Council in 1856. Only one of the 1856 sample was still on the Council in 1862.

More will have to be said later about that remarkable phenomenon of the 1870s, the total disappearance of professional men from the Council. Nothing like that could have been anticipated by looking at the steady contingent of between five and seven members that had always featured

[1] George Tatham, Spanish leather manufacturer, whose political role is discussed on pp. 214 ff.

TABLE 15. *Leeds Town Council 1852–76: selected occupations*

	1852		1856		1862		1872		1876	
	No.	%	No.	%	No.	%	No.	%	No.	%
Lawyers	4	6·2	5	7·8	3	4·7	—	—	—	—
Doctors	—	—	—	—	3	4·7	—	—	—	—
All Professions	5	7·8	5	7·8	6	9·4	—	—	—	—
Textile merchants	10	15·6	8	12·5	8	12·5	4	6·2	3	4·7
Metal industry	5	7·8	8	12·5	7	10·9	5	7·8	6	9·4
Metal industry (large firms)	4	6·2	6	9·4	3	4·7	4	6·2	4	6·2
Leather	2	3·1	2	3·1	3	4·7	5	7·8	6	9·4
Dyers	1	1·6	3	4·7	4	6·2	2	3·1	1	1·6
Retailers	9	14·0	9	14·0	5	7·8	11	17·2	12	18·7
Food retailers	6	9·4	4	6·2	2	3·1	6	9·4	5	7·8

on the table before. But in 1862 the position of the professional men had already changed in one significant respect. It was the first time that none are found in the sample years among the inner ring of committee chairmen.[2]

This group of between ten to twelve members had previously always included two professional men. In fact Tottie and Baker in 1842 and Hope Shaw in 1852 had been the most active policy-making members of the Council. One reason why this is no longer so in 1862 is that out of six professional men only two were Liberals. Without totally monopolising the committee chairs the Liberal party used its control of the Council to retain most of them for its members. The exclusion of Conservatives from the aldermen's bench by giving the seniority to the Liberal members had the same effect. In the years around 1862 while the Radical wing of the Council was led by a coal merchant,[3] other prominent figures were cloth merchants, a wine and spirit merchant, a dyer and a toll contractor.

In 1872 the composition of the Council stands in many ways in marked contrast to that of 1852–62, and the new features are largely confirmed in 1876. Textile merchants now no longer provide a substantial proportion of Council members, while the leather industry provides more than ever before, reaching a peak in 1876 with nearly 10 per cent of the Council. Both these changes are in line with the changing economic structure of the town which is examined in Appendix II. But there are other changes which do not lend themselves to explanations of that kind.

The most obvious has already been mentioned. It is the total disappearance of the professional men. By 1882 there was a recovery with one doctor and three lawyers among the members but even then the number was still somewhat below the previous figures ⟨*see* figure 6⟩. The second feature that calls for comment is the proportion of shopkeepers, which reached unprecedented levels in the 1870s, rising sharply in relation to 1862 and exceeding the previous peak reached in the 1850s. Neither of these changes can be explained in terms of changes in the economic structure of the town, but need to be seen against the politics of the time.

In the administration of the town the years immediately after 1850 saw an outburst of activity. The construction of the drainage system

---

[2] For the purpose of investigating the inner ring of committee chairmen, the samples were in each case drawn from two consecutive years. In this case they were 1861 and 1862. The total number was ten. Chairmen of sub-committees are not included.

[3] R. M. Carter, ex-Chartist, clr. 1850–62, ald. 1862–74, M.P. for Leeds 1868–76. See below, pp. 215–17. He was a clr. again from 1879–82.

between 1850 and 1855 has already been mentioned. In 1851 the Council decided to build a town hall, a project which dragged on until 1858. In 1851 they also embarked on the purchase and extension of the water-works, and built a covered market between 1853 and 1855.[4] In the case of the town hall the Council was responding to impulses generated elsewhere in the town.[5] The purchase of the waterworks was primarily the achievement of Alderman John Hope Shaw.

Hope Shaw was a solicitor and, like Tottie before him, included in his highly respectable practice a fair amount of election work for the Liberal party. His work as mayor's assessor in the Revision Court, which heard appeals against the overseers' compiling of the electoral register, dis-qualified him for membership of the Council. It was too important to the party for him to give it up or else he would have been elected to the Council well before 1844. That year he did resign from the post and straightway became an alderman. He was a man of intellectual distinction and of eminence in his profession.[6] Unlike most of the Liberal leaders of that generation he was a Churchman, a generous supporter of church schools and missions and even a member of that select inner group of Leeds social leaders, the trustees of the Leeds parish church. He had supported Marshall in the 1847 general election but fortunately for the town he was not due for re-election as alderman until November 1850.

Leeds was supplied with water by a private company but under the Act of 1837, which created it, the Corporation had the right to purchase at any time after June 1849. In 1851 drought left the town seriously short of water and it became apparent that the company had for too long put off the search for additional supplies. It commissioned an inquiry, but even before the presentation of the engineer's recommendations, Hope Shaw had been responsible for a long and very able report sub-mitted to the Town Council. He argued that, since new and extensive works would have to be undertaken, there was every reason why the Council should now take up its option to purchase the company. He

[4] Asa Briggs, *Victorian Cities*, chapter 4 for a detailed study of the building of the town hall; Jean Toft, 'Public Health in Leeds in the Nineteenth Century', chapter 9 for the waterworks; Corporation Report Book and Minute Book, Leeds Improvement Act, for the building of the market.

[5] Asa Briggs, *Victorian Cities*, pp. 156–64, 168–70 for the role of Dr. J. D. Heaton oper-ating both through the Leeds Improvement Society and the Leeds Philosophical and Literary Society.

[6] He was one of the earliest presidents of the Provincial Law Association, and on the Council of the Incorporated Law Society. He was prominent in the Leeds Philosophical and Literary Society and seven times president. Also president Leeds Mechanics Institute, vice-president Yorkshire Union of Mechanics Institutes. R. V. Taylor, *Biographia Leodien-sis*, pp. 520–23; *L.M.*, 30.4.1842, p. 6.

8

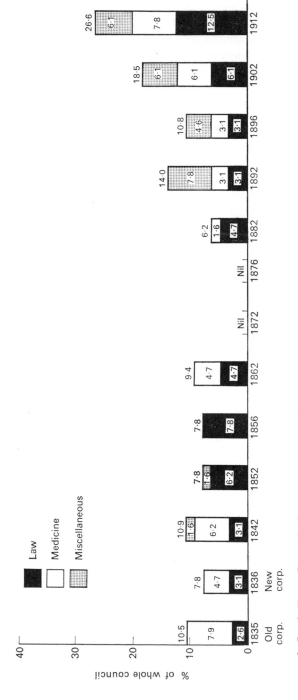

FIG. 6. *Leeds Town Council 1835–1912: the professions*

pointed out that the Corporation was able to raise the capital at 4 per cent instead of the 6 per cent dividends that the company would have to pay. In any case the Council, having recently begun to construct an elaborate system of sewerage for the town, had a direct interest in an ample supply of water under its control with which to flush the drains. The report ended by rehearsing all the arguments that had been advanced by Edwin Chadwick and others before the Royal Commission on the Health of Towns in 1844–5 in favour of municipal control.[7]

On the strength of these arguments the Council decided to buy and the purchase was completed by November 1852. Hope Shaw became chairman of the waterworks committee which commissioned a second investigation into available sources of water. In 1854 the merits of the rival schemes were hotly debated in the Council and in the press. The former finally rejected the scheme for bringing water from the River Washburn which Hope Shaw had championed. They decided to pump it from the river Wharfe instead, despite the dubious quality of the water and the prospect of further pollution from the fast growing communities along its bank.[8] Hope Shaw resigned from the committee and did not stand again for the Council when his term of office expired in 1856. Since he died in 1864 he never knew how completely his judgment was to be vindicated. In 1865 the quality of the water was so strongly condemned by an inspector from the Medical Department of the Privy Council that the Corporation commissioned a further inquiry into sources of supply, and belatedly adopted a scheme to take it from the River Washburn after all.[9]

It looks as if in the municipal administration of Leeds, as of so many other towns, the years immediately following 1850 began with a vigour which it proved hard to sustain and ran by the middle of the decade into the sands of incompetence. F. H. Spencer, author of *Municipal Origins* (1911) and at one time research assistant to the Webbs, who read through all the report books of the Corporation from 1835–99, spoke of the volume covering the years 1852–9 and dealing with the duties under the Improvement Act as giving 'a general impression of dull incompetence and lack of efficient officers', contrasting it with the business-like and

[7] Corporation Report Book, Leeds Improvement Act, 6.8.1851; *L.M.*, 23.10.1851.
[8] J. M. Rendel, *Report as to a further Supply of Water to the Town of Leeds* (Leeds, 1854); *L.M.*, 29.7.1854, 12.8.1854.
[9] Dr. H. J. Hunter, 'On the Sanitary State of Leeds', *Eighth Report of the Medical Officer of the Privy Council, appendix* 6; P.P., 1866, xxxiii, 648 *L.M.*, 2.10.1865; Corporation Report Book, Leeds Improvement Act, V, 11.9.1866.

active impression made by the volume for 1847–51.[10] Certainly the manner in which the two boldly conceived schemes of the 1850s, the building of the town hall and the improvement of the water-supply, were actually carried out, seems to bear him out.

We know how the public health administration looked in 1865 to an informed outsider capable of making comparisons with other towns. Dr. Hunter's report to the Medical Department of the Privy Council indicates carelessness, and the complacent acceptance of low standards:

> 'To the eyes of an inspector who had just left Newcastle and Sunderland, and who in the same week visited Sheffield, Leeds in August 1865 presented a surprising sight, bringing to remembrance the condition of many English towns of twenty years ago, but finding hardly a standard with which to be compared in the present state of any great town.'

The creator of the worst nuisances was the Corporation's night-soil department itself. The whole administration of the Nuisance Removal Acts was perhaps the worst in proportion to the importance of the town which had come to the knowledge of the Privy Council's Medical Department. Only the Board of Guardians emerged with any credit from the inquiry. It was they who had attempted to enforce the removal of nuisances, not the Town Council, and it was with reluctance that Dr. Hunter pointed out that they had in fact been exceeding their legal powers. The Nuisance Removal Act of 1855 had placed the sole responsibility for this on the Council.[11]

The first reaction of the Council to the publication of Hunter's report had been entirely defensive,[12] but on second thoughts they made a genuine attempt to meet the criticism. They took steps to improve the water supply by putting in hand a new scheme of considerable size. They applied to Parliament for a new Improvement Act, which included power to appoint a medical officer of health, and in the spring of 1866 appointed Dr. Robinson to the post. Robinson was able to start an energetic regime of nuisance removal. The vast accumulation of filth, which Hunter had seen overflowing from the middensteads and scattered in thoroughfares, had gone when the next inspector from the Medical Department visited the town in 1870. Although he still found much to criticise, it was clear that considerable energy had been shown

[10] *Webb Loc. Gov. Col.*, volume 262, General Observations.
[11] *Eighth Report of the Medical Officer of the Privy Council*, pp. 23, 226–45.
[12] Leeds Corporation Report Book, V, 2.12.1865.

in several areas of public health administration since Dr. Robinson's appointment.[13]

There was quickened activity in other spheres as well. In 1866 the Corporation became the highway authority and by 1870 had abolished all turnpike tolls within the borough. The same years saw the only major schemes of street improvement undertaken by the Corporation prior to the 1890s—the widening of Boar Lane and the extension of Briggate, the two principal streets in the centre of the town.[14] Such schemes were beneficial in the long run, and the increased rateable value which they created would one day enable the Corporation to recoup itself for the outlay of £118,000 on the Boar Lane and Briggate works. However, in the short run they had to be paid for. In 1867 the Corporation rates for the township of Leeds reached 4s. 10½d. in the £, the highest total so far, largely because of increases in the highway and improvement rates. This was an increase of 9d. over the previous year. As recently as 1863 the figure had always been below 4s. ⟨*See* table 16.⟩

TABLE 16. *Leeds township 1858–80 : rates in the pound*[15]

	Total Corporation rates*			
1858	3s. 5½d.		1869	3s. 10½d.
1859	3s. 4d.		1870	3s. 8½d.
1860	3s. 7½d.		1871	3s. 6½d.
1861	3s. 8d.		1872	4s. 1d.
1862	3s. 11d.		1873	5s. 10½d.
1863	4s. 0½d.		1874	5s. 11½d.
1864	4s. 1½d.		1875	6s. 0½d.
1865	3s. 8d.		1876	5s. 5¼d.
1866	4s. 1½d.		1877	5s. 8d.
1867	4s. 10½d.		1878	5s. 6½d.
1868	4s. 4½d.		1879	4s. 11½d.
			1880	5s. 3d.

* This does not include the poor rate. From 1871 onwards it includes the school rate, levied on behalf of the School Board, but no longer includes the gaol rate, which was henceforth paid out of general taxation. These figures are consistently higher than those for Birmingham, but this is a matter of no significance. At a time when rateable value was assessed by innumerable independent bodies whose methods varied greatly no useful comparison is possible between the rate in the £ in different towns. I have therefore not constructed a comparative table for Birmingham and Leeds. The figures for Birmingham are printed in J. T. Bunce, *History of the Corporation of Birmingham*, II, 47.

13 J. N. Radcliffe, *The Sanitary State of Leeds, with particular Reference to Diarrhoea and Fever* (1871). See also Jean Toft, 'Public Health in Leeds'. Among the action taken at this time was the cleaning out of some of the worst 'becks', i.e. tributary streams of the Aire, flowing through the town. From one of these were removed the carcases of seven cats, eleven rats, seventeen dogs and six pigs.

14 Corporation Report Books, Leeds Improvement Act, Report of Purchase of Property Committee, Report of Parliamentary Committee, 9 November 1869.

15 I am grateful to Professor Asa Briggs for allowing me to use his figures extracted annually from *The Leeds Mercury* and *The Corporation Abstract of Account*. The figures for 1858–70 are also to be found in *L.M.*, 26.10.1870, p. 4.

Such a sudden and considerable increase in the rates would have been difficult to get away with at the best of times. But these were times of political unsettlement caused by the franchise issue and the immediate consequences of the 1867 Reform Act. The result was the Leeds Municipal Reform Association, founded in 1868 to secure change in the local system of government 'principally with a view of lessening expenditure and securing greater municipal purity'.[16] It wished to abolish aldermen and spoke the language of democratic radicalism.

When the Town Council decided in February 1868 to adopt the Public Library Acts which entitled them to spend the product of a 1d. rate, the sensitivity of the public to matters of expenditure became quickly apparent. The advocates of provision for public libraries had a strong case, for the Corporation possessed 2,700 volumes already, not to mention the complete files of the local newspapers, all buried away in a cellar of the town hall. However, at a public meeting on the 11 March the opposition to the levying of even the smallest compulsory rate was strong and loud, led by a Liberal town councillor, a pawnbroker. After a second count the resolution in favour of the new departure was carried by the narrowest of majorities. The Act was adopted, but the Council took the hint and voted against any action for the moment. In January 1869 the advocates of the library were defeated yet again on the grounds that the burdens of the ratepayers should not be increased.[17] This caution is understandable for that very day the visitors' gallery was filled with militant ratepayers. They had petitioned against increases in the salaries of the town clerk and the chief constable, but without success.[18]

At the following municipal elections the Municipal Reform Association demonstrated their power and their discontent with recent policies by defeating the two retiring Liberal councillors in the West ward. It was a contest conducted 'not for party purposes but for the principle of economy'. 'The upper section of the Liberals in the ward', explained one of its sponsors, 'had paid rather too little consideration to the lower section', but he anticipated that in future all would be united under the banner of economy and retrenchment. Elsewhere the emphasis of the successful candidates was much the same, and the election was generally

---

[16] Letter in *L.M.*, 31.3.1868.

[17] *L.M.*, 12.3.1868, 4.4.1868, 2.1.1869. A library committee was at length appointed in August 1969 after an appeal from Sir Andrew Fairbairn, M.P. A librarian was appointed June 1870 and arrangements made to rent the old Infirmary as a central library, and rooms in two outlying mechanics' institutes as branch libraries.

[18] *L.M.*, 2.1.1869.

regarded as a warning to the Council. Next June, when the finance committee recommended an increase in the borough treasurer's salary, there were ward meetings and another ratepayers' deputation. This time the Council bowed to the storm and refused the increase although it was supported by nearly the whole bench of aldermen. In August the Municipal Reform Association held a public meeting attended by a thousand people and decided to form branches in all wards in order to send to the Council 'men of honest principles, of economy and retrenchment'. The elections were again fought prominently on the issue of economy. In two wards the retiring Liberals, a large local employer and a prominent Radical politician respectively, were defeated for failing to oppose the increase in the treasurer's salary. The Association's attempt to repeat their triumph of the previous year in the west ward was, however, beaten off.[19]

The leaders of this protest movement were overwhelmingly shopkeepers or estate agents. In 1872 and 1876 there were four estate agents on the Council. We have already noticed the marked rise in the number of shopkeepers at that date.

It is a curious comment on the momentum that had been generated that it took some time for the vociferous critics of municipal expenditure to catch up with events. The Council had been quick to see the writing on the wall and by 1869 the rates were a whole shilling less than two years before. They continued to fall and in 1871 were lower than at any time since 1859. Yet, as the *Mercury* commented on publishing these figures, no-one would have guessed this from the speeches of the Council's critics in 1870.[20]

This financial success was short-lived but it may explain why the Council embarked almost at once on further ambitious projects. In 1871 on the recommendations of the medical officer 293 houses were pulled down in Wellington Yard, the area that had featured notoriously in every epidemic since 1832. It had been singled out for special condemnation in the Local Government Board report on the sanitary state of Leeds that had just been published, and was the site of an open midden 21 ft. by 5 ft. 10 in. and 6 ft. deep. A few years before a drunken man had fallen in and had suffocated in it. Another three acres were cleared elsewhere some time before 1878. Small though this was by later standards or in comparison with Birmingham, Glasgow and other towns at

---

[19] *L.M.*, 2.11.1869, p. 8, 6.6.1870, 13.8.1870, 2.11.1870, p. 3.
[20] *L.M.*, 26.10.1870, p. 2.

the time, it was the first piece of deliberate slum clearance by the Corporation and the only work of this kind until 1895.[21]

Most spectacular of the projects undertaken in this period was the purchase of Roundhay Park, the 800 acre estate on the north-east of the borough, which had been put up for sale by its owner. Its acquisition for the town was very much the personal achievement of John Barran, mayor from 1870–72. It must be regarded as a bold and imaginative investment for the future, since the park with its splendid lakes[22] was at the time almost inaccessible from the town, and 20 years later the Corporation had to lay on a special tramway service to take the people there. Barran used both his money and his position in the town to make the project acceptable. The founder of the mass production ready-made clothing industry, for which Leeds was to become famous, his career was one of the most spectacular economic success stories of the day. By 1872 he was a large employer of labour and a wealthy man. His sheer ability and personal charm gave him for a few years a commanding position in the Council and it was a serious loss when he was elected to Parliament and resigned in 1877.[23] It would not be out of place to compare him with Joseph Chamberlain, for there are many similarities. But unlike Chamberlain he was alone and not part of a municipal movement and when he went into Parliament he left no successors behind.

The purchase of Roundhay Park added 3d. to the rates and other projects added more. From 1873 onwards ratepayers in Leeds township were paying 1s. per £ more than in the peak year of 1867 and 2s. above the levels of that happy interlude in 1870–1 ⟨*see* table 16⟩. The rates continued to rise until 1875, but by then the pressure from the ratepayers had built up and this period of activity came to an end. The Council had on more than one occasion come to grief and given a handle to their critics. This had naturally reinforced the demands for economy, so that ill-considered expenditure and cheese-paring shortsightedness tended to alternate.

[21] *L.M.*, 1.4.1871; J. N. Radcliffe, *The Sanitary State of Leeds*, p. 13; F. M. Lupton, *Housing Improvement: a Summary of Ten Years Work in Leeds* (Leeds, 1906), p. 11.

[22] Some of Barran's critics said that 'there was too much water bought at land prices'. Frank Kidson, 'Leeds in the Making XVII', *Y.E.P.*, 26.6.1914.

[23] John Barran, elected clr. 1853, ald. 1868–77, Liberal M.P. for Leeds 1876–85, for Otley division of Yorkshire 1886–95. He had come to Leeds in 1842, worked for a pawnbroker who was a town council member, set up as a pawnbroker on his own and by 1852 had added a business as tailor and outfitter. Instead of bespoke tailoring he manufactured for the wholesale market, using mainly outworkers at first. The basis of his great success was the systematic application of the division of labour to the manufacture of clothes. He soon concentrated his workers in a factory. By 1878 he had a factory with 15,000 sq. ft. of floor space. *Leeds Sketches and Reviews* (1900), pp. 21–5; David Ryott, *John Barran's of Leeds 1851–1951* (Leeds, 1951).

In 1870 Leeds had found that it could no longer pour its untreated sewage into the River Aire. As at Birmingham the Corporation was forced to take action by a court injunction. Eager to do something they entered precipitately into a contract with the so-called Native Guano Company for the application of their patent chemical process. Three months later the Royal Commission on River Pollution published their report in which they exposed the uselessness of the process in question, but by then it was too late for Leeds to withdraw from its commitment without much further expense and delay. The next four years saw all sorts of experiments, and by 1877 the Corporation possessed a sewage farm of twenty-six acres worked on less spectacular principles.[24]

To solve its financial problems the Corporation bought out the two local gas companies in 1870, inspired by the well-known success of Manchester. The Council spent £763,225 and then discovered that the equipment was so worn out that the operations ran at a loss. In 1873 and again in 1874 the works had to be subsidised out of the rates to the tune of £14,000 in all. There was nothing wrong with the policy and it paid handsomely in the long run. What was wrong was the valuation at which the purchase had been made.[25]

Such mishaps indicated a lack of technical competence among the advisers of the Corporation. Hence it is not altogether irrelevant that it was on the salaries of its officials that the Council's zeal for economy was most often exercised. Committees commonly found their recommendations on salary levels both for existing officers and for new appointments ignored by the Council as a whole. Such a miserly policy was bound to be detrimental in the long run. Thus in 1874 the governor of the gaol, who during his twelve years of service had reduced the cost of management and been generally most satisfactory, was refused an increase of £100 per annum, although his salary compared unfavourably with that of men in places of less importance. In 1875 it was the turn of the stipendiary magistrate to suffer, although he also had a strong case. In 1877 both these officers' claims were once more put forward and once more turned down. In 1878 the claims of the gas engineer and the inspector of paving work were rejected, despite the pleas of their committees, and that of the detectives passed only by the mayor's casting vote. In 1879 the gas engineer obtained his increase but the watch committee were forbidden to advertise for a detective superintendant at

[24] Jean Toft, 'Public Health in Leeds', pp. 240.
[25] Joseph Chamberlain in 1874 was to make a point of referring to the experience of Leeds as an example of how not to do it.

£200 per annum. They knew it was not worth offering less for a suitable man and preferred to make do with what they had got.[26]

The similar case of the medical officer of health is particularly instructive since in this instance it is possible to trace a direct connection between cause and consequence. Dr. Robinson had been appointed in 1866 at a salary of £500 per annum. This was still his salary in 1872 when the new Public Health Act authorised the Local Government Board to contribute 50 per cent of the salary of medical officers and inspectors of nuisances, provided it was consulted on matters of appointment and dismissal. True to its traditional distrust of central government control, Leeds Corporation refused to apply for the grant. In the course of the debate it became apparent that the ability to check the actions of an overzealous medical officer was a power highly valued by the members of the Council, and that there had been recent occasions when it had been employed to prevent him from closing cellar dwellings.[27] A few months later Dr. Robinson, whose work had been highly praised by the inspector from the Local Government Board the previous year, left to take up an appointment elsewhere at a salary of £2–300 per annum more than he had been getting. Undeterred, the Council advertised for his successor at £400 a year. The appointment was filled by Dr. Goldie, whose incompetence and long-standing neglect was to be revealed in 1889.[28]

These debates on expenditure are instructive for the quality of the arguments used, and for what they reveal of the mental processes of the members of the economy group. In 1870 a grocer, recently elected as a critic of high rates, disposed of a request from the magistrates for additional accommodation in the women's wing of the borough gaol: 'Let the magistrates reduce the number of public houses and they would soon reduce the number of prisoners.'[29]

This is a crude expression of a point of view that was to become of great importance. The men who set the tone in the Leeds Town Council over the next twenty years were inclined to be pre-occupied with the close connection, as they saw it, between temperance, economy, and social progress. There had been a teetotal party on the Council since the early 1860s, who sponsored occasional petitions on matters of licensing

---

[26] J. S. Curtis, *The Story of the Marsden Mayoralty* (Leeds, 1875), pp. 39–41, 101–3; *L.M.*, 8.2.1877, 2.5.1878, 8.8.1878, 2.1.1879.
[27] *L.M.*, 7.12.1872. On the controversial subject of cellar dwellings in Leeds see also H. J. Hunter, pp. 237–8 and J. N. Radcliffe, p. 31.
[28] *L.M.*, 8.6.1873. For the events of 1889, see below, part II, chapter 1.
[29] *L.M.*, 10.2.1870.

policy.[30] Its spokesman was George Tatham, a large leather manufacturer and a Quaker, who had been a councillor since 1856. One way
to measure the growing influence of this party is in terms of the Council
members who belong to the Leeds Temperance Society. In 1854 there
had been two, by 1868 there were fifteen. The sample for 1876 included
eighteen, and that for 1882 twenty-one.[31] But measured in terms of
votes the teetotal party was actually larger. When Tatham proposed in
1871 that the Corporation petition Parliament in favour of local option
he carried the day by twenty votes to nineteen. In 1872 when Roundhay
Park was bought by the Corporation, Tatham immediately proposed
to bar the sale of all intoxicating drink from the park but the Council
compromised by only banning the sale of spirits. They were anxious
to encourage the inhabitants to use the large but very inconveniently
situated park, five miles from the centre of the town, and knew that to
ban the sale of beer was not the way to do it. The following year, when
they proposed to let the Roundhay Mansion within the park as a 'hotel',
Tatham returned to the attack with a petition from over 11,000 inhabitants against the sale of intoxicating drink in the park. In the subsequent
division the teetotal party once again numbered twenty but they were
defeated. Thereafter the annual debate over the renewal of the Roundhay Hotel licence became a measure of the strength of the strict teetotal
party. In 1884 they actually passed a resolution not to re-apply for the
licence by twenty-eight votes to twenty-four. It was a short-lived
triumph, despite the support of an editorial in the *Mercury*, for a month
later the Council rescinded its decision by twenty-nine votes to twenty-
eight. Those twenty-eight votes recorded the high-water mark of the
party's strength, but in 1889 they were still able to muster twenty-four
on a day when Tatham was away ill.[32]

The growth of this militant temperance opinion in the Town Council
was an aspect of changes coming over Leeds Liberalism at this time.
The United Kingdom Alliance agitating for local option was one of
several pressure groups in favour of more radical policies who were
particularly active in the years after the 1867 Reform Act. Their supporters found their natural home in the more radical of the two Liberal
organisations in the town, the northern branch of the Reform League,
led by Alderman Carter and supported prominently by George Tatham.
Strained relations with the more moderate supporters of Edward

[30] E.g. *L.M.*, 1.9.1862; MSS. Corporation Reports, V, 5.3.1869.
[31] Leeds Temperance Society, *Annual Reports*, 1831–1900.
[32] *L.M.*, 1.4.1871, 15.8.1872, 2.1.1873, 7.2.1884, 7.2.1889.

Baines, M.P., who controlled the Leeds Liberal Registration Association, were patched up with some difficulty in 1868 and Baines and
Carter were nominated jointly as Liberal candidates for the general
election. Yet only the week before the truce Tatham had succeeded in
blocking the re-election of three aldermen associated with the moderate
Liberals and replaced them by men taken from a list of reliable Radicals.[33]

In 1870 disagreement over Forster's Education Bill broke the precarious unity of the party once more. Baines had originally been a member of the Manchester-based National Education Union in defence of
denominational education, and he fully supported Forster's Act. The
Radicals took the line of the National Education League and attacked
clause 25, which enabled school boards to pay the fees of certain children
at denominational schools. They carried the day in the nomination for
the School Board elections in December 1870. Until November 1872,
when Baines gave up his support of the 25th clause, the education issue
was the chief bone of contention among Leeds Liberals. However, as
Bruce, the Liberal Home Secretary, fumbled in Parliament during 1871
and 1872 over the reform of the licensing laws, the estrangement between Baines supporters and the proponents of a radical licensing policy
ran along much the same lines as the earlier quarrels had opened up.
Baines, although himself a long-standing teetotaller, consistently opposed the Bills on local option introduced into the House of Commons
by the representatives of the U.K. Alliance.[34]

By 1874 the breach between Baines and Radical opinion in the town
had reached such a point as to rule out any co-operation during the
general election. There were other grounds of disagreement, but it is
significant that the rival Radical candidate put up against Baines was
F. R. Lees, the local agent of the U.K. Alliance.[35] This challenge proved
fatal to Baine's political career, for although Lees came bottom of the
poll, he split the Liberal vote and lost Baines his seat. Carter was now the
sole Liberal M.P. for Leeds, and when in 1876 a single political organisation, the Leeds Liberal Association, was set up on the new model
popularised by Birmingham, power rested squarely with his supporters.

---

[33] *L.M.*, 17.11.1868, 10.11.1868. The victims were Kitson (machine maker), Botterill
(dyer) and Titley (flax spinner). They were replaced by Barran (clothier), Addyman (cloth
merchant) and Shepherd (machine-tool maker). For the divisions in the Leeds Liberal
Party at this time see J. R. Lowerson, 'The Political Career of Sir Edward Baines', unpublished M.A. thesis, School of History, University of Leeds, 1965.

[34] Lowerson, 'Sir Edward Baines', pp. 243–50.

[35] J. R. Vincent, *The Formation of the Liberal Party* (1966), pp. 124–6 for Baines' letter
dated 13 March 1874 in which he explains just how many sections of Leeds Liberalism he
had managed to antagonise.

The first president of the Association was Alderman John Barran, one of the three good Radicals of 1868. When Carter went bankrupt in 1876 and resigned his seat, it was Barran not Baines who succeeded him.[36]

These events set their stamp on the dominant attitudes among the Liberals on the Town Council. As we have seen, militant teetotal views became common among them. In November 1877 it was still possible for a licensed victualler to be adopted as a Liberal candidate and elected in the East ward but he decided not to stand again in November 1883. In the same year on the defeat of a large wine and spirit merchant, owner of several hotels and many public houses, a popular patron of sport and a town councillor since 1871, the *Mercury* explained that being in the drink trade had harmed him politically. They were the last members of the trade among the Liberal councillors. As the hold of the new leaders tightened, other Liberal sympathisers were alienated from local politics.[37] In Leeds as elsewhere, as Liberalism came to be identified with the militant temperance cause, so the drink trade looked to the Conservatives as their defenders and the Conservatives to the drink trade as their allies.[38]

For a short time in the early 1870s it looked as if the Conservatives might come to dominate the Council. The candidature of William Wheelhouse in 1868 for the Parliamentary seat, a popular man from outside the inner circle of Conservative politicians, had attracted new blood into the local party and stimulated vigorous reorganisation. The alliance with the drink trade helped them, as did the internal divisions among their Liberal opponents. By 1873 they numbered twenty-eight councillors. But success evaded them once more, and the capture of a parliamentary seat was followed by defeat in the municipal elections. They had counted on controlling the election of aldermen in November 1874 and so seizing the majority at last. Instead they were badly beaten in the wards and this was repeated in the succeeding years. By 1876–7 there were only a dozen Conservatives left.

---

[36] *Memoirs of Sir Wemyss Reid 1842–1885*, ed., Stuart J. Reid (1905), pp. 219–22.

[37] There is some evidence that the moderate supporters of Baines returned to take office in the Leeds Liberal Association soon after 1876. See A. W. Roberts, 'Leeds Liberalism and Late-Victorian Politics', *Northern History*, V (1970), 131–56. They do not seem to have taken a comparable interest in the Town Council.

[38] *L.M.*, 2.11.1883. The licensed victualler was Owen Geenty, the wine and spirit merchant Adam Brown of Brown, Carson & Co., whose business is described in *Leeds Illustrated* (1892). See book I, part I, p. 35, part II, pp. 149 ff for temperance and municipal politics. Also Brian Harrison, *Drink and the Victorians*, especially chapter 13 for a careful discussion of this identification with the political parties in the national setting.

By the late 1870s the survivors of the older generation of aldermen had become politically quite overwhelmed by the newcomers. Something like a change of generations took place in those years and it was clinched with the simultaneous retirement in 1883 of three aldermen, Luccock (stuff merchant), Kelsall (cloth merchant) and George (dyer). Luccock and Kelsall had been on the Council since the early 1840s, George since the early 1850s.

Even more indicative of the new regime was the election of Tatham as mayor in November 1879. Both by wealth and by seniority he had been long qualified for the office. He had refused it in 1875 because he considered that neither the Council nor the public were sufficiently in sympathy with his teetotal principles. On being urged again in 1879 he judged that the times had changed:

> 'If the people of Leeds wished for their Mayor a Quaker and a teetotaler of strong convictions, who would lead them during the next twelve months in a line of self-denial, sobriety, economy and efficiency, he could not refuse.'

He would not serve wine at his dinners nor any form of alcohol at any time. On hearing this the assize judges declined the customary invitation to dine with the mayor, but agreed to come to breakfast instead.[39] Thereafter the custom of mayors barring alcoholic drinks from civic functions became common in Leeds.

The year after Tatham became mayor, A. W. Scarr became an alderman. Like Tatham he belonged to the dominant group that stood for the combination of economy and temperance but he was the most conspicuous of them all and represented, even as he caricatured, their characteristic qualities. Of all the indomitable self-made men of mid-Victorian Leeds 'Archie' Scarr was the epitome.[40] His father had been a bankrupt grocer from Burnley, a Methodist local preacher, who came to Leeds in 1840 and sold vegetables in the open market on Vicar's Croft. The son helped and gradually worked up the business to prosperity. Although he had no equal in the market as a salesman, Scarr often declared that it was not what he earned but what he saved that first set him on his feet. Thrift was his passion and he used to be laughed at even by the market folk for his old, greasy, patched clothes. In middle life he would wear a grey and greasy billy hat, patched where a joker had once burnt a hole

---

[39] Speech on taking office, *L.M.*, 10.11.1879; *Leeds Biographer* (1892), p. 33.
[40] Herbert Yorke, *A Mayor of the Masses. History and Anecdotes of Archibald Witham Scarr* (Leeds, 1904).

in it. Finding that vegetables were too dependent on the season, he took up dried fruit as a speciality, selling figs, 't'Scriptur frewt'. His sales talk was for many years the leading entertainment of the market. When in 1857 Vicar's Croft was turned into a covered market with permanent shops, he rented four of them and added confectionary, grocery, hardware and crockery to his lines. By the late 1880s he was a wealthy man and occupied eight shops in the market, two branch stores in the poorer parts of Leeds, as well as market shops in Barnsley and Bradford, selling a long list of goods, 'all of an exceedingly popular character', as a contemporary description put it.[41] By then he was employing thirty assistants, but was still to be seen regularly in the market, haranguing his customers, touring from stand to stand laying down the law, approachable by anyone, 'the monarch of the market'.

He first entered public life as a temperance orator, a line in which he was to win great local fame. At open-air meetings on Woodhouse Moor, or at the Temperance Hall in York Street, Scarr was a regular attraction with his powerful voice, his peculiar gestures and his wonderful gift of repartee. His subject on these occasions would quite as often be thrift as temperance; together the two formed his philosophy of life. Like many of his contemporaries he received his training as a speaker at Parker's Coffee House in Briggate, where every evening a debate was held on some current topic of social or political interest ⟨see plate 34⟩. The convivial atmosphere of Parker's, whose owner had himself been a Chartist and town councillor in the 1850s, was for the municipal politics of Leeds much what the *Woodman* was for Birmingham in the same period. In this environment 'Archie' Scarr grew up, a Chartist as a youth, a member in the 1860s of the Leeds Parliamentary Reform Association, the Reform League, and inevitably in the end on the executive committee of the Leeds Liberal Association. His first venture into municipal politics was through the Municipal Reform Association. In 1869 he organised the distribution of pamphlets for them. In 1870 he was one of their candidates in the West ward, but refused to have any truck with public houses, even the Liberal ones. Such disregard for traditional methods was fatal. He was beaten that year, and again in the following one, but in 1872, standing as usual on the platform of economy, he was returned for the North-East ward.

Once in the Council nothing could keep 'Our Archie' down. He spoke nine times at his first Council meeting, and kept up an average of seven times per meeting for the first four occasions. Five years later to his

[41] *The Industries of Yorkshire*, part I (1888), p. 96.

bitter chagrin he was narrowly defeated in the nomination for alderman. His friends staged a protest meeting in the town hall, and at the next elections in 1880 he obtained his promotion. By then his contribution to the Council debates had already been formidable. A few months later *The Leeds Mercury* singled him out on the occasion of his opposition to the provision of public abattoirs as 'Mr. Alderman Scarr, who has constantly opposed almost every local improvement that has been proposed within recent years.'[42] His record justified the claim. It was no different in 1895, when the changes in the municipal politics of the borough put an end to his career. Even at the height of his power Scarr was never chairman of anything more than a sub-committee, and the important policy proposals were seldom his. He could, however, be relied upon to criticise, to rally the timid, the uncertain and the cussed and to give them a weight which their mere numerical superiority on the Council would not have lent them. The frequent overruling of committee recommendations by the full Council, of which instances are given on pp. 213–14 and owed much to the role of 'the inevitable Mr. Scarr', as the *Mercury* called him on one such occasion.[43]

The prospect of Scarr as mayor led to some foreboding not only among his enemies, but after an undignified debate in full Council he was installed in November 1887. The respectable portion of the town was shocked to see the mayor still presiding at the market, but the people loved him, not least for his accessibility there. It was said that in his capacity as a J.P. he signed the naturalisation papers of more Jews than any other magistrate in Leeds. He refused as a matter of course to serve alcohol, and the assize judges declined his invitation to dinner, and on this occasion even to breakfast. They need not have worried at being compromised, for during his year of office he made an effort to moderate his tongue (except at temperance meetings), and confounded his critics by being not at all a bad mayor. In addition to the usual entertainment he gave a monster gala in Roundhay Park, such as had only been given once before. Indeed by bringing him more closely in touch with the officials at the town hall his year of office served to make him less unsympathetic to their claims. As he himself put it to one of them, he 'didn't know at you fellus hed soa much work to do'.[44]

[42] *L.M.*, 15.2.1881.
[43] *L.M.*, 8.2.1877.
[44] Obituary, *Y.E.P.*, 5.2.1904. The dialect is reproduced as quoted but it is almost certainly false. There was a tendency for reporters to exaggerate the quaintness of his language. In conversation he used 'fairly standard' English, and it was only when excited or when interrupted that he lapsed into a 'mixture of Lancashire and Yorkshire with a strong dash of Scarr in it'. Yorke, p. 174.

It should not be supposed that the men who ran the Leeds Town Council in the 1880s were all as colourful, as eccentric, or as likeable as Scarr. But, it would have required great dynamism to have overcome so powerful a brake built into the system, and there was no sign of that. The leading Liberals on the Council were mostly in sympathy with the Tatham/Scarr mentality, though they might well be embarrassed by some of Scarr's eccentricities.

Like him many of them were Methodists. Of the twenty-one committee chairmen in 1891–2 it has been possible to trace the church affiliation of fourteen, and eight of those were Methodists. The rest were one Church of England, three Unitarians, one Congregationalist and one Quaker. At least fourteen were regular members of the teetotal lobby. In the Council as a whole the church affiliation of twenty-seven out of the forty-three Liberals is known. Of these fifteen were Methodists, four Church of England, three Unitarians, two Quakers, two Congregationalists and one Baptist. This preponderance of Methodists is in great contrast to the insignificant role of Methodism in Birmingham, but it looks at first sight like a Leeds version of the great influence exercised by certain Dissenting churches over the Birmingham Town Council. However, the appearance is deceptive for the Council members came from widely scattered churches. Even when we bear in mind that for Methodists the important organisation is the circuit rather than the individual church, it makes no difference. The members were in fact drawn from a whole range of Methodist denominations.[45] What we are seeing is rather the reflection of the great numerical preponderance of Methodists of all kinds in the religious life of Leeds, reinforced by the under-representation of the Established Church in the Liberal party.[46] Appendix III shows that according to the census of church attendance in 1851 Methodists accounted for 41·5 per cent of all Leeds churchgoers, the highest proportion to be found among the eight largest provincial towns in England.

Nor do any of the other churches in Leeds serve as an important source for the recruitment to the Council. This is made clear by the figures just quoted. Tatham's prominence in municipal politics as the standard bearer of militant teetotal Liberalism does not indicate any marked involvement in municipal service by the Quaker meeting. Significantly, the same can be said of the Unitarians at Mill Hill Chapel,

[45] Four Wesleyans, six United Methodist Free Church, three New Connexion, one Primitive and one unspecified.
[46] The religious affiliation of ten Conservative Council members out of a total of twenty-one is known. Nine were Church of England and one a Wesleyan Methodist.

who had furnished many leading Council members in the first generation after 1835, but who contribute relatively few in this period. Edwin Gaunt, a small Radical cap manufacturer who had made good, had been on the Town Council since 1861. He was an active Holbeck politician whose main connection was really with the non-denominational Zion Sunday schools at New Wortley in the Holbeck ward, where he was in turn pupil, teacher and superintendant. James Lowley, a high-quality bespoke shoemaker of the old sort, had been on the Council since 1873. John Ward, wealthy wholesale provision merchant, who was chairman of the sanitary committee from 1886–95, had joined the Council in 1877 and was to be an important figure in the Liberal camp until his death in 1908.[47] All three gave long service and Gaunt and Ward were active and influential men, but only Ward was an important figure in Mill Hill. His example seemed to have had little effect. Between 1877 and 1895–6, when the Conservatives inaugurated their regime by inviting a Lupton to the aldermen's bench and a Kitson to the mayor's chair, the recruitment from Mill Hill had almost dried up.[48]

When questioned in 1899 'various old councillors' said that until the Conservatives came to power in 1895 'the Council was predominantly teetotal and Sunday school and that these views were a *sine qua non* of having influence in Council or even obtaining official appointment.[49] But it is clear that the institutional basis for this situation was not provided by the churches, but rather by the party, and perhaps by the Temperance Society.

In terms of administration the Council, whose character we have

[47] Edwin Gaunt, clr. 1861–70, 1873–4, ald. 1874–98. He was mayor in 1885–7 and was knighted on the occasion of the Queen's Golden Jubilee. President Holbeck Temperance Society. His firm, Gaunt & Hudson, was small in the 1860s, but employed c. 400 outworkers by the 1890s.

James Lowly, clr. 1873–6, ald. 1876–92. He was shoemaker to the Queen and the Royal Family, imported from France in addition to making his own. A highly respectable man of no great economic standing. He was not at any time an office-holder at Mill Hill.

John Ward, clr. 1877–86, ald. 1886–95, 1896–8, 1904–8, mayor 1888, 1892, 1902. President Leeds Liberal Federation 1894–1908, knighted for political services 1906. Mill Hill Chapel warden 1885–6, 1888–9, appointed Trustee 1901. Died 1908. For his sanitary work see below, pp. 248–49.

[48] Arnold Lupton, a town councillor in 1889 and Mill Hill pewholder, was, however, not caught by the sampling method. One factor contributing to the decline in the influence of Mill Hill was the seepage from Unitarian families into the Established Church, which occurred everywhere towards the end of the century. Thus James Smithson Lupton, an alderman in 1872, 1876 and 1882 was not connected with Mill Hill although most members of his family were. John Henry Wurtzburg, Conservative ald. in 1898 and churchwarden at St. John the Evangelist also belonged to a Mill Hill family.

[49] Answer to questionnaire, Q . 17, II. 'Political and religious opinions or parties, with details of past changes in this respect'. See also Report of the Webbs' interview with C. F. J. Atkinson, for a reference to meetings in 'a coffee tavern in Briggate'. Both in *Webb Loc. Gov. Col.*, volume 265.

described kept the machine going but did little more. They wrestled somewhat inconclusively with the sewage problem and the pollution of the River Aire. They refused altogether to increase the police force between 1879 and 1893, and in 1878 adopted the Baths and Washhouses Act and then took no action on it. In 1876 they reversed the policy adopted ten years before in response to Dr. Hunter's report, and gave the work of emptying ashpits to a contractor. This decision to disband their own force of night-soil men was an economy measure and followed repeated attacks on the sanitary committee for its extravagance. They accepted the lowest tender for this work which bore directly on the health and the death-rate of the town, and so made almost certain that it should be skimped. At least one contractor went bankrupt, and in 1889 it was discovered that one of his successors had failed to use disinfectant as he was supposed to do.[50] They took no steps to control the building of back-to-back houses, and between 1869 and 1883 resisted all demands for the provisions of public abattoirs.[51] In 1879 their vacillation in the face of pressure from the butchers over the removal of the cattle market from the centre of the town drew complaints about the Council's timidity from the normally tolerant *Mercury*.[52] They took no action under the Artisans' and Workmen's Dwellings Act, and although they possessed powers to build working-class houses under the Leeds Improvement Act of 1869 they naturally took no action on this matter either.

Two achievements must be placed over against this dismal record. The first was the gradual filling in of the middens or ashpits, which had been identified by the Local Government Board inspector in 1871 as probably the chief cause of the unhealthiness of the town, and their replacement by communal water-closets, which he had recommended as 'the more seemly method of excrement disposal'. This was a process that went on slowly over two decades, as it did in most towns at this time with significant effects on the urban death rates.[53]

[50] Debates on this subject are to be found in *L.M.*, 2.3.1876, 2.1.1880, 8.6.1882, 2.10.1883, 30.9.1886. *L.M.*, 4.7.1889 for the final scandal. The contract system was once more replaced by direct labour in 1890.

[51] MSS. Corporation Reports, VI. Cf. Janet Blackman, 'The Food Supply of an Industrial Town. A Study of Sheffield Public Markets 1780–1900', *Business History*, V (1962), pp. 83–97 for an urban slaughter-house crisis in the 1870s in Sheffield parallel to that in Leeds.

[52] *L.M.*, 17.4.1879, p. 4; 5.6.1879, p. 4. Similar complaints by a minority within the Council, e.g. clr. Emsley, 'the Council of late seemed to be much given to the consideration of how not to do things'. *L.M.*, 6.6.1879, p. 3.

[53] See J. Toft, 'Public Health in Leeds in the Nineteenth Century'. The process could, however, not have been completed by 1890 in view of the debate over the cleaning of ashpits and the decision to employ direct labour once more in March 1890. *L.M.*, 6.3.1890.

The other achievement was the erection in 1886 of a municipal art gallery. This provides the exception that proves the rule, for on this occasion the inertia of the Council was overborne by a one-man campaign waged with skill and determination from within the Liberal establishment. The Corporation had occasionally been the recipient of works of art presented to the town, which were displayed in the town hall as well as the circumstances permitted. It was not a satisfactory arrangement and did not encourage local collectors to make donations. It was in order to persuade the Corporation to provide a real art gallery that T. W. Harding, himself a local collector, stood for the Council in 1883. He was one of the largest manufacturers of textile machinery in Leeds, connected by marriage with some of the richest capitalist families in the West Riding, and was chairman of the Headingley Ward Liberal Association. In 1866 a committee under his guidance recommended the erection of a building for £8,000 to be serviced out of the library rate. The plan was approved and Harding became chairman of the building committee. When the gallery was opened in 1888 he arranged among his friends and the public at large for a loan collection to be put on display. He himself presented several pictures and was to do more for the adornment of the town in the 1890s. So strong was his personal position that even his adherence to Liberal Unionism and consequent resignation from the Council in November 1888 did not shake it. He remained the indispensable chairman until the formal opening of the building, and was subsequently co-opted to the library and art gallery committee, an unprecedented step in Leeds.[54] Harding's career between 1883 and 1888 shows what an able man of good standing could achieve, if he was prepared to make the effort. It is not surprising that with the fall of the Liberals in 1895 he was one of the first to be nominated to the bench of aldermen.[55]

Death rates in the Borough of Leeds per thousand, given by the Leeds medical officer of health in his *Annual Report* (1912), were as follows:

1865-9	28·9	1890-94	21·1
1870-74	27·9	1895-9	19·8
1875-9	24·6	1900-1904	18·6
1880-84	22·9	1905-9	16·4
1885-9	21·1		

[54] 'Let 'em come int' at front door, as I did, if they want to be on the Art Committee' had been Scarr's attitude, when a proposal in 1886 to co-opt members was defeated. F. R. Spark, *Memories of my Life* (Leeds, n.d. [1913]), p. 19.
[55] For T. W. Harding, clr. 1883-8, ald. 1895-1904, Colonel, Leeds artillery volunteers, see *Leeds Biographer* (1892).

When we compare the Council as it was in the late 1880s with what it had been in the early years of the reformed Corporation, we are bound to be struck by the contrast. The social and economic composition of the Council now stood in a very different relation to that of the community. The decline in the representation of the social and economic elite had been gradual, accelerated during the 1840s and the 1870s and never significantly reversed. However tentative the classification 'large' and 'small' must be in some cases, the contrast is such that a 3 per cent margin of error would not seriously affect it.

In 1892 the Council contained six men who had some claim to rank as large businessmen by the standards of the contemporary Leeds economy. In 1842 the figure was approximately twenty-four, and in addition there were two gentlemen of independent means who were not just retired businessmen.[56] The professional men, whose absence we had noticed in 1872 and 1876, had returned. There were four in 1882 and nine in 1892. The latter compared well with the seven who had served in 1842. At the other end of the scale the difference is also not as striking as in the case of large businesses. There had been eight that can be identified as small businesses in 1842; now there were fourteen. It is the middle range that had grown in representation, and it is from there that most of those who took the lead in the Council were drawn. In the two-year period 1892–3 out of a total of twenty-one committee chairmen, two were large businessmen and two professional men, i.e. 19 per cent of the total.[57] This was far less than ever before. In 1842–3 and 1851–2 the figure had been in the region of 50–60 per cent; in 1861–2, 1871–2 and 1882 between 30 and 40 per cent.

We have already used the number of J.P.s among the town councillors to indicate the changing social standing of the Council membership in the period 1836–48. Appointments to the bench continued to be made from among the leading citizens until the 1880s, when lord chancellors began to widen the social range of the body of magistrates. Until then the number of J.P.s on the Council continues to be a useful indicator. Table 17 shows how the numbers fell throughout this period, but rose again in 1892 as a result of generous additions by both Liberal and Conservative governments in the 1880s and in 1892 itself.

Another set of considerations is introduced, if we look at the membership of the Leeds Philosophical and Literary Society. Founded in 1818

---

[56] See p. 195 for 1842 and table 19, part II, p. 267 for 1892. The assessment is fairly generous in both cases.
[57] See table 20, part II, p. 267.

TABLE 17. *Leeds magistrates' bench and Town Council 1861–92: overlap of membership*

Date	Total no. of J.P.s	No. on Council
1861	42	6
1871	25	4
1876	33	4
1881	41	4
1885	46	3
1892	59	8

by some of the town's most distinguished citizens and deliberately non-party in its composition, this society continued to attract all those members of polite society with intellectual interests, whether scientific, literary or historical. Despite the greater range of leisure activities available in the 1890s, it had not yet lost this position by the end of the century.[58] Table 18 shows the number of Town Council members at different dates who belonged to the society. The remarkably high number in the early years tells us something about the kind of person whom the Council attracted in the first generation after 1835.

TABLE 18. *Leeds Philosophical and Literary Society and Town Council 1842–1902: overlap of membership*

Date	No.	Per cent of Town Councils
1842	27	42·1
1862	17	26·5
1892	5 or 6	7·8 or 9·4*
1902	8	12·3

* It is not clear whether Alderman William Firth took over the membership which had originally been that of his father.
Source: Leeds Phil. & Lit. Society, *Annual Reports.* Membership of the Society is taken from membership lists for the same year as the Town Council sample, except that the first line is taken from that for 1840–41. In the following year the Society went into a temporary period of decline.

To judge from the whole range of evidence in this chapter it appears that in terms of business ability and of local standing the Council had reached a nadir by the second half of the 1880s.[59] The history of municipal government in Leeds was therefore in marked contrast to that of

[58] For the history of the Society see E. Kitson Clark, *History of 100 Years of Life of the Leeds Philosophical and Literary Society* (Leeds, 1924).
[59] There is further evidence for this in the MSS. volume of Corporation Reports. The volume covering the years 1869–90 shows a sharp deterioration for 1884–7 not only in the quality but in the quantity of reports.

Birmingham. The trends in the two towns had largely moved in opposite directions. The kind of situation that had characterised Leeds in the early years was now found in Birmingham, while the later developments in Leeds had reduced the Council there to a position more like that of Birmingham in the first two decades.

This is, however, not the end of the story. The 1890s saw a new departure in the history of Leeds, which led to rapid changes in the composition of the Council. The hold of the Liberals on the municipal government of the borough was broken for the first time since 1835. At the same time and as part of the same movement the social composition of the Council was drastically changed. From the point of view of municipal administration, the decade saw innovation and improvement. Insofar as Leeds ever had a period resembling the Chamberlain era in Birmingham municipal history, this was the one.

What happened, why it happened and how, is the subject of the next part of the book. To avoid repetition we shall incorporate the analysis of the changing composition of the Council from 1892 to 1912 into the detailed study that follows.[60]

[60] See chapter 3, pp. 167–74.

Part II
The New Era and After, 1889-1914

I

Mismanagement

Two incidents provided the occasion for a new start, an outbreak of typhoid in 1889 and a labour dispute at the corporation gas works in the following year. The mismanagement first of one and then the other undermined public confidence in the established regime.

I

The typhoid epidemic broke out in Headingley in July 1889. It was ultimately traced to a dairy from which a youth, who had been feeling unwell and had subsequently gone down with the disease, had recently been dismissed. There were rumours that the medical officer of health had been slow to follow up information and to stop the supply of infected milk. In consequence the sanitary committee set up a committee to inquire into the events and to report also on the administration of the sanitary department in general, for which the medical officer was responsible.[1] The rumours were proved correct. Personal pique had prompted Dr. Goldie to countermand the emergency measures taken by the chief sanitary inspector on his personal initiative, and this had led to the distribution of another complete delivery of the infected milk. The medical officer found a relentless critic in the editor of *The Leeds Mercury*, who wrote that Dr. Goldie has 'conspicuously failed in the discharge of his duty. It is not right that an officer capable of such failure should be maintained at the head of the department responsible for the public health in a town of 350,000 inhabitants.' Not satisfied with the attack on the medical officer, the editor criticised the state of

[1] *L.M.*, 9.7.1889, p. 5.

public health in the town as illustrated by the Registrar-General's latest comparative statistics, and urged the sub-committee to be energetic in its inquiries.[2] These inquiries revealed that Dr. Goldie had indeed been neglecting his duties for a long time. It will be remembered that he had been appointed during the economy campaign of 1872-3 at a paltry £400 per annum.[3] What had been sown in those years was now being reaped. The *Mercury*, which had condemned the salary at the time as inadequate, now had the satisfaction of saying, I told you so. 'Those who appointed him must have known that at the salary offered no medical man of the intellectual and moral calibre needed would be at all likely to undertake the duties of the office.'[4] Dr. Goldie's dismissal was inevitable and the *Mercury* was determined that the same mistake should not be repeated. In several articles it urged the Council to follow the example recently set by the West Riding County Council and to pay a salary high enough to attract a good man.

The anxiety that found expression in the *Mercury* did not confine itself to the replacement of an incompetent official. The investigations of the sub-committee into the sanitary administration of the borough, once begun, let loose a flood of complaints, much of which found an outlet in the correspondence columns of the press. As the *Mercury* observed, 'the public mind is now deeply stirred by the necessity for a searching reform in the whole system'. The investigation revealed abuses which were the result of dividing responsibility between the sanitary committee, the sewerage committee and the buildings clauses committee, each of which pursued their own policy in utter disregard of what the others were doing. A reorganisation of the committee system which would give wider responsibility to the sanitary committee and to the medical officer of health was badly needed.

Typhoid in Headingley, the supposedly healthy suburb for the well-to-do, seemed more shocking even than typhoid in Hunslet or in Holbeck would have been. It brought the town's dependence on the corporation sanitary department home to the vocal and influential section of the public, and opened a gulf between it and the Council. This was revealed

[2] *L.M.*, 10.7.1889, p. 4.
[3] See above, part I, p. 214.
[4] *L.M.*, 23.7.1889, p. 4. See *L.M.*, 8.6.1873 for hostile comment on Dr. Goldie's original appointment.

MAP 4. (opposite). *Borough of Leeds 1885*.
    Source: P.P., 1884-5 [C. 4287-I], xix. p. 297.

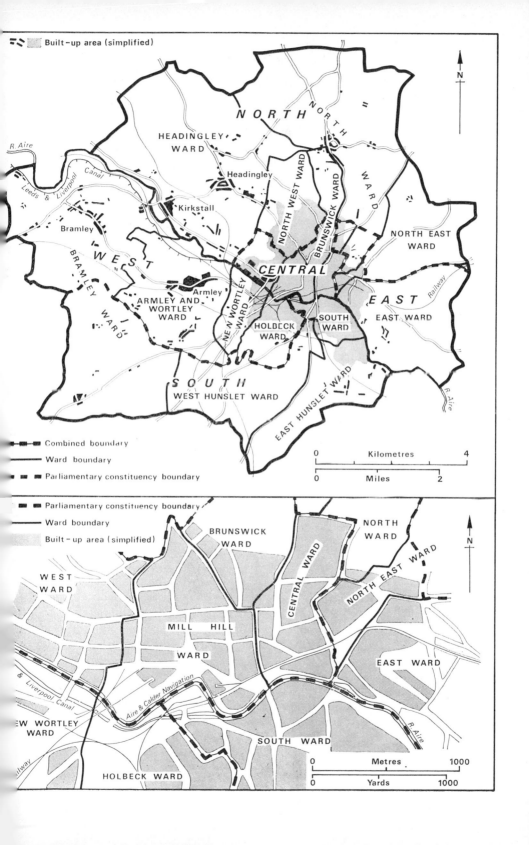

Built-up area (simplified)

NORTH

HEADINGLEY WARD

NORTH

Headingley

R. Aire

Leeds & Liverpool Canal

Kirkstall

NORTH WEST WARD

BRUNSWICK WARD

NORTH WARD

Bramley

WEST

NORTH EAST WARD

CENTRAL

Armley

BRAMLEY WARD

ARMLEY AND WORTLEY WARD

NEW WORTLEY WARD

EAST

HOLBECK WARD

SOUTH WARD

EAST WARD

Railway

SOUTH

WEST HUNSLET WARD

EAST HUNSLET WARD

R. Aire

Combined boundary
Ward boundary
Parliamentary constituency boundary

0   Kilometres   4

0   Miles   2

Parliamentary constituency boundary
Ward boundary
Built-up area (simplified)

BRUNSWICK WARD

NORTH WARD

WEST WARD

CENTRAL WARD

NORTH EAST WARD

MILL HILL WARD

& Liverpool Canal

Aire & Calder Navigation

EAST WARD

R. Aire

EW WORTLEY WARD

Railway

SOUTH WARD

HOLBECK WARD

0   Metres   1000

0   Yards   1000

when a deputation from the Leeds Philosophical and Literary Society waited on the Council urging them to take vigorous action and offering to contribute 'such moral forces as they possess to any effort made by the Council to protect the public health'. That the Philosophical and Literary Society did possess some moral force cannot be doubted. It was the meeting point for those of the leading citizens of Leeds with more intellectual interests. Its president, who led the deputation, was Pridgin Teale, the chief surgeon at the Leeds Infirmary and a fellow of the Royal Society.[5] Only one town councillor (Edmund Wilson) had been present when the Council of the Society decided to send the deputation. The Town Council, far from welcoming the signs of an awakened sanitary opinion in the town, objected to being lectured to by outsiders and spent some time discussing whether to admit them at all. Its members were distinctly on the defensive and a sharp discussion ensued. *The Leeds Mercury* strongly commended the deputation and agreed with them that this was the moment to take advantage of the aroused state of public opinion to make progress. Talbot Baines, its editor, had in fact been a member of the deputation.[6]

When the salary of the future medical officer of health came up for debate, it became even clearer that, whatever may have happened to public opinion in the town, it had not greatly affected the majority of the Town Council. Speakers voiced their contempt for scientific opinion, and made it plain that they expected their medical officer to have little power of initiative for independent investigation. The spokesman for the sanitary committee said that they wanted a man who would come when called for by the inspectors of nuisances and added: 'to do that a man did not require much scientific knowledge'. Such a cool lead from the committee encouraged those who thought that much less was required. One speaker would have preferred four additional sanitary inspectors and no medical officer at all, another wanted several part-time appointments. Scarr was convinced that the epidemic would not have broken out, if the sons and daughters of the middle-class population of Headingley had not been brought up 'as hot-house plants', while Tatham thought that not doctors but universal sobriety was the answer. The Committee proposed a salary of £700 per annum, compared with the £680 that Dr. Goldie was receiving in 1889. Goldie had,

[5] A book written by him in 1879 points to a long-standing interest in the improvement of house-drains for the sake of the health of the inhabitants. T. Pridgin Teale, *Dangers to Health: A Pictorial Guide to Domestic Sanitary Defects* (London and Leeds, 1879).
[6] *L.M.*, 26.7.1889, p. 3.

however, had to provide his own transport and also been responsible for the inspection of diseased cattle. His successor was not to be responsible for the cattle, and would have transport provided, but it was assumed that he would be mainly in his office, visiting districts only 'if the inspectors reported on any place from time to time'. An amendment to recruit at £900 per annum was overwhelmingly defeated, so was another suggesting £800. Thus the expectations of the *Mercury* were rudely shattered. Both Birmingham and the London County Council were at that time paying their Medical Officer £1,000 per annum, Liverpool was paying £1,000 and another £700 to his deputy. Manchester had just raised theirs to £850 and the West Riding's recent appointment had been at £800 per annum. Yet the appointment cost Leeds more than any of these authorities had to pay, since the Council was still adamant in refusing any contribution from the Local Government Board.[7]

By good fortune the Corporation obtained a better man than they deserved. The advent of Dr. J. S. Cameron, formerly a medical officer of Huddersfield, saw the beginning of new zeal in the Sanitary Department. He succeeded in persuading the Council to transfer a wide range of duties to his department, wrote informative reports and was generally regarded as 'too zealous by half'. His relationship with the Council was not always cordial, but there can be no doubt that his advent was an important step in the improvement of the sanitary work of the Corporation. Other steps were soon to follow.

It is worth noting that the small minority on the Council who had been overwhelmingly defeated in this attempt to engage of a medical officer of health at £900 per annum contained a disproportionate number of Conservatives. Not that the public health issue, as it was debated in July-August 1889, was a party issue either in the town or on the Council. But it was among the Conservatives that the only medical man then on the Council, J. S. Loe, was found,[8] as well as a sanitary engineer, Slater, a specialist in drains. They were both critical of the sanitary work of the Council, and over the issue of the medical officer's salary were joined by Willey and Gordon, the two professional men who were among the three most prominent members of the Conservative group.

---

[7] In its leading article commenting on the debate the *Mercury* described Scarr's speech as 'a disgrace to the Corporation. It represented the spirit of British Philistinism in its most offensive and blatant form.' *L.M.*, 8.8.1889. For the refusal to accept a grant from the L.G.B. see above, part I, p. 214.

[8] B. G. Heald, a Liberal surgeon, was elected to the subsequent municipal election in November 1889.

There were leading sanitary improvers, however, also among the Liberals. Edmund Wilson, who had sponsored the deputation of the Philosophical and Literary Society, has already been mentioned. There was also F. R. Spark, who had joined Slater in criticising the work of the sanitary committee quite early during the epidemic. As for public opinion out of doors the vigorous lead given by *The Leeds Mercury* would have made it difficult to think of the issue in party terms.

When the municipal elections fell due a few weeks later concern for the health of the borough was still alive enough to add an element of public interest to the lethargic performance that had become customary of late. But the usual Liberal *versus* Conservative party fight seemed more than ever irrelevant, and the *Mercury* pleaded that in the public interest the re-election of Slater, the Conservative sanitary engineer, should not be contested.[9] Not for the first time the editor mused on the inappropriateness of conducting municipal elections strictly on party lines, and he tentatively suggested that some organisation separate from political parties might be brought to bear on 'the elevation of municipal life'.[10] As far as Slater was concerned the appeal was ignored by the Liberal Association, who put up a candidate against him, but failed to dislodge him from his seat. The Conservatives behaved very similarly in Headingley against a Liberal sanitary reformer, the universally respected Quaker, William Harvey. *The Yorkshire Post*, while it regretted the introduction of party politics, thought that in view of the behaviour of the Liberals there was 'nothing for it but to meet politics with politics'.[11] The party organisations were too firmly committed to fighting municipal elections to let the editor of the *Mercury* or anyone else divert them from sending their troops into battle, and it was the Conservatives' determination to win a party advantage that ultimately did most to improve the municipal life of the town.

Such developments lay still in the future. In November 1889 the sole Conservative victory was ironically gained by a man who championed the Holbeck pig-keepers against restrictions imposed by the sanitary committee. 'Vote for Musgrave and Home-fed bacon' was what pulled in the votes. The actualities of Holbeck politics were far removed indeed from 'the new spirit . . . in our sanitary administration' for which the *Mercury* had appealed.

---

[9] *L.M.*, 2.11.1889. He had recently been employed by the Gladstones to put the drains right at Hawarden Castle.
[10] *L.M.*, 21.10.1889.
[11] *Y.P.*, 2.11.1889.

II

The second crisis that undermined public confidence was to rebound more plainly to the advantage of the Conservative party. It broke in the summer of 1890, although it had been in preparation since the winter before.

The dispute at the municipal gas works which began on 1 July 1890 was made possible by the organisation in the previous year of a local branch of Will Thorne's Gas Workers and General Labourers' Union.[12] When this union presented the gas committee in October–November 1889 with a demand for eight-hour shifts and the engagement of additional men to take over some of the duties previously carried out by the stokers, the committee might grumble but was forced to yield. A strike would have plunged the town in darkness during the long winter nights and the Town Council could not contemplate the social dislocation that this would have produced. 'Their time would be in the summer' Alderman Gilston, the committee chairman, explained to the Council. That would be the moment 'to make a permanent arrangement with the men'. In the meantime the committee merely waited, while refusing to embody the enforced concessions in the form of detailed rules for display in the works. In December they replied to a query from the Union that the rules would be drawn up 'at the earliest convenience' but did nothing. When a dispute arose over the men's pay for the Good Friday holiday, the committee refused to deal with a deputation that included Cockayne, the branch secretary of the Union. They sent it away and wrote a formal letter through the town clerk to say that they would deal only with their own employees. With the approach of summer the labour force was reduced as usual to a mere quarter of that needed in winter. The longer days reduced the demand for gas, which, it should be remembered, was primarily used for lighting purposes. Now, the committee felt, was the time to act, and on 1 June they issued a set of rules, not designed to give expression to the settlement of November, but to modify it on their own terms. The former, it was reckoned, had increased the cost of gas production by $42\frac{1}{2}$ per cent, the latter was meant to bring it down again by one-fifth.[13] The committee could not have expected to obtain the consent of the men. Their treatment of the Union had shown

---

[12] For a treatment of the dispute as it affected the growth of a socialist movement in Leeds see E. P. Thompson 'Homage to Tom Maguire' in A. Briggs and J. Saville (eds.), *Essays in Labour History* (1960).

[13] *L.M.*, 11.7.1890, p. 3.

9

that they had no thought of negotiating a settlement. They had turned the tables on the men and were prepared to use the same methods as had been applied to them in the winter. The rules were accompanied by a notice asking the men to signify their willingness to abide by them. When there was no reply, the gas committee gave fourteen days' notice, due to expire on 1 July, and began to recruit a new labour force. Two days before giving notice, Gilston did, however, approach the Chamber of Commerce and asked whether this was not a suitable case for a conciliation board. The Chamber had recently set up a committee to study means of creating such a board in Leeds and they were in touch with the Leeds Trades Council. But the board did not yet exist, and in any case the Gas Workers' Union had definitely decided to have nothing to do with the project.

On the same day as the notices went out, the gas committee set up a sub-committee of seven men to deal with the dispute on their behalf. The gas committee as a whole consisted of twenty members, four of whom were Conservatives, but so habitual had the exclusion of Conservatives from positions of power become that the seven men chosen for the sub-committee were all Liberals. No doubt they were the men who stood nearest to Gilston, the chairman, for the latter dominated his committee.

There was always a surplus of stokers in the summer and the sub-committee expected little difficulty in recruiting labour. In a sense they were right. In Leeds itself the influence of the Union had become too great for success, but once they got in touch with agents in Manchester and London the 500 odd places were soon filled. The only problem was to get the men to the gas works on 1 July. It was here that things went wrong.

The previous night about 450 men arrived from Manchester in a special train. They were intended for the New Wortley works, but in view of the hostile crowds that had assembled it seemed too dangerous to march them straight there. Instead they were lodged in the town hall for the night, while requests for reinforcements were sent out to neighbouring towns and barracks. It was raining, the gas lamps were out and the newly recruited men made a gloomy sight as they trudged in columns of four through the night.

The London contingent arrived in the early hours of 1 July. Their train steamed through the siding at Meadow Lane Works where a strong reception committee had assembled to give the blacklegs a rough welcome and unloaded at Leeds Central Station. The men were marched under a strong escort to Meadow Lane, there was a short but sharp battle between police and pickets and the men were inside. But the pickets climbed on the walls and neighbouring roofs and addressed the men in the yard. By the early afternoon about seventy to eighty of the men had climbed out and joined the strikers, leaving a mere fifty to operate the works. In the evening a full scale attack was made but it was repulsed with many broken heads on either side.

Meadow Lane was, however, not the main focus of interest. New Wortley was the bigger works, and its labour force was inside the town hall while the crowds gathered in the square in front. As the crowds swelled, the chief constable became convinced that nothing short of a military escort would ever suffice to get the men to work. It was necessary to wait for the arrival of the troops.

After spending the night in the town hall crypt the men were provided with beer and sandwiches for breakfast and allowed upstairs into the large concert hall, where they were given a recital by the borough organist. When this palled, an informal smoking concert was arranged by Alderman Scupham who had been detailed to attend to the men's comfort. Councillor Hunt sang several songs including *Rule Britannia*, and the men joined in the chorus 'Britons never, never, never shall be slaves'. The words were somewhat ambiguous under the circumstances, but no doubt the song was chosen for its rousing tune. There was also a 'characteristic rendering of *Auld Lang Syne*' by Councillor Hunt who seemed to have had a reputation in this field. It was not very dignified, but a crowd of over four hundred rough labourers with nothing to do had to be kept happy somehow. They got bored soon enough and tried to go out for a stroll; some of them even offered to fight their way to work without assistance. It was perhaps just as well that for high tea there was only cocoa provided with which to wash down the sandwiches.

The watchers at the New Wortley gas works hoped anxiously that, if the men were to be marched from the town hall, it would be before the surrounding factories discharged the workers for the day. Yet 4.30 p.m. passed and still the mounted troops from the barracks had not arrived. It was 7.40 p.m. before the chief constable with all his reinforcements on the spot began the operation. No worse time could have been chosen, for by then the streets, not least the streets around the gas works, were swarming with crowds in which the idle sightseers and the roughs out for their fun mixed with determined pickets.

The procession that set out from the town hall square could seldom have had its equal in the streets of Leeds. The gas workers marched four abreast flanked on either side by police in double file. These in turn were protected by the troops both mounted and unmounted, while mounted police formed the outermost barrier. The remainder of the cavalry and police made an advance guard and a rear guard. Between the main body of men and the rear guard drove two hired cabs occupied by the mayor and his fellow magistrates. Thousands of people followed the procession. However, all was not as impregnable as it seemed. As the column passed under a railway bridge not far from the gas works, large lumps of coal, bricks and railway sleepers rained down upon it. The strikers, who had stationed themselves up there, had found a train laden with coal in a siding and had helped themselves. Many of the marching men were most terribly injured, the procession broke up in disarray and by the time the blacklegs got inside the gate of the works even those still uninjured were convinced that they would not be safe. Here, as at Meadow Lane, the pickets were allowed to climb the walls and address the men. The result was that most of the blacklegs climbed over the wall and joined the strikers. The order to the cavalry to clear the streets came too late to affect the course of events, although not too late to injure a number of harmless bystanders. The following day a mere seventy men were left inside the works.[14]

Such bungling was surely the fault of the chief constable, but the odium fell on the gas committee. To his great distress, Gilston, at other times a popular Liberal politician, had to have police protection after being dangerously hustled by the crowd. There were more battles on 2 July in defence of the gas works. At Meadow Lane the attackers took the outer gate off its hinges and almost carried the day. But reinforcements arrived in time and the presence of the cavalry did much to quieten the town.[15] Indeed some of the blacklegs, who had gone over to the strikers, changed their minds and returned to work. The rest were sent home at the Union's expense, and before departing were addressed by Will Thorne himself who had come to Leeds.[16]

It could be argued that by 3 July the gas committee had got the situation under control. Some gas was being manufactured, protection of the blacklegs was assured and a report came in that more men could be recruited from Manchester. But that would be to reckon without the effect that the disorders had had an opinion, not least on opinion within the Council.

[14] *L.M.*, 2.7.1890, p. 8.
[15] *L.M.*, 3.7.1890, p. 8.
[16] *L.M.*, 3.7.1890, p. 8, 4.7.1890, p. 8.

Up to the day after the battle the conflict had been conducted entirely by the seven members of the sub-committee. They had not even reported back to the gas committee itself. From 2 July onward the opinion of the Town Council as a whole became relevant. On that day the leading personalities of the Chamber of Commerce took the initiative and brought the two parties together. This was an achievement, for up to then the gas committee had refused to have any dealings with William Cockayne, the Socialist secretary of the Yorkshire district of the Union. There were two meetings on successive days, and by 4 July a compromise had been worked out, which was accepted by both sides. The gas committee was left with the task of satisfying the claims of the remaining blacklegs many of whom had long-term contracts. But they were happy to take compensation and left Leeds in good spirits without any further mishap.

On the men's side the settlement was greatly facilitated by the conspicuous ability of Cockayne and the influence that he had over his followers. By the gas committee on the other hand the pressure of political opinion was strongly felt. The comments of the local press had from the first been highly critical of the action taken. The *Mercury's* leader on the day after the battle, while voicing the 'shame and indignation' of the inhabitants at 'the brutal and disgraceful scenes which were witnessed in these streets yesterday' strongly criticised the gas committee for not taking all possible steps to bring about a settlement in a conciliatory manner, nor yet taking the measures necessary to make a warlike policy successful.[17] Its treatment of the whole episode was remarkably objective and did justice to the gas workers' point of view. There was no tub thumping about law and order or the right to work. *The Leeds Express*, the popular Radical paper, practically made itself the voice of the men and attacked the action of the gas committee in no uncertain terms. Its editor, F. R. Spark, was himself a member of the Town Council, and during the subsequent debates showed himself well briefed by the gas workers whose case he presented in the Council chamber. Walter Battle, the other Liberal newspaper proprietor on the Council, also strongly supported the men.

The attitude of the Liberal press is relevant not least because the Conservative group in the Council immediately dissociated itself from what had been done and launched a strong attack on the gas sub-committee. The fact that this body had been exclusively composed of

[17] *L.M.*, 2.7.1890, p. 4.

Liberal party stalwarts now acquired a new significance. John Gordon, the Conservative councillor, gave a strong lead to his party colleagues to adopt the role of champions of the people and to disassociate themselves from the blundering and lack of diplomacy that had characterised the political majority. He strained every rule of procedure in order to put a vote of censure on record at the earliest possible moment, and after three stormy debates he had won his point. The majority of the Council was pushed into identifying themselves with the action of Gilston and his associates ⟨*see* plates 32, 33⟩. Among the critics were a few Liberal names like Spark and Battle and practically the whole of the Conservative group.[18] Most of this was hindsight. Originally only one Conservative had protested against the adoption of the revised rules, and only two had objected to the setting up of the sub-committee with full powers. But it was convenient hindsight and aligned the Conservatives with a large body of opinion outside the Council which irrespective of party was critical of what had been done. No amount of arguing by Gilston that in the long run the town had saved money by opposing the Union in this way could prevent the stock of the Council from sinking in the estimation of the town.

'We have passed through a most serious crisis, and the result of what has taken place may be felt in this town for many days, weeks and possibly months to come', commented Edmund Wilson.[19] He was right, and the results began to appear in the municipal elections of that year. The loss of six Liberal seats made the number of Conservatives equal to that of Liberal councillors, for the first time since 1874. However, for the moment Liberal control of the Council was still secured by the votes of the sixteen aldermen.

The Yorkshire Post, the Conservative paper, had launched the election campaign with four and a half columns of attack, headed 'The Leeds Corporation. Another Year of Peddling Incompetency'. Although the indictment was exaggerated and could be refuted on several points, there was enough substance in it to hurt. It provided ammunition for the Conservative candidates during a brisk campaign which attracted an unusual amount of attention. For once the arguments actually dealt with municipal matters and this was probably the most important innovation of all. Municipal elections had traditionally been fought as an abstract exercise in party politics.

The Conservatives' indictment ranged over a wider field than the

---

[18] *L.M.*, 3.7.1890, p. 8, 4.7.1890, p. 8, 11.7.1890, p. 3.
[19] *L.M.*, 4.7.1890, p. 8.

dispute with the gas stokers, dealing also with sanitary matters, electric lighting, tramways, and the policy of street improvement.[20] It was certainly not hard to find instances of incompetence. One will suffice. Several years had elapsed since the question of a public supply of electricity for Leeds had first been raised. The Council had power to undertake the supply itself or to license a private company, and it appointed a committee of inquiry to go into the matter. By any standards this was one of the crucial issues of the day, yet on three occasions the committee of inquiry had had its report referred back for further consideration. The question came up for the fourth time less than four weeks before the municipal election of 1890. The report of the committee advocated a municipal undertaking. The committee chairman moved the adoption of the report but explained that he disagreed with it. The seconder, while complaining about the vague and confused way in which the matter had been brought before the Council by the chairman, also disagreed with it. It then transpired that attendance at the committee had been so poor that the report had been drawn up practically on his own by Alderman Spark, who was described as a strongly biassed man and obviously carried no weight on the Council. This is at first sight surprising since Spark was certainly a great deal more coherent and informed than anybody else who spoke. The Council rejected the report and decided to allow electricity to be supplied by any private company willing to take the risk.[21] The *Mercury* was upset at this decision which concerned what it recognised as 'the illuminant of the future', but it was even more pained by the level of the debate. 'Defeat in this matter' wrote its editor, 'would have been pardonable if the resolution of the committee had been negatived after a discussion worthy of the occasion. Defeat after such a discussion was a confession of weakness which every burgess who has the best interest of the borough at heart must regret.'[22]

When the election results were announced, even *The Yorkshire Post*, partisan though it naturally was, recognised that the Liberal party had been 'condemned more for their bungling and blundering and general incapacity and failure in municipal matters than for their politics'.[23] Something was happening in the town that transcended party, a feeling of uneasiness at the quality of local government and the capacity of the

[20] *Y.P.*, 23.10.1890, p. 6.
[21] *L.M.*, 7.10.1890, p. 3.
[22] *L.M.*, 7.10.1890, p. 4.
[23] *Y.P.*, 3.11.1890, p. 4.

men who were in control. Unfortunately elections fought in party terms could not in the nature of things give a true reflection of such feelings. It was the marginal wards that naturally suffered the casualties. Solidly Liberal wards were not going to change unless and until the movement of opinion was also reflected within the structure of the party organisation itself. That day was not yet. In consequence the election of 1890 produced ironic results. Councillor Henry, chairman of the South Leeds Liberal Association, was safe at Holbeck although he had been a member of the ill-fated gas sub-committee. It was Edmund Wilson, possibly the most outspoken advocate of good government that the Council possessed, who went down in defeat in the marginal Headingley Ward. A leading solicitor in the town, a sanitary and housing reformer, a man of education and culture, it was indeed ironic that he should have been defeated in an election waged against the incompetence of the Council, of which he was so conspicuous an exception. *The Leeds Mercury* had appealed to the parties, as it had done in 1889, not to oppose outstandingly progressive councillors merely on party grounds, but once more had been ignored.

The municipal election of 1890 was an important event in the transformation of Leeds municipal politics which is the subject of this part of the book. It was important not so much for what was achieved as for the opinions that were voiced, for the diagnosis of the situation that existed at the time.

'It has been notoriously difficult of late years', wrote the *Mercury* with reference to Edmund Wilson's defeat,

> 'to induce citizens of station and culture to undergo the fatigues of municipal service, coupled with the annoyance of a rough and tumble election fight every three years. . . . The result has been to lower materially the average standard of discussion in our local parliaments, and also to injure the efficiency and keep down the enlightenment of corporate administration.'

This general indictment is made more specific when the writer turns to catalogue the contribution made by Wilson:

> 'Here and there there have been found gentlemen of cultivation and social influence ready to face all the drawbacks and disagreeables [sic] of municipal contests and municipal government . . . and Mr. Edmund Wilson has been prominent amongst them. . . . He has contributed an element of breadth and liberality to the consideration of . . . affairs by the Council, and he has conspicu-

ously striven to maintain in its debates some approach to the dignity which ought to characterise the proceedings.'[24]

Conservative opinion, as expressed in *The Yorkshire Post*, did not differ from this diagnosis of the failings of the Council, and its prescription for improvement was couched in terms of the same virtues. But in one crucial respect it was more realistic. It saw that the main reason for the mediocrity of the Council was the composition of the bench of aldermen. These were maintained in power by the Liberal majority, and only by eroding that majority could they be removed. To the *Mercury's* appeal to allow candidates of conspicuous fitness to be returned without opposition, *The Yorkshire Post* replied in effect that an admirable Liberal or two might have to be sacrificed. For the crucial task was to remove the aldermen, and so take power out of incompetent hands.[25]

There was another difference between the two papers. *The Yorkshire Post* represented the views of the local leaders of the Conservative Party, but the priorities so clearly expounded in the *Mercury* were certainly not shared by the leaders of the municipal Liberal Party. Otherwise Wilson could easily have been brought back into the Council by offering him an aldermanic vacancy. Several such vacancies occurred, particularly in 1892, and not all were pre-empted by the convention that ex-mayors who were still councillors should be promoted at the first opportunity. No such seat was offered to Wilson. He remained prominent in the public life of the town but 1890 effectively put an end to his municipal career. The reason for this is as simple as it is important. When the Conservatives captured power in 1895 the councillors deliberately refrained from promoting themselves, but with small exceptions used the opportunity to recruit men of standing from outside. The Liberals had not shown such self-denial for a long time. According to someone well placed to know, for at least thirty years before 1895 these elections had been strictly by seniority without any reference to calibre or eminence. It was impossible, so it was said, to by-pass the oldest sitting Liberal councillors without running the risk that the rejected men would break up the party.[26] These were the kind of conventions that made it impossible for the dominant Liberals to respond adequately to the new breezes of public opinion which had began to blow. Nothing but electoral defeat could purge them.

[24] *L.M.*, 3.11.1890, p. 4.
[25] *Y.P.*, 3.11.1890, p. 6.
[26] *Webb Loc. Gov. Col.*, volume 265, questionnaire, Q. 16.

In 1899, looking back upon the experience, a Liberal councillor admitted as much to Beatrice Webb:

> 'The Liberals had become fossilized. The same men were elected time after time Aldermen and Chairman of committees. One man was Chairman of a committee for fifteen years. The Unionists have done a great service in clearing the Aldermen's bench: when we return to power we shall begin with a fresh choice of men.'[27]

[27] W. Womersley in interview with B. W., 15.4.1899, *Webb. Loc. Gov. Col.*, volume 265.

2

Public Health Issues

The events of 1889–90 indicate the main lines of subsequent development. The awakened concern over public health and the appointment of a new medical officer, no less than the Conservative attack on the calibre of the entrenched majority contained potentialities for change that were not exhausted by the events that gave them their initial impetus.

Dr. Cameron had not been content to sit in his office waiting to be consulted by the inspectors of nuisances. He had taken the initiative and drawn attention to the Marsh Lane-Quarry Hill area in north-east Leeds consisting of 33 acres with a particularly high fever rate. In September 1891 he officially reported it to the Council as an insanitary area within the meaning of the Housing Acts of 1875 and 1890.[1] In the same month appeared the first of five articles on 'The Health of Leeds' especially commissioned by *The Leeds Mercury*, which provided the reading public with a picture of the same district. The district contained about 7,700 people living in small back-to-back houses frequently massed around tiny courts to which the sun seldom penetrated. The average density was 200 persons to the acre but parts with 274 and even 314 persons to the acre could be found. The detailed description of lack of light and air, of infant mortality and bad privy accommodation, with which the first of the articles abounded, was supplemented a few days later by lurid statements about drink, prostitution and opium addiction among the inhabitants. As a social investigation it was crude by the best standards of its time, but it made its impact, if one may judge from letters to the press. Its chief point was driven home repeatedly, namely that nothing short of complete clearance would do.[2]

[1] *L.M.*, 15.9.1891.
[2] *L.M.*, 26.9.1891, p. 10; 3.10.1891, p. 3; 9.10.1891, p. 8; 16.10.1891, p. 8. See especially the first, third and fourth articles.

It took the Corporation until 1895 before they decided to follow this advice. The sanitary committee produced a scheme for dealing with the area section by section, and the Corporation embarked on the work of clearance. Little did they guess then what problems the Council would run into over the re-housing of the inhabitants, nor what money it would finally spend. In 1901 the area to be dealt with was extended to 68¼ acres and when the war stopped the work 3,893 houses had been demolished. In the 1930s after another burst of activity the famous Quarry Hill flats rose on the site of the former 'insanitary area'. This is not the place to tell the complex story of slum clearance in Leeds. The important fact is that in 1894–5 the Council did finally reach the point of commitment. Only five men voted against the scheme, and only two of these were Liberal aldermen.[3]

A big issue of the years 1890–95 was whether the notification of infectious diseases should be made compulsory. Had such a system been in force during the typhoid outbreak of 1889 the source of the infection could have been traced more easily and quickly. The Infectious Diseases Notification Act (1889) appeared therefore to be entirely suited for adoption in Leeds. However, when Alderman Ward, the Liberal chairman of the sanitary committee, in December 1890 proposed the adoption of the Act the Council referred the matter back for further consideration. It was looked upon as a mere fad, an intrusion of officialdom into the privacy of the home, and since notification was likely to be followed by admission to an isolation hospital it was also seen as an infringement on individual liberty. The interesting thing is that the local doctors were not at all keen on the innovation.[4] So although the Act was adopted in Birmingham, Bristol, Liverpool, and Hull, while a similar system had been in operation in Manchester and Bradford since 1881, the matter was not raised again in Leeds until June 1893.[5] Even then the Council refused to act. When in November 1893 the Reverend J. W. Horsley, sanitary reformer from Woolwich, was invited to Leeds by the recently founded Leeds Sanitary Aid Society, he took time off from criticising the local housing to comment that 'it can hardly be believed by people outside Leeds that the authorities of such a large and important city

---

[3] One of these was A. W. Scarr. In party terms the minority consisted of three Liberals and two Conservatives. *L.M.*, 4.4.1895. For slum clearance in Leeds see F. M. Lupton, *Housing Improvement. A Summary of Ten Years' Work in Leeds* (Leeds, 1906); City of Leeds unhealthy areas committee, *Reports 1902–1909*, development committee, *Reports 1910–1915*; City of Leeds, *A Short History of Civic Housing* (Leeds, 1954).
[4] *L.M.*, 4.12.1890.
[5] See Memo from the Leeds Sanitary Aid Society, listing fourteen large English towns where compulsory notification had been adopted. *L.M.*, 14.2.1894.

have not yet adopted the Infectious Diseases Notification Act'. In February of the following year, a third attempt by Alderman Ward and Dr. J. S. Loe was finally successful, although only by a narrow margin. The Council on that occasion received petitions from no less than three deputations. Of these the most significant came from the faculty of the Leeds medical school, who explained that whatever opposition there had been among the local doctors in the past had now disappeared, and that at a recent meeting the profession had shown itself unanimously in favour. This deputation had been preceded by a most influential body sent by the Leeds Sanitary Aid Society and led by the vicar of Leeds, who also spoke in favour of compulsory notification. Besides these two bodies the hostile deputation led by the professor of mining from the Yorkshire College made less impression than a similar deputation had made the previous year. The voting on this occasion as on most others had no relation to party. Leading Conservatives as well as leading Liberals were found on both sides of the division.[6]

More significant than anything that was happening within the parties were the efforts of the body to which passing reference has already been made, the Leeds Sanitary Aid Society. Founded in 1892 in the wake of the revelations made by *The Leeds Mercury*, it was a non-party body designed to create a public opinion in favour of more vigorous action by the Corporation in matters of public health. Its president was the Conservative vicar of Leeds, who had come to the town in 1888 determined to emulate R. W. Dale of Birmingham whom he much admired.[7] Its two honorary secretaries were drawn from each side of the political divide, and so were its eleven vice-presidents who included Edmund Wilson, Liberal ex-councillor, and John Ward, Liberal chairman of the Corporation sanitary committee. But the overlap with the personnel of the Town Council was remarkably small. In 1894, when the membership of the society stood at 100, it included no more than two Town Council members. Another councillor had been a member in 1893 but had stopped his subscription.[8]

If the Town Council provided few members, the Leeds Philosophical and Literary Society provided many. Of the one hundred members in

---

[6] *L.M.*, 2.11.1893, 8.2.1894, p. 3, 15.2.1894, p. 3.

[7] Canon Edward Stuart Talbot, vicar of Leeds 1889–95, previously Warden of Keble College, Oxford, and subsequently in turn bishop of Rochester, Southward, and Winchester. As he once explained, he was a Conservative, but a Conservative with a bad conscience. Gwendolen Stephenson, *Edward Stuart Talbot* (1936), pp. 69–70.

Leeds Sanitary Aid Society, *Annual Reports 1893–?* The two councillors were John Ward and B. G. Heald. The third councillor was Walter Battle, also a Liberal. His name does not appear in the lists of members after 1893.

1894 thirty-four were also subscribers to the Society. This included a high proportion of the scientific men in the town, for at least eleven of them were either doctors, professors or fellows of the Chemical Society. It is also remarkable how many of the men who actually ran the Philosophical and Literary Society were connected with the new body. It included the president, both vice-presidents, both honorary secretaries and four out of the ten Council members. In the winter of 1894-5, when the Town Council was still undecided whether to embark on the clearing of the Quarry Hill insanitary area, Edmund Wilson, both a Council member of the Philosophical and Literary Society and a vice-president of the Sanitary Aid Society, gave a lecture on 'slums' to the former. It was rare for the lecture programme of this body to deal with social and economic problems on its own door-step.[9]

The Sanitary Aid Society also drew heavily on the local Protestant clergy both Anglican and Nonconformist for its support. This was in addition to the Philosophical and Literary Society, for strangely enough out of the twenty clergymen who subscribed to the Sanitary Aid Society only two belonged to the other body. Between them these two groups accounted for more than half the membership of the Sanitary Aid Society. It is plain that sections of the community had been mobilised who had not before been active in Corporation matters. In 1889 the Philosophical and Literary Society had offered to support the Town Council in any efforts to protect the public health of the town. They had been treated with suspicion and repulsed. Now they had mobilised themselves and the Council was soon to feel the difference.

During the municipal elections of 1892 the Sanitary Aid Society had made a rather vague appeal to the public on a non-party basis, but in 1893 it set more seriously about the task of influencing the elections. It proposed four public health issues on which electors should obtain pledges from the candidates.[10] One of these was the compulsory notification of contagious diseases, another the adoption of a clearance scheme for the 'insanitary area'. It will be remembered that both these issues were at last dealt with satisfactorily soon after. A third matter was the poor design of the street gullies which caused them to become minor cess pools. Ineffectual complaints had been made about this in

---

[9] Leeds Philosophical and Literary Society, *Annual Reports*, using the membership for 1892-3 for comparison; E. Kitson Clark, *The History of 100 Years of Life of the Leeds Philosophical and Literary Society* (Leeds, 1924), p. 197.
[10] *L.M. Supplement*, 14.10.1893.

the press since at least 1889. At last in 1894 the Council agreed to replace them by a more satisfactory design.[11] The policy of organised pledging seems to have brought results.

The fourth issue raised by the Sanitary Aid Society was not brought to a satisfactory conclusion quite so soon. They had asked for the systematic inspection of the whole town and the appointment of additional sanitary inspectors for this purpose. Not until 1899 did the Town Council accept that this was necessary. But for the Sanitary Aid Society the intervening years were not a time of passive waiting. From its beginning the Society had undertaken house-to-house inspection by volunteers, primarily looking for instances of defective drains. In 1893 571 houses had been visited and 136 complaints submitted to the Health Department. In the absence of any increase of the official inspectorate, the Society appointed its own salaried inspector in 1894. The following year he visited 1,253 houses and reported 558 defects; in 1896 altogether 2,278 houses were inspected under the auspices of the Society and 279 defects reported.[12] In undertaking this work at their own expense the Society had intended to find out whether there was need for more systematic inspection than was being provided by the authorities. The information which they collected made it only too clear that there was such a need. They had discovered numerous defects which had been allowed to remain because the Corporation possessed too few men to inspect house drains systematically, although faulty construction was notorious. Nor were they able to revisit all the houses on which notices for improvements had been served. It was common for landlords to ignore the notices and to remain undetected. One property owner said in 1899 that as they were printed on one side only he found them useful as scrap paper.[13]

In 1898 the Society finally gave up their independent inspection for lack of funds. They did not give up their pressure on the Town Council, in which they were supporting throughout the efforts of the medical officer of health. 1898 was a year of financial stringency in which the sanitary committee had £5,000 lopped off their estimates. But victory came at last in 1899. The Town Council agreed to appoint seven additional inspectors with the comment that 'there was a general feeling that something should be done in the direction of carrying out a systematic house-to-house visitation'. One of the new inspectors spoke Yiddish so

[11] *L.M.*, 26.10.1894, p. 7.
[12] Leeds Sanitary Aid Society, *Annual Reports*.
[13] *Webb. Loc. Gov. Col.*, volume 265, questionnaire, Q. 109.

as to be able to work among the recent immigrants from Russia and Poland who crowded into the Leylands slums.[14]

Not all the causes which the Society championed were equally successful, and after 1903 it ceased to exist. But there can be no doubt that it caused the Town Council to mend its ways and to adopt courses which it had previously rejected. Enjoying the support of an influential section of the town, it created a public opinion which the two parties struggling for an electoral advantage could not and did not ignore. The very closeness of the party struggle helped to make both sides more sensitive to what was going on in the town.

It had once seemed sufficient to quote the comparative death rates of the nine largest towns in the United Kingdom, which the Registrar-General published regularly, to reassure the public that all was well. In this table Leeds almost always showed up favourably. As has been said already in connection with Birmingham, such statistics did not discriminate enough to serve any but the crudest purposes. What is particularly relevant in this case is that they took the local government boundaries at their face-value forgetting that the arbitrary way in which these had been arrived at vitiated any straight comparison between towns. The historic area of Leeds contained even in the fourth quarter of the nineteenth century much open land, whereas the densely inhabited area was spilling well over the boundaries of Liverpool and Manchester. In 1878 when Leeds had the second lowest death-rate among the nine cities it also had the second lowest rate of persons per acre.[15] By the 1890s a better informed public had learnt to look beyond such crude measures of adequacy and had lost much of the complacency that had once characterised the town.

[14] *L.M.*, 5.5.1898, 6.4.1899.
[15] Leeds Corporation, *Report of the Medical Officer of Health* (Leeds, 1878), p. 9.

3

The Party Struggle

We need to bear in mind the growth of a new public opinion in the town in order to understand the political struggle which had begun in 1890. As the margin between the two parties in the Council narrowed, their struggles acquired a new intensity. But at the same time the standards by which the parties condemned their opponents were also being transformed, and it is this that is so significant. The argument was now first and foremost about municipal issues, and this in itself was new. What is more, the municipal debate was no longer focussed on economy, as had been the case before. It was now about efficiency and adequacy of services.

In this respect the election of 1891, more bitterly contested than any municipal election had been since the 1840s, marked another advance on the practice of the previous year. Mindful no doubt of the wild attacks that had appeared in *The Yorkshire Post* the year before, the *Mercury* published a series of articles on 'The Liberal Administration in Leeds'.[1] They were exceptionally full and informative and largely based on information supplied by the chairmen of the more important committees. Although they were distinctly defensive and laudatory in their tone, they did provide the public with new and easily digestible means of information on the work of the corporation.

The result of the election cheered the Liberals for they gained two seats. Three Labour candidates, appearing for the first time and including Cockayne the gas workers' leader, were all defeated.

The Liberals on the Town Council, had, however, definitely been put on the defensive. They defended themselves chiefly by pointing to the progress made since the 1860s or even the 1840s. The Conservatives included one or two who were anxious to appear in the role of municipal innovators. Lowden, Edmund Wilson's vanquisher at Headingley,

[1] *L.M.*, 27.10.1891, 29.10.1891, 31.10.1891.

scored a marked success in this respect by taking up the matter of public baths. Although the Baths and Washhouses Act had been adopted by the Corporation in 1878 no action had ever been taken. It was highly unusual for a town such as Leeds to have neither public baths nor wash-houses and Lowden moved for the appointment of a committee to deal with the matter. After initial hesitation the resolution was passed unanimously. Public baths were definitely accepted and two were to be built straight away.[2]

The next electoral innovation followed in 1893. The Liberals came before the electors for the first time with a municipal party programme, agreed upon by almost all Town Council members and candidates. Nothing like it had ever been known on either side before. The nine-point programme is worth examining:

1. The immediate clearing of insanitary areas, with due regard to the provision of accommodation for persons displaced by demolitions.
2. Cleansing of the River Aire and the prevention of house-flooding.
3. The extension of public baths.
4. The provision of a better, cheaper and more extended tramway service, with reasonable conditions of labour for tramway employees.
5. The letting of Corporation contracts only to such firms as in their respective trades pay the standard rate of wages, and work fair hours.[3]
6. Inclusion of a due proportion of labour representation in all elected public bodies.[4]
7. The abolition of gas-meter rents.
8. A free public reading room for every ward.
9. Economy in the administration of all departments of City affairs by the Council, with due regard to efficiency.[5]

Not least remarkable is the fact that the ritual reference to economy was consigned to the last item while slum clearance headed the list. The publication of this programme, far from setting off a controversy over the desirability of the items, caused the Conservatives to protest that their opponents had merely stolen their own ideas. The long debates over who was to get the credit for first raising each point made one thing

[2] *L.M.*, 3.12.1891, 4.8.1892. Public baths and wash-houses had been pioneered in Liverpool in 1842, introduced in Birmingham in 1848 and Manchester in 1876.
[3] This was an elaboration of the Fair Wages resolution passed by the Council in August 1891. The demand for such a policy had come from the Leeds Trades Council.
[4] This Lib.–Lab. clause was a way of fighting off the Independent Labour party candidates. It lead to the adoption of Owen Connellan, secretary of the Leeds Trades Council, a compositor, as Lib.–Lab. candidate for the East ward in 1895.
[5] *L.M.*, 21.10.1893, p. 12.

quite clear. A new emphasis in municipal politics had emerged such as would not have been seriously considered four years before.

In 1894 the Liberals again issued an agreed programme. Points 3, 5, 7 and 8 of the 1893 version had been dropped on the ground that they had been carried out.[6] The most important change, however, was the adoption of a new item—the municipalisation of the tramways. It was this issue which for the moment dominated municipal politics. Once again a policy had been imposed on a recalcitrant council by organised agitation outside.

Horse-drawn trams had been in operation in Leeds since 1871 when a tramway company obtained a twenty-one years' lease from the Corporation. There was considerable friction between the company and the highways committee of the Town Council over the repair of the roads, as well as widespread dissatisfaction with the service being provided. The Corporation therefore refused to renew the lease and tried to negotiate for the purchase of the fixed stock. This proved difficult and in the end the price was fixed by arbitration. The transfer of ownership took place in February 1894. Even before that date the Corporation had laid its own tram lines from Sheepscar to Roundhay so as to provide access to Roundhay Park for the population at large. The tramway company had always refused to provide this service, and in 1891 the line was leased to a licensee of the Thompson Houston Company, who provided an experimental electric service. The purchase of the main undertaking was also intended as a prelude to leasing it out again to a suitable operator. When the Leeds Social Reform Union, the Trades Council and the local branch of the I.L.P. called in October 1893 for the lines to be municipally operated, as they were at Huddersfield, the Council was definitely not interested. At a Council meeting in January 1894 no one spoke in favour of municipal management. It was understood that the Corporation would take over the management temporarily, while the roads along which the lines ran were being put in order and a lessee was being sought.[7]

The local Labour and Socialist bodies who believed in municipal management as a permanent policy were not content to leave the matter there. They insisted on the mayor calling a town meeting, and there a resolution in favour of municipal control was carried with only a score

---

[6] With regard to point 7, two public baths were in process of construction. Further action was being deferred to see whether the use made of these justified the erection of any more. *L.M.*, 19.10.1894, p. 8.

[7] *L.M.*, 28.10.1893, 4.1.1894.

of dissentients. Both the president of the Trades Council and representatives of the Labour Church were on the platform, and the principal speakers came from the same quarter. 'Got up by the Socialists' was how one councillor described the meeting subsequently. Of the three members of the Town Council who spoke, two were strongly opposed to the resolution. The following day the Town Council received petitions in favour of municipal control from the Trades Council, various trades unions but also from several ward Liberal associations. These were received in stony silence, while a few petitions in favour of leasing were greeted with expressions of approval. There was a debate and the decision to lease the tramways to a company was confirmed by forty-one votes to thirteen. It was not opposition to municipal control on principle that led to this decision but rather doubts whether the Corporation would be able to manage the undertaking successfully. Memories of the troubles that had followed the municipalisation of the gas and of the water works weighed heavily with the Council, whose members clearly had little faith in their own business capacity. In a leading article the *Mercury* commented scathingly on 'a cowardly decision'. It suspected that the Council's members were reluctant to take on the management because 'they were afraid of pressure being brought to bear upon them to do a great many undesirable things.'[8] There was something in this. When the Council subsequently decided to retain the management of the tramways a new factor entered municipal politics. The question of what fares should be charged on different sectors of the line serving different wards of the city became for a time matter of debate both in the Council and in the wards at election time.[9]

Between February 1894 when this debate took place and the publication of the Liberal Election Programme in October the Leeds Liberal Federation's executive committee and the Liberal members of the Council slowly and reluctantly yielded to the view pressed on them by the ward associations. In October at practically the last moment the advocates of municipal tramways won the day on the executive committee by a narrow majority.[10] At first it looked as if the pessimists had been right. Immediately on taking control the Corporation had to improve the working conditions of the drivers and conductors, whose long hours and low wages had obtained much publicity in the town. Thirty-eight additional men were employed to make a more humane system of

[8] *L.M.*, 7.2.1894, p. 5, 8.2.1894, 15.2.1894.
[9] See for instance *L.M.*, 7.4.1894; *Y.P.*, 31.10.1899, p. 7; *Y.P.*, 7.12.1899.
[10] Leeds Liberal Federation, executive committee minutes, 6.7.1894; 7.9.1894, 14.9.1894, 4.10.1894. Leeds City Library, archives department.

shifts possible. Moreover much of the equipment, including the horses, was found to be worn out and had to be renewed. The first eight months' operations yielded a loss of £404. But the town rang with praises of the improved service and there seemed every chance that the following year would see a good profit, as indeed it did.[11]

It seemed for a moment as if the municipalisation of the tramways would provide the two parties with a genuine difference over policy. But the moment passed. Twelve months later the Conservatives were no longer prepared to challenge the issue. It was in fact the Conservative-controlled Council that obtained Parliamentary powers in the Leeds Tramway Act of 1896 to regularise the temporary arrangement. Although Huddersfield and Glasgow had adopted the principle of municipal management before them, tramways was a field in which Leeds was well to the fore. Its electrified line to Roundhay was the first in the country, and as early as 1895 the decision was taken to extend electric traction to the whole undertaking.[12] The profits from a greatly extended municipal tramway system were to play a useful role in prolonging the period of municipal improvement in the history of the town.[13]

In these closely fought elections the Conservatives gradually gained ground. By 1894 they had eight more councillors than the Liberals. Only the mayor's casting vote stood between them and control when the next election of aldermen was due in November 1895. In the municipal elections of that year they gained another two seats. On the subsequent retirement of eight aldermen their majority was assured and sixty years of Liberal rule came to an end.

How would the Conservatives use their power? The first test came at once with the election of the mayor and of the new aldermen. Their action on this occasion was significant for its contrast with Liberal practice. It showed the victorious party sensitively attuned to the new emphasis on recruiting a different type of man to the Council. The first Conservative mayor since the Municipal Corporations Act was W. L. Jackson, since 1880 M.P. for North Leeds, former Financial Secretary to the Treasury (1885–91) and Chief Secretary for Ireland (1891–2). He was the head of the largest firm of leather tanners in Leeds and indeed in the U.K. Since 1870 Leeds had been the most important centre of tanning in Great Britain, and in 1890 the eight largest firms there

[11] *L.M.*, 24.10.1894, 15.10.1895.
[12] *L.M.*, 16.10.1895. For a treatment of municipalisation and electrification of tramways in Britain as a whole see A. L. Lowell, *The Government of England* (1912), II, chapter 44.
[13] See below, p. 276.

were at the height of their prosperity.[14] Jackson's had been built up overwhelmingly by his own exertions. It had been of no great size in 1858 and was on the verge of bankruptcy, when at the age of seventeen he took charge on his father's death. By 1895 he was also chairman of the Great Northern Railway, and in the very first rank of Leeds businessmen. A prominent Freemason, a devout Churchman and supporter of the extension of church work in Leeds, one of the earliest promoters of the Yorkshire College which was to become the University, Jackson had gained the esteem of all sections of the community by his personal intervention when the Liberator Building Society failed in 1892. His proposals for more efficient audit and financial control over building societies, which were the result of his investigation, had become law in the Building Societies Act of 1894.[15] Yet it was even more than respect for a leading citizen that inspired the choice. Jackson was no stranger to Council work. He had been a town councillor from 1869–81, i.e. during the time of the previous Conservative municipal revival. In 1873, when the party had been within one vote of controlling the Council, he had been their candidate for mayor. They were beaten off and from 1874 their numbers declined rapidly and this deprived Jackson of his chance. Although only thirty-three at the time, he had been leader of the Conservatives on the Council and generally regarded as far and away their ablest man.[16] His election in 1895 was in part a gesture of restitution towards the disappointed party leader of bygone days.

There were therefore two aspects to the first Conservative nomination. On the one hand the payment of a party debt, on the other a deliberate attempt to raise the standing of the office of mayor by electing to it an outstanding citizen. The first of these is remarkable only for the tenacious political memory that it showed; it is the second that calls for comment.

I THE CHOICE OF ALDERMEN

The selection of the eight new aldermen revealed a similar preoccupation. Prudence may well have counselled that it was safer to bring men in from outside the Council than to risk too many bye-elections in the wards. Only three of the seats were given to those who had represented the party on the Council during the long years of opposition. Loe, the surgeon, and Walker, a butcher, were still councillors; Harland,

---

[14] W. G. Rimmer, 'The Leeds Leather Industry in the Nineteenth Century', *Thoresby Society Publications*, XLVI (1961), 145.

[15] 'Jackson, William Lawies, Baron Allerton', *D.N.B.*, 1912–21 (1927).

[16] J. S. Curtis, *The Story of the Marsden Mayoralty* (Leeds, 1875).

another butcher, had retired only the year before and was now brought back.[17] The other five aldermen, all chosen from outside, were among the leading industrialists of the city. They were the heads of three of the largest engineering firms, the biggest brewer and a leading woollen manufacturer. Two of them, Harding and Lupton, had been nominated by the Liberal Unionists, the other three were prominent Conservatives.[18] Their recruitment was a policy avowedly designed to strengthen the City Council, 'by the introduction of citizens of weight and standing'.[19]

'It is the curse of Leeds that its Corporation lags a generation or two behind the enterprise of its manufacturers and merchants', *The Yorkshire Post* had written in 1890. It had appealed to the best men in the town to come and fight the battle in the wards.[20] But the Conservative election successes had tended rather to increase the number of quite small businessmen, including licensed victuallers, at the expense of the heads of middle-sized firms within the Leeds economy. The proportion of heads of really large businesses or of professional men had not changed at all. The introduction of the new aldermen redressed the balance, which had been tilted in the other direction at the very time that the Council was being criticised for its lack of businessmen of standing. The Liberals had not been slow to draw attention to the contrast between what the Conservatives said they wanted to achieve and the candidates they put up for election. The trouble, one suspects, was that the prospect of fiercely fought ward elections in the hard hitting atmosphere that the closer margin between the parties had generated was not very congenial to the men of social standing in the Conservative party. The great advantage of obtaining at last the disposal of aldermanic seats was that the party could and did recruit those who, in the words of *The Yorkshire Post* 'are ready to give their services to the city when they can do so without insult, but who will not "wade through dirt to dignities".'[21]

---

[17] J. S. Loe, first elected January 1880; William Walker, first elected November 1878; Thomas Harland, first elected November 1869 during a fracas over the removal of the cattle market from North Street.

[18] Colonel T. W. Harding, of Harding, Richardson, Rhodes & Co. Ltd., F. W. Lawson, of Samuel Lawson & Sons, both manufacturers of textile machinery. Reginald Wigram of John Fowler & Co., Steam Plough Works, Hunslet. C. F. Tetley of Joshua Tetley & Son Ltd. F. M. Lupton of William Lupton & Co. For Harding see above, Part I, p. 224. Lupton was chairman of the Leeds and County Liberal Unionist Club, Lawson vice-president of the Leeds Conservative Association. Wigram had been president of the Leeds Conservative Association 1881–6 and remained a powerful member of the committee. Tetley was president of the South Leeds Conservative Association.

[19] *Y.P.*, 30.10.1895, p. 4. Leeds had become a city in 1893.

[20] *Y.P.*, 3.11.1890, p. 6.

[21] *Y.P.*, 30.10.1895, p. 4.

Once more, as in 1890, considerations of quality and party control did not altogether coincide. The eight Liberals who were swept off the Council included John Ward, chairman of the sanitary committee, who, it was generally agreed, ought to have been retained on grounds of calibre. When a few months later a vacancy occurred among the remaining Liberal aldermen, the Conservatives did not press their advantage but helped to bring Ward back into the Council. Behind this action was the conviction, then generally expressed by the Conservative leaders, that the aldermanic bench should properly be shared between the parties. The same view had been held by the Liberals in 1835 but neither then nor now did it survive long in the party struggle for control of policy.

When the next aldermanic elections were due in 1898 the Council was delicately poised 32 : 32, and the Conservatives decided that taking all the seats had its merit after all. Two of the retiring aldermen were Conservatives already—Cooke, who had conveniently changed his party allegiance during his term of office, and Gordon, the Conservative leader on the Council, who had been given a vacancy in 1896. The six retiring Liberals had to make way. Neither Ward nor Emsley, the solicitor whom *The Yorkshire Post* had once singled out as a model to be followed,[22] were proof against party considerations.

Their places were taken by five Conservative councillors and one recruit from outside. The time had come to reward the troops, but even so the opportunity was taken to bring in at least one distinguished outsider. J. H. Wurtzburg was of the same type as the recruits of 1895. Managing director of a large engineering firm, he was also a vice-president of the Leeds Conservative Association. He had been educated at the University of Bonn and was a man of historical and archaeological scholarship. In addition he was a prominent Churchman and associated with many bodies in that sphere, as well as a patron of friendly societies. He had been nine years a member of the Leeds School Board, and chairman until 1897 when the Liberals recaptured the majority and he lost his seat. The election to the aldermanic bench of one so recently freed from other duties showed the Conservative party determined not to waste its talented and public-spirited officers. The five men promoted from within the Council could not lay claim to the social or economic position of Wurtzburg, but two of them were fairly substantial

---

[22] 'The presence of a few more such men in the Corporation would afford a guarantee of a vastly wiser and more dignified system of governing the borough than that which has obtained for many years.' *Y.P.*, 11.11.1889, p. 6.

manufacturers.[23] The remainder belonged to a different category—a retired licensed victualler representing the influential liquor wing of the party, a building contractor and a wholesale grocer.[24]

The dismissal of the entire body of Liberal aldermen may have caused the loss of one or two generally respected men, but it certainly cleared out the dead wood. It had indeed done more than that. When the Liberals came back in 1904 they had learnt their lesson.[25] Of eight seats that they obtained, only two went to councillors of the old type.[26] One went to an energetic councillor of only two years' standing,[27] three to complete outsiders[28] and one was used to bring John Ward once more back into the Council. This mixture, in such contrast to practice in the past, was an attempt to 'satisfy the reasonable ambitions of men from within, and . . . to try, if they could, to satisfy the opinions of the people outside'. We are not left in any doubt what these opinions were:

> 'The Liberal party in the Leeds City Council are doing what they can to redeem their promise to bring business ability to bear on the administration of the city's affairs. Apart from the members of the Council who have been chosen as Aldermen and whose services to the city entitle them to a place in the municipal House of Lords, the other selections made are men who have proved their ability by the success with which they have managed their own affairs.'[29]

Hepton, Mathieson and Portway, the three outsiders, were none of them important figures in the local Liberal organisation. Portway had once in the late 1880s been on the committee of the Liberal Association, but the *Mercury* could describe them all as men who had up to the time of their nomination not taken any part in political and municipal life. It was in the Chamber of Commerce that they had been prominent and in the economic life of the town.[30]

Thanks to the agility with which the Liberals had once more adapted

[23] Joseph Lowden, cloth dyer and finisher, who employed 200–250 hands. Thomas Willey, retired wholesale clothing manufacturer.

[24] J. F. Carter, Thomas Hannam, Alfred Knowles.

[25] By a concordat between the parties arranged that year the Liberals obtained eight aldermen, the Conservatives seven and Labour one.

[26] Robert Pickersgill, pawnbroker, elected clr. 1883; Peter Laycock, fairly large cloth manufacturer, elected clr. 1887.

[27] J. R. Ford, solicitor.

[28] A. F. L. Hepton, clothing manufacturer; Ewing Mathieson, iron founder; G. R. Portway, woollen manufacturer.

[29] *L.M.*, 14.11.1904, p. 6; 12.11.1904, p. 6.

[30] Portway, whom the Conservative evening paper called 'a citizen of the best type', had also been prominent in the management of the General Infirmary, the Leeds, Skyrac and Morley Savings Bank, and in local Congregationalist bodies.

themselves to the standards set by their political opponents, the changes of 1904, significant though they were in party terms, made little difference to the social composition of the aldermanic bench. The ejection of three large businessmen and one accountant from among the Conservatives was fairly balanced by the accession of three large businessmen and one solicitor on the Liberal side.

2 THE CHOICE OF MAYOR

The changes in the recruitment of aldermen had more effect on the social composition of the City Council than the concurrent changes that occurred in the choice of the mayor. But the two sprang from the same mental climate, and reacted on each other. Not only did the new bench of aldermen provide a new reservoir to draw on for the exacting and expensive office of mayor, but the decision to look outside the Council for mayoral candidates created for the first time a previously unsuspected avenue for recruitment to long term municipal service on the aldermanic bench.

The nomination of Jackson in 1895 was no isolated instance but the beginning of a new policy towards recruitment for the mayor's office. In the following year, so as to emphasise that this was not primarily a party issue, the Conservative majority nominated Sir James Kitson, *grand personnage* of the Leeds Liberal Party. Kitson had been President of the National Liberal Federation from 1883–90 and host to W. E. Gladstone on his visit to the town in 1881. He was head of the Airedale foundry, the largest of the locomotive-making works in Leeds, employing 1,400 men in 1890, as well as of subsidiary firms.[31] Unlike Jackson, he had never been a member of the Town Council before, although a public figure in the town for many years, serving as governor of the Leeds Infirmary and president of the Chamber of Commerce. He came in fact from a prominent local family which for three generations was to provide Leeds with much of its unpaid public service. His father, the founder of the family fortune, had been a town councillor and alderman from 1854–68, mayor in 1860–62.[32] For James Kitson the elder, moving as he did among the Unitarians at Mill Hill Chapel, it was a natural step to stand for the Council and to sit among the Luptons and Luccocks, where only a few years before a Stansfeld, a Tottie and a Clapham had

---

[31] British Association, *Handbook for Leeds and Airedale* (Leeds, 1890), p. 98. See also E. Kitson Clark, *Kitson's of Leeds, 1837–1937* (1938).

[32] He had been a clr. already for a few months in 1851 but was defeated at the November elections.

held sway. For these were the established families of two or three generations' standing, whose leadership he acknowledged and whom he hoped to emulate. Sir James, on the other hand, although he remained true to the public service tradition in which he had been reared, had not included the Town Council, nor had any other second-generation Kitson. It was the New Era policy of the 1890s that brought the family back into the Council chamber: Sir James as described, and his nephew F. J. Kitson as Lord Mayor in 1908–9 and then as a Liberal alderman for several years.

Neither Jackson nor Kitson continued their connection with the Corporation beyond the year that they served as mayors.[33] Their function had been to give a new lustre to the office. Their immediate successors were all drawn from the ranks of the Conservative aldermen recently recruited to the Council: Tetley the brewer, Harding and Lawson from among the engineers. The only nomination that at all resembled the older practice was that of John Gordon in 1899. Gordon more than anyone else had been the architect of the Conservative revival in the Council. He had led the party there since the mid–1880s and seized his opportunities with skill and great perseverance. Yet he had been in no hurry to take for himself valuable positions of prestige that could be used for the implementation of the new policy. He did not become an alderman till December 1896. When he was nominated for Lord Mayor in 1899 it was clear from the comments of his sponsors that he could have had the honour long before. Gordon had in fact been anxious to continue the policy of choosing eminent men and had only accepted nomination at forty-eight hours' notice when other negotiations had broken down. He hinted that he could ill afford to spare the time from his accountant's business.[34] His term of office was a mere interlude in the new policy, and an accidental one at that. After Alderman F. W. Lawson's year had expired in 1901 the party fell back again on an outsider of standing, Ambrose Edmund Butler, managing director of the Kirkstall forge, one of the largest employers in the town.

The municipal election in November 1901 had left the narrowest of margins between the parties and the re-election of the outgoing Conservative aldermen was obtained only by the Lord Mayor's casting vote. Butler never really lived down the indignation that this partisan act drew down upon him from the Liberals. Although their nomination

---

[33] On the occasion of the Diamond Jubilee in 1897 during Kitson's term of office the title was changed to Lord Mayor.
[34] *Y.P.*, 10.11.1899, p. 4.

had always been a party matter, the mayors once installed in the chair had invariably made a point of being above party. Similarly the opposition, after registering its protest at the principle that excluded them from the honour, had always been careful to treat the chair with respect and submit to its rulings. Butler, an ardent Conservative, was prepared to face the opprobrium of a breach with tradition, but thereafter things could hardly be the same again.[35] In the light of the narrow party balance and the bitter feelings of the previous year a concordat was arranged in 1902 whereby the nomination went alternatively to the two parties.

Butler was the first of several lord mayors who were elected to a vacant aldermanic seat during their year of office and remained on the Council subsequently. Others were the Conservative nominee for 1903–4, Arthur Currer Briggs, a wealthy colliery owner, F. J. Kitson, the Liberal Lord Mayor in 1908–9 already referred to, and William Penrose Green, a big engineering employer and Conservative nominee for 1909–10.

When they were once more able to nominate lord mayors the Liberals did not return to their earlier practice, any more than they did with the election of aldermen. They followed by and large the new precedents that had been established by their opponents. They did bring back John Ward for a third term of office in 1902 followed by another spell as alderman. He had been President of the Leeds Liberal Federation since 1894 and was knighted in 1906 for his political services. But their nominee in 1904, Robert Armitage, had only been a councillor for one year. His claim rested not on seniority in municipal service but on his economic standing as director of the Farnley Iron Company and on his philanthropic work south of the river.[36] Two years later they returned to the past in choosing Joseph Hepworth, the clothing manufacturer, who had served on the Council during the 1890s and been ejected from the aldermanic bench in 1898. By 1906 he was seventy-two, and by reviving the teetotal practices of the past proved an embarrassment to the party leaders who were very conscious of the changed political atmosphere.[37] The next three Liberal nominees were F. J. Kitson (1908–9) of the Monkbridge Iron and Steel Company, William

---

[35] In addition to being a strong party man Butler commended himself to the majority on the Council by being a man of great wealth who would be able to shoulder the extra expense of the office during the Coronation year.

[36] On 12 October 1904 when he attended the executive committee meeting of the Leeds Liberal Federation as mayor-elect it was his first time and he was formally welcomed accordingly. Leeds Liberal Federation, executive committee minutes Leeds City Library, archives department. For his position in South Leeds see *Y.P.*, 10.11.1904, p. 4.

[37] George Ratcliffe, *Sixty Years of It* (Hull, 1935), chapter 25.

Middlebrook (1910–11), a solicitor and M.P. for South Leeds, and A. W. Bain (1912–13) a wealthy insurance broker. They were all from outside and unlike Hepworth had had no previous connection with the Council. J. E. Bedford of the Airedale chemical works, Lord Mayor in 1914–15, was a councillor of four years' standing.[38]

In thus conforming to Conservative practice the Liberals really made a virtue of necessity. Their action in the nomination of lord mayors is of less significance than in the parallel case of the aldermen, because they had so little choice. There had been some mayors in the past who had marked their term of office by lavish expenditure. H. R. Marsden's mayoralty in 1873–5 was long remembered in this context. His public generosity included a water gala on Roundhay Lake and earned him a statue raised by public subscription, when he died suddenly a few months after his term of office.[39] A. W. Scarr, whose election had caused such public scandal in 1887, seems to have compensated by being more than usually generous.[40] But these were exceptions. Harding told the Webbs in 1899 that before 1895 mayors had as a rule not spent large sums. But since then they had spent several thousand pounds a year in office, and the public had come to expect heavy subscriptions.[41] There are no accounts against which to check this assertion, but the impression given by a reading of the newspapers confirms the view that the succession of wealthy men in the second half of the 1890s raised the general level of expectation. Sir James Kitson had presented the Corporation with an enamelled badge for the Lady Mayoress. Harding at the end of his term in office in 1899 presented a badge decorated with diamonds, rubies, sapphires, and emeralds for the Lord Mayor 'after the fashion of those worn by lord mayors of London, Liverpool, and he thought some other cities'.[42] In 1906 when Joseph Hepworth's teetotal principles prevented him from serving wine at his dinners, he donated £500 instead for the provision of meals to school children. When the Education (Provision

---

[38] The complete list of Conservative nominees after the concordat of 1902 were Arthur Currer Briggs (1903–4) colliery owner, Edwin Woodhouse (1905–6) cloth manufacturer, Wilfred Hepton (1907–8) clothing manufacturer, William Penrose Green (1909–10) engineer and ironmaster, William Nicholson (1911–12) building contractor and Edward Brotherton (1913–14) chemical manufacturer.

[39] J. S. Curtis, *The Story of the Marsden Mayorlty* (Leeds, 1875).

[40] Herbert Yorke, *A Mayor of the Masses. History and Anecdotes of A. W. Scarr* (Leeds, 1904).

[41] S. W. and B. W. 'Interview with Lord Mayor, T. W. Harding' 1899. *Webb. Loc. Gov. Col.*, volume 265. Before 1877 there was no Corporation cutlery, glass, or china for the mayor's use when he entertained officially. He had to hire this at his own expense, but what was provided was often homely rather than elegant, wine being drunk out of tumblers for instance. Herbert Yorke, p. 58.

[42] *Y.P.*, 10.11.1899, p. 4.

of Meals) Act of 1906 met this need during the school terms, Penrose-Green, Lord Mayor in 1909–10, provided free meals for poor children during the Christmas holidays. His successors in 1910–11 and 1911–12 did the same, while disclaiming any intention of setting a precedent.[43]

Admirable though this was, it limited the range of choice for the office. The Liberal party in particular was often hard pressed to find a suitable candidate. One year the whips went round to twelve men in turn before finding one who would accept.[44] The need to look for candidates from outside had the disadvantage that it gave the Council a chairman not accustomed to its business. In March 1912 the Liberals therefore decided in the public interest to provide future lord mayors with a salary of £1250 per year. They were supported in this by the Labour members but the Conservatives were strongly opposed. It was one of the few issues over which the voting was on strictly party lines and since the Liberal-Labour combination had a majority, the proposal was accepted. Liverpool and Birmingham were already paying salaries to their lord mayors, but other large towns and all smaller towns clung to the older practice of unpaid service. In November 1912 the Conservatives made the matter one of the two issues at the municipal election and captured seven seats. This changed the party balance and caused a temporary reversal of policy until all parties finally accepted the principle in 1917.[45]

Writing in 1921, when the novelty of salaried mayors had not yet worn off, Charles Masterman saw a conflict taking shape in England between two rival interpretations of the mayor's role. On the one hand, he explained, a new and 'professional' ideal was being set up by those who saw the mayor primarily as the chairman of the Council, presiding over it with briskness and impartiality. But at present most of the cities are not prepared for so drastic a break with 'the ancient ideal', which sees the mayor as 'a kind of "good uncle", or fairy godmother to all the citizens. He sits in the Mayor's Parlour . . . and people come to him with any kind of request or grievance or demand for advice. Every charity or athletic society or school entertainment requests his presence and his subscription.'[46]

The choice was never made in such a logical manner. As with other features of local government in twentieth-century England the old has prominently survived in the partial acceptance of the new, and both

[43] *Y.P.*, 10.11.1906, p. 10, 10.11.1910, p. 8.
[44] See George Ratcliffe, *Sixty Years of It*, chapter 25, for the troubles of the Liberal whip in this connection.
[45] *Y.P.*, 30.3.1912, 4.9.1913; *Leeds Council Proceedings*, 3.10.1917.
[46] Charles Masterman, *How England is Governed* (1921), pp. 71–3.

have impeded the development of forms of municipal leadership more positive and more truly professional than either. But how ancient was the ideal that Masterman described as such in 1921 ? In Leeds it seems to owe many of its most prominent features to late-Victorian innovation, though innovation deeply tinged with notions of an older England, of patronage and munificence.

The impact of these changes on the composition of the Council is well brought out in the following table.

TABLE 19. *Leeds City Council 1892–1912 : selected occupations*

	1892		1902		1912	
	Nos.	%	Nos.	%	Nos.	%
Professions	9	14·0	12	18·5	17	26·6
Large businessmen	6	9·4	15	23·1	9	14·0
Total	15	23·4	27	41·0	26	40·6

The chairmen of Council committees provide us with a smaller group and one more representative of those who took the major part in decision making. In the two-year period 1892–3 there were twenty-two chairmen, of whom the overwhelming number were heads of medium-sized businesses. One or possibly two were heads of large businesses, two were professional men. In 1902–3 out of a total of seventeen chairmen of committees certainly five and possibly seven were heads of large businesses, while one was secretary of a large joint-stock company. Three were professional men. In 1911–12 a total of twenty-one chairmen included five or possibly six heads of large businesses and five professional men. In simplified tabular form it looks like this:

TABLE 20. *Leeds City Council 1892–1912 : chairmen of Council committees*

	1892-3	%	1902-3	%	1911-12	%
Total no. in sample	21	100	17	100	21	100
Professions	2	9·5	3	17·6	5	23·8
Large businessmen	2	9·5	8	47·1	6	28·6
Total	4	19	11	64·7	11	52·4

The first of the three samples shows the Council at the height of the old Liberal regime, the second at the height of the new Conservative one. By 1911–12 the party balance was delicately poised. The Conservatives provided the chairmen in 1911 but in the following year lost control temporarily to the Liberals, who replaced most of the chairmen by their own nominees. The last sample is therefore drawn fairly evenly from both the main parties.

A comparison between the two tables shows that after 1895 power on the Council fell largely into the hands of the large businessmen and the members of the professions. In 1892–3 these two groups provided a slightly smaller percentage of committee chairmen than their numbers on the Council would have warranted. In 1902–3 and in 1911–12 they provided a percentage considerably in excess of their share of the Council as a whole.

In the leadership of both municipal parties the professional men played a role out of all proportion to their numbers. From the beginning the Conservative revival was led by John Gordon, the accountant. When the Liberal victory deprived him of his aldermanic seat in 1904, Charles Wilson, another accountant, had already made such a position for himself that he was the inevitable successor.[47] At the same time the party appointed C. F. Tetley, the brewer, as vice-chairman and another accountant together with a manufacturing chemist as party whips.[48]

The Liberal party weathered the storm under the lead of politicians from the stronghold of Leeds Liberalism in Holbeck and Hunslet, south of the river. These were owners of small or medium-sized businesses,[49] but in the course of the Liberal recovery they allied themselves with professional men from north-west Leeds who could and did give the lead in the promulgation of policy.[50]

How do the figures in table 19 compare with those for Birmingham? The percentage of large businessmen on the Leeds Council in 1902 is strictly comparable with what Birmingham had known in the 1880s and 1890s. The lower figure recorded for 1912 is still only just below those for Birmingham in 1902 and 1912.[51] Judged therefore by the degree to which it recruited large businessmen for municipal work, the New Era produced much the same effect as the Chamberlain movement but for a much shorter time.

[47] Clr. 1890–1907, ald. 1907–28, 1929–30, knighted 1923, M.P. Central Leeds 1923–9, Charles Henry Wilson was the most powerful figure in Leeds politics in his generation.
[48] R. A. Smithson, E. A. Hirst.
[49] E.g. Joseph Henry, party leader 1895–1904 and possibly longer, a Holbeck ironfounder; George Ratcliffe, party whip, a Holbeck confectioner; Herbert Brown, party leader from some time before 1909–11, pawnbroker, Hunslet Road and elsewhere.
[50] E.g. J. R. Ford, solicitor, clr. for Headingley, party leader from 1912 onwards; F. Kinder, from Kirkstall, in turn yarn merchant, barrister and worsted spinner. One of the strongest personalities on the Council, he lacked the tact necessary for a successful party leader and his term of office was short.
[51] The Birmingham figures are given on pp. 34 and 39.

What does continue to rise in Leeds, as it had done in Birmingham, is the involvement of professional men in municipal service. In 1902 and 1912 the two bodies contained a very similar proportion of members drawn from the professions, as a comparison of figure 2, pp. 44–5 with figure 6, p. 206 will show. In Birmingham this rise did not merely reflect an increase in the professional men active in the city but greatly exceeded it. Appendix I shows that the same is true of Leeds. Nor are the two towns unique in this respect. E. S. Griffith has recorded a marked increase in professional men on the Liverpool City Council between 1900 and 1910, and G. W. Jones has done the same for Wolverhampton between 1903 and 1914.[52] It seems to have occurred no matter whether the recruitment from the professions in preceding years had been high as in Liverpool and Birmingham or low as in Leeds.

Once again we can compare the presence of professional men on the Council in this period with what happened after 1918, as we did for Birmingham. The figures available are for the full membership of the Council over consecutive periods, and are therefore not directly comparable with any drawn from sample years. But since the series begins in 1888, it is possible to use figures constructed on the same principle for both pre- and post-war councils.

TABLE 21. *Leeds City Council 1888–1953: the professions**

Years	Whole Council		Labour party		Other parties	
	No.	%	No.	%	No.	%
1888–1905	30	14·7	—	—	30	15·5
1906–1918	34	21·4	—	—	34	26·8
1919–1928	32	20·9	2	3·6	30	30·9
1929–1935	31	20·3	7	10·9	24	27·0
1936–1944	32	21·2	5	7·9	27	31·0
1945–1953	35	19·0	10	9·9	25	30·1

* This table is constructed from figures given in Brenda M. Powell, 'A Study of the Change in Social Origins, Political Affiliation and Length of Service of Members of the Leeds City Council, 1888-1953', unpublished M.A. thesis, Department of Social Studies, University of Leeds (1958), pp. 105, 138, 140. The range of occupations included is slightly wider than elsewhere in this book. The table includes three journalists, one stockbroker, one retired officer of the armed services, one retired elementary-school headmaster, the wife of an administrative-grade civil servant and three clergymen. The clergy were all Church of England and all belonged to the Labour party. They include the most famous of the Labour councillors of this period, the housing reformer the Reverend Charles Jenkinson. Clergy had only become eligible for seats on the City Council since 1925. It must also be borne in mind that wives have been counted under the profession of their husbands. They account for 6 per cent of the total given here over the period as a whole.

[52] F. S. Griffith, *Modern Development of City Government*, II, appendix 13; G. W. Jones, *Borough Politics*, tables XI, XII.

The marked rise in the percentage of professional men which the sampling method had revealed is also shown here in the contrast between the periods 1888–1905 and 1906–18. Thereafter the percentage hardly fluctuated until after the Second World War. Whereas in Birmingham the numerical growth of the Labour party reduced the proportion of professional men on the Council in the years between the wars, this did not happen in Leeds. For one thing, the other parties came to rely more heavily on recruitment from the professions than had been the case even from 1906–18. For another, the municipal Labour party itself was recruiting among the professions far earlier than in Birmingham. It is a remarkable fact that in the years 1929–35 10·9 per cent of the Labour members of the Council were professional people.

No analysis of the state of the Council in 1912 is complete without a reference to the presence of manual workers and trade union officials. In 1902 the representation of the working class had still been of insignificant proportions and channelled through the Liberal party. By 1912 one Council member in ten was a manual worker or trade union official, a higher proportion than in Greater Birmingham, and again in contrast to Birmingham they belonged with one exception to the Labour party. The single Lib.–Lab. councillor survived only until the following November. The Labour party enjoyed a recognised position on the Council with nine councillors and one alderman.

What impact did the stirrings of political consciousness in the world of labour have on the nature of municipal politics and the functioning of municipal government? The introduction of trade unionism into the municipal gasworks and the repercussions of the dispute of 1890 have already been discussed.[53] It was the inability of the older municipal leaders to conceive of any form of labour relations other than those which they had always known that proved so damaging to them. That the Conservatives were able to turn the gas dispute to their advantage was not due merely to a capacity for fishing in troubled waters. It was mainly due to their leader's quick recognition of the fact that, as he put it, 'they were long past the time when any public body could afford to ignore a Trade Union'. In saying this he was not just acquiescing in a new political fact, but recognising the merits of the new developments. He saw that once the older concept of employers' discipline had been challenged, trade unions, including the new ones that were spreading into occupations previously neglected, provided welcome opportunities for social

[53] See above, pp. 237 ff.

TABLE 22. *Trade union officials and manual workers on Leeds City Council 1896–1912*

Date	1896				1902				1912			
	No.	%	Lib.	Lab.	No.	%	Lib.	Lab.	No.	%	Lib.	Lab.
T.U. official	—	—	—	—	1	1·5	1	—	3	4·7	1	2
Foreman and skilled	1	1·5	1	—	2	3·1	2	—	3	4·7	—	3
Unskilled and semi-skilled	—	—	—	—	—	—	—	—	1	1·6	—	1
Total	1	1·5	1	—	3	4·6	3	—	7	10·8	1	6*

* The remaining four members of the Labour party were insurance agent or manager (2), bookseller and commercial traveller (1), cooper and cask merchant (1).

progress. 'No-one could discuss a question or come to a settlement with a rabble, whereas if they had an organised body there was a possibility of an arrangement being arrived at.'[54]

For the Liberals, who prided themselves on their traditional links with the aristocracy of labour, it was easier to recognise the merit of new demands, when they appeared under the sponsorship of the Trades Council.[55] When during the municipal election of 1890 the Trades Council asked for a Fair Wages clause in all corporation contracts, it was granted before the next municipal election.[56] A more elaborate version, which covered hours as well as wages, was promised in the Liberal election programme of 1893.

After 1895 the chief link between the City Council and the Trades Council was its secretary, Owen Connellan. He was a compositor, sponsored by the Labour Electoral Association, a Lib.–Lab. body set up to ensure the Labour representation promised in the 1893 Liberal programme. When he joined the rival Labour Representation Committee in 1904, it had to be recognised that all hopes of tying Labour representation to the Liberal party were dead. The first Independent Labour Party candidate had been elected to the Council in the previous year. In 1904, when an agreement was reached between the parties about the election of aldermen, the Independent Labour group was accorded recognition and given the right to nominate one person. There were ten Labour members in 1907. Then came a temporary set-back, but by 1912 double figures had once more been reached, and in 1914 there were fourteen in all.[57]

The period dealt with in this part of the book ended as it had begun, with a major dispute between the Corporation and its workmen. This occurred in December 1913 and at its peak involved 4,434 men or 80 per cent of all Corporation workmen.[58] The strike was conducted by

[54] Clr. Gordon moving a vote of censure on the gas committee. *L.M.*, 3.7.1890, p. 8.
[55] E. P. Thompson has drawn attention to the strained relations between the Leeds Trades Council and the new Socialist-led movements in the 1890s. 'Homage to Tom Maguire', in A. Briggs and J. Saville (eds.), *Essays in Labour History* (1960).
[56] This was a clause in all Corporation contracts stipulating that the contracting firm pay the standard rate of wages. *Y.P.*, 24.10.1890, p. 4; *L.M.*, 6.8.1891.
[57] See appendix IV for details.
[58] Corporation of Leeds, *Report of the Special Committee on the Strike of Municipal Workmen 1913–14* (1914). See also J. E. Williams 'The Leeds Corporation Strike in 1913', in A. Briggs and J. Saville, eds., *Essays in Labour History 1886–1923* (1971).
In 1913 the Corporation employed:
Officials   Male   2,245 including   630 teachers
              Female 1,851 including 1,715 teachers
Workpeople Male   5,506
              Female   579
Financial Statistics 1913, City Treasurer's Archives.

the Federal Council of Municipal Employees, whose secretary, Walter Wood, was a town councillor at the time. The numbers involved show how successfully trade unionism had spread among the municipal employees. By embracing workmen from different municipal departments in one organisation, unionisation quickly revealed anomalies and led to a demand for uniformity of treatment. The City Council had set up a consultative committee with this object in November 1910, but after the strike this loose structure was replaced by a strong general purpose committee to deal with personnel matters in all departments. Its chief executive officer, the former tramway manager, had shown himself to be a strong man during the crisis. In this way the role that the Corporation played as a large employer of labour led to a demand for uniformity, accountability and rationalisation of procedure.

By 1914 the Corporation stood not only *vis à vis* the ratepayers and their representatives, as it had done since 1835. It also stood *vis à vis* its employees and these too enjoyed their representation on the Council. The strike had demonstrated that the Labour group saw themselves primarily as spokesmen for the men. The dual role of Walter Wood, conducting a strike against the Council of which he was a member, was paralleled by the attitude of the Labour group as a whole. In 1911 during an earlier strike of tramway workers their secretary who was also a councillor had been in the same position. The strike merely emphasised what the general run of debates showed to be the case on most occasions. Indeed the Conservatives tried hard to exclude the Labour group from membership of the General Purpose Committee set up to deal with labour matters, on the grounds that they belonged on the other side of the negotiating table. The Liberals did not think it wise to give institutional form to such an interpretation of the Labour councillors' role and allocated one of their own places to a Labour member.[59]

Up to 1914 independent Labour representation in Leeds, therefore, meant primarily the representation of a new interest, that of the workmen employed by the Corporation. Otherwise the policies of the Labour group were less distinctive. They stood for the extension of municipal activities into areas of private enterprise—the use of direct labour by a public works department instead of private contractors, the possible creation of a municipal coal supply in competition with private coal merchants. The Liberals also advocated the use of direct labour on grounds of economy, like the Progressives on the London County Council before them. In a study that ends in 1914 the beginnings of

[59] *Y.P.*, 10.11.1911, p. 4, 28.3.1914.

Labour representation therefore do not assume the significance that they would acquire in a longer perspective. Its most important contribution to the working of the municipal corporation, while it raised anxious questions about the nature of representation, led to policy repercussions primarily in the field of labour relations.

4

The Cost of Improvement

'From the appearance of the Liberal Programme last year we shall come to date a new era in the history of the civic life of Leeds.'[1]

So wrote the *Mercury* in 1894 and in a sense this was true. However, the acceptance of the programme with its promises to provide additional services implied also a willingness to pay for them. In the first year of the New Era this simple conclusion, obvious to the finance committee, was unpalatable to the Council as a whole, for it would have meant putting up the rates. In 1895 the conclusions could no longer be avoided. Not only did the estimates for the coming year exceed the product of an unchanged rate, but there was also a deficit from the previous year to be taken into account. Boothroyd, the Liberal chairman of the finance committee, therefore proposed to raise the city rate by 3d. and the consolidated rate by 2d. in the £. This was bound to cause frowns and in fact there was fierce opposition in the Council. The majority irrespective of party preferred to follow the lead of Charles Wilson, the Conservative accountant, and to leave the rates unchanged. 'Of a distinctly Micawberish character' was how the *Mercury* described the arguments used, and it added

'It is bad business for our rulers to shut their eyes to the inevitable growth of expenditure which will have to be met in future years.'[2]

Charles Wilson's initiative in saving the ratepayer probably helped the Conservatives to victory in November. But how was a Conservative chairman of the finance committee to solve the problem that had baffled his Liberal predecessor? It looked as if the New Era might quickly give

[1] *L.M.*, 27.10.1894.
[2] *L.M.*, 2.5.1895, pp. 3, 5.

way to a new ratepayers' reaction, according to the familiar pattern. But John Gordon, the accountant and Conservative leader on the Council, who succeeded Boothroyd, had an answer which was as unoriginal as it was effective. Like Joseph Chamberlain before him and many others too, he appropriated the profits of the gasworks to keep the rates level in the face of rising expenditure. In 1896 he appropriated £18,000. In 1897 he rang the changes by taking £18,000 from the profits of the waterworks instead. In 1898 he decided to take £9,000 from each, and in 1899 the *ad hoc* arrangements of the previous years were given a permanent form. The gas committee created a depreciation fund of £10,000; the waterworks committee a similar one of £7,000. All profits over and above this were to be automatically paid into the City Fund. In these ways a total of £429,000 was transferred to the City Fund in aid of the rates during 1896–1904, the years of Conservative ascendancy, drawn from the profits of gas, water and tramways.[3] Although the Birmingham Corporation had always drawn the line at making a profit on the sale of water, there was nothing original in what the Leeds Conservatives were doing. In this as in many other respects, the New Era was a belated attempt to take a leaf out of Birmingham's book.

Obvious though the measure would appear to have been, and standard practice though it was in many towns, the Conservatives' financial policy now became the main target of attack for the Liberal opposition. Previously finance had not produced straight party voting; in this matter it did. The Liberal party committed itself to the principle that the trading operations of the Corporation should not be used to subsidise the ratepayer. This was probably little more than the automatic reaction of a party that had seen their opponent pull the ace of spades from his sleeve. It was to the 'electioneering dodging' that objection was taken, and it was the principle that the Conservatives should go to the ratepayers for what money they require that was proclaimed.[4]

Was there anything more substantial in this opposition? The policy adopted by the Conservatives did of course imply that the gas and water consumers and the tram passengers were paying instead of the ratepayers. Although the groups did greatly overlap they were not identical, nor was the financial burden distributed identically. There was one obvious ground for objection. The Corporation of Birmingham had in 1875 laid down the principle that the waterworks should not be regarded as a source of profit, since cheap water was of fundamental importance

[3] *L.M.*, 7.5.1896; 7.5.1897; 5.5.1898; 2.3.1899, p. 6; 28.10.1904, p. 8.
[4] *L.M.*, 5.5.1898; 7.5.1897.

to the health of the town.[5] Sanitary reformers whether Liberal or otherwise could well have objected to the new Conservative policy on those grounds, but they did not. In Birmingham in the 1870s the problem had been to persuade the poor to use Corporation water instead of the tainted water from local wells. There was no such problem in the Leeds of the 1890s, and water was generally considered cheap and plentiful enough for its use to be taken for granted by all sections of the population. In fact relatively little was heard about the hardship of water consumers, and even less about that of the tram passengers. The argument, insofar as it was at this level at all, focused on the pricing policy of the gas committee. It was the gas consumer who was chiefly regarded as the sufferer from the new policy.

Since the purchase of the gasworks in 1870 the municipal gas committee had tried to keep prices as low as possible. Profits when made were paid into the Borough Fund, losses when they occurred were made good out of the Borough Fund, but there had never been a policy, such as that deliberately pursued in Manchester over several decades, of fixing prices so as to make a sizeable profit. The objective had been to break even but to be a little on the safe side. Between 1871 and 1891 profits had totalled £124,590, losses £76,794 leaving a favourable margin of £47,796. Most of these profits were made before 1886. Since then increasing wages and worsening trading conditions had led to much narrower margins and even to losses.[6] What the gas committee prided itself on, especially in the last decade of the Liberal ascendancy, were not large profits but low prices and high quality. Between 1871 and 1892 the price of gas had fallen from 3s. 6d. to 2s. 2d. per thousand cubic feet, while the candle power had been improved and discrimination against the small consumer abolished. In that year Manchester Corporation was selling gas of an identical quality at anything between 2s. 8d. and 3s. 2d. per thousand.[7]

This policy of keeping the profit margin low led to a £13,000 deficit in 1892 when coal prices suddenly rose. In the following year the committee reluctantly put up its price by 2d. per thousand, but softened the blow for the small consumer by abolishing gas meter rents as promised in the Liberal programme. Two years' trading served to wipe off the deficit and enabled the committee to cut the price back to its former level.[8]

[5] J. T. Bunce, *History of the Corporation of Birmingham*, II, 408.
[6] *L.M.*, 29.10.1891; 28.10.1893, p. 12.
[7] *L.M.*, 29.10.1891, p. 8; 28.10.1892, p. 7.
[8] *L.M.*, 25.10.1892, p. 5; 29.10.1894, p. 7; *Y.P.*, 23.10.1895, p. 3.

In Manchester the single-minded pursuit of the opposite policy had enabled expensive improvements and ambitious water undertakings to be financed from the gas profits. It had also produced an opposition movement of gas consumers, first noticeable in 1856 and organised into a gas consumers' association in 1859. This body succeeded in having its representatives elected to the Council, forcing a reduction of gas prices and the cessation in 1862 of the subsidy which had been made to the Waterworks Department throughout the previous ten years. These representatives of the gas consumers in the Manchester of the late 1850s and early 1860s were mostly shopkeepers, and they entered the Council quite self-consciously as shopkeepers in contrast to the merchants, manufacturers and professional men who had made policy on the Manchester Town Council before.[9]

Was there, it might be asked, a connection between shopkeeper municipal politics and a policy of low gas prices? The principal use of gas even in the 1880s was for light, not for power. The need to keep their premises well lit in the winter evenings may have made shopkeepers especially sensitive to higher gas prices. But since there is ample evidence that they were also highly sensitive to higher rates, there is probably not much in this contrast. It is unlikely that the alternative policies adopted by the two parties in Leeds reflected sensitivity to different social groups and their conception of the public interest. The failure of the Liberals to take this way out of their financial impasse may be ascribed rather to lack of flexibility and imagination. One thing is certain, that the contrast had nothing to do with long-term differences between Leeds Liberals and Conservatives as such. In 1853 Liberal aldermen, when debating whether to buy out the Gas Company, had been attracted to the project by the prospect of using the profits to subsidise the rates,[10] and in 1871 the Conservative *Yorkshire Post* had rejected a suggestion that the purchase of Roundhay Park be financed from the profits of the gasworks, proclaiming that 'there is but one object to which the profits of the gas can with propriety be devoted, namely the lowering of the price of gas'.[11] Other circumstances breed other opinions, and, as so often, the polarisation of opinion through the party system at any one time was more important than continuity of party principles.

There were two further reasons why the new Conservative regime was able to sustain the higher rate of expenditure which characterised

[9] *Webb. Loc. Gov. Col.*, volume 158. There are passing references in Radford and Russell, *A History of Local Government in Manchester*, II (1940), 199, 203.
[10] Speeches of Alds. Hepper and Luccock, *L.M.*, 12.2.1853, p. 9.
[11] Leading article, *Y.P.*, 1.11.1871.

the New Era. It benefited under the scheme of assigned revenues, which had been introduced in 1888 by Goschen as Chancellor of the Exchequer. This scheme was intended to provide local authorities with an expanding revenue drawn from taxation instead of the tied Exchequer grants for certain specified services which they had received previously. It was expanded in 1890, and provided the Corporation with a revenue which grew from £35,135 in 1889/90 to £58,431 in 1908/9. This increase was independent of and in addition to the specific grants for education, which the Corporation received after it had taken over the duties of the School Board under the 1902 Education Act. After 1909 the assigned revenues ceased to expand, as the policy of 1888 was reversed and the claims of local authorities on the yield of taxation limited to a specific sum.[12]

The same period that saw this increase in the revenue drawn from taxation also saw a remarkable increase in the yield of the local rates. After 1897 the assessed rateable value of the city began to grow much faster than had been the case since the 1870s. The 1880s had been years of stagnation. After 1889 matters improved, but they improved to a much greater extent after 1897, as can be seen by comparing the years 1897–1905 with the two eight-year periods that immediately preceded. This growth ceased after 1905 and was followed by stagnation even greater than that of the 1880s.

TABLE 23. *Borough of Leeds : growth in the assessed rateable value*

1881-9	7·8%
1889-97	19·1%
1897-1905	37·1%
1905-12*	2·7%
1905-13†	7·6%

Source: Financial Statistics, Rateable Value in the Several Townships, Leeds City Treasurer's Archives.

* 7 year period only.
† Includes an extension of the city area.

This remarkable contrast between the growth rate before 1897 and after was not due to any change in the system of assessment. The work of assessment was done by seven different authorities in different parts of the city, none of which were under the control of the Corporation. It was widely held in the late 1890s that this multitude of separate bodies made for inefficiency and lax assessment.[13] In view of these figures it is

[12] City of Leeds, *Annual Accounts* 1889–90 ff. For the changing policy in respect of Exchequer Grants see Maureen Schulz, 'The Development of the Grant System', in C. H. Wilson (ed.), *Essays in Local Government* (1948).
[13] For instance speech by Clr. Battle in *L.M.*, 2.5.1895, p. 3 and comments reported in *Webb Loc. Gov. Col.*, volume 265, questionnaire, Q. 79.

hard to believe this, at least for the 1890s. When in 1904 the number of authorities was reduced to four, the change was followed by a sharp fall in the annual growth rate.[14]

Operating within a favourable growth-situation and using the trading profits of the Corporation, the Conservatives managed to maintain the momentum of the spending committees. For seven years they kept the rates steady, but by 1902 the slack had been taken up and still expenditure continued to increase. Now the rates really came under pressure. They rose by 4d. in 1902. Two years later the Corporation was forced to float a loan at a time of high interest rates and the rates climbed to 6s. 7½d. in the £. They had been 5s. 11d. three years before. ⟨Table 24.⟩

TABLE 24. *City of Leeds 1894–1914: rates in the pound*

Year	Corporation rates	Education rates	Total
1894-5	4s. 9d.	1s. 1d.	5s. 10d.
1895-6*	4s. 7½d.	1s. 2½d.	5s. 10d.
1896-7	4s. 7½d.	1s. 2½d.	5s. 10 ⌐.
1897-8	4s. 7d.	1s. 3d.	5s. 10d.
1898-9	4s. 7d.	1s. 3d.	5s. 10d.
1899-1900	4s. 6½d.	1s. 3½d.	5s. 10d.
1900-01	4s. 6½d.	1s. 3½d.	5s. 10d.
1901-2	4s. 6½d.	1s. 4½d.	5s. 11d.
1902-3	4s. 10½d.	1s. 4½d.	6s. 3d.
1903-4	4s. 11d.	1s. 5d.	6s. 4d.
1904-5	5s. 2d.	1s. 5½d.	6s. 7½d.
1905-6†	5s. 8d.	1s. 6d.	7s. 2d.
1906-7	5s. 10½d.	1s. 6½d.	7s. 5d.
1907-8	5s. 7d.	1s. 7½d.	7s. 2½d.
1908-9*	5s. 4½d.	1s. 9d.	7s. 1½d.
1909-10	5s. 4½d.	1s. 9d.	7s. 1½d.
1910-11	5s. 9d.	1s. 10d.	7s. 7d.
1911-12	5s. 8½d.	1s. 10d.	7s. 6½d.
1912-13	—	—	7s. 4½d.
1913-14	—	—	7s. 4½d.

The year ran from June to June.
* First year of Conservative majority.
† First year of Liberal majority.
Figures taken from *Y.P.*, 18.10.1911, p. 10 and City of Leeds, *Annual Accounts*.

[14] The area of the City of Leeds was included in four Poor Law Unions—Leeds, Holbeck, Hunslet and Bramley. Each of the last three had its own assessment committee. In the Leeds Union each of its four constituent townships had their own assessment committee. By the County Borough of Leeds Confirmation Order (1904) the four townships within the Leeds Union were amalgamated, and the number of separate assessment authorities thereby reduced by three. The City of Leeds acquired a single assessment authority when the four unions were amalgamated under the Leeds Corporation Act 1924.

Finance was the most prominent issue at the municipal elections in November 1904, which lost the Conservatives their control of the Council. The party organisers thought that the increase in the rates and the high expenditure had made their supporters reluctant to bestir themselves, and they were almost certainly correct. The Liberals made their come-back by promising rigorous economy and an end to 'financial mismanagement'. It was an open secret that Gordon had strained normal accounting practice to minimise the deficit in the published accounts, knowing that to raise the rates any further would be political suicide. Even the Unionist nominee for Lord Mayor referred critically to 'irregularities' in the presentation of accounts and called for more care and economy.[15]

The Liberals had no panacea for these ills. They had swept in as critics of laxity, but the way of probity was to pay on the nail. It was unfortunate for them that the growth in the rateable value fell off shortly after they took over. In the course of two years they raised the rates by as much as their opponents had done in ten, while insisting that it was all their predecessors' fault and that they were only putting the figures straight. Finally in 1907 the two main parties reached agreement over the drawing up of the estimates and the financial difficulties of the Corporation ceased for the moment to furnish the ammunition of party warfare. In the words of the *Mercury* the concordat was 'designed to raise the finances of the city above the considerations of party advantage and place them on a sound business footing'.[16] Only the small Labour group protested that too many concordats were dangerous.

1907 marked the end of the period that had begun in 1890. Financial elasticity had already gone some years before, and during the last phase the Council, conscious that every such decision would push up the rates, was reluctant to extend its commitments. It was only a conjunction of special circumstances that kept up the momentum until 1907. The building of a new water reservoir and of a purification plant for sewage could not be avoided. In addition the change in party control once more introduced new brooms into the administration. It led to a radical reorganisation of the city engineer's department, whose growth had not kept pace with the sharp increase in its work. Two additional engineers were appointed at the highest level and almost at once discovered serious design-errors in the plans for the new reservoir. With this reorganisation the New Era may be said to have come to an end.[17]

[15] *L.M.*, 29.10.1904, p. 8; 10.11.1905, p. 6.
[16] *L.M.*, 28.6.1907.
[17] *L.M.*, 5.10.1905, pp. 5, 6; 20.10.1905, p. 6; 6.9.1906, p. 6; 26.10.1907, p. 3.

Before it passed, the New Era had, however, left its mark on Leeds over and above anything mentioned yet. One outcome of the new spirit was City Square, and its statues proclaimed the new interest of the wealthy in the provision of public amenities by the Corporation. In the 1880s the Coloured Cloth Hall had seemed a mean survival from an age before public buildings had become conspicuous by their spacious proportions.[18] When it was demolished and part of the land bought by the Crown for a general post office, the remainder was to be left as an open space. Only the Quebec estate now blocked the creation of a much larger square, which would abut on the L.M.S. railway station and welcome the visitor on his arrival. In April 1891 the Council decided against purchasing the estate for £35,000. But the new winds of public opinion had begun to blow and in October the Council yielded by a narrow majority. The price offered (£33,000) was still regarded as too high, but the desire in the town for a dignified public square had become too strong to be denied.[19]

In 1896 plans for the lay-out of the square, privately commissioned by Alderman T. W. Harding, were adopted.[20] They included a site for a central equestrian statue and for other monuments, and within a few months Harding had offered to present a statue of the Black Prince, together with four pairs of female figures each representing Morn and Eve and holding electric globes aloft. The Black Prince was chosen because an equestrian statue demanded a subject with heroic associations. Like the nude figures of Morn and Eve an equestrian statue carried the overtones of Renaissance city decoration and civic patronage. Subsequently Harding added two statues of Leeds worthies[21] and some more sculptured bronze lamp standards, including four in the shape of the Corporation mace ⟨*see* plate 20⟩. Two further statues were presented by two other benefactors, one of whom was Councillor Richard Boston, chairman of the committee responsible for the scheme.[22] But it was all very much Harding's project, and he watched over its progress with paternal care. By the time it was completed he had retired from the Council and from Leeds, but he took rooms in the railway hotel overlooking the square to be able to supervise personally the erection of the

---

[18] T. Wemyss Reid, *A Memorial of John Deakin Heaton, M.D.* (1883), p. 19.
[19] *L.M.*, 18.4.1891, 2.10.1891, 21.10.1891.
[20] *L.M.*, 2.7.1896, p. 4. Thereafter see *Corporate Property Committee, Minutes*, 1896–1905.
[21] Dean Hook and Joseph Priestley.
[22] John Harrison and James Watt. The latter was the gift of Mr. Richard Wainwright. The statues including the figures of Morn and Eve have survived, but the mace-shaped lamp standards have been removed.

statues. He went so far as to pay for a uniformed attendant to look after the monuments for the first two years. When people began to strike sulphur matches on the bare ladies, the Council put up a notice to warn them off and continued to employ the attendant. It was a fitting gesture that Harding was made a freeman of the city on the same day on which the square was formally opened ⟨*see* plate 21⟩.

5

The Springs of Improvement

It is clear from the narrative that much of the momentum behind the New Era sprang from the rivalry of the two political parties. It was because the party organisations saw their opportunities and took them that innovation became possible; it was because of the eagerness of the rivalry that innovation was so rapid. Leeds had of course been familiar with party rivalry in its municipal politics for a long time. Since 1835 practically all municipal elections had been fought between Liberals and Conservatives.[1] Yet there is a difference. In the past the stake had been the positions of prestige that control of the Council could confer, the offices of mayor and aldermen as well as the minor pieces of patronage that occasionally went with it. It had hardly ever been any municipal policy as such. A cry for economy, the shibboleth of opposition, was often enough found in the mouths of the Conservative minority, but it was just as much the cry of discontented Liberals. In this way party became the basis of municipal politics without having much, if any, bearing on matters of municipal administration. *The Leeds Mercury*, as the leading Liberal paper, naturally welcomed Liberal victories, but it could not help deploring the whole process. 'The political character of these elections', wrote the editor in 1870, 'has given them a feature, which we think is to be regretted, but we seem to drift hopelessly into the current year by year.'[2] He knew very well the reason for this state of affairs, and had explained it some years before:

'There is in Leeds no one prominent municipal object of great public interest for or against which the different parties can rally.

---

[1] The all-embracing hold of party conflict on the politics of Leeds, whether at the Parliamentary, municipal or vestry levels, is the principal conclusion of Fraser's study of the years 1830–52. D. Fraser, 'Politics in Leeds 1830–1852', *passim*.
[2] *L.M.*, 25.10.1870.

18 George Goodman (1792–1859), woolstapler, in his regalia as the first mayor of the reformed Corporation in 1836. Unlike some such corporations that of Leeds did not sell off the symbols associated with the old order. The use of the seventeenth-century mace and the general manner of representation in the grand style emphasise the continuity with the patrician days of the old Corporation. Goodman became mayor three times more, was knighted in 1852, and elected M.P. for Leeds from 1852–7. From a painting by J. Simpson, dated 1836, now hanging in the Civic Hall.

20 & 21 City Square, Leeds: *right* two of the four lamp standards modelled on the Corporation mace which formed part of the elaborate symbolism of the square, as designed by William Bakewell on the instruction of Colonel T. W. Harding, the donor. From the A. W. Franks Collection of Photographs by courtesy of the Leeds Civic Trust. (*Photo: Dorchester Photographers, Leeds*). *Far right* the opening of the square and the unveiling of the statue of the Black Prince, 1903. From a photograph in the Leeds Central Library.

19 Leeds from the direction of Holbeck Junction in 1868. The Town Hall was as prominent from the edge of the town as a medieval cathedral. From the *Illustrated London News*, lii (1868), 532–3.

The first generation:

22 & 23 These two professional men among the leaders of the Council complement the picture of George Goodman, woolstapler (18). (*top left*) John Hope Shaw (1793–1864), attorney, who was elected to the Council in 1844 and became mayor three times before retiring from office in 1856. From a portrait in the Collection of the Thoresby Society. (*bottom left*) Robert Baker (1804–80), surgeon and factory inspector, one of the professional members of the Council from 1836–43, and the leading instigator of municipal action to purge the town of insanitary conditions. He helped to establish the Leeds Statistical Society in 1838 and made important contributions to various inquiries into public health. From a portrait included in the grangerised edition of Edward Parsons, *The Civil . . . History of Leeds, &c.* (1834), I, p. 158.

The middle period—Liberal Temperance leaders:

24 & 25 Archibald William Scarr (1827–1904) (*top right*), as he appeared during his mayoralty in 1887–8. He was elected to the Council in 1872 and became an alderman in 1880. His municipal career lasted to 1895 but he was never chairman of a Committee. From a photograph in the Lord Mayor's Collection in the Civic Hall. (*top far right*) Archie Scarr as the epitome of the self-made man of Leeds in the nineteenth century, the thrifty greengrocer who became a wealthy mayor. From a watercolour sketch of him in *Our Public Servants* (Leeds, n.d. [*c.* 1892]), No. 11.

26 & 27 George Tatham (1815–92), leather manufacturer, who entered the Council in 1856 and was three times mayor between 1879 and 1882. (*bottom right*) As depicted in a watercolour sketch from *Our Public Servants* (Leeds, N.D. [*c.* 1892]), No. 9, and (*bottom far right*) from a photograph of him as mayor in the Lord Mayor's Collection in the Civic Hall.

Conservatives and Liberal Unionists of the New Era:

28 (*top left*) Colonel T. Walter Harding (1843–1927), engineer, Liberal Unionist, who was responsible for the acquisition of the municipal art gallery. From a photograph of him as lord mayor in 1898–9 in the Lord Mayor's Collection, Civic Hall.

29 (*above*) Charles Francis Tetley (1848–1934), a brewer, president of the South Leeds Conservative Association, elected alderman from outside the Council in 1895. He became deputy leader of the Municipal Conservative Party from 1904. From a photograph of him as lord mayor in 1897–8 in the Lord Mayor's Collection, Civic Hall.

30 (*bottom left*) John Gordon (1854–1925), accountant. Leader of the Municipal Conservative Party in the 1890s and until 1904. From a photograph of him as lord mayor in 1899–1900 in the Lord Mayor's Collection, Civic Hall.

31 (*right*) Charles Henry Wilson (1859–1930), accountant. He succeeded Gordon as leader of the Municipal Conservative Party in 1904. Councillor for the North ward from 1890–1907 and an alderman from 1907 until his death. He was M.P. for Leeds Central from 1923–9 and the leading figure in Leeds politics in his generation. This cartoon dates from the municipal election of 1905. The coloured original is in the Leeds Central Library.

The General Gordon of the Council leading the attack on the Gas Committee.

I've whitewashed that there sub-committee

till it's as clean as if nowt had ever happened

ALDERMAN MAJORITY

A Champion Whitewasher.

NORTH WARD

The Great F.O.S.

32 & 33 The Council and the gas dispute of 1890, a serious crisis for the dominant Liberal group, as seen by *The Yorkshireman*, 16 July 1890. (*above right*) Alderman Peter Gilston, chairman of the sub-committee that mishandled the dispute, relying on the bloc of Liberal aldermen to defeat the resolution of condemnation, tabled by John Gordon, the Conservative leader (*above left*).

34 Parker's Temperance Hotel, Briggate, in the late 1890s, the centre of Temperance Liberalism in the previous generation, when it had been known as Parker's Coffee House.

Still less is there any broad principle of municipal action—regulating and controlling all our local legislation—on which the members of the Council have ranged, or very well could range, themselves on opposite sides. Thus the basis of party organization is not easily found in municipal questions.'[3]

Party zeal provided the workers in elections when no other considerations would have done so. The same diagnosis could have been made for any decade between 1840 and 1890.

The important municipal objectives in the 1890s were often put forward by altogether different bodies in the town, but it was the party organisations who took them up and incorporated them into their programmes. Since, however, party ambition was primary and devotion to municipal issues a mere means to success, no party ever retained the monopoly of a promising cause for more than a year or two. Locked in battle, the two rivals were quick to learn from each other, so that conflict made them more alike. At the same time they were quick to spot new issues in an attempt to keep ahead of their rival. It was party conflict that brought about the rapid acceptance of new attitudes.

In identifying the rival ambitions of the political parties as the source of momentum, we are also pointing to the main source of recruitment for municipal service in this period. Recruitment was by the party political association at ward level, often with the active participation of the central party organisation, and the recruits so found were with certain exceptions that have been mentioned from among the party activists.

If we would understand the reasons for the vigorous municipal conflict, we must therefore seek it primarily not in the municipal sphere, but in the national and local factors which weakened the appeal of Liberalism and spurred Conservatives on to increased action in organisation and electoral work. It was this that enabled them to seize their opportunities when they arose in 1889 and 1890, and to convert them into a political campaign.

There are signs of this increased vigour and ambition in the minutes of the Leeds Conservative Association. In 1886 and 1887 the executive committee held long discussions in consultation with ward chairmen on how to fight municipal elections, and in December 1887 adopted a scheme for working municipal elections on a uniform system throughout the borough.[4] If, in the words of *The Yorkshire Post*, the Liberals in

---

[3] *L.M.*, 2.11.1863.
[4] Leeds Conservative Association, minutes, 7.7.1886, 8.11.1880, 19.12.1887. Leeds City Library Archives.

1890 were condemned more for their failure in municipal matters than for their politics, it was due to the vigour of the Conservative organisation that municipal discontent turned into Conservative votes.

The strength of the Conservatives in the late 1880s and early 1890s may be compared with the upswing that occurred in 1837–41 and again in the early 1870s. The similarities are clear. In each case the local Conservatives profited from a weakening in the Leeds Liberal party, which was a local reflection of national developments. However, at least as significant is the difference between this occasion and the two previous ones. In the earlier periods the Conservative gains at municipal elections had indicated the mounting strength of the party which reached a climax and found its natural fulfilment in the return of a Conservative M.P. at the general election. This happened in July 1841 and again in February 1874. The shock that this administered to Liberal complacency led on both occasions to Liberal successes at the next municipal elections. The trend of municipal elections over the following years rapidly reduced the Conservatives once again to insignificance on the Council.[5]

The 1890s saw a similar drift towards the Conservatives, which led in 1895 to an increase in the Conservative share of the vote in all the five Leeds constituencies. It reached its climax in 1900, when the Conservatives won East Leeds from their opponents. But the municipal elections are now no longer a reliable indicator of this trend. Although the parliamentary drift continued until 1900, the municipal drift in favour of the Conservatives stopped sharp in 1895. From 1896 until 1904, when the Liberals regained control of the Council, there was not a single year during which the Conservatives had a net gain of seats at the municipal elections. The difference between this and the two earlier occasions is probably due to another difference that went with it. This time the municipal drift in favour of the Conservatives led to a conspicuous municipal triumph. The fact that in November 1895 the Conservatives obtained control of the Council and elected their own aldermen administered the sort of shock that in the past had been left

[5] For a contemporary comment on the relation between Parliamentary victory and municipal defeat in 1874 see John Gorst, Conservative principal party agent, to Disraeli, 2 December 1874: 'The municipal elections of this year appear to furnish additional evidence of the precarious tenure of our position in the Boroughs. It is worth notice that we seem to have lost ground in places like Bath, Ashton, Colchester, Leeds and Wakefield, which in the late General Election expressed their condemnation of the late government; and to have gained ground in places like Bolton, Bradford, Hastings and Rochdale, where the movement of repulsion had not spent itself in a Parliamentary victory.' Quoted in H. J. Hanham, *Elections and Party Management. Politics in the Age of Disraeli and Gladstone* (1959), p. 389.

to the general election. If thereafter the trend of municipal and parliamentary politics part company, it may be that the municipal triumph had provoked its own reaction which expressed itself through the municipal elections. By the mid-nineties municipal voting was no longer a mere reflection of changing party effectiveness in national politics. For the first time municipal politics had acquired its own momentum.

What happened after 1904? A mere thirteen months separated the municipal triumph of the Liberals in November 1904 from their triumph at the general election in December 1905. This makes it difficult to distinguish the effect of the one from that of the other. In November 1905 the Liberals lost two seats to Labour and so did the Conservatives, so that the sole intervening municipal election tells us nothing by which to test the theory. But after December 1905 the Conservatives rallied, just as the Liberals had always done after signal defeats. Their vigorous compaigning gave them control of the Council once again in 1908. From 1909 they lost councillors again steadily at every election until the Liberals regained control for a short moment in November 1911, thereby setting the pendulum swinging once more in the opposite direction.[6]

The Liberal recovery in municipal elections after 1895 was closely supervised by the Leeds Liberal Federation. From 1896 onwards it became normal for the executive committee and its inner cabinet to concern itself with the provision of suitable candidates for the wards. Regular reports of the state of preparation were required from the ward associations from the spring of the year until the contest in early November. Although the choice of candidates remained in the first place with the ward associations, the central body actively searched out candidates and sent delegations to persuade suitable persons to make themselves available. The central party organisation seems to have been particularly active in these matters between 1896 and 1901. Thereafter the Liberal members of the City Council, now formally organised under a leader, deputy and two whips, made themselves increasingly responsible not only for the conduct of municipal politics but also for the recruitment of candidates.[7]

Rivalry between the two principal political parties played a far more

[6] In 1913, the last municipal election before 1919, the Labour gains slightly confuse the pattern. See appendix IV for the distribution of seats annually between the parties from 1889–1914.

[7] Leeds Liberal Federation, minutes of the executive committee 1894 ff. minutes of the cabinet 1897 ff. Leeds City Library Archives. On the last mentioned part see especially cabinet minutes, 18.3.1901, 2.5.1904; executive committee minutes, 27.5.1908.

important role in the New Era in Leeds than in the Chamberlain movement in Birmingham municipal politics a generation before. In Birmingham the municipal changes had come about by the displacement of power within the Liberal party and owed little to any challenge from the Conservatives except as a pretext for ruthless action. In the particular circumstances of late-Victorian Leeds the narrow margin between the parties facilitated the adoption of new men and new attitudes. The new men were in general abler than their predecessors, and the new attitudes made for a bolder and more effective use of resources by the Corporation. Not that this always follows from the mere fact of political change. In this instance political change opened the door to improvement, because influential sections of the community had accepted views about municipal action that were becoming normal in the nation at large, and were judging the local administration accordingly. Thereafter, the determination of both parties to compete for the support of this body of opinion led to a situation where the very alternation of party control contributed to the improvement. For the acceptance of common objectives focused the party rivalry on the means to achieve them, and meant that on both occasions a change in the party control added further momentum to one and the same process.

This consideration brings us back to the ideas themselves. Here the debt of Leeds to the earlier generation in Birmingham is very striking. It is to be found in the objectives, and indeed in the whole way in which these objectives were stated. The demand for men of standing, especially for the heads of large businesses, to serve on the Council, the reliance on the profits from municipal trading to keep down the rates, the clearance of the insanitary area as the principal achievement of a vigorous policy of public health, all point to the similarity between these two movements in municipal reform.

Yet it is exactly this similarity that reveals the profound differences between them. The Birmingham movement had been the discovery of something fresh, a new vision of the role that representative local authorities could perform in civilising England. Much more than any specific measure, it was this ideological dimension that was the real novelty. In this respect there was nothing new in Leeds, and it is significant that the New Era produced no body of thought comparable to the sermons or speeches of Dawson, Dale and Chamberlain. The campaigns were fought in terms of the commonplaces of the day—the desire for party supremacy, the need to keep the party organisation active between general elections, as well as those handed down from Birmingham and

288

long ago passed into general currency. This is not to deny that what was done was new for Leeds. In terms of accepted standards Leeds in the 1890s had a leeway to make up. Yet the movement was essentially imitative. It never had 'the freshness and charm of a discovery' that the Birmingham movement had possessed for its protagonists.[8] This may well be why it left no abiding tradition nor served as an inspiration in later years, but petered out when the financial resources were used up and party zeal had run its course.

From the perspective of the mid-twentieth century this failure to bring to the Leeds of the 1890s the freshness of vision that had characterised local government in the Birmingham of the 1870s may appear less surprising than it should. We are accustomed to seeing local authorities acting in practice increasingly as agents of the central government, and to look to the latter for important new departures in social policy. The circumscription of the independent role of local government is one of those profound structural alterations, which lend to the views of the 1870s all the charm of an age well past. Yet despite the important changes that occurred between the 1870s and 1890s to sap the vigour of independent local life, it would be a mistake to assume that by the 1890s the day had already passed when local authorities could take important independent initiatives. The subsequent decline owed much to the increasing dependence of local authorities on financial subsidies channelled by government departments for specific services. It was in part the abandonment after 1909 of the policy of providing local government with an independent expanding revenue additional to that furnished by the rates, the policy inaugurated by Goschen in 1888, that made its dependence on the initiative of the central government inevitable. The twenty years from 1889 to 1909, when total revenue at the discretion of local authorities was expanding faster than ever before, were the last moment when such a reinterpretation of the role of local government would have been, at least administratively, possible.

With the help of the historian's hindsight one can identify the areas of social policy on which such a fresh vision might well have focused at the time, in Leeds or any other city. A generation later among the functions of local authorities two were especially prominent, housing and the provision of educational and health services for the young. Both stemmed from an awareness of social needs that first took shape in that particular way in the generation before 1914, however much they drew

[8] R. W. Dale in R. A. Armstrong, *Henry William Crosskey. His Life and Work* (1895), p. 248.

on older traditions. To have emphasised the duty of local authorities and to have pioneered provisions in either of these areas could have been the hallmark of a local authority capable of the freshness of vision to which we have referred.

This is what distinguished the London County Council in the period of Progressive party rule from 1889–1907. It is true that the Progressive movement was an attempt to find a municipal expression for civic pride and to do for London what had already been achieved in the best of the provincial cities. It is equally true that there were marked limitations in practice to the policy of municipal housing, on which the L.C.C. embarked in the 1890s. But the fact that the obligations were stated and a beginning made to see how far they could in practice be fulfilled does distinguish the Progressive era in London from the municipal developments in Leeds, which were exactly contemporary to it.[9]

Something like this can also be said about the interest taken in Bradford in the welfare of the young. The fight of the I.L.P. under the leadership of F. W. Jowett for school meals, for medical inspection, and for school baths was inspired by a conception of the needs and the potentialities of the children of the poor, which had much of the freshness of vision that had once led to the transformation of local government in Birmingham. In Margaret McMillan it possessed a prophet, whose words had the power to open men's eyes and inspire action.[10]

These references to contemporary developments elsewhere, however sketchy, should remove some of the force of the objection to a comparison between the events in Leeds in the period after 1890 and what had happened in Birmingham a quarter of a century before. Although the local bodies in London and Bradford came up much sooner against the limiting factors of central government control of finance than had been the case in the 1870s, their experience demonstrates that local authorities had not lost the power of initiative at this period.

Naturally the comparison which we have attempted in this book has its limitations. We have been able to trace the long-term consequences of the Birmingham reform movement and to note how far its momentum carried over into the next generation. This cannot be done for Leeds, if only

[9] For the L.C.C. under the Progressive party and in particular for the work in housing, see A. G. Gardiner, *John Benn and the Progressive Movement* (1925). John M. Stevens, 'The London County Council under the Progressives 1889–1907', unpublished M.A. dissertation, University of Sussex, 1966, emphasises the limitations of the policy. Also useful, Sir Gwilym Gibbon and Reginald Bell, *The History of the London County Council 1889–1939* (1939); William Saunders, *The History of the First London County Council* (1892).
[10] Albert Mansbridge, *Margaret McMillan, Prophet and Pioneer* (1932); Fenner Brockway, *Socialism over Sixty Years. The Life of Jowett of Bradford 1864–1944* (1946).

because the New Era occurred towards the end of the period chosen for detailed analysis. It would be safe to say that its long-term consequences in terms of recruitment were not great. But it must be remembered that they were affected by the general disruption of the First World War and the increasingly prominent role played thereafter by the Labour party in municipal politics. The occupational composition of town councils in an age when the Labour Party had become one of the principal contenders for political power was to depend on the balance of parties in an obvious and primary sense such as did not apply to the eighty years that have been studied in this book.

BOOK III
THE WIDER SETTING

I

Looking Abroad

Writing of the government of American cities in the years covered by our two case-studies of English municipal reform movements, Richard Hofstadter identified 'two thoroughly different systems of political ethics':

> 'One, founded upon the indigenous Yankee-Protestant political traditions, and upon middle-class life, assumed and demanded the constant, disinterested activity of the citizen in public affairs, argued that political life ought to be run, to a greater degree than it was, in accordance with general principles and abstract laws apart from and superior to personal needs, and expressed a common feeling that government should be in good part an effort to moralize the lives of individuals while economic life should be intimately related to the stimulation and development of individual character. The other system, founded upon the European background of the immigrants, upon their unfamiliarity with independent political action, their familiarity with hierarchy and authority, and upon the urgent needs that so often grew out of their migration, took for granted that the political life of the individual would arise out of family needs, interpreted political and civic relations chiefly in terms of personal obligations, and placed strong personal loyalties above allegiance to abstract codes of law or morals. It was chiefly upon this system of values that the political life of the immigrant, the boss and the urban machine was based.'

Edward Banfield and James Wilson accept this distinction, and much of their excellent study of city politics in the U.S.A. pivots on it.[1]

---

[1] Richard Hofstadter, *The Age of Reform* (New York, 1955), p. 9. Edward C. Banfield and James Q. Wilson, *City Politics* (Cambridge, Mass., 1963).

This conflict between mutually incompatible notions of how towns should be governed was the most striking feature of American municipal politics for much of the nineteenth and early twentieth century. For those who accepted the Yankee-Protestant tradition it created 'the problem of American city government', as it was often called. In England American city politics were almost universally condemned from the same point of view, and those interested in municipal government were worried lest the American virus should infect English municipal life.[2]

For a study of English municipal life the model that is so valuable for explaining American urban politics also has its use, but it is a negative one. By its inappropriateness it underlines the narrower limits within which municipal conflict was carried on in England. Except perhaps in Liverpool, there is little trace of Hofstadter's second system of political ethics.

That is not to say that there was no 'corruption' in English municipal politics, i.e. no offences against the dominant system of values. But this took different forms and had different consequences. The most common form was bribery of the electorate with money and with drink. In constituencies where this existed it usually persisted for a long time and was difficult to eradicate.[3] In fact it had all the characteristics of a rival system of political ethics. Voters expected to be bribed, everybody knew it and the electoral process worked in practice on this assumption. But in contrast to American machine politics, the English candidate for office used his own resources or those of his party, never the resources of the town. Bribery was with drink and money, hardly ever with jobs or favours to be given when in office. This meant that electoral corruption did not lead to the corruption of the municipal administration. The rival system of political ethics affected the way men obtained power, but not usually the way in which they used it. It is this that made it in practice so different from the extensive, highly organised corruption to be found in American cities.

Liverpool is perhaps the one English town to which this does not fully apply. Those who know where to look might find there traces of an immigrant ethos with a boss and a machine geared to its special needs. But so far no-one has looked at the history of the town from that point of view, and it is therefore no more than a hunch that might well be

---

[2] Examples of this are quoted on pp. 157 and 328–9.
[3] See H. J. Hanham, *Elections and Party Management. Politics in the Time of Disraeli and Gladstone* (1959), chapter 13 for examples of persistently corrupt Parliamentary constituencies. In Leeds municipal politics the North ward had a reputation for corruption which continued for many years.

proved wrong. The power of Archibald Salvidge, the best known Liverpool party-boss, being Conservative and Orange, was certainly not based directly on any immigrant ethos.[4]

The most common form of corruption by English town councillors once they had been elected, was the jobbing of contracts. It was the direct consequence of the belief that town councils should be recruited from local businessmen. Such people were likely to be involved as private persons in business very similar to that which they had to undertake as public servants. In small places, where the choice of firms for public contracts was limited, such jobbing was particularly common. But there are few big cities which did not have the odd scandal of this kind. They are rarely found in the official histories, but those who go to newspapers will come across them.[5]

Because the dangers sprang so directly from the dominant insistence on municipal service by the business community and were so obvious, much energy and ingenuity went into building up defences against it. By the Municipal Corporations Act of 1882 a business contract with the corporation automatically disqualified a man from sitting on the council. The law extended to the partners of a firm but said nothing about the directors of limited liability companies. What had been intended as a severe safeguard proved therefore increasingly irrelevant. Furthermore little could be done about arrangements less formal than partnerships which gave a sitting councillor an interest in a contract. In 1933 Parliament found that by closing the loop-holes it would make the grounds for exclusion so broad as largely to exclude the local business community from the council. The Local Government Act therefore removed all disqualifications of this kind, and merely required the councillor to declare his pecuniary interest and to abstain from speaking and voting on the matter.[6] It is clear that neither the overtly harsh law of 1882 nor the lenient one of 1933 really disposed of the problem. This was beyond question the vice inherent in the English system and it is surprising that there was not more of it. It is certain that it never emerged as a rival set of norms capable of maintaining itself in the face of public

[4] For Salvidge see Stanley Salvidge, *Salvidge of Liverpool. Behind the Political Scene 1890–1928* (1934). B. D. White, *Corporation of Liverpool*, pp. 87–90 refers in passing to small ward bosses in the years 1842–70.

[5] There was a case in Leeds in 1901. For cases in Manchester in 1869, 1871 and 1880, see 'Manchester 1838–1900' in *Webb Loc. Gov. Col.*, volume 158. For a good discussion of the problem see W. I. Jennings, 'Corruption and the Public Service', *Political Quarterly*, IX (1938).

[6] W. O. Hart, *Hart's Introduction to the Law of Local Government and Administration*, 6th ed. (1957), pp. 116–17.

exposure. In this sense there was one system of political ethics and not two.

For English municipal politics the options were all variants within Hofstadter's first system. Patricians versus plebeians, improvers versus economists, private enterprise versus carefully controlled public works, these were the choices that English municipal electors made. A study such as this does not deal with the dramatic contrasts that existed on the American scene. English municipal reform movements could be charged with moral passion, as we have seen, but they were not the 'crusades against vice' that the term implied in contemporary America.

Another respect in which the movements we have studied differed from the municipal reform movements of the American Progressive era, was that there was little belief in England that good government could be preserved by the adoption of new constitutional procedures. The belief in the referendum or other such procedures as the guarantee for good government has no parallel in England. Hofstadter, writing of the American Progressive reform movements, commented that 'in their search for mechanical guarantees of continued popular control the reformers were trying to do something altogether impossible—to institutionalise a mood.'[7] There was no such illusion in England. Municipal reform was understood to be the creation of a mood, or at least of a sense of duty, and its survival was believed to depend on the creation of a tradition of thought and behaviour.

In terms of the English experience the most dramatic alternative to the concept of local government which we have studied had been tried in Oldham in the thirty years prior to about 1842. There we find a native and genuinely different system of political ethics based on militant working-class Radicalism. Its aim had been to control the organs of popular government and thereby the police and the poor law in the interests of higher wages. The control of the police made it possible to intimidate employers by the systematic use of violence and thereby to raise average wages in the cotton industry in the 1820s and 1830s by as much as 10 per cent compared with those current in Manchester. In the mid-1840s this 'corrupt' use of local power was broken from the outside and disintegrated from within and was never seen again.[8] Oldham may have been unique in the degree of control that working-class Radicals

---

[7] Hofstadter, *Age of Reform*, p. 264.

[8] John Foster, 'Capitalism and Class Consciousness in earlier nineteenth century Oldham', unpublished Ph.D. thesis, Cambridge 1966. There is a brief resumé in John Foster, 'Nineteenth Century Towns—A Class Dimension', in H. J. Dyos (ed.), *The Study of Urban History* (1968).

obtained over the organs of government, but the same tendency was to be found elsewhere at the time. Hence the distrust of popular government as expressed in the imposition of property qualifications for the franchise by the Sturges Bourne Act of 1818, the Poor Law Amendment Act of 1834 and the Municipal Corporations Act of 1835.[9] In the Leeds of the 1830s and 1840s, although the vestry could be captured by militant working-class Radicals, the other organs of government could not, and it was there that the powers that really mattered had been placed.

The case of Oldham is a reminder that until the 1840s quite far-reaching disagreement existed about systems of political ethics in some places on the far left of the political scene. But thereafter it survived hardly even as a spectre, so rapidly and totally had the possibility of such action been eliminated.

A different range of considerations is brought into focus, when we compare the English municipal experience with that of the industrial towns of Germany, and more specifically those of Prussia. There was enough similarity between the systems of local government in the two countries in the nineteenth century to make such a comparison possible, and the existence of several studies of German towns similar to this one is a challenge to do so.

Whatever may have been the condition of the central government, municipal government in Prussia had been designed since the reforms of Stein in 1808 to encourage the participation of the citizen body. The Prussian Municipal Ordinances of 1831 and 1856 are in this respect not so different from the English Municipal Corporations Act of 1835. Both provided the towns with a council of unpaid, part-time representatives elected by the tax-paying citizens.[10] The major differences between the two systems were two: the sharper separation of the process of administration from that of representation, and the greater role played by professional civil servants.

In Prussian towns responsibility for the formulation and execution of policy rested not with the town council (*Stadtverordneten*) but with a

---

[9] S. and B. Webb, *The Parish and the County* (1906), p. 154 for the Sturges Bourne Act.
[10] Helmuth Croon, *Die gesellschaftlichen Auswirkungen des Gemeindewahlrechts in den Gemeinden und Kreisen des Rheinlands und Westfalens im 19. Jahrhundert* (Cologne and Opladen, 1960) for details of franchise qualifications. The best description of German municipal government at the turn of the century written in English is W. H. Dawson, *Municipal Life and Government in Germany* (1914). The authoritative study of the political theory of local government in Germany is Heinrich Heffter, *Die Deutsche Selbstverwaltung im 19. Jahrhundert* (Stuttgart, 1950).

smaller body, the *Magistrat*, headed by the *Buergermeister*. The members of the *Magistrat* consisted of a mixture of salaried officials and honorary members. Both were chosen by the town council, for six years if honorary and for twelve years in the first instance if salaried. The honorary members were not unlike a combination of aldermen and long-standing committee chairmen, a combination common enough in an English borough. But once elected, they were responsible to the *Buergermeister*, not to the council.[11] The latter controlled the purse, but although it could make policy suggestions, it could normally not implement them. For this reason its representative functions were supreme over all other considerations to a degree not true of the English town council.

The same point is reinforced by the other difference between the two systems. In the *Buergermeister* the Prussian towns possessed a chief for whom there was no English equivalent. Not only were his powers greater than those of any person connected with municipal government in England, but he was also a trained professional civil servant. Some of the *Magistrat* were like him salaried civil servants, and the key posts of finance, public works, and education were always filled by professionals. But in the nineteenth century it was generally assumed that the majority of the *Magistrat* would be substantial citizens holding their offices in an honorary capacity and reinforced only where necessary by the professionals. Membership of the town council could and did lead to election to the *Magistrat*. The council attracted and was meant to attract the substantial citizens.

To sum up, although the ability of the Prussian town council to affect the actual government of the town was less than in England, and the power of salaried professional officials was greater, the expectation in Prussian as in English towns was that the substantial citizens would stand for election and serve in an honorary capacity both on the full Council and the executive body.

The towns that have been studied in the western provinces of Prussia fall into two groups.[12] On the one hand there are those in which an

---

[11] This was so in the western provinces of Prussia. In the eastern provinces the *Magistrat* acted corporately and the *Buergermeister* was formally only *primus inter pares*. The difference is immaterial for our purposes, since it did not affect the relationship of the *Magistrat* to the council.

[12] Helmuth Croon, 'Die Stadtvertretung in Krefeld und Bochum im 19. Jahrhundert', in Richard Dietrich and Gerhard Oestreich (eds.), *Forschungen zu Staat und Verfassung. Festgabe fuer Fritz Hartung* (Berlin, 1958), pp. 289–306; Wolfgang Hofmann, *Die Bielefelder Stadtverordneten* (Luebeck and Hamburg, 1964); Wolfgang Koellmann, *Sozialgeschichte der Stadt Barmen im 19. Jahrhundert* (Tuebingen, 1960).

upper class of merchants controlled a long-established textile industry, and whose social structure was subsequently transformed by mechanisation and organisational changes and by the founding of additional industries. In these respects the experience of such towns as Krefeld, Bielefeld, and Barmen is reminiscent of that of Leeds, Nottingham, or Leicester. On the other hand the coal-mining and steel-making towns of the Ruhr, such as Bochum, were the rapid creation of the industrial revolution itself. They were more like Merthyr Tidfil and other towns of the South Wales coalfield.

In the older towns which possessed a town council already in the 1830s and 1840s this body faithfully mirrored the economic and social elite of the community. Wolfgang Hofmann, the historian of Bielefeld, described the first election under the municipal ordinance of 1831 as 'legitimising the long-standing group of leading citizens'.[13] What happened thereafter in the second half of the century was strongly affected by the introduction of the peculiar three-class electoral system, which dated from 1845 in the Rhineland and from 1850 in the other provinces of Prussia.

This system divided the total electorate into three classes according to the amount of taxes paid by each person. The first class contained as many of the largest taxpayers as between them accounted for one-third of the total tax-revenue. The second those medium-sized taxpayers who between them contributed the second third of the revenue. The third class contained all the rest. This form of division produced enormous contrasts between the numerical size of the classes, but despite this each class elected one-third of the town council members. The system gave the wealthiest citizens secure control of at least one-third of the Council, and limited the political power of the small taxpayers, who, however numerous, could not elect more than one-third of the councillors. This franchise had some paradoxical consequences especially in Westphalia, where the vote could be exercised on behalf of corporate tax-payers, i.e. of limited liability companies. In years when the profits of the big local firms were poor some voters found themselves promoted to another class, only to fall back again when profits and therefore tax-liability recovered. The introduction of tax-reforms in 1891 intended to reduce the burden on the recipients of small incomes also reduced their political power in the local elections. In the Rhineland the third class had previously contained between 75 and 80 per cent of the electorate in most towns, but in the late 1890s contained more than 90 per

[13] Hofmann, *Die Bieletfeldet Stadtverordneten*, p. 120.

cent.[14] In this situation each third of the council membership reacted to its own particular electorate in a very different way.

In Krefeld the petty bourgeoisie whose political self-consciousness had been roused in 1848, made an appearance in the Council as representatives of the third class in 1849 and 1850, but far from maintaining themselves, disappeared again.[15] As late as 1867 the overwhelmingly Liberal Council was still with only two exceptions composed in all three sections of the leading silk merchants and manufacturers and of the professional men with whom they were connected by marriage and social intercourse. By 1877 this was no longer so. The representation of the third class had now been taken over by master craftsmen and smaller businessmen, most of whom belonged to the middle range of incomes and voted in the second class, but not in the first class as their predecessors had done.

Two fundamental changes that had taken place in the intervening decade explain the contrast. One was the transformation of the local silk industry from a domestic system employing weavers living in the outlying villages to a factory system which brought them into the town. The other was the outbreak of the *Kulturkampf*, which by setting Catholics against Protestant Liberals opened a deep chasm in the political life of many industrial towns of the Rhineland and Westphalia. In Krefeld the industrial entrepreneurs were Protestant, while the surrounding countryside and the lower ranks in the town itself were Catholic. Under these circumstances it was easy for the Catholic petty bourgeoisie to become the spokesmen for the immigrant workers against the Liberal Protestant upper class. Krefeld provided a majority for the Catholic Centre party in the Reichstag elections of 1871. By 1877 the same process had transformed the representation in the third section of the Council. But as the Catholic population rose in wealth, and in their turn produced successful entrepreneurs and professional men, so towards the end of the century the members of the third section also rose in social and economic status.

The first section of the Town Council did not alter at all in its social composition before the turn of the century. In the second the defence of Liberal politics was undertaken by widening the range of candidates to include other sections of the economy. But most of these enjoyed close ties with the old families through common membership of elite social clubs.

Similar discrepancies between the three sections is to be found in

[14] Croon, *Auswirkungen*, pp. 18–20.
[15] Croon, *Krefeld und Bochum, passim.*

Bielefeld, a mainly Protestant industrial town with a minority of Catholic immigrants.[16] Here the petty bourgeoisie, i.e. innkeepers, dealers, and master craftsmen were by the 1850s already in permanent control of the third section. The big businessmen were able to retain their position in the first two sections, but as a result of the economic transformation of the town linen merchants found themselves alongside factory owners both in textiles and to some extent in engineering. The professions entrenched themselves strongly in the second section.

The phasing in Bochum, a coal and steel town, dominated by one overwhelmingly powerful steel-company, the *Bochumer Verein*, is slightly different again.[17] But here too from about the 1860s the directors from the mines as well as the steel-works are found in person on the Council. The *Bochumer Verein* even used its hold over the voters in the third section to place its leading personnel there. From 1869–92 the director-general of the company sat as one of the representatives for the third section. It was in the second section that some of the variety of middle-class occupations not directly connected with the large works found their representatives.

It is apparent that the Prussian municipal electoral system made it far easier for the social and economic elite to maintain a dominant position in the town council, if they wished to do so. The distaste for competing in the rough and tumble of ward elections, often expressed by the upper-class families in English towns, was here eliminated from consideration. But despite certain penalties for refusal of office no electoral system could ensure their participation, if other considerations than a distaste for democracy led them to abstain.

The available studies of West German industrial towns leave us in no doubt that the leading families willingly accepted the role sketched out for them by Stein and those who followed in his tradition. Since in these towns the patrician class of merchant entrepreneurs were Protestant, no matter whether the surrounding area was Catholic, as in Krefeld, or Protestant, as in Barmen and Bielefeld, their sense of public service expressed itself in very Protestant formulas and was for some time reinforced by an identification of economic pre-eminence with honorary office in both church and town. In Barmen, Bielefeld, and Krefeld the institutions of the Protestant churches helped to maintain and to transmit this sense of obligation on the part of the upper class.[18]

[16] Hofmann, *Die Bielefelder Stadtverordneten* especially pp. 39–40, 123–30.
[17] Croon, *Krefeld und Bochum*, pp. 293, 296–8, 301–3.
[18] This is particularly well described in Koellmann, *Barmen*, pp. 108 ff. But see also Croon, *Krefeld und Bochum*, pp. 292–3.

The same identification with the public life of the town was found among the Jewish merchants of Posen in the eastern province of Prussia. Here too the institutions of social life reinforced and perpetuated a strongly developed sense of duty and identification with the community on the part of a wealthy minority.[19]

In fact at least as important as the churches in reinforcing and pre-serving the earlier traditions of honorary service in the German towns were the social clubs. The historians of the West German towns, Croon, Hofmann and Koellmann, all draw attention to the role which these bodies played in articulating the social structure of the town.[20] In each of them there was one such club, called *Concordia*, *Ressource* or simply *Societaet Nr. 5*, membership of which distinguished those who belonged to the elite from those who did not. These bodies provided a common meeting-point and an effective way of transmitting the dominant ethos. Other clubs of the same kind existed for those lower down the social scale, shaping their social life by means of common activities such as music and rifle-shooting. The historian of nineteenth-century Birmingham or Leeds has no such simple sociological guide to follow, partly because he is dealing with bigger and therefore more complex communities, partly maybe because of the greater fluidity of the English social scene. He must look for bodies less rigid in their class composition or less all-inclusive which fulfilled similar roles in English cities. This is a disadvantage for the student of society, but not necessarily for the society itself.

There is evidence that after 1900 the commitment to honorary public service which had characterised the leading families of the industrial towns of Westphalia and the Rhineland came under pressure and was much eroded by 1918. In Barmen, Krefeld, Moenchen-Gladbach, and Aix-la-Chapelle patrician families with long-standing traditions of muni-cipal service began to turn away, nor were their places taken by newer families of the same standing. On the contrary the representatives of class I were drawn increasingly from salaried employees of the big firms, members of the professions, wholesale merchants, and journa-lists, i.e. often men who stood in a position of clientage towards the big industrialists of the town.[21]

[19] Moritz Jaffé, *Die Stadt Posen unter Preussischer Herrschaft. Schriften des Vereins fuer Sozialpolitik*, volume 119, part 2 (Leipzig, 1909).
[20] Croon, *Krefeld und Bochum, passim;* Hofmann, *Die Bielefelder Stadtverordneten*, especially pp. 40–45; Koellmann, pp. 112–14, 122–3, 212 ff.
[21] The list is taken from the case of Krefeld, where Croon analyses the phenomenon with some care. Croon, *Krefeld und Bochum*, p. 303. The case of Barmen is discussed more cursorily in Koellmann, pp. 121, 267. For Moenchen-Gladbach and Aix-la-Chapelle, see Croon, *Auswirkungen*, pp. 38–9.

As in England the writers on the subject of local government had no hesitation in describing this as a process affecting German towns in general. The explanations they provided were similar to those given by English writers since the 1870s—the greater demands of business, the involvement in organisations on a national rather than a local scale, and the withdrawal from the towns in which the money had been made.[22] It may be assumed that these considerations did affect the willingness of the social and economic elite to continue with honorary local service.

But there were other towns, Bochum and Remscheid in the West, Posen in the East, where these changes had not taken place before the old system disappeared in 1919.[23] In Bielefeld the old-established public-service families from the linen industry also continued to play their old role, but withdrew from the Town Council into the *Magistrat*, where the real power increasingly lay. But their example was not followed by the large employers in the more recently established engineering industry, whose willingness to participate in the public life of the town was much less. Earlier in the book the author had commented on the resistance shown by the social institutions of upper-class life in Bielefeld to the pioneers of the new engineering industry, and had spoken of a disjunction between the economic and social elite that had come about during the closing years of the century.[24] The Kitsons had been more fortunate in the reception they received from the established woollen merchants at the Mill Hill chapel and the Leeds Philosophical and Literary Society.

We have already noticed how the Prussian three-class system provided other strata of propertied society than the highest, an assured place on the Council.[25] In those towns where there was no really powerful Centre party to appeal to Catholics across the class divisions the Social Democrats were able also to place manual workers and trade union officials on the Council. Compared with its position in the Reichstag the party was weak on the municipal councils and their successes came late, since the simple universal manhood suffrage of the Reichstag elections placed fewer obstacles in their way. In Bielefeld the first manual worker was not elected until 1896. But by 1913 there were three

[22] In particular Hugo Preuss, *Die Entwicklung des deutschen Staedtewesens* (Leipzig, 1906), I, 373–4.
[23] Croon, *Auswirkungen*, p. 39; Croon, *Krefeld und Bochum*, pp. 301–3; Jaffé, *Posen*, pp. 414–17.
[24] Hofmann, *Die Bielefelder Stradtverordneten*, pp. 38, 124–6.
[25] The legal requirement that half the council consist of house-owners also contributed to this.

trade union officials and five manual workers, comprising about half the third section and 19 per cent of the whole Council.[26]

In many respects the condition of German municipal government was such as to arouse admiration in England. As policy-making and administration became more exacting, it had been easy for German municipalities to strengthen the salaried professional element in the mixed *Magistrat*. The assured position of the upper classes in a council of mixed social composition under the direction of trained professionals came nearer to the ideal put forward by John Stuart Mill, which is discussed in the next chapter, than anything to be found in England. But this is not the whole picture.

The Prussian three-class system enabled the upper class to remain on the town councils, but it did so by insulating them from the impact of democracy. Secure behind the barrier of the electoral system, they were not forced to make adjustments to the political processes of a society in which social deference was not automatic and leadership could be retained only by those able to identify themselves imaginatively with the aspirations of others not of their own kind. When in 1919 the barrier of the special franchise was removed, they were swept away by the political movements to which they had remained strangers. 1919 in municipal politics saw not only a political revolution, placing the Centre party or the Social Democrats firmly in power, but also a revolution in the social composition of the councils.[27] In an article, 'Liberalism and the City in Nineteenth-Century Germany',[28] James Sheehan has argued most perceptively that between 1880 and 1918 this protection enabled the Liberal elite of the German towns to use the town councils as a refuge from a world whose changing character they deplored. They used them as Englishmen, but particularly Americans, in a similar frame of mind have used the voluntary community organisations, and they surrounded municipal government (*Selbstverwaltung*) with a very similar halo of superior virtue.

None of this can be said of those from the social and economic elite who served on English town councils in the same historical period. There were fewer of them, as we have seen. Since the English system of local government relied heavily on the elected personnel for the making and execution of policy, this had unfortunate effects on the quality of the administration especially in some places and in some periods. But

---

[26] Hofmann, *Die Bielefelder Stradtverordneten*, pp. 130-1, 173.
[27] Croon, *Auswirkungen*, p. 48.
[28] *Past and Present*, No. 51 (May 1971), pp. 116-37.

the English electoral conditions ensured that those who held the positions of councillors and aldermen had proved themselves capable of operating in the world of mass politics. Certainly in the big cities, with which this book is primarily concerned, those who were elected, whatever their social and economic position, knew how to live in the world of democratic parties and to think in categories that could unite men of different social and economic experiences.

2

Town Councillors: the History of an Ideal

When we ask ourselves what characteristics town councillors were expected to possess at the beginning of the historical period covered in this book, we shall not have far to search for an answer. Ideals are often taken for granted and not expressed, but at certain times they break the surface for all to observe. Such a time were the 1830s in England. The Royal Commission on Municipal Corporations of 1833–5, the controversy to which its report gave rise, and the parliamentary debates on the Municipal Corporations Bill of 1835 provide a wealth of evidence. They are particularly suited to our purpose, since they provide not isolated statements but a complete debate. They demonstrate the common ground shared by those who engaged in it, as well as the issues on which they disagreed.

It was generally agreed that ideally town councillors possessed two or possibly three crucial characteristics. They were men of *station* or *respectability*, they were men of *substance* or *property* or *wealth*, and they were men of *intelligence* or *education*. They were never merely intelligent without being also men of station and substance. It was station or respectability that appeared on all occasions as the indispensable criterion, and it was substance or property that was most commonly linked with it.

This was as true of the Reformers engaged in the debate as of the defenders of the established order. For instance a Radical assistant commissioner to the Royal Commission criticised the Corporation of Boston, Lincolnshire, in the following terms:

'Many dissenters who reside in the town are persons of considerable property and respectability, and occupy stations in life from which common councilmen are usually selected, but none of them have ever been admitted to the Corporation.'[1]

In Gloucester the Radicals complained that

'the character of the magistracy is lowered, and its efficiency impaired, by the exclusion of many respectable and instructed persons.'[2]

When Tories defended the existing state, they disputed the alleged facts presented by their critics, never the relevance of these facts to the indictment. Boston Corporation challenged the accuracy of the commissioners' report before the House of Lords. Its town clerk testified that aldermen were 'respectable and substantial men . . . some of them men of large property'. Bath Corporation claimed that its members were 'Persons of Property and Station in Life', and Liverpool Corporation that they were 'Men of Station, Education and Substance'.[3]

This was the common ground. What was in dispute was the propriety of excluding men on the grounds of party or religion, who were otherwise qualified. The *Report* of the Royal Commission condemned the composition of the corporations because:

'Since the repeal of the Test and Corporation Acts, and the removal of the civil disabilities of the Catholics, very few instances occur in which either Catholics or Dissenters, who often form a numerous, respectable and wealthy portion of the inhabitants, have been chosen into the governing body of the corporation.'[4]

Reformers pressed for election by a wider constituency instead of co-option by those already in office. They did so, not because they believed that anyone was as good as anyone else, but 'so that all in equal station

---

[1] *Municipal Corporations in England and Wales. Royal Commission 1st. Report*, appendix, part IV, p. 2152; *P.P* 1835 (116), xxvi, 74.
[2] *Municipal Corporations in England and Wales. Royal Commission 1st. Report*, appendix, part I, p. 62; *P.P.* 1835 (116), xxiii.
[3] *Municipal Corporations Bill. H.L. Inquiry. Mins. of ev.*, p. 304; *P.P.*, 1835 (H.L. 141.1), xli.
[4] *Municipal Corporations in England and Wales. Royal Commission 1st. Report*, p. 36; *P.P.*, 1835 (116), xxiii, 1.

should enjoy equal privileges and be subject to equal duties'.[5] To understand this emphasis on station and substance we need to remember what the function of municipal corporations had principally been. They had been first and foremost bodies of magistrates. They had been secondly owners of corporate property.

They had been bodies of magistrates, just as in the counties J.P.s were at one and the same time judicial and administrative officers. At a time when administration had been thought of as the judicial distribution of onerous duties among the citizens, this combination of what we now consider to be distinct functions had seemed natural.[6] By the second quarter of the nineteenth century this assumption that had once dominated the theory of local government was beginning to fade. Under the Municipal Corporations Act of 1835 the judicial functions could for the first time be taken away from the Corporation and vested without a sense of incongruity in a separate bench of borough magistrates. The bodies that emerged from the process of reform could therefore be regarded as first and foremost owners of corporate property. They were made answerable to the rate-paying householders for the way in which they administered this property and employed its revenues. In relation to the community at large they had only one administrative function imposed on them by statute, the provision of a police-force. Whatever further function they might undertake depended on the initiative of the corporation in the past, differed greatly from place to place, but hardly belonged to the essence of a municipal corporation. Most of what was later to be regarded as the essential administrative duties of a municipality were carried out, if at all, by *ad hoc* improvement commissioners and similar bodies.

In the long run this hiving off of the judicial functions to a separate bench of borough magistrates was to have important consequences. But that took time, and in 1833–5 much of the thinking about municipal government was strongly influenced by the long association of the corporation with magistrates' duties. Nor was the connection severed in 1835 with a clean sweep. The Bill originally provided that the appointment of the borough magistrates by the Crown should be on the nomination of the town council. This was dropped under pressure from the

---

[5] 'Petition to the House of Commons by the undersigned Bankers, Merchants and Householders of Liverpool for Corporation Reform', quoted in *Municipal Corporations in England and Wales. Royal Commission 1st. Report*, appendix, part IV, p. 2704; *P.P.*, 1835 (116), xxvi. They described themselves in the petition as 'possessing great wealth and property in the town and yielding to none in intelligence and moral worth'.

[6] See the classic exposition in S. and B. Webb, *English Local Government*, volume IV. *Statutory Authorities for Special Purposes* (London, 1922), chapter V.

House of Lords, but the Whig government nevertheless pledged itself to obtain such nominations. What is more, the Act made the mayor *ex officio* a borough magistrate and chairman of the bench.[7]

In such a context the primary emphasis on the respectability that was associated with status is understandable. The report on Hastings brings out the connection very clearly:

> 'The mayor and greater number of resident jurats have generally been tradesmen, unqualified, however estimable in their private stations, to discharge the duties of magistrates or judges. . . . The manifest dependence of the municipal authorities on the guidance of their own officers could scarcely have failed to lower the respectful feeling essential to a due administration of justice.'[8]

Sir Robert Peel had already in 1832 called for the reform of municipal corporations in the interest of the 'better maintenance of public peace'.[9] This was the pivot of the measure in 1835 as far as he was concerned, and it was by this touchstone that he judged the fitness of the corporations:

> 'No system of Municipal Government . . . will promote the object for which alone it ought to be designed . . . the maintenance of public order, the pure administration of justice, or the harmony and happiness of the societies to which it is to be applied, unless its direct tendency be to commit the management of Municipal affairs to the hands of those who from the possession of property have the strongest interest in good government, and, from the qualification of high character and intelligence, are most likely to conciliate the respect and confidence of their fellow citizens.'[10]

By linking the possession of property explicitly with the maintenance of public order, and making the administration of justice and the harmony of society dependent on the respect and confidence enjoyed by those in office, he demonstrates very clearly the perspective from which a Conservative looked at the matter. The foundations of respect were for Peel

[7] S. and B. Webb, *English Local Government*, volume III. *The Manor and the Borough* (London, 1908), pp. 739–47. See John Stuart Mill's statement that municipal government and the administration of justice should be entirely separate and his criticism of the Bill for failing to make a clear-cut separation. 'Parliamentary Proceedings of the Session', *London Review*, I, 2 (1835), 518–24.

[8] *Municipal Corporations in England and Wales. Royal Commission 1st. Report*, appendix, part II, p. 999; *P.P.*, 1835 (116), xxiv. 'Jurats' was a term for members of municipal corporations. It is synonymous with aldermen.

[9] 3 *Hansard* XIII, 386 (4 June 1832), quoted in S. and B. Webb, *Manor and Borough*, p. 699.

[10] 3 *Hansard* XXVIII, 571 (5 June 1835).

less clearly a matter of station, and more of character and intelligence. But 'intelligence and respectability' had been the formula he had used earlier in the same speech, and a few days later he was to speak of 'persons of wealth and respectability'.[11]

The parliamentary debates of 1835 provide also much evidence for the connection between the view that councillors should be men of substance and their role as trustees of corporate property.[12] Once again the agreement to be found among M.P.s and peers of every shade of political conviction, when they turned to the question of what characterised a suitable member of a municipal corporation, is most striking. Although there were debates in both Houses over the Conservative insistence on a property qualification for councillors, an insistence which the Whig government strongly opposed, this was a disagreement about means, not ends. Both sides wanted to secure 'Members of a certain stamp of respectability', 'substantial persons', men 'of respectable standing in society', etc. The Whigs believed, however, that it was unnecessary to introduce a formal property qualification to obtain this result. 'If you left this office without qualification, the voters would naturally elect the most respectable person.' They finally made a tactical concession and accepted the Tory amendment, but protested to the end that they would have preferred the Bill without it. Their objection stemmed from considerations of political psychology. The purpose of the reform was to produce a 'community of feeling' between the great body of the people and the members of town councils. The absence of this sense of identification had been 'the supreme complaint laid against the old corporations'. It was for this reason that they were unwilling to introduce an 'exclusive principle' into the Bill.[13]

II

During the 1850s, as so often since, the personnel of town councils repeatedly attracted critical comment. It seemed to many observers that there had been a change for the worse since 1835. Others were equally disparaging if less nostalgic. They judged what they saw around them by the same ideals as had been expounded in the 1830s. The plight of municipal government they ascribed to an ignorant electorate, often enlarged well beyond the intentions of the framers of the 1835 Act, and

[11] *3 Hansard* XXIX, 100 (30 June 1835).
[12] *3 Hansard* XXIX, 114, 119 (30 June 1835).
[13] *3 Hansard* XXX, 485–6, 490–2, 495 (14 August 1835).

too easily seduced by drink from its proper respect for men of station and property. They noticed that men who possessed these qualities had become reluctant to stand for election. While deploring such lack of public spirit they were quick to add that this was largely the consequence of the disgraceful conditions that prevailed in ward politics and in the council chamber.

Such was the view of the 1859 select committee of the House of Lords on the operation of the Small Tenements Rating Act (1850). The language of the witnesses whom it examined leaves no room for doubt that they shared the basic assumption that had been expressed in 1833–5. In Weymouth, it was alleged, 'the more respectable inhabitants' had been replaced by others of 'inferior station and intelligence'. In Scarborough the more respectable inhabitants were said to be unwilling to come into the Town Council. The inquiry into the composition of Boston Town Council was once again conducted in the language familiar from 1835, the more respectable inhabitants being identified with the principal merchants and tradesmen. A witness from Exeter claimed that there was quite a different class of men in the Council from what there had been at the time of the first election in 1835. 'At that time we had the heads of the city and now . . . gentlemen will not come forward.'[14] A witness from Warrington saw the issue as between gentlemen of high standing and men very inferior in character.[15]

Not all these assertions would stand up to impartial investigation. The select committee had been set up to make a case against the enfranchisement of small occupiers who were not direct ratepayers, and those who testified before it were chosen with this object in view. We are interested in them not as witnesses to municipal conditions in their towns but to the survival of the values of the 1830s.

Similar expressions can be found in local newspapers throughout the country. The replacement of substantial and respectable men by people 'lower in the scale' was, to put it bluntly, regarded as a deplorable lapse. Manchester Town Council, dominated since its inception by respected merchants, found itself increasingly under pressure from an 'economy' party led by and largely composed of shopkeepers. In 1861 this group tried to reduce the salary of the town clerk and their action led to public protest meetings and much strong feeling. *The Manchester Guardian* devoted a leading article to the matter:

[14] Robert Newton, *Victorian Exeter 1837–1914* (Leicester, 1968) largely bears out the truth of this assertion.
[15] *Operation of the Small Tenements Rating Act 1850, Select Committee H.L. mins. of ev.*; *P.P.*, 1859, Session 2 (56), vii, 269.

'If the respectable section of citizens feel themselves annoyed and humiliated by such discussions as Mr. Bennett has raised, we have no comfort for them. It is all their own fault. If they will allow the municipal wards of Manchester to become rotten boroughs in the gift of pot-house orators, they must take the inevitable consequences. If they want an illustration of the state of affairs which their indifference is creating, let them ask any American friend to tell them something about the Corporation of New York. They will find that by a process similar to that which is being followed here, this body has become a civic nuisance, and a national disgrace . . . and so it will be with us if the language used at the last election is understood to be the passport to success.'[16]

Ten years previously a Manchester Conservative, his perception sharpened by political opposition, had deplored a situation in which 'in each ward . . . the patronage is falling into lower, and centering in fewer hands from year to year'. He had blamed the apathy in part on the domination of Manchester politics by one party 'with its accompanying want of wholesome rivalry', but in all other respects his diagnosis agreed with that of the *Guardian*.[17]

This sort of language, whether from Liberal or Conservative, was by then, however, only one side of the argument. There was another point of view. As long as the financial responsibilities of municipal corporations had been mainly concerned with the management of the corporate property, men of substance, who would bring to public life their own experience of the administration of large property, had been the most eligible of candidates. When, however, municipal bodies began to undertake the provision of increasingly expensive services often involving the creation of large capital works, as in the case of drainage, the position changed. The profits from corporate property could hardly ever provide the necessary funds, and corporations had to resort more and more to the levying of rates. They increasingly became engines of direct taxation. In these circumstances a council composed of rich men was now not necessarily a thing to be desired by all and everyone. It is possible to identify the emergence of a rival point of view. Rich men, although certainly large ratepayers, could afford municipal extravagances that would crush the smaller man. They were, therefore, hardly the proper

[16] *The Manchester Guardian*, 18 November 1861.
[17] 'Neglect of Municipal Duties', Letter by 'A Burgess', *The Manchester Guardian*, 15 October 1851.

guardians of the interests of the small tradesmen, heavily rated for their shops, whose savings were often invested in a house or two.

During the 1850s, and occasionally already in the 1840s, the steep rise in the rates that followed the adoption in one town after another of necessary but expensive sanitary duties, provoked the rise of municipal parties of 'Economists'. We have met examples of this in Birmingham and Leeds. Their intervention often led to the replacement of 'substantial men' by shopkeepers, publicans and other representatives of the hard-pressed ratepayer.[18] Their language was a direct challenge to the notions which we have met so far.

'The upper section of the Liberals in the ward had paid rather too little consideration to the lower section,'

said the sponsor of one such revolt against extravagant gentlemen in Leeds,

'but he anticipated the result of that day's proceedings would be to unite both parties more closely and more firmly under the banner of economy and retrenchment.'[19]

Impartial observers of such contests detected the appearance of a new form of legitimacy. A harmony of interests was to be attained by balancing the social composition of the Council between the large men and the small:

'A corporation of merchants and shipowners and thoroughly educated gentlemen is no doubt very nice in the abstract . . . but the attraction would be merely on the surface . . . the thing would not work. There would be no drag chain upon any amount of extravagance in small things. . . . At the same time the scale may be overbalanced in the other way. There may be too many representatives of the hard working ratepayers, and too few of the representatives of the mercantile community.'[20]

[18] E. P. Hennock, 'Finance and Politics in Urban Local Government 1835–1900', *Historical Jl.*, VI (1963), pp. 212–25.

[19] Speech by G. A. Linsley, *L.M.*, 2 November 1869, p. 8.

[20] *Hull Advertiser*, 27 October 1860. The Corporation of Hull was more or less dominated by Economists from the early 1850s to the end of the century. In the 1850s the leading merchants and shipowners were operating outside the Town Council, which was chiefly composed of shopkeepers. In an attempt to obtain the vesting of the docks in the hands of trustees, they tried at various dates in the 1850s, to enter the Town Council, but were usually unsuccessful. The above quoted article is a comment on such an attempt. The dock dues provided Hull Corporation with a substantial income even after they had been reduced in 1852. The shopkeepers as ratepayers were therefore in a very strong position in meeting the challenge to their municipal supremacy. There was only one limiting consideration—the prosperity of the town. 'The shopkeepers must be careful not to drive away the shipowners and merchants from the port' (*Ibid.*, 25 October 1850).

This comment is at least as interesting for what it does not say as for what it does. It would have been easy to interpret mid-century Hull municipal politics as a conflict between dock-users and ratepayers over the source of the Corporation's revenue. Instead it is regarded as a conflict between two attitudes of mind—that of the substantial town elite and that of those on whom the burden of the rates fell most severely.

The same point was made by a Wolverhampton shopkeeper, a town councillor, in 1903. Opposing the costly system of electric tramways, which was the pet scheme of a committee chairman who was a large businessman, he said

> 'It frequently happened that when matters of this kind were taken in hand by men of easy circumstances and in possession of great wealth—they could not find that consideration for struggling tradesmen and shopkeepers and hard working artisans, who had to get their living and reside in the town, that was desirable.'[21]

Here is the dissenting point of view—the other side of the argument —claiming for the small man, heavily burdened by the rates, particularly the small shopkeeper, legitimacy as a town councillor.

It would not be hard to show that the persistence with which this claim was made is equalled only by the persistence with which it was rejected. 'Small shop element was what he disliked. Down with everything was their motto', said the energetic medical officer of health for Plymouth in 1900, and recounted how, the tradesmen on the council told him, when he advocated the compulsory notification of whooping cough, that he was only after half-crowns for his professional brethren.[22]

But there is more to the matter than that. Those who rejected the claims of shopkeepers, or perhaps even those who grudgingly accepted them, did not merely continue to repeat the arguments of the 1830s in favour of men of station and substance. From the 1860s new standards emerged by which to judge the suitability of town councillors. Strictly speaking there were two points of view. There were those who thought that the model for the ideal councillor was the successful businessman. There were others who thought of councils as bodies with essentially a mixed social composition, which served to educate their members in political wisdom.

---

[21] G. W. Jones, *Borough Politics. A Study of the Wolverhampton Town Council, 1888–1964* (London, 1969), p. 121.
[22] Notes on interview with Dr. Williams; *Webb Loc. Gov. Col.*, volume 112.

III

If corporations were to be great undertakings, providing services on a scale comparable with those of the most adventurous entrepreneur, raising loans and assuming the disbursement of great sums, then service on their chief committees demanded skills normally to be looked for in successful businessmen. 'Economists' might object to municipal ambition, but even they could not avoid the need to dispose of sewage and of flood water, to straighten thoroughfares for the growing number of horse-drawn vehicles, to pave and scavenge, and to enlarge the gaol. These had become the inescapable tasks of municipal corporations. The only question was how well they would be performed. Seen in this perspective there was a true economy, and a false, and the latter was that of councils that were 'penny-wise and pound-foolish'. Success in such undertakings demanded boldness as well as caution, a willingness to think big as well as shrewd attention to detail.

In insisting that the virtues of the businessman were the necessary qualifications of the town councillor, men could agree who differed strongly on matters of policy. It was not necessary to be an 'improver' to believe that proper attention to the accounts, and a knowledge of how best to fund your clamorous overdrafts, were sterling qualities. As for the men who wished to provide good pavements, good water and good drains or some costly symbol of civic aspiration in a world in which the ultimate political arbiter was the ratepayer, they too could not afford to trust in dreams of a new Athens and pay no attention to the balance sheet.[23] Seen in such terms there would be room for disagreement on which kind of business attitude should be dominant, caution or enterprise. The issue between improvers and economists, the central issue of local government politics at the time, was fought out on just such common ground.

At its most philistine this perspective could lead to an exaltation of business attitudes to the exclusion of all else:

> 'Fill the Council Chamber with lawyers, and you will have a Babel of confused sound. Fill it with doctors, and the whole borough would start with amazement at the unpractical character of men whose minds must needs, in order to reach success, be concentrated on their noble profession. Fill it with journalists, and—the idea makes me laugh until my pen is broken. Successful businessmen

[23] See the discussion of this in E. P. Hennock, 'Finance and Politics', *Historical Jl.*, VI (1963), 212–25.

of age sufficient, experience ripened, honesty unimpeachable, and the devotion to the work, are the right men to send to the Council. Nor does a high degree of education, so-called, appear to me to be a necessity.'[24]

But the claim that the government of a town is a business to be run exclusively 'by businessmen on business principles' is not a common one in England. The idea stemmed from the U.S.A., where it implied a rejection of the claims of politicians to run the town on the spoils system. It was an American journalist who applied the formula to the Birmingham of Joseph Chamberlain in explanation of its success as 'the best-governed city in the world'.[25] The spokesmen for the Birmingham municipal ideal were not anxious to assert the exclusive rights of businessmen to a council seat. For them the emphasis on the duty of successful businessmen to serve their fellow citizens on the Council was a remedial one. It had to do with the important role of businessmen on a council of mixed social composition, not with the notion of a business city run exclusively by businessmen.

In this sense they were disciples of John Stuart Mill, and it will help to place them if we look first at Mill's ideas. In *Representative Government* (1861) he turned his back on all exclusive claims, even that of men of station and substance, to the representation on town councils. No lover of a 'shopocracy', he nevertheless accepted the fact of shopkeepers on local government bodies and found a carefully circumscribed justification for their presence.

The starting point of Mill's thinking on the subject was his conviction that it was the duty of government to educate citizens in their political responsibilities. Local government he regarded as particularly suited to this purpose on account of the wider participation of social classes in its work, and because the safety of the State was less immediately endangered by defective administration than was the case with the central government. This view of local government as a school of political capacity made him more tolerant than most who have so far been quoted of the motley composition of elected councils, as they really were. But there were limits:

---

[24] J. S. Curtis, *The Marsden Mayoralty* (Leeds, 1875), p. 77.

[25] 'It is above all else a business city, run by businessmen on business principles'. Julian Ralph, 'The-Best Governed City in the World', *Harper's Monthly Magazine*, June 1890. Cf. a laudatory article, 'The Municipal Government of Berlin', *Local Government Jl.*, XXVI (20 November 1897), which refers to the American theory but argues for a heterogeneous council of men of ability.

'A school supposes teachers as well as scholars; "the utility of the instruction greatly depends on its bringing inferior minds into contact with superior".'

He was consequently much preoccupied with inducing what in another passage he called 'persons of a high class either socially or intellectually' to take a share in local administration. He advocated plural votes for those of large property, as already existed for Boards of Guardians and Local Boards of Health, but pinned his hope chiefly on concentrating the entire local business of the town in one authority, so as to attract 'the best minds of the locality' by the scope that it would give them,

> 'who are thus brought into perpetual contact, of the most useful kind, with minds of a lower grade, receiving from them that local or professional knowledge they have to give, and in return inspiring them with a portion of their own more enlarged ideas, and higher more enlightened purposes.'[26]

It might be thought that such an emphasis on the social and intellectual elite was in a straight line from the debate of 1835 and the 1859 select committee. So it was, but with a difference. What had once been a claim to exclusive possession had now become a remedial emphasis, an emphasis on the crucial element that was liable to be missing.

The emphasis on leavening local government bodies by persons of a high class socially or intellectually survived among Mill's disciples. It can be found in G. C. Brodrick's essay 'Local Government in England' published under the auspices of the Cobden Club in 1875 and republished in a new edition in 1882. The author was a Liberal historian, fellow and later warden of Merton College, Oxford, an acknowledged expert in his day.

Surveying the general characteristics of local government as it then existed, he concluded that

> 'the Local Government of towns is almost entirely in the hands of shopkeepers and struggling professional men, engaged in busy callings and with few hours to spare for public business.'

and added in explanation that 'no class has less concern for self-government in towns than the commercial aristocracy.'[27] This should not be accepted as a true statement in all cases. It certainly applied neither to

[26] J. S. Mill, *Representative Government* (1861), chapter 15.
[27] George C. Brodrick, 'Local Government in England', in *Local Government and Taxation in the United Kingdom. A Series of Essays*, ed. J. W. Probyn (1875), pp. 70–2.

Nottingham nor to Leicester.[28] But we are here not concerned with the accuracy of Brodrick's statements, merely with what they reveal about his values. The essay, written in the assured tone of the expert, contains not a single scrap of evidence. There is no indication that Brodrick ever looked for any or that he doubted that these things were self-evident and known to informed observers of the social scene.

He did not approve of the situation that he described and wished to change it. Like John Stuart Mill he wanted to concentrate all the powers of local government into a single body and for the same reason. 'Men of education, independence and leisure' would be more willing to serve on a body of that kind, especially if it included the management of schools.[29] 'It is not certain that men of this class are to be found at all in every borough and rural district', he added, but he brushed such doubts aside and concentrated on mobilising the talent that was available. In the provincial manufacturing towns this meant looking to the 'richest capitalists, the commercial aristocracy'. He valued them, not primarily because they were businessmen, but because they were aristocrats of a kind, and discussed their role together with that of the landed aristocracy as parallel cases. It was on account of their 'education, independence and leisure', that he regarded them as 'eligible candidates' and 'good materials for the Town Council'.[30]

There can be no doubt where Brodrick put the emphasis or what he meant when he used such phrases. Yet in the last analysis, as with John Stuart Mill, there is a distinction to be made between the theory and the emphasis. Others too had a rightful place on the Council. They might need to be restrained from 'short-sighted extravagance alternating with short-sighted parsimony' and other more venal follies[31] but they had their role to play:

> 'By accustoming representatives of all classes to work together daily for public but non-political objects, they would strike at the root of those class prejudices, mainly springing from mutual ignorance, which are not corrected, if they are not rather aggravated, by

[28] R. A. Church, *Economic and Social Change in a Midland Town. Victorian Nottingham 1815–1900* (1966), pp. 370–3; evidence on Leicester assembled in E. P. Hennock,' Finance and Politics', pp. 218–19.

[29] Brodrick, 'Local Government', p. 80. Mill's proposals for all-purpose authorities had been recommended by the Royal Sanitary Commission in 1871, and became the orthodox view until at least 1929.

[30] Brodrick, 'Local Government', pp. 70–1.

[31] Brodrick, 'Local Government', p. 64.

the rare and boisterous association of rich and poor voters at Parliamentary elections.'[32]

The same distinction between the full theory of local government representation and the practical emphasis applies to points of view contemporary to those of Mill and Brodrick but less academic and intellectualised than theirs, in particular that formulated in Birmingham in the 1860s and 1870s and studied in detail in part II of this book.

For the second edition of the Cobden Club Essays on *Local Government and Taxation* the editor had approached Joseph Chamberlain for an authoritative contribution, and had been passed on to J. T. Bunce, editor of the *Birmingham Daily Post*, and intimate collaborator in the Birmingham municipal reform movement.[33] His essay on 'Municipal Boroughs and Urban Districts' is an expression of the view of the Birmingham school in its maturity:

> 'The true municipality should completely grasp the life of the community, and in doing so should aim at expressing the communal idea—one for all, all for one. The work of the town, according to its means, should be done with such completeness as to leave no source of danger or evil unchecked, no material defect uncured, no intellectual want uncared for. It should be done with such regularity of method as to ensure the steady and easy working of the complex machine; with such stateliness of manner as to dignify the corporate life; with such a spirit of earnestness, and thoroughness and self-sacrifice, as to raise the general tone and standard of public service to the highest level; and with such unity of feeling as to bind all classes together with a real sense of belonging to a community worthy of being served, and honoured, and obeyed.'

The ideal council should be recruited from all men of character and ability,

> 'not restricted to one class, for the artisan should find his place beside the manufacturer, the shop-keeper beside the professional man, the representatives of culture and those blessed with the enjoyment of wealth and leisure beside the representatives of commercial activity and industrial labour.'

In practice how was this to be achieved?

> 'Such community in this matter needs the help of its best men . . . qualified by education and capacity. . . . They are usually found

[32] Brodrick, 'Local Government', p. 95.
[33] Joseph Chamberlain to J. Thackray Bunce, 26 July 1881, Chlain. MSS. JC 5/8/58.

in sufficient number to give tone to the local governments, and they can be induced to give their services, if the right means are employed.'[34]

It was thirteen years since Bunce's paper had welcomed the candidature of Joseph Chamberlain as

'a large ratepayer, a man of thorough business habits, enlarged views and marked ability, belonging indeed to precisely the class of burgesses most desirable to the Council.'

The right means of attracting such men, thought Bunce, was to give them something important to do. Like many local government reformers at the time he wanted to increase the scope of the Town Council by making it the sole local governing body. The view that to attract good men to the council was to increase the scope of its work was indeed a central belief of the Birmingham school.

By 1890 the emphasis which had originated in Birmingham had become something like orthodoxy. We know how it dominated the minds of both political parties in Leeds during the New Era and it is remarkable for how long it has managed to survive. It found classical expression in 1921 in the inaugural address of a famous lord mayor of Manchester, Ernest Simon, later Lord Simon of Wythenshaw and a distinguished exemplar of the creed:

'Every Athenian citizen profoundly believed in and loved his city, and was prepared to work and, if necessary, die for her. To serve the city was the object of every man, and those who served her best were held in the highest honour, while those who did no public work were regarded with contempt. That was the secret of the greatness of Athens.

The contrast with Manchester is depressing. A few days ago I was talking about the work of the City Council to a most successful Manchester businessman who has a large house in Cheshire and hunts three days a week. He said, 'Of course it takes all sorts to make a world, but it is curious that there are people who seem to like the kind of work you do on the City Council. I believe it must be due to the ambition of their wives!'

'Can we do anything to counteract this attitude?', he asked. One remedy might be an extension of the city boundary:

[34] J. T. Bunce, 'Municipal Boroughs and Urban Districts', in *Local Government and Taxation in the United Kingdom. A Series of Essays*, ed. J. W. Probyn, 2nd ed. (1882), pp. 302, 304–5.

'Our most successful citizens quite naturally go out to live in beautiful surroundings in Cheshire, and so, as regards their homes, are lost to the city. I suggest that we ought to follow the example of Birmingham which recently extended its area. We should in this way keep our best businessmen, who have many of the qualities most needed in public life, as full citizens.'[35]

It will be obvious to the reader of the contemporary press that the view that the ideal town council contains a considerable proportion of the leading businessmen of the town is still alive in the England of the mid-twentieth century. So is the anxiety over the obvious gap between this ideal and the reality.

In 1951 James Beattie, Mayor of Wolverhampton, said

'He was disappointed at the failure of representatives from big industrial businesses in the town to enter the Council. Such men with special experience of large-scale management and administration he regarded as invaluable to the Council.'[36]

Behind much talk about the declining calibre of local councillors since some unspecified point in the past lurks just such a definition of the term. When, for instance, Voice and Vision Ltd. produced a memorandum on *Public Relations for Local Government* for the Association of Municipal Corporations in 1960 they claimed that

'The majority of local government officers to whom we have spoken raise the point that the standard of those presenting themselves for council elections has declined over the past decade.'[37]

The memorandum saw this in terms of the absence from among the candidates of directors and senior executives of large and medium-sized companies. In a more sophisticated analysis published in 1962, L. J. Sharpe was careful to repudiate any such simple identification of calibre with occupational status:

'Such qualities as integrity, political nous, will power, judgment, local knowledge and so on—all would need to be taken into account in any realistic assessment of a councillor's calibre.'

[35] 'The Citizen and his City'. Speech by the Lord Mayor of Manchester, Alderman Ernest Simon, 9 November 1921 (Manchester, 1921), pp. 3–5.
[36] *Wolverhampton Express and Star*, 21 May 1951, quoted in G. W. Jones, *Borough Politics*, p. 151.
[37] Voice & Vision Ltd., *Public Relations for Local Government. Memorandum for the Association of Municipal Corporations* (1960) quoted in L. J. Sharpe, 'Elected Representatives in Local Government', *British Jl. of Sociology*, XIII (1962), 202.

But he added

> 'There are certain qualities which are clearly relevant to a coun-
> cillor's function and which are measurable. It may be reasonably
> argued . . . that a man who holds a position of executive responsi-
> bility in private life, or is used to making administrative decisions,
> or has had professional training, would on the whole be better
> equipped as a councillor than someone who wholly lacks this kind
> of experience, notwithstanding the fact that other less tangible
> qualities are important and that these are not the prerogative of any
> one occupation.' [38]

IV

What in the light of our investigation so far has been the status of
professional men? Were they considered fit and proper persons to
represent a ward?

There is until the most recent years no unambiguous answer to this
question. At the beginning of the period not all professional men were
respectable or substantial citizens, while some undoubtedly were. This
was indeed the distinction that mattered.

'In order to get a more respectable and higher class', suggested a
witness before the select committee of 1859 on the Small Tenements
Rating Act,

> 'I would require that the town councillors should be persons who
> were rated to a higher amount, so that the parish doctor, or the
> clerk to the Poor Law Guardians, could not get into the Town
> Council.'[39]

On the other hand there were many attorneys such as T. W. Tottie of
Leeds, who were undoubtedly men of station and substance and whose
fitness for the highest municipal office was never in doubt.

When the emphasis on station and on wealth began to change and be

[38] L. J. Sharpe, 'Elected Representatives', p. 204. G. W. Jones quotes an ex-councillor in
Wolverhampton who 'complained of "deadbeats" on the Council, council-house dwellers
who had never signed a four-figure cheque and who had never even possessed a cheque-book.
He was especially bitter about the appointment as Mayor of . . ., whom he castigated as an
old-age pensioner, often on the dole, whose last job had been to open and close the gates
of the gas works'. *Borough Politics*, p. 151.

[39] *Operation of the Small Tenements Rating Act 1850, Select Committee H.L. mins. of ev.*,
Q. 537; *P.P.*, 1859, Session 2 (56), vii, 269.

replaced by a demand for men capable of managing great undertakings, the same doubts persisted. For many they were a poor second-best to the businessmen. The comment quoted on pp. 317–18 makes the distinction with humour and complete assurance. By Brodrick's standard those generally serving on the councils, 'struggling professional men, engaged in busy callings and with few hours to spare for public business', also left much to be desired.[40]

The steep increase in the actual proportion of professional men on the Leeds City Council from the 1880s onwards was accompanied repeatedly by reservations:

> 'What a motley lot the Conservatives proposed to substitute. There were publicans, licensed victuallers, architects, a doctor, members of other professions, but among the lot there was not one who was a manufacturer or a large tradesman.'[41]

In 1899 a Conservative candidate was criticised for being not a businessman but a lawyer, and throughout the decade there were complaints that the business centre of Leeds was represented by accountants and lawyers but not a single businessman.[42]

Once again this is not just a Liberal party point of view. In 1906 the Conservative *Yorkshire Post* wrote enthusiastically of a Conservative candidate:

> 'It is often said that the City Council contains too much of the professional element. In Mr. Sheldon the electors have a businessman pure and simple, whose success in his own particular sphere is a guarantee that he would bring to the affairs of the city the same acumen that he has used in the affairs of his own concern.'[43]

This may seem a strange attitude to take. Were accountants and architects, lawyers and doctors not particularly well qualified by all the standards that applied to businessmen? In the twentieth century it has usually been assumed that this was so. Thus in 1960 *The Economist*, lamenting the alleged decline in the calibre of borough councils, lumped them both together and explained:

> 'The business and professional classes . . . are becoming increasingly disinterested in borough government. Working in one local

---

[40] See above, pp. 13, 15.
[41] Ald. Edwin Gaunt (Liberal), *L.M.*, 26 October 1892, p. 7.
[42] *Y.P.*, 31 October 1899, p. 7.
[43] *Y.P.*, 30 October, 1906, p. 10.

government unit and sleeping in another, they confine their citizenship to an occasional grumble about the rates.'[44]

In his discussion of the quality of elected representatives in local government, L. J. Sharpe makes the same juxtaposition of the manager and the professional man.

In very recent years a distinction has again occasionally been made, but this time to discriminate in favour of the professional man. The Enquiry undertaken for the Maud committee on *The Management of Local Government* reported that in the boroughs which were visited, both parties spoke of the lack of candidates from the professions, who, it was said, if they could be found, had exceptionally good chances of success. One witness, himself a councillor and a businessman, 'thought that big businessmen often had insufficient vision. He valued most highly as a qualification for a councillor a professional or university training.'[45]

V

When after 1880 manual workers increasingly claimed the right to be town councillors, the theory of local government as it had been expounded since the days of John Stuart Mill was well adapted to the new development. The view that a socially mixed council was a school for political wisdom made it easy to accept working men of 'ability and character', such as W. J. Davies of Birmingham or Owen Connellan of Leeds, particularly since as leading figures in the local Trades Council they possessed an undoubted constituency-appeal:

> 'It is not always that a working man candidate is able to enlist the enthusiastic support of his fellow men, and when he succeeds in such a marked degree as Mr. Toller, it is only reasonable to assume that he possesses qualities above the common. There is no reason why the Secretary of the gas workers should not do as useful work in the City Council as a lawyer or a pork butcher.'

So wrote the Unionist *Birmingham Daily Mail* on one such occasion, despite the fact that both the lawyer and the pork butcher had been Unionist candidates.[46]

[44] *The Economist*, CXCIV (30 January 1960), p. 413.

[45] Ministry of Housing and Local Government, *Committee on the Management of Local Government* (1967), volume V. Margaret Harrison and Alan Norton, *Local Government Administration in England and Wales, an Enquiry carried out for the Committee*, chapter 3, §§ 118, 90.

[46] *Birmingham Daily Mail*, 29 November 1897, partly quoted in Asa Briggs, *Victorian Cities* (1963), p. 238. For Davis and Connellan see above, pp. 54 and 272.

Such a welcome did, however, have its limits. True, J. S. Mill and his disciples had acknowledged the right of all sorts of groups to participate in municipal administration. But participation was one thing, domination was another. Just as they had never accepted the sort of policies and conduct that sprang from shopkeeper domination, so now many of those who were prepared for a working-class presence strongly repudiated the policy implications of working-class domination. This was of course due first and foremost to the big issues of principle on which the municipal politics of the period were polarised. Working-men councillors tended to demand more collective provision and give less scope to private enterprise, but this was a preference which they shared with other collectivists. In addition there were reservations about working men councillors *qua* working men, and it is these which I want to consider for the purposes of the present discussion.

The greatest innovation made by the early working-men councillors to municipal politics had almost nothing to do with collectivism: it was a Labour matter pure and simple. In many towns Labour representation meant at first largely the representation of municipal workmen by their trade union spokesmen. We have noticed that this was the case in Leeds, and Leeds was no isolated instance. In Wolverhampton the Labour party re-entered municipal elections in 1913 after a period in the doldrums and they did so as the champions of the corporation employees, on whose behalf they campaigned for a minimum wage of 25s. a week.[47] The examples could easily be multiplied. Efforts to organise municipal workmen on trade-union lines were in practice greatly helped by the use of political pressure through the electoral process. It was thereby possible to organise the unskilled in municipal employment, when similar organisations collapsed in other sectors of the economy.[48] It was also often possible to obtain concessions which private employers were not willing to grant. Labour representation was therefore of great importance to the trade union movement at a certain stage in its history, for local authorities could be used as pacemakers. Concessions obtained from them became precedents in dealing with employers elsewhere.

Strictly speaking such town councillors are most usefully thought of not as manual workers but as union organisers, who may or may not still have been employed as manual workers. In one sense the recruitment of men such as these was an innovation. Previously representative

[47] G. W. Jones, pp. 48–9.
[48] E. J. Hobsbawm, 'British Gas Workers 1873–1914', in *Labouring Men* (1964), p. 172 refers to this factor in passing.

government in towns had meant one of two things: the actual representation of the ratepayers, and the virtual representation of the inhabitants at large seen as consumers of the corporation's services. Municipal politics had moved within the field of tension created by these two interpretations. The representations of corporation employees was different from either, and by these terms of reference it was something smaller, an attempt at the assertion of sectional interests against the common good. In another sense, it could be argued it was not such an innovation after all. Sectional interests particularly affected by municipal policy had been found before on the council: trade unionist councillors were in this respect no different from councillors who were market traders, licensed victuallers or hackney-coach proprietors. Such men existed and had existed for a long time. There are even political theories which would justify their presence, and according to which they would indeed be 'fit and proper persons'. But that was not how local government was thought of in England at the turn of the century. By the standards of theories then accepted such groups were suspect. Their notion of representation seemed defective and potentially subversive of the idea of local government.

An example of a person sympathetic to a working-class presence on the council, who nevertheless expressed this view, was Joseph Chamberlain. In the same month that *The Birmingham Daily Mail* had welcomed the secretary of the gas workers to the council, Chamberlain addressed himself in public to the question 'whether it is possible that these institutions (of local government) may yet be worked to our harm?'

Like all who hoped much from local government, he was alarmed by the notorious corruption of many American cities, and anxious to ward off similar evils from British towns. He argued that the crucial difference between the two systems lay in the treatment of local government employees, both salaried officials and wage earners. After dealing with the former, he turned to the even more serious danger that he believed would follow from paying wage-earning corporation employees more than their market rate:

> 'There is an idea rising up in the minds of certain of the working classes of this country that a man who becomes . . . employed by a public corporation is to have a better pay than his fellow workmen, doing precisely the same work under a private individual. I protest against that doctrine . . . It is fatal to good government.'

The result would be

> 'to create a privileged class of workmen, to whom public office is
> in itself a distinct advantage and in that case there will be an
> inevitable temptation . . . to make this privileged post a reward
> for political services.'

Poor work and the multiplication of jobs for political reasons—in this
lay the whole secret of the failure of American local institutions. He
warned his hearers not to abandon 'the business-like and honourable
system upon which our public work is now conducted', and made a
special appeal to the working classes on the grounds that the work of
public bodies, which was carried out principally for their benefit, would
suffer.[49]

Chamberlain appealed to the working classes in their role as consumers
of the municipal services to abandon the furtherance of sectional interests. Others accepted such a situation as a new fact of political life.
Opponents of the extension of municipal trading and of a policy of direct
employment (as opposed to putting municipal work out on contract to
private firms) gained additional support by pointed to their possible
political consequences.[50]

This kind of Labour representation, so different from what we now
mean by the phrase, became less significant as the creation of national
negotiating machinery in the years after 1918 removed from the council
the responsibility of deciding the wages of its servants. In Wolverhampton there was a crisis in 1920 over the acceptance or rejection of an agreement negotiated by a Whitley council, but that proved to be the last
occasion—except for an isolated incident in 1941—on which Labour
councillors had to champion the corporation employees. Thereafter all
parties accepted the machinery of negotiation and a chapter in the
history of Labour representation was closed:

> 'From the 1920s, therefore, the trade unions did not have to deal
> directly with the Council to advance the claims of their members,
> so that they had less need of the assistance of Labour Councillors
> to support their objectives.'[51]

[49] Joseph Chamberlain, 'Speech on receiving the Freedom of the City of Glasgow,
8 November 1897', *Local Government Jl.*, XXVI (13 November 1897), 734.

[50] That was the moral which the editor of the *Local Government Journal* drew from
Chamberlain's speech. See also the Leicester Corporation gas manager in 1900: 'Undoubtedly further municipal employment was a dangerous thing. The men had votes and
their votes were sought after, and it became more and more difficult to manage them'.
Interview by F. H. Spencer; *Webb Loc. Gov. Col.*, volume 163.

[51] G. W. Jones, pp. 306–7.

Since the creation of Whitley Council was a national phenomenon the same must have been true of other towns.

In their demand for the maximum collective provision of services and generous financial treatment for corporation workmen, the characteristic politics of working-men councillors appeared to be in direct contrast to those associated with small-shopkeeper politics. Yet there was one respect in which the two were very similar, in their determination to achieve economy at the expense of the salaries of corporation officials. Towards the officials the characteristic policies of the first generation of working-men councillors was the exact reverse of that adopted towards the workmen.

In Wolverhampton between 1894 and 1929 scarcely a year passed in which the Labour representatives did not oppose increases in the salary of corporation officials. They argued, for instance in 1894 and 1898, that the need of the workmen was so much greater that all salary increases should be opposed until a minimum wage had been granted.[52] In Leeds before the First World War, Labour councillors regularly opposed salary increases and in Manchester the I.L.P. entered municipal politics in 1893 with a two-point programme, of which the reduction of the salaries of corporation officials was one.[53] In the 1920s the need to find a new town clerk led to conflict over the salary to be offered. Comparable cities were paying £3,000 per annum and the Manchester committee recommended £2,500 rising to £3,000 over the next three years. The Labour group opposed any salary over £1,500, and one of its members explained that if a labourer was worth £3 a week, no man on earth was worth over £30.[54] In Wolverhampton similar views were expressed in the 1920s, the maximum conceivable being £1,000 per annum.

Such policies had been characteristic of shopkeeper economy movements for many years, and then, as later, had been the consequence of electing men who had no experience of running large and complex undertakings. The demand that municipal policy should be in the hands of large businessmen had been ever since the middle of the nineteenth century strongly grounded in fears of this kind of economy.

The opposition to officials' salaries still characterised working men's attitudes on the councils after the particular preoccupation with the wage claims of corporation workmen had ceased. In Wolverhampton it was such a bitter issue that in 1936 all salary decisions were transferred

[52] G. W. Jones, p. 306.
[53] *L.M.*, 1.8.1907; *Y.P.*, 4.2.1909; *Y.E.N.*, 1.5.1912; *Manchester City News*, 16 September 1893.
[54] Ernest Simon, *A City Council From Within* (1926), p. 140.

to the general purpose committee so as to avoid vituperation in the open council.[55] But ultimately, as in the earlier case, the establishment of negotiating machinery on a national scale did much to remove these issues from the forefront of debate. In time the local Labour parties also came to accept the view that it was worth giving salary increases to able officials, and managed to impose this policy even on those of its members who retained the older attitude.

Thus by the end of the 1930s the attitude of manual workers towards professional salaries, which had once loomed so large, was no longer of significance to the conduct of local government. A second objection to working-class councillors had thereby become a matter of history.

Between the wars Labour party spokesmen far from turning their back on the customary criterion by which councillors had been judged, responded to criticism by claiming that Labour-controlled councils were more competent than any others. The view that businessmen possessed special ability which enabled them to achieve municipal efficiency with due regard to economy was strongly repudiated. Not only were Labour councillors more sensitive to the needs of the under-privileged; they were better administrators too. In 1934 a series of articles in the *Daily Herald* described the achievements of local authorities with Labour majorities. It naturally dwelt on their success in providing badly needed services, but also repeatedly pointed out that this had been accompanied by reduced rates, owing to the administrative and financial skill of the Labour members. 'Labour administration has meant many things to Sheffield and among them are solvency' was the punch-line of an article entitled 'Saving a Debt-Ridden City'. Similar instances of financial rectitude and skill were recorded for Barnsley, Rotherham, Wigan, Thornaby-on-Tees, Swansea and Lincoln.[56] The charges of administrative and financial incompetence which critics of Labour councillors were wont to make were with great gusto hurled back into their teeth. Herbert Morrison, in a foreword to the book made much the same point:

> 'From the varied ranks of Labour we have discovered a considerable number of administrators of real capacity. Sometimes they have been what are known as educated people; sometimes what are known as uneducated. I have found that one cannot generalize

[55] G. W. Jones, p. 307.
[56] H. R. S. Phillpott, *Where Labour Rules* (1934). There was a contributing factor not mentioned in the book. In 1933 the bank rate stood at 2 per cent. Between 1914 and 1930 it has hardly ever dropped below 4 per cent. This enabled all public authorities to reduce their annual debt charges.

about the respective administrative capacities of these two types.'[57]

VI

Since the 1830s there has been no shortage of opinion, as we have just seen. Although it was not uncommon to support such opinion with the help of selected instances, systematic evidence has been hard to come by. Hence the value of G. W. Jones's recent study of the Wolverhampton Borough Council, for he tried to assess the quality of all the members serving on the Council in a series of sample years stretching from 1888–9 to 1962–3.

The assessment was of course no more than the author's impression, but it was based on a careful consideration of available evidence. Councillors were placed into one of four classes. A was for those outstanding figures who made a mark on the Council as a whole, on many aspects of its work and not in just one committee. B was for those who made a significant contribution in more than one field on the Council, although more narrow in range than class A. C was for those who made some mark although usually only in one committee, while D was those who made little or no impact at all. Since the author was himself not quite happy about the consistency with which he had been able to distinguish between classes A and B, it may be safer to take the two together. Nor was he satisfied that he had been able to apply the same method to those who had entered the Council only a short time before.[58] We have in consequence omitted his figures for the year 1962–3.

The resultant figures are remarkably consistent over the period and provide little evidence for a decline in the calibre of councillors in this borough.

TABLE 25. *Wolverhampton 1888–1954: quality of specific councils**

Percentages

Type of councillor	1888-9	1903-4	1919-20	1929-30	1945-6	1953-4
A&B	39	37	31	31	26	30
C	17	23	31	32	30	33
D	44	40	38	37	44	37

* Taken from G. W. Jones, *Borough Politics*, p. 161.

[57] Phillpott, pp. v–vi.
[58] G. W. Jones, *Borough Politics*, p. 161.

Does Wolverhampton provide any evidence for the view that linked the calibre of councillors with their occupation? Dr. Jones's tables have been re-worked with the help of further information provided by him. The category 'Retired' has been as far as possible eliminated by re-allocating members to their former occupation. Secondly the category 'Drink' has been eliminated. Brewers have been added to the figures for manufacturers and a wine and spirit merchant has been added to that for shopkeepers.

TABLE 26. *Wolverhampton 1888–1954: quality of council members correlated with occupation**

Occupation	Absolute Figures				Percentages		
	A & B	C	D	Total	A & B	C	D
Manufacturer	35	22	26	83	42	27	31
Shopkeeper	12	27	31	70	17	39	44
Publican	0	4	9	13	0	31	69
Professional	16	12	12	40	40	30	30
Administrative (R.)	8	4	5	17	47	24	29
Administrative (N.R.)	6	8	7	21	29	38	33
Manual Worker	18	10	25	53	34	19	47
Woman	4	2	5	11	36	18	45
Occupation before retirement unknown*	3	0	1	4	75	0	25
Total	102	89	121	312			

* Re-worked from G. W. Jones, *Borough Politics*, tables XXI, XXII. I am most grateful to Dr. Jones for providing the additional information. Administrative occupations are divided according to the responsibility they carry into managerial and supervisory (R) and clerical (N.R.). (See Jones, p. 113). The last group, which is residual, also includes a retired farmer under A & B. N.B. It is a peculiarity of this table that individuals are counted each time they appear in one of the six year-samples. Long-serving members appear therefore two or three times in the columns of absolute figures and affect the percentages accordingly. Thus the six trade union officials mentioned on p. 334 appear eleven times in the table.

There are two conclusions that one can draw from this table. A councillor's occupation is obviously no guarantee that he will make or fail to make a significant contribution to the work of the Council. All groups have provided members who were of no consequence. Dr. Jones himself came to the conclusion that there have been so many exceptions to any assertions correlating occupation with calibre that occupation is useless as a basis for generalisation.[59]

[59] G. W. Jones, *Borough Politics*, p. 153.

The fact remains that some occupations have provided more of the valuable members than others. Over the total number of Councils one-third of the members fell into classes A and B. This gives us a norm for each occupational group and therefore some measure of the degree to which each has diverged from it. Although there was no group that provided more members in A and B than in C and D, administrators (R), manufacturers and the professions were well above the norm, while publicans and shopkeepers were very much below.

These figures would throw more light on the theoretical discussion were it possible to make any distinction between large and small manu-facturers. Unfortunately Dr. Jones provides no systematic information on this point. He does, however, state in the text that in the 1930s the great ironmasters and metalware manufacturers, employing a large labour force, who had formed the majority of the industrialists so far, no longer joined the Council. They gave way to lesser men in charge of smaller enterprises.[60] If on the strength of this, we concentrate on the four councils between 1888 and 1930, the figures for manufacturers (still including the brewers) are as follows:

	A & B	C	D	Total
Nos.	31	13	32	66
Per cent	47	20	33	100

Manual workers in table 26 also include six salaried trade union officials. Taken together they stand at about the norm for all groups. But taken separately the percentages diverge very sharply.

	A & B	C	D	Total
T. U. officials	91	0	9	100
Manual workers	19	27	57	100

Dr. Jones was greatly impressed by the skills which the trade union officials brought to the Council. Their recruitment clearly made a major impact on it. It is when skills are joined to convictions that obstacles are moved.

[60] G. W. Jones, *Borough Politics*, p. 109.

3
The Present State of the Question

I

The language which has been quoted for the 1930s still presupposed that administrative and financial skills loomed large in the qualities demanded from the ideal councillors. This was to ignore what has been one of the most striking features of local government in the twentieth century, the constantly increasing importance of the official. We have already referred in the introduction to the extent to which in the past elected members had performed duties which have since then fallen to officials. Together with the parallel growth in the supervisory and policy-making role of central government departments, this development has had far-reaching consequences for the role of the elected members in local government. It therefore also has implications for the question, what characteristics councillors ought ideally to possess, since such a concept can have meaning only in relation to the role that councillors are expected to perform.

The increasing importance of the officials has played havoc with any clear-cut notions, such as had existed in the past, and has left the whole subject enveloped in a mist of ambiguity. It proved to be one of the key problems which between 1964 and 1967 confronted the Maud committee, appointed 'to consider in the light of modern conditions how local government might best continue to attract and retain people (both elected representatives and principal officers) of the calibre necessary to ensure its maximum effectiveness'.[1]

This committee and the subsequent Royal Commission on Local Government under the same chairman, by mounting a great inquest into the nature of English local government, have provided the evidence for a systematic discussion of the present state of the question.

[1] Ministry of Housing and Local Government, *Committee on the Management of Local Government* (1967), volume I. *Report of the Committee.*

335

The Maud committee found that there was no agreement on the role that councillors ought to play in local government *vis à vis* the officials. At one extreme were those who saw them as a board of directors and policy makers, at the other those who thought of them as watchdogs to ensure that the officers did not go astray or spend public money extravagantly. The idea that they should act largely as a consumer council was deplored by one witness, but explicitly asserted by the authors of a survey report prepared for the committee. Numerous intermediate positions ranged themselves along this spectrum.[2]

To make matters more difficult none of the views put forward were logically altogether consistent. The one most commonly held stated that policy was the province of the members and its implementation the responsibility of officers. Yet in his written evidence Mr. D. N. Chester rightly pointed out that this distinction could not be made in practice, and that the elected member had to concern himself with detail as well as principle, since a succession of detailed decisions may eventually constitute a policy. Unless these details were watched, it would be the officials, not councillors, who were the policy-makers.[3] Others thought that councillors, though lacking the professional expertise to make administrative decisions, could judge them by their results. But the authors of the *Enquiry* pointed out that councillors must commit their authorities to heavy expenditure before results can be achieved, and can hardly do so if they lack the skills to understand the implications of their actions.[4]

The theoretical confusion about the role of councillors is mirrored in the practice of many local authorities. The *Enquiry* quoted an officer of a fairly large authority who said,

> 'long experience had taught him that what most of his committee wanted was not to discuss the important issues but to have a "cosy" talk on matters of detail on which they could express themselves with more fluency . . . an illusion of contributing when they are really doing nothing.'

[2] *Ibid.*, volume V. Margaret Harrison and Alan Norton, *Local Government Administration in England and Wales, an Enquiry carried out for the Committee*, chapter 3, §§ 87–8; *ibid.*, volume II. Louis Moss and Stanley R. Parker, *The Local Government Councillor, an Enquiry carried out for the Committee by the Government Social Survey*, p. 2. These will usually be referred to in the text as the *Report*, the *Enquiry* and the *Survey*, and cited in the footnotes as *Maud Committee*, I, V and II respectively. It is important to note that they are by different authors and often represent different points of view.

[3] *Maud Committee*, I, chapter 3, § 109; V, chapter 9, § 16.

[4] *Maud Committee*, V, chapter 3, § 106.

Descriptions of a similar kind are too numerous to quote. The *Report* reviewing the evidence as a whole came to the conclusion that

> 'the virtues of committees are, at present, outweighed by the failures and inadequacies of the committee system. . . . The system wastes time, results in delays and causes frustration by involving committees in matters of administrative detail. The system does not encourage discrimination between major objectives and the means to attain them, and the chain of consequential decisions and action required. We see the growth of business adding to the agenda of committees and squeezing out major issues which need time for consideration with the result that members are misled into a belief that they are controlling and directing the authority, when often they are only deliberating on things which are unimportant and taking decisions on matters which do not merit their attention.'[5]

In the absence of a clearly identified end, attention shifted to the machinery of local government itself. From the councillors' point of view the characteristic machinery was the committee. Although officials complained about the ultimately aimless way in which committees worked, there was little dissatisfaction among councillors themselves and much evidence that they valued the time so spent.[6] But committee meetings were valued for reasons with which the officers had little sympathy, and which had more to do with feelings of sociability than with decision-making. One chief officer noticed that the council was 'a bit of a club for members. They actually seemed to like those interminable discussions.' Another said that 'meetings were more of club evenings than anything else and members were often visibly disappointed if they did not drag on long enough'.[7]

If this is how councillors feel about their role, they are likely to judge the requisite qualities accordingly. One can understand why, when asked what personal characteristics were necessary to make a good council member, they cited qualities of sociability—broadmindedness, patience, impartiality, a sense of humour, a pleasant personality, being

---

[5] *Maud Committee*, V, chapter 3, §§ 78, 82, 83, 95–9; I, chapter 3, § 128.

[6] *Maud Committee*, I, chapter 6, § 494, based on II, table 4.5; V, chapter 3, §§ 66, 78–83. See the same conclusions reached in J. Blondel and R. Hall, 'Conflict, Decision-Making and the Perception of Local Councillors', *Political Studies*, XV (1967), 322–50, especially p. 333.

[7] *Maud Committee*, V, chapter 3, § 80. The apparently useless quest for detailed information, which many officials noticed and deplored, had also more to do with the psychological satisfaction obtained by the councillor from being 'in the know' than with any operational concern, § 82.

a good mixer and speaker—much more often than any others. A mere 7 per cent of all councillors regarded education, specialised knowledge and qualifications or organising ability as the *main* requirement, while more than three-quarters thought them too trivial to mention at all.[8]

Here, it might be argued, is the contemporary answer to the question about the fit and proper person. But that would be going too fast. The majority opinion among elected members does not tally with what other people expected from them. We shall find that what emerged from the total investigation was not uniformity but diversity of opinion.

Before turning to other views it is important to do justice to this one. It cannot have been entirely new. Local government having been organised on the committee system since 1835 at least and conducted according to committee procedure, the qualities of sociability were certainly appreciated in council chambers in the past. But never had they loomed so large in the total picture. With the growing power of the officials and the consequent ambiguity about the councillor's role in policy making and administration, committee skills as such could acquire an importance in the definition of the good councillor greater than ever before.

Under these circumstances a different set of people emerge as the ideal councillors, while others appear less useful. Occupations which put a premium on rapid decision-making of an autocratic kind might easily unfit a man for committee work. A medium-sized firm whose structure was not so complicated as to require much co-ordination between different decision-makers, a wholesale merchant or perhaps a high street shop, belong to this class. G. W. Jones's study of Wolverhampton quotes a comment on a highly successful businessman, who had been a failure on the Borough Council and resigned, that 'he was a man who lived on his nerves, was used to taking rapid decisions and therefore did not fit into Council work'.[9] The really large modern business, operating through subsidiary divisions on a national or international scale, might differ rather less in its requirements. But the time-consuming nature of much committee-work as at present found in local government, and the inability to order priorities in the light of a commonly identified objective, would, as the Maud committee pointed out, be frustrating to people used to reaching decisions quickly and accustomed to thinking in terms of broad development rather than personalities.[10] Unable to get their way, they might well be markedly less successful on

---

[8] *Maud Committee*, II, pp. 75–6, table 2.27.
[9] G. W. Jones, *Borough Politics*, p. 154, footnote.
[10] *Maud Committee*, I, chapter 3, § 129; chapter 6, § 496. See also V, chapter 3, § 84 for the same opinion.

the council than in their other occupations, nor remain councillors for very long.

On the other hand, local government authorities are not the only institutions organised on the committee system. It is a common feature of bodies which place a premium on consent, and this includes a whole range of voluntary associations. Such bodies have often been valued exactly because they provided an education in democracy of a kind that most people did not obtain from their work. The relevance of this to trade unions with their representative organisation at branch, district and area level should be obvious. Both here and in the democratic organisation of the Labour party at ward, borough and constituency level, Labour candidates, whatever their actual occupation, frequently obtain the training to fit them as councillors. Studies of the selection procedures in recent times for the Manchester City Council, the borough councils of Wolverhampton, Newcastle-under-Lyme and Banbury all make the point that Labour candidates had been drawn from people closely associated with the running of the local party or other institutions of the democratic Labour movement.[11] G. W. Jones has argued that on account of this training Labour activists, whatever their formal occupation, are likely to make successful councillors. He quotes the testimony of a Wolverhampton Conservative to the ability of the trade union officials, whom he regarded as making excellent chairmen. Their experience in handling trade union committees, in drafting and presenting reports, and the training given them by their unions, he considered, fitted them well for council work.[12] The enquiry for the Maud committee also found witnesses who defined a good councillor in terms of his committee skills.[13]

There is something in this argument. All representative government places a high value on consent, and this is what a committee is well adapted to produce. Under contemporary conditions the qualities demanded from councillors are more than ever those of an intermediary able to conciliate different points of view. It can be argued that this requirement places a premium on experience obtained from occupations in which the individual acts in some sense as a broker. A number of

---

[11] J. M. Bochel, 'The Recruitment of Local Councillors: A Case Study', *Political Studies*, XIV (1966), 360–64; Frank Bealey, J. Blondel and W. P. McCann, *Constituency Politics. A Study of Newcastle-under-Lyme* (1965), chapter 17; Margaret Stacey, *Tradition and Change. A Study of Banbury* (Oxford, 1960), chapter 3; G. W. Jones, *Borough Politics*, pp. 97–8, 129–30.
[12] G. W. Jones, *Borough Politics*, pp. 152, 157.
[13] *Maud Committee*, V, chapter 3, §§ 93, 97.

recent studies, mainly American, have drawn attention to the way in which such 'brokerage' occupations facilitate participation in politics.[14]

The views of G. W. Jones, the majority view among serving councillors, these were but two among the great diversity of views collected for the Maud committee. It is the diversity that is so striking. The confusion about the role that councillors should play is mirrored in the confusion about the standards by which their calibre should be assessed. Whereas in 1835 it was not hard to find the common criteria to which both sides in the political debate appealed, we are faced in 1967 with a much wider scatter of opinion. But it is not a random scatter. There is a pattern to be discerned.

We know already from other sources that the point of view exemplified by Lord Simon of Wythenshaw is still alive. The *Enquiry* found it particularly among older people and in areas in which there had been rather more continuity in the traditions of public service than was now usual.[15]

More common was the value placed on intellectual qualities. We have already met the witness who thought little of big businessmen, and 'valued most highly as a qualification for a councillor a professional or university training which enabled a man to seize on the essentials of any problem'. Others wanted 'clear purposeful discussion with a good level of understanding', the ability 'to think clearly and explain why he was voting in a particular way', the ability to read a report, etc. A witness who rejected professional or occupational qualifications in favour of a 'wider general education' belonged essentially to the same school of thought. Many of them ascribed importance to higher education in fostering these qualities; others were more doubtful. Teachers, with a formal education but without much experience of affairs, could be niggly and lacking in a sense of proportion, while insight and judgment or a grasp of the issues involved could sometimes be found in a factory worker and others with a restricted formal education.[16] This is just the kind of disagreement one would expect in the 1960s, when the educational system is meant to select people with high intellectual qualities and train them in these skills, but has obviously not succeeded over the relevant period of the last thirty years or so.

[14] Robert E. Lane, *Political Life* (Glencoe, 1961), pp. 331–4; Lester W. Milbraith, *Political Participation* (Chicago, 1965), pp. 124–5; H. Jacob, 'Initial Recruitment of Elected Officials in the U.S.—a Model', *Jl. of Politics*, XXIV (1962), 709.
[15] *Maud Committee*, V, chapter 3, §§ 100, 104.
[16] *Maud Committee*, V, chapter 3, §§ 90, 95–98, 102.

Over against this demand for general intellectual qualities stood another, equally insistent, for some kind of specialist knowledge. Without it, it was widely held, councillors were incapable of making informed decisions in the many fields for which they were responsible, or even of appraising the practical consequences of an officer's suggestions. The list of such requirements was long: finance, technology, educational policy, administrative science, sociology and computer techniques were all specifically mentioned, and no doubt others could have been added.[17] Much of this evidence came from the officials, many of whom, it seems, would like councillors with whom they can share a common language. 'It is just like talking to another officer' said one of them, describing his best committee member. 'He can produce arguments which will make an officer change his mind', said another in praise of a retired colonial civil servant. The authors of the *Enquiry* and the Maud committee itself were very sympathetic to this point of view.[18]

It is not difficult to recognise in this demand for relevant specialist knowledge the modern extension of that preference for business experience and the business mind, which was so frequent in the nineteenth century and early twentieth century, and can still be found. The assumptions are the same; it is the duties performed by the modern local authority that have become more varied. As in the days of J. S. Mill and Joseph Chamberlain, of Brodrick and of Simon, a large body of opinion still believes that 'fit and proper persons' are men of intellectual quality or valuable occupational skills or both.

II

This whole tradition stands now no longer unchallenged. A completely different criterion has been advanced, that of inclusiveness. It was clearly expressed by Louis Moss and Stanley Parker, the authors of the *Survey*.

> 'The direct responsibility of local government for services designed to meet the needs of many sections of the population can only be effectively discharged if people with first-hand knowledge of all sections of the community are represented on councils.'

They based their view on the difference, as they saw it, between the functions of Parliament and those of local authorities.

[17] *Maud Committee*, V, chapter 3, §§ 92, 105, 106.
[18] *Maud Committee*, V, chapter 3, § 92; I, chapter 6, § 511(b).

'Local government by definition necessarily requires a closer connection between local representatives and the management of the services of a relatively small area; it is concerned only with local issues and not with such wide issues of state as defence or foreign affairs. The activities of local councils are specified by statute, and increasingly the work of local councils is concerned with improving the quality of living conditions and ameliorating the personal difficulties of individuals in their areas. For the writers it seems that these special features of local government, in contrast to central government, require personal experience of all the varied circumstances and opinions of the local electorate which are unlikely to be available if small sections of the population play a disproportionate role in local government.'[19]

Even G. W. Jones, who had devoted a whole chapter of his book to discussing the calibre of Wolverhampton borough councillors in terms of the skill with which they performed their duties, allocating each to a category of excellence, felt the need to provide a corrective to what might otherwise seem too 'élitist' an approach.

'A representative body, if it is to be truly representative, should not contain just the talented or the competent. It should represent everyone, even the politically uninterested and apathetic, who form the majority of the population. A Council consisting overwhelmingly of individuals in categories A and B would not be representative.'[20]

The same ideas are found whenever concern is expressed at the under-representation or over-representation on the council of socio-economic groups, age-groups or one of the two sexes by comparison with the population at large.[21]

---

[19] *Maud Committee*, II, pp. 2, 7.

[20] G. W. Jones, *Borough Politics*, p. 162. Categories A and B were the highest in his fourfold division of councillors according to the quality of their contribution. See above, p. 332.

[21] E.g. Brenda M. Powell, 'A Study of the Change in Social Origins, Political Affiliations and Length of Service of Members of the Leeds City Council, 1888–1953' (unpublished M.A. thesis, Department of Social Studies, University of Leeds, 1958), especially chapter 11. This is the earliest example known to me of what has since become a common preoccupation of writers on local government. Both the new preoccupation and the old are often found side by side in recent discussions, e.g. in 'Representation and Community: An Appraisal of Three Surveys', *Royal Commission on Local Government in England 1966–1969*, volume III, appendix 7. 'If it is found that some people are prepared to give voluntary service and leadership to the community, but not in local government, then not only are they under-represented on the councils, but also potential talent and service are lost.' (§ 8). See also § 2. Unfortunately the study here quoted has no satisfactory way of answering the interesting question that it raises.

These writers are operating with a theory of representation which differs profoundly from that customary in earlier discussions of representative government. This is surely the consequence of changes that have taken place in the scope and administration of local government. For the authors of the *Survey* it was its responsibility for the quality of the local environment and for the personal welfare services that especially characterised modern local government. In making general regulations for the common good the preferences of individuals must inevitably by sacrificed. But it is of the essence of the personal welfare services and similar provisions that the diverse needs of individuals and families should be met. It is always true that only he who wears the shoe knows where it pinches, but in matters such as these it is more than ever important that administrators be confronted with the views of those for whose benefit they are supposed to act. This is to put the case at its strongest. In addition, over a wide range of its planning duties the council makes regulations aimed at the supposed needs of particular areas or groups of people.

In matters such as these the councillor is expected to speak on behalf of the community, to be aware of opinion likely to affect policy, whether such opinion is organised or not:

> 'Insofar as a council may be expected to serve as a sounding board for the community for proposed policies, concern with the degree to which it is representative is surely justified . . . A situation can . . . arise where important groups in the community are alienated from the local authority because they lack a voice or a spokesman on the council. Where this happens it falls upon the officers alone to interpret their interests to the council—a position fraught with difficulties.'[22]

Expressed in these more limited and negative terms this is not far from the standard argument for democratic representative government. The question is, to what extent the ability of councillors to formulate policy, to direct and control the affairs of the authority, should be sacrificed to their role as representatives. Now that central government departments have assumed many of the policy-making and supervisory functions, while powerful officials carry out much of the directing and controlling (and policy-making as well), the answer to this question can be very different from what was accepted in the past. It has become possible to

[22] *Maud Committee*, V, chapter 3, § 18.

regard a town council as being like a consumer council, not a board of directors.

There are, however, two drawbacks to the view that the Council should be composed of a faithful cross-section of the consumers of local government services. One is a matter of logic, the other of policy. It is strictly speaking impossible to reproduce in any council 'the personal experience of all the varied circumstances and opinions of the local electorate'. Such language is an argument for government by town meeting, if it is anything. The usual way of talking about representativeness, as if it were to be achieved by reproducing the proportions of the Registrar-General's social classes or socio-economic groups, or by having the same proportion of women on the council as in the electorate obviously does not meet the argument on which, for instance, Moss and Parker base their case. What about epileptic women with illegitimate children, or widowed old-age pensioners driving an invalid's carriage?

Secondly the theory presupposes a willingness to acquiesce in the trends which have increasingly removed the powers of direction from the hands of elected members of local authorities, and possibly even to speed them up. As we shall see, those who reject the theory largely do so because they want to reverse these trends. But once they are accepted and it is recognised that local councils operate now largely within a nation-wide power system, the older priorities can be pushed into the background and all sorts of new perspectives are possible. More recent than the Maud committee is a study of the problem which actually welcomed the reluctance of the social and economic elite of Bristol to serve on the City Council and saw local councils as valuable correctives to the position of dominance occupied elsewhere in British society by the wealthy and the educated:

> 'Without their local political participation, the role of the working class in our common society would be greatly the poorer, reduced to little more than to be followers, the led, in every sphere political as well as economic and social, wherever influence is exercised. The economic and political notables have so much, must they be given more? . . . A society in which power and position are divided in some pluralist way is more likely to survive, and even be worthier of survival, than a social system in which position and power are monopolised.'[23]

[23] Roger V. Clements, *Local Notables and the City Council* (1969), p. 199.

III

This last quotation already takes us beyond the range of opinion available to the Maud committee, although it fits into the pattern that we have discovered. The evidence reveals a fundamental split between a recent theory which values inclusiveness and a traditional one which values skills. Within the traditional theory itself we find a scatter of views, polarised between an insistence on specialist occupational skills and intellectual ability in general. Unfortunately it is unlikely that the standards demanded in order to fit the older theory to the exacting requirements of modern conditions would in practice be found among many councillors. The newer theory escaped this difficulty by demanding a merely representative role from councillors, but did so at the cost of hastening rather than opposing recent trends in favour of both central control and the professionalisation of local government.

The Maud committee's own recommendations were an attempt to obtain the best of both worlds without the drawbacks of either. Their principal contribution was to make a distinction between the role of a small management board of five to nine members and that of the committees of the council. The management board was to formulate the principal objectives and the means to obtain them, it was to direct and control all the work of the corporation. The committees were to be deliberative and representative bodies only.[24] Having concentrated the most exacting functions in a body of not more than nine members, they felt no need to water down the qualities required. These they defined as *both* 'the capacity to understand increasingly complex technical, economic and sociological problems', *and* 'the ability to innovate, to manage and direct; the personality to lead and guide public opinion and other members; and a capacity to accept responsibility for the policies of the authority.'[25]

One must be impressed by the inclusiveness of that list, and also by the relevance of the qualities demanded. It may look at first as if the committee in identifying the general skills required had chosen to ignore some of the intellectual abilities so strongly insisted on by many witnesses. But the difference may be more one of language than of substance, for in practice the role as they defined it obviously required brains as well as personality. There is some ambiguity here, as might be expected from such a document at such a date. The committee

[24] *Maud Committee*, I, chapter 3, §§ 158–67.
[25] *Maud Committee*, I, chapter 6, § 511.

protested their belief that 'these qualities are not dependent on education or social background but can be discovered in all levels of society.'[26]

The concentration of responsibility in the small management board left most councillors with a less exacting role:

> 'The functions of the generality of members on council are to deliberate, and to contribute ideas in accordance with their individual abilities, to criticise, to question and to represent the interests, grievances and views of the electorate.'

> 'They have also the power to vote on those major items which are referred to them and they have power to bring a matter to the council by question or by motion. It is our view that by being freed from the heavy burden of present committee business members will be able to spend more time on "constituency" work.'[27]

The emphasis was on the duties of the representative. But this did not mean that the committee accepted the new view of what is meant by the term:

> 'It is neither possible, nor in our opinion is it desirable, that councils should in some way be representative of all the varying interests, economic groups, income or education levels in the community.'

They reaffirmed the older belief that representation was a matter of political skill, not a function of social statistics. All councillors needed

> 'the capacity to understand sympathetically the problems and points of view of constituents and to convey them to the authority and, at the same time, to interpret and explain the authority's policies and actions to those whom they represent. These we believe are the qualities of the good representative.'[28]

The contribution of the Maud committee to the debate about the meaning of 'fit and proper persons' depended thus essentially on the distinction between the role of the management board and that of the committees. For a small minority they set standards of the same kind as in the past, but more exacting than ever. They rightly believed that nothing less will reassert for the elected members their traditional role under contemporary conditions. For the majority they accepted the

---

[26] *Maud Committee*, I, chapter 6, § 512.
[27] *Maud Committee*, I, chapter 3, § 212.
[28] *Maud Committee*, I, chapter 6, §§ 508, 511.

probable consequences of the electoral system as they found it, expecting them to possess, in addition to integrity, mainly political skills as representatives of the consumer.

Not everyone agrees that it is either possible or desirable to make the distinction on which this argument depends. Whereas the establishment of some kind of management board has been generally welcomed, there has been widespread objection to the status and functions assigned to the committees. Sir Andrew Wheatley's dissenting opinion, recorded in the *Report*, has in these respects found much support outside, including that of so distinguished an expert as D. N. Chester. The latter has accused the committee of greatly oversimplifying the distinction between policy-making and representative functions and in consequence of making committees and their chairmen completely ineffective.[29]

The implications of this for the calibre of the general body of councillors have filled the critics with dismay. Sir Andrew Wheatley expressed the belief that

'unless the members as a whole are given a worthwhile part to play, a function which must inevitably involve direct participation in formulation of policy, local government will not attract members of the quality that are needed.'[30]

Objections of this kind explain why up to 1969 not a single county borough had accepted this item in the Maud reforms. The Bath Council agreed with their town clerk when he said,

'The Management Board involves a concentration of power and decision making in a small proportion only of the Council . . . The Council may feel that this might lead to discontent, dissatisfaction, and a general feeling of frustration, and tend to discourage men and women of high calibre from submitting themselves to the electorate.'

Much the same objection was made at Bury.[31]

The Royal Commission on Local Government in England, under the same chairman and with some overlap of membership, drew the obvious conclusion and retreated from the dreadful clarity of the earlier statements. The establishment of a management board (now called a central

---

[29] D. N. Chester, 'Local Democracy and the Internal Organization of Local Authorities', *Public Administration*, XLVI (Autumn 1968), p. 297.

[30] *Maud Committee*, I, *Note of Dissent by Sir Andrew Wheatley*, section A, p. 155.

[31] Quoted in R. Greenwood, A. L. Norton and J. D. Stewart, 'Recent Changes in the Internal Organization of County Boroughs, part I, Committees', *Public Administration*, XLVII (Summer 1969), 153-4.

committee), they said, need not deprive the other committees of their policy-making function. They welcomed variety and experiment. The sharp differentiation of roles between the few and the many, and the equally sharp differentiation of skills that followed from it, was blurred. They still made distinction between some councillors and others, but this has become a matter of degree and not of kind. It relates to the 'varying degrees of involvement in committee work, not to supposed difference of ability'.

The Maud committee's point that there were different kinds of excellence was forgotten in the anxiety to evade criticism:

> 'We do not underrate the qualities likely to be required for *all* elected members of the new authorities. All the committees . . . will need competent and conscientious members.'[32]

This was not redefinition but retreat. The retreat is understandable in view of the opposition aroused by the original proposals.[34] These had had all the merits and all the dangers of simplicity.[35]

This study in the history of an ideal ends therefore as it began, with a great inquest into the nature of English local government. Each has provided a conspectus of the standards by which the suitability of councillors were judged. Each has illustrated the ground common to all, as well as the points of disagreement. It must be obvious how much more confusion there is about these standards, and how much greater the disagreement in 1967–9 than in 1835.

There is a further contrast to be made between these two enquiries. Little if any anxiety was expressed in 1835 over the recruitment of suitable personnel. Not so in 1967, when the anxiety on this point was so great as to lead to the very setting up of the Maud committee. It was the 1830s that were the exception in this respect, and the confidence that was then expressed belonged to an age that was about to pass. By the 1850s people had begun to ask how councillors of the right calibre could possibly be found. The criteria for councillors have changed since then, but that anxiety has not been set at rest.

[32] *Royal Commission on Local Government in England 1966–1969, volume I Report*, chapter XII, § 506. The whole passage discussed is §§ 490–96, 504–6.

[34] E.g. The Greater London Group, *Local Government in South-East England* (1968), *Royal Commission Local Government in England, Research Study*, No. 1.

[35] In this respect, as in many others, Mr. Derek Senior's *Memorandum of Dissent* from the *Report of the Royal Commission on Local Government in England* is bolder than the *Report* itself. It does not abandon the view that there are two kinds of excellence and that they are relevant to different functions of local government. He tries to use this distinction to support his argument in favour of two kinds of local authorities responsible for different kinds of services. See volume II, §§ 345–9. The passage is too short, however, to permit him to work out the implications of the distinction for the management of either type of authority.

Appendices

APPENDIX I: THE STRENGTH OF THE PROFESSIONS IN THE TOWN AND ON THE COUNCIL 1841-1912: BIRMINGHAM AND LEEDS

(a) *Birmingham: the professions 1841-1912: numbers in the town and on the Council*

	1841(a)	1852(b)	1861(c)	1871(d)	1882(e)	1892(f)	1901(g)	1912(h)
Accountants	25	28	51	80	102	160	225	262
Architects	22	36	65	65	87	121	161	190
Other surveyors	24	45	24	39	51	47	68	89
Attorneys/solicitors	127	152	171	192	234	301	359	365
Barristers	6	2	2	6	20	22	27	33
Physicians	13	15	20	17	32	50	98	} 382
Surgeons	109	131	128	138	159	179	210	}
Dentists	11	20	23	30	63	70	82	92
Veterinary surgeons	7	9	13	8	11	11	11	14
Consulting engineer	—	—	—	—	2	9	26	49
(i) Total practising in the town	344	438	497	575	761	970	1,267	1,476

								pre-1911 area	post-1911 area
(ii) Male population 20 yrs. + (¹)	47,361	61,276	75,884	87,165	100,064	121,899	141,585	146,106	232,664
(iii) (i) as a per cent of (ii)	0·726	0·715	0·655	0·660	0·761	0·796	0·895	1·01	0·634
(iv) Per cent of professions on Town Council	1·6	4·7	7·8	7·8	10·9	19·4	18·0	21·5	23·3
(v) Ratio (iv) : (iii)	2·2	6·6	11·9	11·8	14·3	24·4	20·1	21·3	36·8

Notes to table (a)

Sources

(a) *Pigot's National and Commercial Directory of Warwickshire, Leicestershire, Rutlandshire, Staffordshire and Worcestershire* (December 1841).
(b) *Slater's Directory of Birmingham and its Vicinities 1852-53* (Manchester, 1852).
(c) *Corporation Directory of Birmingham* (Cornish: Birmingham, 1861).
    Doubtful figures checked against *Kelly's Post Office Directory of Birmingham* (1860).
(d) *Kelly's Post Office Directory of Birmingham* (May 1871).
(e) *Kelly's Post Office Directory of Birmingham* (February 1882).
(f) *Kelly's Directory of Birmingham* (May 1892).
(g) *Kelly's Directory of Birmingham and Suburbs* (March 1901).
(h) *Kelly's Directory of Birmingham including the Suburbs and the Borough of Smethwick* (April 1912).
(i) Drawn from Census Reports for the years, 1841, 1851, 1861, 1871, 1881, 1891, 1901, 1911.

From 1871 the directories list all the partners in a firm of solicitors separately; for 1841-61 they do not. The number of cases where this makes for uncertainty is few and the following conventions have been followed:

A & Co counted as 2,
A & Son counted as 2,
A & Sons counted as 3,
A, B & C counted as 3.

1892 and 1901 'Physicians' includes all those listed as 'Physicians and Surgeons'.

N.B. Since it has not been possible to obtain the number of teachers from the directories, they have been omitted in preference to using the very differently based figures given in the occupational tables of the census reports. They are however, included in the enumeration of the Town Council (line iv) for 1892 and 1912.

(b) Leeds: the professions 1841–1912: numbers on the Council

	1841[a]	1851[b]	1861[c]	1872[d]	1881[e]	1891[f]	1901[g]	1912[h]
Accountants	17	19	22	54	70	59	91	116
Architects	14	21	23	} 91	67	71	96	87
Other surveyors	12	21	22		23	23	28	24
Attorneys/solicitors	89	94	96	106	132	146	187	207
Barristers	2	5	6	6	14	28	22	23
Physicians	13	11	12	? 53	12	} 142	96	} 245
Surgeons	67	78	72	79	98		118	
Dentists	5	14	15	31	36	49	32	39
Veterinary surgeons	7	4	4	10	9	11	11	12
(i) Total practising in the town	226	267	272	? 430	341	529	681	753
(ii) Male population 20 yrs. + (j)	38,020	45,246	54,336	67,451	79,279	95,577	117,880	126,412
(iii) (i) as a per cent of (ii)	0·594	0·590	0·501	? 0·637	0·430	0·553	0·578	0·596
(iv) Per cent of professions on Town Council	10·9	7·8	9·4	0	6·2	14·0	18·5	26·6
(v) Ratio (iv):(iii)	18·4	13·2	18·8	0	14·4	25·3	32·0	44·6

Notes to table (b)

Sources

(a) Pigot's National and Commercial Directory of Yorkshire (August 1841).
(b) Slade and Roebuck, Directory of the Borough and Neighbourhood of Leeds, (Leeds, June 1851).
(c) William White, Leeds Directory (1861).
(d) Thomas Porter, Topographical and Commercial Directory of Leeds and Neighbourhood (Provincial Directories Co., November 1872).
(e) Kelly's Directory of Leeds and Neighbourhood (1881).
(f) Slater's Directory of the West Riding of Yorkshire (Manchester 1891).
(g) Kelly's Directory of Leeds (1901).
(h) Kelly's Directory of Leeds (1912).
(j) Drawn from Census Reports for the years, 1841, 1851, 1861, 1871, 1881, 1891, 1901, 1911.

From 1881 the directories list all the partners in a firm of solicitors separately. The same applies to accountants from 1901, and to doctors for the year 1891. When this is not the case, the same conventions have been followed as for table (a).

APPENDIX II: THE STRENGTH OF CERTAIN INDUSTRIES IN THE TOWN AND ON THE COUNCIL 1841–1912 : LEEDS

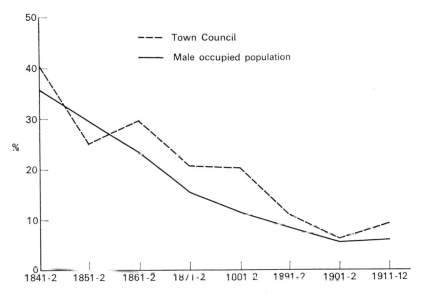

(a) *Textiles*

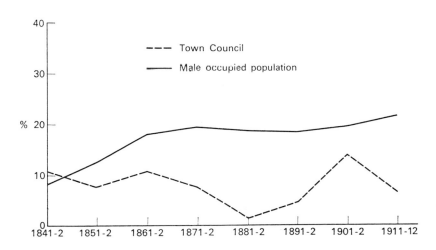

(b) *Non-precious metals*

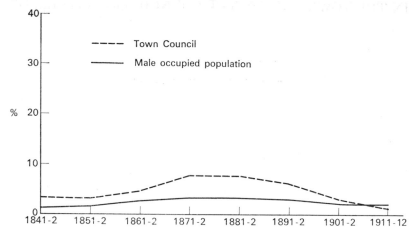

(c) *Leather*

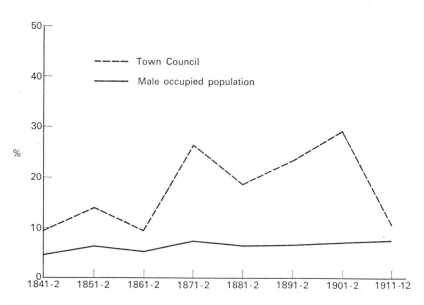

(d) *Food, drink and lodging*

354

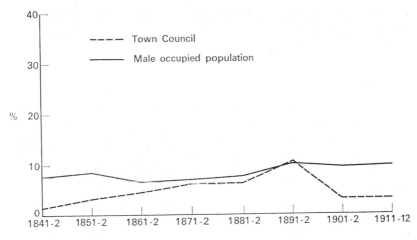

(c) *Dress*

The figures for the male occupied population are those compiled by W. G. Rimmer in 'Occupations in Leeds, 1841–1951', *Thoresby Society Publications*, L, 113 (1967). For 1871 figures are available only for the male occupied population over the age of twenty.

These graphs are especially useful for comparisons of the decennial rate of change in the Town Council and in the economy of Leeds. Since no census figures are available for the mid-decades, the figures relating to the composition of the Council in 1836, 1856, 1876 and 1896 have also been excluded.

Textiles

Except for the year 1851 the drop in the percentage of Council members engaged in the textile industry is only slightly faster than that in the share of the industry in the local economy. The 1890s, when the fall on the Council accelerated, is the period that saw the marked increase in the ratio of professional men, as indicated in appendix I.

Non-precious metals

This graph plots the growth in the importance of the local engineering industry and should be compared with the fall in the importance of the textile industry. But in this instance the changes on the Council do not run parallel with those in the town; between 1861 and 1881 they run counter to it. The marked rise in the following two decades, but particularly in the 1890s, should be seen in part as a compensation for the earlier

355

trend. The shape of the graph between 1861 and 1901 is consistent with the theory that entrepreneurs first build up their fortune and only subsequently take up public service.

Leather

Like engineering this is an industry rising to importance during the nineteenth century, although being capital-intensive its importance is not as clearly represented by the occupation figures. Until 1902 the changes on the Council follow and slightly exaggerate the changes in the occupation figures. It is remarkable that this graph does not indicate the time-lag which we have noticed in the case of engineering. If the behaviour of the engineers is to be regarded as normal, then a special explanation must be found for that of the leather manufacturers. They were of course particularly vulnerable to any regulations aimed at limiting the pollution of the river Aire and its tributaries.

Food, drink and lodgings

The changes in the Town Council appear to have no relation to the position of this important group of occupations in the local economy. As in the case of the professions the changes in the economy are minimal, while the strength on the Council fluctuates very considerably. Both groups of occupations furnished a higher proportion of the Council in most years than their numerical strength in the town would lead one to expect. Placed in a privileged position for obtaining office, this group also has unusual inducements for doing so, being affected by the Council's control of the markets as well as by Temperance politics. In consequence the fluctuations on the Council are to be explained mainly by considerations other than changes in the local economy.

N.B. For the purpose of this graph cornmerchants and cornmillers have been included, but they are only of marginal importance compared with food retailers, wholesalers operating in the markets, licensed victuallers, wine and spirit merchants and brewers.

Dress

The rise of the ready-made clothing industry, particularly in the 1880s, hardly shows up in this graph, which deliberately excludes women.

APPENDIX III: THE COMPARATIVE STRENGTH OF RELIGIOUS DENOMINATIONS IN THE EIGHT LARGEST BOROUGHS OUTSIDE THE METROPOLIS 1851*

		L'pool %	M'chester %	B'ham %	Leeds %	Sheffield %	Bristol %	Bradford %	N'castle %
Group A	C.E.	39·7	32·1	47·9	33·2	30·8	45·5	20·7	39·2
	R.C.	35·4	27·1	6·9	7·7	10·1	6·6	13·2	15·0
	Wesleyans	6·8	11·5	10·5	25·4	25·1	5·8	20·7	7·9
Total for Group A		**81·9**	**70·7**	**65·3**	**66·3**	**66·0**	**57·9**	**54·6**	**62·1**
Group B Orthodox	Other Meths.	5·6	7·8	5·0	16·1	13·6	11·4	16·8	10·7
	Congists.	4·1	9·7	9·4	8·8	10·8	16·3	13·0	4·4
	Baptists	2·4	3·6	10·9	5·5	6·0	8·6	12·3	5·9
	Presbs.	3·8	5·3	1·0	—	—	—	2·0	13·5
Total for Group B		**15·9**	**26·4**	**25·3**	**30·4**	**30·4**	**36·3**	**44·1**	**34·5**
Group C Heterodox	Unitarians	0·9	1·8	3·7	1·2	2·3	1·5	0·6	2·1
	Quakers	0·3	0·7	1·2	0·8	0·3	1·0	0·8	1·1
Total for Group C		**1·2**	**2·5**	**4·9**	**2·0**	**3·4**	**2·5**	**1·4**	**3·2**
Isolated Congregations		1·2	0·3	3·4	1·2	0·3	3·3	—	0·2
Total for all Protestant Dissent		**18·3**	**29·2**	**34·6**	**33·6**	**34·1**	**42·1**	**45·5**	**·9**

Protestant Dissent

* Compiled from figures in Horace Mann, ed., Religious Worship in England and Wales. Part of the Census of Great Britain for 1851. (1854).

Explanatory note

These figures are the result of a census of attendance at places of worship, undertaken in 1851, the only year in the nineteenth century for which suitable returns are available. They are expressed as percentages of the total number of attendants. The census provided figures for morning, afternoon and evening attendances, and I have computed these on a uniform system into a single figure to represent the approximate number of attendants. I decided not to follow the system adopted by Horace Mann, who added 55 per cent of the afternoon attendances and $33\frac{1}{3}$ per cent of the evening ones to the figure for the morning. That system gives a weight to the afternoon Sunday school, which would be misleading for my purpose. I have therefore taken only the morning and evening attendances, and added 55 per cent of the smaller figure to the total of the larger. Only in the case of the Quakers, with whom afternoon meetings took the place of evening service in all towns but Bristol, have the afternoon figures been used.

The resulting percentages should be treated with very great caution. Their reliability is impaired by three factors in addition to the arbitrary nature of the computation.

1. No figures of attendance which relate to one Sunday only can be considered a reliable guide to the number of adherents in any town
2. Between one and six places of worship per town failed to make any returns. I have not attempted to compensate for those omissions.
3. The figures were supplied by the ministers of the places of worship who were inevitably interested parties. Since the experiment of a religious census was never repeated under the auspices of the Registrar-General, it is difficult to test their accuracy. The figures collected by Andrew Mearns in *The Statistics of Attendance at Public Worship, as published in England, Wales and Scotland by the Local Press* (1882) relate to a period thirty years later, and are rendered useless for the present purpose by the omission of Manchester, Birmingham, and Leeds. A comparison in the case of the other five towns makes the 1851 figures not implausible, except that for Liverpool the number of Roman Catholics was probably too high. When all the necessary reservations have been made, however, the high proportion of Unitarians and Quakers in Birmingham and of Methodists in Leeds relative to the other towns, would still be a striking fact, and it is primarily to illustrate this that the table has been compiled.

APPENDIX IV: THE STRENGTH OF THE POLITICAL PARTIES ON THE LEEDS CITY COUNCIL 1889-1914

Date	Liberals			Conservatives			Labour			Indep.		
January	Clrs.	Ald.	Total	Clrs.	Ald.	Total	Clrs.	Ald.	Total			
1889	32	16	48	16	—	16	—	—	—			
1890	30	16	46	18	—	18	—	—	—			
1891	24	16	40	24	—	24	—	—	—			
1892	27	16	43	21	—	21	—	—	—			
1893	24	16	40	24	—	24	—	—	—			
1894	20	16	36	28	—	28	—	—	—			
1895	20	16	36	28	—	28	—	—	—			
1896	18	8	26	30	8	38	—	—	—			
1897	23	8	31	25	8	33	—	—	—			
1898	23	7	30	25	9	34	—	—	—			
1899	26	—	26	22	16	38	—	—	—			
1900	26	—	26	22	16	38	—	—	—			
1901	27	—	27	21	16	37	—	—	—			
1902	28	—	28	20	16	36	—	—	—			
1903	30	—	30	18	16	34		—	—			
1904	29	—	29	18	16	34	1	—	1			
1905	31	8	39	14	7	21	3	1	4			
1906	29	8	37	12	7	19	7	1	8			
1907	26	8	34	14	7	21	8	1	9			
1908	18	8	26	21	7	28	9	1	10			
1909	15	8	23	29	7	36	3	1*	4*	1	—	1
1910	15	8	23	27	7	34	5	1	6	1	—	1
1911	18	8	26	23	7	30	6	1	7	1	—	1
1912	20	8	28	19	7	26	9	1	10			
1913	15	8	23	26	8	34	10	1	11			
1914	13	6	19	24	9	33	14	2	16			

* Alderman Buckle was repudiated by the Labour Party in July 1908 but not replaced until his term of office expired in November 1910.

Years printed in **bold** type indicate a change in the party control of the Council as a result of the elections in the *previous November*.

359

APPENDIX V: TURNOVER OF MEMBERS OF THE LEEDS TOWN COUNCIL

(a) *Those with* 10 *years' service or multiples of ten as a percentage of the possible total.*

Council of	10 years	20 years	30 years
1852	14	—	—
1862	19	8	—
1872	23	9	3
1882	22	**13**	**5**
1892	**39**	3	3
1902	26	5	—
1912	23	3	—

(b) *Those with* 15 *years' service as a percentage of the possible total.*

Council of	15 years
1852	6
1856	14
1872	13
1876	16
1892	17
1896	15
1912	13

These figures should be compared with table 9, p. 55., which gives the same information for Birmingham. The repeated fluctuation in the strength of parties on the Leeds Town Council, in the 1840s, the 1870s and from 1892-1912, produced a markedly faster turnover of members than in Birmingham.

If we take the Leeds figures in their own right, the highest turnover occurred in the period 1836-52, as both the ten-year and the fifteen-year column show. At the other end of the scale, the Council in 1892 was the product of ten to fifteen years of the lowest turnover in these three generations. It showed to an unusual extent the influence of the recruitment that had taken place in the 1870s. The small number of those on the Council of 1912 who had been elected before 1892 indicates the clearing out of the older members that had taken place in the 1890s.

A Note on Methods

The statistical information on the composition of the two town councils is drawn from twelve samples. Eight of these were taken at decennial intervals, showing the total membership of the council in the January after the census year. Municipal elections occurred at the beginning of November, and by the following January the election of aldermen had been completed, and bye-elections held to fill up vacancies created thereby among the councillors. The remaining four samples show the council in mid-decade at twenty-year intervals, i.e. in January 1836, 1856, 1876, and 1896. The first of these dates represents the first council elected under the provisions of the Municipal Corporations Act. (For Birmingham, whose charter was not granted until 1838, the equivalent date used is 1839.)

Throughout the period studied the Leeds Town Council normally consisted of 64 members, 48 councillors and 16 aldermen. But in 1896 and 1902 the election of a mayor from outside the Council raised the numbers in the sample to 65. The Birmingham Town Council also consisted of 64 until 1891 when it was increased to 72 (54 councillors, 18 aldermen). In 1911 the creation of Greater Birmingham raised its size to 190 (90 councillors and 30 aldermen). In addition there is a sample of 38 persons, being the unreformed Corporation of Leeds in 1835, the year of its abolition.

The occupations of Council members were taken either directly from the statutory declaration that each was required to make on taking office, or from printed lists based on these sources. Self-declared occupations are, however, notoriously untrustworthy, and work based solely on them is of limited value. They have therefore been checked by means of directories. It was customary for those who had retired from a gainful occupation to describe themselves as a gentleman or esquire. In all these cases attempts have been made to trace them back in the directories, and to classify them under their former occupation. The category 'retired' does not feature in the book, and the few gentlemen who still remain were men habitually living a rentier's life on a private income.

For the purpose of this study, professions have been defined as comprising the practitioners of law and medicine, accountants, architects, surveyors, consulting engineers, and graduate teachers. The medical profession includes physicians, surgeons, dental surgeons, and veterinary surgeons. Apothecaries, who might have been regarded as practitioners of medicine at the beginning of the period, do not appear on either council at any time. This problem has therefore been ignored and they are excluded from the calculations in appendix I. Consulting engineers appear in Birmingham directories only from 1882 onwards and on the Council only by 1896. There is therefore no danger of anachronism in this case. There are no non-graduate teachers on either council in the sample years. Clergy were precluded by law from election to borough councils until 1925 and are therefore excluded from consideration. The only officer of the armed services to feature in the samples sat on the Birmingham Council in 1839 and has been specially identified.

Bankers and bank managers have not been included among the professions but among the businessmen. Journalists in the early period, such as the editor of *The Northern Star*, were printers and stationers as well as editors, and have been treated as such. By the end of the period, when a journalist who was not also a printer appears in the Birmingham sample for 1912, he has been singled out for comment and not included in the professions. Brokers and agents of various kinds have also not been counted among the professional men. This applies in particular to the auctioneers and estate agents who are found on both councils most of the time, as well as to the stock and share brokers who are rarely found.

The professions have therefore been conservatively defined, at least by twentieth century standards. In the case of this concept, which changes to such an important degree between 1835 and 1912 it has been necessary to find a compromise between faithfulness to the notions of the time and the need to preserve uniform categories for the sake of comparison. In practice this has proved less difficult than might have been expected. But it would have been far more difficult had the study not ended when it did. This needs to be borne in mind when any comparisons are made between figures given in this study and those available elsewhere for the more recent period. The way in which this affects the interpretation of figure 2, p. 45 and table 21, p. 269 is explained in the relevant footnotes.

A distinction has occasionally been made in the text between leading professional men and those less prominent in their profession. In the case of the Birmingham study this distinction is based on a systematic analysis of the honorary officers and council members of the regional professional associations. In the case of the Leeds study the distinction is not used systematically and is based on contemporary comment, where this is available.

Women only qualified as town councillors in 1907. There were none on the Leeds Council in 1912 and two on that for Greater Birmingham. Miss Margaret Pugh, a spinster, has been put into a separate category of her own. Mrs Ellen Pinsent, the wife of a barrister, has been included among the professional people.

An attempt has been made to classify Council members by the size of their business at the time that they were serving on the Council, or else at the time that they retired from business. In view of the scale on which the Corporation operated it appeared useful to know whether the administrative experience of members had been in the largest, medium or smallest businesses then operating in the town. This was done by identifying the owners or directors of the really large or really small businesses, since the extremes were easiest to find as well as most obviously relevant. Even so the difficulties to be overcome were considerable, both on the conceptual and on the practical level. Because of the differences between various kind of businesses no simple criterion for size was satisfactory. Nor was it possible to aggregate all the different criteria that might be relevant, since the material was too fragmentary to permit this. It has been necessary to work with what was available and to use common sense.

(i) *Numbers employed* This was the most commonly available information. Parliamentary Papers of one kind or another have been useful for establishing some basic standard for the economy of Birmingham and Leeds, as well as yielding information on the firms of councillors. Some of the most useful have been listed in the Note on Sources. Most of the information has been drawn from more ephemeral local material and from trade periodicals.

(ii) *Size of the works or number or size of machines employed* This was relevant for certain kinds of firms and this information was sometimes available.

(iii) *Capital employed* These figures were sometimes available especially towards the end of the century, as firms became public companies.

(iv) *Size of the estate on death*   Wills have not been used systematically, and the figures available in obituaries, etc., have been difficult to interpret.

(v) *Rateable value of business premises*   The rate books for Leeds have been lost, and this proved a serious obstacle to the study of that city. The rate books for Birmingham have been used for certain occupations where this criterion seemed to be appropriate, especially for shop-keepers. In this case the median value for the central shopping streets and for shops in outer areas was first established, and any specific business was measured against this scale.

In all these respects the fact that I was trying to identify only the extremes was a great help.

In the frequent absence of information on the particular firm the problem has been approached generically, judging the size of the firm by that normal in the industry concerned. For instance, the manufacture of jewellery in Birmingham was essentially an industry carried out in small workshops. The exceptions, like Elkington Brothers, were few and easy to identify. This approach had great advantages where it was applicable.

A Note on Sources

The work of classification has been possible only on the basis of research into the economic history of the region already undertaken by other scholars. In the course of the work on Birmingham I have relied heavily on the material collected by Mrs Barbara D. M. Smith of the Faculty of Economics and Commerce, Birmingham University, in preparation for the 'Bibliography of the Industrial History of the Birmingham District 1860–1900'. This is now available for consultation at the Birmingham University library. I am most grateful for the way in which she placed her card index and her unrivalled knowledge of Birmingham firms unstintingly at my disposal. The most useful introductions to the Birmingham economy in this period are *The Resources, Products and Industrial History of Birmingham and the Midland Hardware District*, ed. Samuel Timmins (Birmingham, 1866); G. C. Allen, *The Industrial Development of Birmingham and the Black Country, 1860–1927* (1929); *V. C. H., The County of Warwick*, VII, *The City of Birmingham*, ed. W. B. Stephens (1964).

For the Leeds study I have used the special catalogue to material on business firms in the Local History Collection of the Leeds Central Library. There are also two published bibliographies: Clive A. W. Ward, 'A Bibliography of the History of Industry in the West Riding of Yorkshire 1750–1914', *Proceedings, Leeds Phil. & Lit. Soc. (Lit. & Hist. Section)*, XIII, part 1 (September 1968); *Yorkshire Business Histories, A Bibliography*, ed. Joyce M. Bellamy (Bradford U. P., 1970). This is the more comprehensive of the two. Particularly valuable has been the work of W. G. Rimmer and R. G. Wilson. W. G. Rimmer, *Marshalls of Leeds, Flax-Spinners, 1788–1886* (1960); 'The Leeds Leather Industry in the Nineteenth Century', *Thoresby Society Publications*, XLVI (1961); 'The Industrial Profile of Leeds, 1740–1840',

'Occupations in Leeds, 1841–1951', *Thoresby Society Publications*, L, 113 (1967). R. G. Wilson, *Gentlemen Merchants. The Merchant Community in Leeds 1700–1830* (Manchester, 1971). M. W. Beresford, W. G. Rimmer, *et al.* 'Leeds and its Industrial Growth', a series of articles published in the *Leeds Journal* 1953–60. They are listed in detail in Ward's *Bibliography*. But the information on the economic standing of the Leeds councillors is less complete than in the case of Birmingham, owing to the more fragmentary nature of the material available to me. This accounts for the statistically less ambitious and more selective treatment of the subject. Hsien Ding Fong, *The Triumph of the Factory System in England* (Tientsin, 1930) is valuable for the study of the size of factories *circa* 1840. It is based mainly on Parliamentary Papers, some of the most useful of which are mentioned below.

The study is based first and foremost on the Local History Collections in the Birmingham Central Reference Library and the Leeds Central Library. Particularly important have been local directories and other reference books, local newspapers, collections of newspaper cuttings, both biographical and others, annual reports of institutions and descriptions of firms. The catalogues of these two collections have been, in addition to the Industrial Bibliography in the Birmingham University Library just referred to, the principal tool for research. I want to pay particular tribute to the excellent work that has been done in indexing and cataloguing the collection in the Birmingham Central Reference Library over many years. For Leeds mention must be made of a useful MS. Index to Obituaries in *The Yorkshire Post*, kept in the Offices of Yorkshire Post Newspaper Ltd., Leeds, to which I was allowed access.

The following manuscript collections have been consulted:

(i) *Municipal Records:* The MS. records, including the Declaration Books, of the Corporation of Birmingham and of the Birmingham street commissioners are kept in the Birmingham Council House. The Proceedings of the Council have been printed since November 1851 and are available in the Central Reference Library. Ratebooks for the borough are also available there.

The MS. records of the Corporation of Leeds and of the Leeds improvement commissioners since 1835 are kept in the Leeds Civic Hall. The main collection is in the care of the committee clerk, but the city treasurer's archives are kept separately. The Proceedings of the Council have been printed only since 1889. The MS. records of the pre-1835 Corporation, including the Declaration Book for 1765–1835, are kept in the Archives Department of the Leeds Public Library. So are the only ratebooks for this period which have survived. They are for Bramley township.

(ii) *Records of Churches consulted:* Carr's Lane Congregational Church, Birmingham, at the Birmingham Central Reference Library; Church of the Saviour, Birmingham, Part of the Dawson Collection at the Birmingham Central Reference Library; Francis Rd., Congregational Church, Birmingham, formerly at Francis Road Church, present whereabouts unknown; Mount Zion Baptist Chapel, Birmingham at the Church of the Redeemer, Hagley Rd., Birmingham; New Meeting and Church of the Messiah, Birmingham, at the Church of the Messiah, Broad St., Birmingham. The People's Chapel, Birmingham, at the People's Chapel, Great King St., Birmingham; Mill Hill Unitarian Church, Leeds at Mill Hill Church, City Square, Leeds.

(iii) *Records of Political Bodies consulted:*

Birmingham Liberal Association } Birmingham Liberal Club }	at the Birmingham Central Reference Library
Birmingham I.L.P. Federation } King's Heath Branch I.L.P. }	at the Birmingham Social Science Library
Leeds Liberal Federation (printed)	at the Central Library, Leeds
Leeds Liberal Federation } Leeds Conservative Association } West Leeds Conservative Association }	at the Archives Department, Leeds Public Library

(iv) *Other Collections:* Chamberlain MSS., Birmingham University Library; Lupton MSS., Archives Department, Leeds Public Library; Marshall MSS., Brotherton Library, University of Leeds; Webb MSS., Local Government Collection, British Library of Political and Economic Science, London School of Economics; Census of England & Wales, 1851, Enumerators' Tallies, Public Record Office, London.

(v) *British Parliamentary Papers:* These have been consulted for most aspects of the subject and the following have been found particularly useful for the classification of firms:

Royal Commission on the Employment of Children in Factories, Supplementary Report, 1834 (167), xix, xx.

Select Committee on the Exportation of Machinery, First and Second Reports, 1841 (201, 400), vii.

Royal Commission on Children's Employment, Second Report, 1843 [430–32], xiii–xv.

Royal Commission on Children's Employment, First Report, 1863

[3170], xviii; Second and Third Reports, 1864 [3414], xxii; Fourth Report, 1865 [3548], xx; Fifth Report, 1866 [3678], xxiv; Sixth Report, 1867 [3796], xvi.

Select Committee (House of Lords) on the Sweating System, First Report, 1888 (361), xx; Second Report, 1888 (448), xxi; Third Report, 1889 (165), xiii; Fourth Report, 1889 (331), xiv; Fifth Report, 1890 (169), xvii.

Royal Commission on Labour, First Report, 1892 [C.6708], xxiv; Second Report [C.6795], xxxvi- Pt. I; Fourth Report, 1893–4 [C.7063], xxxix-Pt. I; Fifth Report, 1894 [C.7421], xxxv.

(vi) *Unpublished University Theses:* M. H. Bailey, 'The Contribution of Quakers to some Aspects of Local Government in Birmingham 1828–1902', M. A., Birmingham, 1952.

G. W. A. Bush, 'The Old and the New. The Corporation of Bristol 1820–1851', Ph.D., Bristol, 1965.

Derek Fraser, 'Politics in Leeds 1830–1852', Ph.D., Leeds (School of History), 1969.

J. R. Lowerson, 'The Political Career of Sir Edward Baines', M.A., Leeds (School of History), 1963.

Brenda M. Powell, 'A Study of the Changes in the Social Origins, Political Affiliations, and Length of Service of Members of the Leeds City Council 1888–1953', M.A., Leeds (Department of Social Studies), 1958.

D. N. Sandilands, 'History of the Midlands Glass Industry with special reference to Flint Glass', M.Comm., Birmingham, 1927.

Jean Toft, 'Public Health in Leeds in the Nineteenth Century. A Study in the Growth of Local Government Responsibility 1815–1880', M.A., Manchester, 1966.

Index

Churches belonging to generally known denominations are listed under the name of the denomination, e.g. Baptists, Mount Zion Chapel, Graham Street, Birmingham.

The names of town council committees and of municipal wards are listed respectively under Birmingham Town Council committees, Leeds Town Council committees and Wards.

Books cited in footnotes are listed under the name of the author or editor. But each book is listed only once, the reference being to the page on which the full title occurs for the first time.

Index

Small Tenements Rating Act, (1850),
Select committee on operation of, 313,
319, 324
Smethwick, 83
Smith, A., 47
Smith, Barbara, M.D., 365
Smith, Eustace, 171
Smith, George, 100
Smith, H. John, 8n
Smith, Henry, 30n
Smith, J. Piggot, 33
Smith, Trevor, 170n
Smithson, R. A., 268n
Snow, Dr. John, 189
Snow Hill, Birmingham, 113
Sociability, see Town Councillors, ideal
characteristics of
Social Democratic party, 305, 306
Social emulation, 30, 171, 173
Social Reform Union, Leeds, 255
Society of the Friends of Italy, 74
Societaet Nr. 5, 304
Solicitors and attorneys, 28, 49, 152, 155
in Birmingham, 25, 28, 32, 33, 94, 350–1
in Leeds, 200, 205, 244, 261n, 262, 265,
352
South Africa, 173
South Wales, 301
Southborne, Edgbaston, 153
Spark, F. R., 224n, 236, 241, 242, 243
Specialised knowledge, see Town Council-
lors, ideal characteristics of
Spencer, F. H., 207, 329n
Spectator, The, 68
Spindles, 193
Spoils system, 318
Stacey, Margaret, 339n
Stadtverordnete, 299
Stansfeld, Hamar, 200, 262
Stationers, see Printers and Stationers
Statisticians, 48
Statistical investigation, Leeds, 188, 189–90
Statues, City Square, Leeds, 282–3, plates
20, 21
Steam engines, 193n
Stephens, W. B., 17n
Stephenson, Gwendolen, 249n
Stein, Freiherr von, 299, 303
Stevens, J. V., 53n, 54
Stevens, John M., 290n
Stewart, J. D., 347n
Stock or share brokers, 269, 362
Street Commission, see Birmingham Street
Commission; Improvement Com-
missions
Street gullies, 250–1
Street improvement, 190, 317
in Birmingham, 30, 31
in Leeds, 196, 209, 243

Street lighting,
in Birmingham, 30, 118
in Leeds, 187, 191
Street widening,
in Birmingham, 105, 109
see also Paving, Road construction
Strike, Leeds corporation employees', 272–3
Study of Urban History, The, vii, x
Sturge, Charles, 90
Sturge, Joseph, 90n, 148, 200
Sturges Bourne Act, (1818), 299
Sunderland, 88, 208
Sunday schools, 83, 94, 142–3, 147, 222
teachers in, 83, 94n, 143, 222
see also Quakers, Severn Street Adult
School, Birmingham
Surgeons, 362
in Birmingham, 28n, 350–1
in Leeds, 188, 189, 234, 235n, 258
see also Doctors; Professional men
Surveyors, 362
in Birmingham, 81, 350
in Leeds, 193, 352
Sutcliffe, Anthony, vii
Swansea, 188, 331
Switzerland, 91
Sword cutlers, 30n

Tailors, 212n
Talbot, Canon Edward Stuart, 249
Tame, river, 34, 107, 110
Tame Valley, 34, 81, 109
Tangye, Richard, 146n
Tanners, 194, 195, 257
Tatham, George, 202n, 215, 216, 218, 221,
234, plates 26, 27
Taylor, James, 18n
Taylor, R. V., 181n
Teachers, 362
in Birmingham, 40, 351
in Leeds, 269n
Tea-dealers, 196n, 198
Teale, T. Pridgin, 234, 234n
Teetotal party, Leeds Town Council, 153,
214–15, 217, 218, 221, 222
Temperance, 102, 140, 141, 153, 214–17,
218, 219, 356
as a factor in Birmingham Municipal Re-
form Movement, 102, 149–53
Temperance Hall, York Street, Leeds, 219
Temperance movement,
Quakers in, 149–50, 152–3, 215
Temperance organisations in municipal
politics, 35, 153, 217n
Temperance Society, Holbeck, 222n
Temperance Society, Leeds, 222
Test and Corporation Acts, repeal of,
(1828), 309
Tetley, Charles Francis, 259n, 263, 268,
plate 29

391

Leeds Town Hall, the most celebrated symbol of
civic pride in Victorian England, as seen from the
south-west. It was designed by Cuthbert Brodrick
and built at great cost. The enormous tower was
the final touch in every sense and was still incomplete when the Queen opened the building in
1858. From an engraving by C. Fenn in the Leeds
Central Library.